T0176718

Advanced
Analytics and AI

Advanced Analytics and AI

Impact, Implementation, and the Future of Work

TONY BOOBIER

WILEY

This edition first published 2018
© 2018 John Wiley & Sons, Ltd

Registered office
John Wiley & Sons Ltd, The Atrium, Southern Gate, Chichester, West Sussex, PO19 8SQ, United Kingdom

For details of our global editorial offices, for customer services and for information about how to apply for permission to reuse the copyright material in this book please see our website at www.wiley.com.

Wiley publishes in a variety of print and electronic formats and by print-on-demand. Some material included with standard print versions of this book may not be included in e-books or in print-on-demand. If this book refers to media such as a CD or DVD that is not included in the version you purchased, you may download this material at http://booksupport.wiley.com. For more information about Wiley products, visit www.wiley.com.

Designations used by companies to distinguish their products are often claimed as trademarks. All brand names and product names used in this book are trade names, service marks, trademarks or registered trademarks of their respective owners. The publisher is not associated with any product or vendor mentioned in this book.

Limit of Liability/Disclaimer of Warranty: While the publisher and author have used their best efforts in preparing this book, they make no representations or warranties with respect to the accuracy or completeness of the contents of this book and specifically disclaim any implied warranties of merchantability or fitness for a particular purpose. It is sold on the understanding that the publisher is not engaged in rendering professional services and neither the publisher nor the author shall be liable for damages arising herefrom. If professional advice or other expert assistance is required, the services of a competent professional should be sought.

Library of Congress Cataloging-in-Publication Data

Names: Boobier, Tony, 1956– author.
Title: Advanced analytics and AI : impact, implementation, and the future of
    work / by Tony Boobier.
Description: Chichester, West Sussex, United Kingdom : John Wiley & Sons,
    2018. | Series: Wiley finance series | Includes bibliographical references
    and index. |
Identifiers: LCCN 2018003398 (print) | LCCN 2018005453 (ebook) | ISBN
    9781119390923 (pdf) | ISBN 9781119390930 (epub) | ISBN 9781119390305
    (cloth)
Subjects: LCSH: Management—Statistical methods. | Artificial
    intelligence—Industrial applications.
Classification: LCC HD30.215 (ebook) | LCC HD30.215 .B66 2018 (print) | DDC
    658.0072/7—dc23
LC record available at https://lccn.loc.gov/2018003398

Cover Design: Wiley
Cover Images: blurred people © blurAZ/Shutterstock;
              hand touch © whiteMocca/Shutterstock;
              hand touch © monsitj/iStock

Set in 10/12pt, SabonLTStd by SPi Global, Chennai, India.

Printed and bound by CPI Group (UK) Ltd, Croydon, CR0 4YY

10 9 8 7 6 5 4 3 2 1

Contents

Acknowledgements

I owe an enormous debt of gratitude to family, friends, colleagues, acquaintances and even strangers who were willing to share their views over the past few years on this most complex and interesting of subjects. It seems everyone has a point of view, which is a good thing.

Thanks also to the staff of Wiley who have produced this book, especially to Thomas Hykiel as the original commissioning editor and subsequently Gemma Valler who brought this project to a conclusion.

I'm especially grateful to my wife Michelle not only for her support but also for her observations and advice, leaving me in no doubt as to the meaning of 'better half'.

This book is especially written for my grandchildren who will live with the consequences of all these changes.

Preamble: Wellington and Waterloo

Let's start with a true story about the Battle of Waterloo, which was fought on Sunday 18 June 1815.

Facing each other were the French emperor Napoleon Bonaparte, who for more than a decade had dominated European and global affairs, and Arthur Wellesley, the Duke of Wellington, who had made his military name during the Peninsula Campaign of the Napoleonic Wars, and ultimately rose to become one of Britain's leading statesmen and politicians.

Waterloo is located about 15 kilometres south of Brussels. On that day, the French army comprised about 69,000 men and faced an opposing force of about 67,000 troops, although this number was to swell to over 100,000 with the arrival of Prussian allies before the end of the day. By nightfall, Wellington emerged as the victor, but nearly 50,000 from both sides were dead or wounded. According to Wellington, this was 'the nearest-run thing you ever saw in your life'.

There are many explanations for his success. One that resonates is that that there is evidence that he was in the area during the summer of 1814, having taken a wide diversion from his route from London to Paris where he was taking up his new role as British ambassador to the court of Louis XVIII. Rather than taking the more direct route from Dover to Calais, he sailed on HMS *Griffon* to the Belgian port of Bergen Op Zoom, accompanied by 'Slender Billy', the 23-year-old Prince William.

He spent two weeks touring the Lowlands, and the valley south of Brussels seemingly caught his attention. There's a suggestion that he stayed at the inn La Belle Alliance, a location that was to play a part in the eventual battle.

At that time there was no hint on the horizon that he would ever fight his old adversary Napoleon, and perhaps his visit was simply the old habit of a retired soldier. During the battle he was so aware of the terrain that he was able to deploy his troops to the greatest effect. During the fighting he took care to allocate particular regiments to protect key defence points, such as Hougoumont. Without these insights, some argue that Wellington's success would have been uncertain.

Two hundred years later, perhaps there is a still lesson to be learned from this encounter.

Whilst we shouldn't think of the introduction of AI to business as being a battle, there are definitely significant challenges ahead. How well we humans prepare and respond to that environment will depend significantly on how prepared we are. Like Wellington, understanding the terrain may not be enough in itself, but it will provide a useful indicator about what might happen and what we should do about it.

This book can't provide all the answers, or even all the questions. Perhaps, at best, all it will give us is some sort of compass in a sea of data and analytics that will provide guidance as to how the world of work will evolve. But in uncertain oceans, isn't a compass still useful?

Introduction

It seems that almost every time we pick up a newspaper or read an online article, there is some reference to AI. It's difficult not to reflect on how it may – or may not – change the way we live and how we will work in the future. As we read the articles, we can become either excited or confused (or perhaps both) about what AI really means, why it's happening, and what will be the consequence.

The articles tend to be either quirky or technical. On the one hand, they suggest how AI can help choose the best and quickest route, keep the elderly from feeling alone, and assist with the best retail choice. On the other hand, technical articles also imply that beneath the covers are numerous algorithms of a complexity that normally gifted humans cannot possibly understand – and that this topic is best left to expert academics and mathematicians with deep statistical insights.

These experts seem at face value to be the people whom we will have to trust to create some sort of compass or road map for all our futures, yet how much do they understand *your* world or *your* work?

AI is a topic that is much more important than a means of simply providing a clever satellite navigation scheme or some form of novelty tool for aiding personal decisions. It is a concept that potentially goes right to the core of how we will work and even how we will exist in the future. As individuals, we should not only feel that we have the right to know more about what this matter is actually concerning, but that we should become contributors to the discussion. Through greater understanding we become more empowered to enter into the debate about the future, rather than leaving it to others. But beyond simple empowerment, don't we also have a duty to become part of the discussion about our future – that is, *your* future?

This isn't the first book about AI and certainly won't be the last. But readers who don't have deep technical, academic qualifications or experience in computer science or advanced mathematics increasingly need to understand what is actually going on, how it will affect them going forward, how best to prepare, and what they can do about it.

It's important to be realistic about the time frame involved. It wouldn't be to anyone's benefit to worry unduly today about a technology that won't be in full implementation for another quarter or half a century, but many suspect it will happen much sooner than that. In many places there is evidence of it already beginning to happen. Industries, professions, and individuals need to be prepared, or to start to become prepared.

A recent paper, 'Further Progress in Artificial Intelligence: A Survey of Expert Opinion', interviewed 550 experts on the likely timescale for development of AI.

In the paper, 11% of the group of eminent scientists surveyed said that we will understand the architecture of the brain sufficiently to create machine simulation of human thought within 10 years. And of these, 5% suggested that machines will also be able to simulate learning and every other aspect of human learning within 10 years. They also predict the probability of the machine having the same level of understanding and capability as a Nobel Prize-winning researcher by 2045.

Of that group, even the most conservative thinkers indicated that they believe there is a 'one-in-two' chance that high level AI 'will be developed around 2040–2050, rising to a nine-in-ten chance by 2075'.[1] Who can really be sure?

It's impossible to make predictions about timing with certainty. Some people might have doubts about implementation timelines proposed by academic experts. On the other hand, businesses that operate in demanding and cutthroat climates are continually looking for competitive advantage, which invariably comes from appropriate technological advances. The drive for competitive advantage, most probably through cost cutting, will force the development timetable. To do so effectively requires business practitioners to better understand technology, and for technologists to have a greater grasp on business pains and opportunities.

As market conditions increasingly accelerate the pace of change, there is a real possibility – or more like a probability – that some professions within certain industries will be using some forms of AI within the next 10 years; that is, by the mid-2020s. Whilst many organisations remain obliged to manage their progress in terms of a series of short-term goals, in strategic terms this date is just around the proverbial corner, and they need to start working towards it now.

Even if the more conservative, longer-term view (that we will not see AI until 2040) is taken, the shift to AI will almost certainly occur within the lifespan of the careers of graduates and interns joining industry today. In their book *The Future of the Professions*, lawyers Richard and Daniel Susskind make the case that professionals (especially those between the ages of 25 and 40) need to have a better understanding of the potential paradigm shift from the influence of technology on the way they work, suggesting that 'professions will be damaged incrementally'.[2]

This is not an issue that will only affect individuals working at that time. Those still working today, who will have finished their full- or part-time employment within a decade, will find their daily personal affairs being increasingly influenced by AI in terms of services provided to them.

The issue therefore may not be what and when, but rather how. The problem may not be of crystallising what we mean by AI, or conceptualising what we can do with it, but rather how it can be effectively and sensibly deployed.

Some of these same issues have already occurred due to the adoption of advanced analytics (i.e. predictive and prescriptive analytics), so we will attempt to consider the question of implementation from a practical point of view. Although the implementation time frame of one decade or even three is not absolute, this book makes the brave assumption that AI in the form of advanced analytics will eventually be with us in one form or another. Regardless of the period of time involved, the book proposes that there are a series of incremental building blocks and an optimum implementation route that should be followed. If organisations are to take advantage of AI within a single decade, then the journey to change needs to start immediately.

Some industries are more likely to be affected by AI than others: those that involve much repetitive decision-making, have extensive back-office functions, or are not specifically customer facing are particularly suited to AI implementation. They will respond and implement at different speeds but changes as a result of AI will lead to an environment of knowledge sharing. It is entirely feasible that we will see the sharing and cloning of complementary technologies used in quite diverse markets, such as consumer goods, retail, financial services, medicine, and manufacturing. Effective transfer of technologies and capabilities from one industry to another may ultimately become one of the most critical types of innovation going forward.

Manufacturing will increasingly and rapidly embrace robotics driven by superadvanced, or cognitive, analytics. But to what degree should specialist professions, such as dentists, surgeons, publishers or even many parts of the creative-arts sector, feel threatened?

There will also be immense cultural issues for the workforce to cope with. To what degree will our traditional understanding of the meaning of *work* change? The book will consider who will suffer (or benefit) the most. Will it be the blue-collar workers, whose role will become partly or fully automated? Will it be knowledge workers, who find that their most valuable personal commodity – knowledge – has become devalued and replaced by super search engines operating in natural language? Alternatively, will it be the business leader, whose authority, based on experience and judgement, will be undermined by systems offering viewpoints on the probability of success of any given decision?

In any event, how will business leaders even be able to lead unless they have personal experience? The very nature of leadership will need to change, and we will look at that as well. What can any – or all – of these groups do to prepare themselves?

Location may also be a key driver for change. In some growing markets, such as Asia and Latin America, new AI technologies could become the first resort for providing services where there has been a massive existing or potential market unsupported by adequate professional talent. The consequence of this could be that relatively immature marketplaces could start to leapfrog established practices to satisfy market need. What might be the implications of creating a new global world order, in terms of the use of machine learning?

We will also think about the impact of change through AI on existing business models. Traditionally, the way of doing work has been relatively linear in nature: one thing happens, and then another thing happens. Will the use of AI herald a change to that modus operandi, and if so, then how? What also will be the impact on traditional views of operational risk (risks of failure of systems, processes, people, or from external events) – especially if the decisions are being made by computers in an automated way?

One of the key enablers for change rests with professional institutions in whose domain is vested the awarding of professional qualifications. Many of these institutions are already struggling with the concept of big data and analytics as they try to convince their members that these trends are more than a fad or hype. In the near future an even greater burden will fall on their shoulders to carry the flag for AI and for new ways of working.

The choice whether to do this or not is not negotiable, insofar as on the whole the younger members of these institutions will increasingly adopt what are described as liquid skills, which reflect a new way of learning, to broaden their personal capabilities. Increasingly, many younger professionals see the ultimate goal of personal development and upskilling as being that of the ability to go solo in the world of work and to earn a crust through value creation rather that a regular paycheck. To what degree will this affect professional institutions and how will AI help – or hinder – this aspiration?

This book is not about the deepest technical details of technology and mathematics – although we will touch on these to give context and raise awareness – but rather aims to help individuals understand the impact on their business environment and their careers. As far as practically possible, it will help practitioners start to 'future proof' their careers against changes that are already beginning to happen, might occur in under a decade, and almost certainly will occur afterwards.

AI is not a subject without potential controversy. Not only are there technical and professional issues to contend with, but there are also some ethical aspects to consider as well. At a broader level, readers will gain a level of insight that allows them to contribute to the wider discussion in a more informed way.

Beyond this, the book aims to help employers supported by professional institutions start to ensure that their employees and their leaders have the right skills to cope with a world of work that is transforming rapidly and radically.

Overall the focus is on raising awareness in individuals, professional organisations, and employers about a future world of work that will be with us sooner or later. My guess is sooner – and that there is no time to lose.

NOTES

1. Muller, Vincent C. and Bostrom, Nick (2016). Future progress in AI: a survey of expert opinion, 553–571. Paper. Synthese Library, Springer.
2. Susskind, Richard and Susskind, Daniel (2015). *The Future of the Professions*. Oxford University Press.

What Do We Mean by *Work*?

SUMMARY

This chapter sets the scene for a new work ethos in a data-fuelled business environment. It considers the evolution of work, taking into account the relationship between employer and employee; the origin and development of the work ethic; and the different motives of the individual in the workplace, especially the young entrepreneur and aging employee. Beyond this, it reflects on the future validity of Maslow's hierarchy of needs and suggests new prioritisations.

INTRODUCTION

The writer H.G. Wells (1866–1946) was no fool. Although he anticipated a journey to the moon in 1901, his writing was more in the nature of scientific romance. He wrote of time machines, war of the worlds, and the invisible man, but beyond all this speculation he thought hard about the impact of change on society. He even imagined a future society whose members at some stage had taken divergent paths: a hedonistic society called the Eloi, focused on leisure and self-fulfilment, and a manual underclass that he called the Morlocks. The Morlocks had regressed into a darker world, even to the point of working underground to ensure that the Eloi would have luxury. It's a dark tale from Wells's *The Time Machine*, about a world many centuries into the future.

Who knows whether Wells will be right or wrong? As we will see later in this book, science fiction writers seem to have an uncanny knack of anticipating the future. We'll never really know whether this is because they put ideas into the minds of man, whether they have some divine inspiration, or whether it's purely coincidental. A professional colleague of mine who describes himself as a futurist tells me it's the easiest job in the world. After all, he says, who today will be around later to say whether the predictions are right or not?

As we consider the whole issue of the influence and application of technology, and specifically artificial intelligence, on work, then we need not only to look forward but also backward. What is this concept of work anyway?

There's no real doubt that the meaning of *work* has continually changed. By way of example, contrast the child working in what William Blake termed the 'dark Satanic Mills' of Victorian England, where there was a constant risk of losing a finger (or worse) in the cotton loom, with those working in the relative safety of the so-called flat white economy of London's Shoreditch today. The flat white economy is a term that references the most popular type of coffee ordered by start-up entrepreneurs, whose idea of working is to forsake a regular salary in favour of the prospect of creating (and ultimately selling) an innovative technological gold mine.

A few decades ago, the ambition of most university graduates was to survive the so-called milk round (an expression used by prospective employers who visit multiple universities – like a milkman delivers milk from house to house – to seek out the best talent). The milk round still exists, but finding a steady job with a linear career path is not the most important thing for some of today's grads. Entrepreneurship informs the zeitgeist of the moment. I recently fell into conversation with a young Canadian woman in her early twenties, working as a guide at the Design Museum in London. On enquiring, I discovered that it was only a temporary job for her, as she was looking to join a suitable start-up in London. What was more interesting to me was that she had quit her job at a leading technology corporation in the United States, forgoing its regular paycheck, to travel overseas and seek her fortune – an ambition, perhaps, indicative of the times.

Entrepreneurship isn't confined to bright young things. Increasingly, major corporations are offloading skill and experience in favour of young, new thinking – even if cost cutting is probably part of the real agenda. Older workers of both genders shouldn't take it personally, even if it may slightly hurt their pride. They too may respond by finding new market opportunities, attaching themselves to start-ups, or even starting something themselves.

For that older generation, the world of work has changed as well. More and more they have needed to understand the impact of change and adapt accordingly. They are like the proverbial old dogs learning new tricks.

There's also a sense of regaining the balance between work and play. For many younger people in the workplace, the division between the two has narrowed, or possibly even disappeared. The expression *working from home* has entered into our vocabulary. At the same time, office-based workers find themselves still working excessive hours, making leisure time something to be grabbed rather than something to which they are entitled. With so many of the big jobs located in the city, regardless of the country, and with city accommodation and commuting so costly, it's really not surprising that the focus of workers is on career advancement and salary improvement. But won't automation and AI undermine that way of thinking, and if so, then how?

How did we find ourselves here? And more importantly, what will this new age of work bring?

SLAVERY OR FREEDOM?

Let's start with slavery. It's an unattractive and disturbing subject. For many ancient cultures, the concept of slavery did not exist. Men apparently did the hunting and women did the rest – which at least seems to suggest some division of labour from the outset. (In honesty, it's a bit uncertain and all we can really do is speculate.) But alongside, and perhaps as a result of, creating divisions of labour, civilisations seem to have created an environment for servitude, and the idea of slavery had established itself by the time of the ancient Greeks and Romans. Sir Moses Finley, professor emeritus of ancient history at Cambridge University, identifies the five key slave societies as being ancient Rome, ancient Greece, the United States, the Caribbean, and Brazil.[1] It's a complex and controversial subject, and Finley makes the point that conditions for slaves were entirely dependent on the owner's disposition, which might be kind, cruel, or indifferent.

There are not many religious arguments in slavery's defense. Finley says that even many early Christians were slave owners, but that slaves' treatment and how these individuals were ultimately looked after was perhaps also a matter of the disposition of the owner. Sometime in the mid-first century the Roman writer Columella wrote about the treatment of slaves, recommending the stick as well as the carrot. Overall there was a general consensus among Romans about the virtues and financial benefits of a balanced approach to servitude (on the part of the owners).

Slavery did not disappear with the fall of Rome. The word itself is derived from the Eastern European word *Slav*, which is a term passed down from very old times. The Latin word for slave, *servus*, is the basis for the term *serf*, which combines the idea of servitude with the right of the individual to have some degree of control over property, if not necessarily ownership of it.

The Roman way of life was to be increasingly undermined by ancient Rome's two-level society. Some historians suggest that it was the moral 'flabbiness' of the ruling class that ultimately resulted in Rome falling to the Germanic hordes in AD 410.

The other side of slavery's coin is *freedom*, a notion which the ancient Greeks recognised as they consulted the Pythia, the priestesses at the temple known as the Oracle at Delphi in upper central Greece. On the walls of the temple there were definitions of the four elements of freedom:

1. Representation in legal matters
2. Freedom from arrest and seizure
3. The right to do as one wished
4. The right to go where one wished.

It follows that one definition of slavery in ancient Greece can be stated by laying out the opposite of these values – for example, that the slave is represented by the master, that the slave must do what the master orders, and so on.

Two thousand years on, the expression *freedom* seems to have taken on a new set of values. Franklin Roosevelt in 1941 spoke of a world founded on four freedoms:

1. Freedom of speech and expression.
2. Freedom of worship.
3. Freedom from want.
4. Freedom from fear.

Some suggest that the final two of these freedoms – *want* and *fear* – have in particular driven the notion of work as we know it. In a consumer-driven society there is a desire not only to feed the family but also to keep up with peers. The notion of *fear* perhaps might be best represented by the anxiety of not being in employment and therefore being unable to buy those essential things, be they for survival or enjoyment. To what degree are we fearful about not being in work and not having an income, and how will that fear show itself in a future technological age?

Perhaps slavery is somehow linked to a struggle of classes and hierarchies, as Karl Marx suggested was the case in his *Communist Manifesto*. He wrote, 'The history of . . . society is the history of class struggle', oppressor and oppressed, 'in constant opposition to each other'.

Yet at the same time it has more often than not been possible for a servant to become a master, especially in a meritocracy. Learning and education seem to be key enablers or catalysts that allow this to happen, but they are frequently coupled with a bit of good fortune, and, from time to time, a helping hand.

The notion of work therefore seems to be unavoidably attached to servitude, through which we gain some form of freedom by not being in need or in fear. The now infamous phrase *Arbeit macht frei* (Work sets you free), forever to be associated with a sinister regime, comes from the title of a 1873 novel by German philologist Lorenz Diefenbach, in which gamblers and fraudsters find the path to virtue through labour.[2]

The opposite of work is leisure. There appears to be a time and place for some downtime of sorts. Few people would begrudge the leisure of others – perhaps provided that the leisure has some degree of moderation and is not flaunted. After all, isn't leisure the reward for work? If we work to earn money for essentials, then isn't leisure one of the ways in which we choose to spend any surplus? And at the end of the day, how do we define work anyway? Maybe the work of a musician or a writer is as hard as that of a miner, albeit a quite different kind of labour. The rock musician David Lee Roth summarizes it like this: 'Money can't buy you happiness, but it can buy you a yacht big enough to pull up right alongside it'.

Perhaps working is not optional but essential. After all, as St Paul put it over 2,000 years ago, 'If any would not work, neither should he eat'.

THE RISE OF INDUSTRIALISATION

Our generation stands in the shadow of the great industrial age. We compare the era of big data with the industrial ages of steam, hydrocarbon, and electricity. The great industrialists, such as Arkwright, Brunel, Carnegie, and Ford, to name but a few, were not only entrepreneurial but also had an ability to make changes happen at scale, even at the price of wringing every drop of sweat from their employees. Some industrialists even recognised the social impact on their employees and created special small communities for them.

Bourneville, a small village south of Birmingham in the United Kingdom was created by the chocolate-making Cadbury family in the 1890s, not only to ensure that their workforce was optimally placed close to the factory, but also to provide facilities such as parkland for health and fitness. The Cadbury family is not unique. Port Sunlight, south of Liverpool, was created by Lever Brothers (now part of Unilever) in 1888 to house its workers and was named after its most profitable product, Sunlight soap.

But even if these worker villages appear to have been created out of altruism, fundamentally they were founded on what we might describe as the *work ethic*. With its origins in Lutheran Germany, the Protestant Martin Luther challenged the Roman Catholic hierarchy in 1517 by nailing *Ninety-Five Theses* to a wall in Wittenberg, in which work he poured contempt on the 'lazy' comfort of the Catholic Church. According to the Bible, God demands work in atonement for original sin – brought about by Adam's eating of the forbidden fruit in the Garden of Eden – and Luther made no secret of that.

Luther had created a new type of religion that combined worship with hard work in demonstrating devotion to God. This was a 'business model' that was to be further reinforced by John Calvin. Calvin was a French theologian who lived at the time of the Protestant Reformation and who, like other Reformers, understood work and service to be a means by which believers expressed their gratitude to God for the redemption of Christ. Beyond this, he implied that economic success was a visible sign of God's grace – an idea ultimately taken further by Max Weber, the German sociologist. Weber wrote *The Protestant Ethic and the Spirit of Capitalism* in 1904, suggesting in it that the Protestant work ethic was one of the underlying (but unplanned) origins of capitalism and the growth of prosperity. Weber's 'spirit of capitalism' is said to consist of a set of values which comprise the spirit of hard work and progress.

What Weber argued was, in effect:

- That religious doctrine compelled an individual to work hard, but in doing so he or she could become wealthy.
- That the purchasing of luxuries was sinful, as were charitable donations (as they encouraged laziness on the part of those receiving the benefit).
- That the best way to reconcile these differences was through investment, which was a nascent form of capitalism.

As we consider the challenges of work not only today but going forward, we often fail to recognise that the underlying driver of hard work might appear to be seated not only in a very traditional approach to servitude, but also in the deep religious beliefs that have become ingrained in our work psyche.

The mood for change was an international movement. Benjamin Franklin, Thomas Carlyle, and John Stuart Mill, amongst others, all had something to say about the rise of capitalism and industrialism. Mill especially 'looked forward beyond (this) stage of Protestant-driven industrialisation to a New Age where concerns for quality, not quantity would be paramount'.[3]

Leap forward more than half a century. In the interim, the world has suffered World War I, during which the generals increasingly turned to industry to supply massive amounts of munitions, and World War II, which Peter Drucker has described as an 'industrial war'. Both of these major events, especially the latter, created the context for a new view of corporations in terms of how work itself functioned. At General Motors, Drucker not only gained a greater understanding about organising work but also about the functions of management. The lessons of the 'industrial' World War II taught many in management about chains of command, hierarchy, and the impact of scale.

Throughout that time, the work ethic remained sound and true. In 1934 General Motors recruited the consultant James 'Mac' McKinsey, who formerly had been a professor of accounting at Chicago University and who formed the McKinsey Company in 1926 at the age of 37. At that time he was the highest paid consultant in the United States, at US$500 per day. Within three years he had died as a result of illness brought on by the pressures of work. It's said he was at the office six days per week, brought his work home on Sundays, and was consumed by his responsibilities. He is seen as an embodiment of the Calvinistic work ethic that we have been describing.

Today, McKinsey Consultants is a very well-known and well-respected company, and the work ethic instilled by James McKinsey seems not to have changed substantially. A 2005 newspaper article in *The Guardian* that discussed McKinsey providing advice to the UK Prime Minister Tony Blair reminded readers that at McKinsey 'hours are long, expectations high and failure not acceptable'.[4] There's no doubt that McKinsey's employees – who are called 'members' (McKinsey calls itself 'The Firm') – are motivated not only by financial reward but by the trust bestowed on them by their clients and the recognition of their peers. For them, work seems to have taken on a meaning beyond drudgery. Some might even say that it is a form of religion.

What makes us want to work, anyway? Abraham Maslow, an American psychologist who was Jewish, was curious about this very topic, and found some enlightenment in the experiences of Holocaust survivors. He wanted to understand what motivated some to survive while others just gave up. He recognised a link between motivation and psychological development. From this he concluded that, in the workplace, employees worked better if they experienced a feeling of self-worth: in other words, if employees felt as if they were making meaningful contributions.

His book *Maslow on Management* was influenced by the work of Henry Murray, who had previously identified what he believed to be the 20 needs of all people, which he explained in his book *Explorations in Personality*. These needs were categorised into five key groups by Murray: ambition, materialism, power, affection, and information (see Table 1).

Maslow refined the work by Murray. He identified five human desires, in what has come to be known as his 'hierarchy of needs', which are (in ascending order): physiological (i.e. hunger and thirst), safety, love, esteem, and self-actualisation. The satisfaction of a need lower in the order allows for the pursuit of the next higher one.

TABLE 1   Murray's table of needs.

Ambition	Materialism	Power	Affection	Information
Achievement	Acquisition	Abasement (apologising and confessing)	Nurturance (caring for others)	Exposition (educating others)
Exhibition (the ability to shock others)	Construction	Autonomy (independence)	Play	Cognizance (seeking knowledge and asking questions)
Recognition (gaining status, displaying achievement)	Order (making things organised)	Aggression	Rejection	
	Retention (keeping things)	Blame avoidance	Succorance (being protected by others)	
		Deference (cooperation and obedience)		
		Dominance		

Source: K. Cherry, Murray's Theory of Psychogenic Needs, *Verywell* (1 January 2015). http://psychology.about.com/od/theoriesofpersonality/a/psychogenic.htm (accessed 4 May 2015)

The highest of these needs, self-actualisation, is described as the fulfilment of the talent of the individual, as expressed by creativity. It is often accompanied by a quest for spiritual enlightenment and a desire to positively transform society.

How do these needs respond to the workplace, and more importantly, to the work ethic? Is it really possible for a worker doing a mind-dulling, repetitive job to be creative and obtain a level of spiritual fulfilment? How might this also apply to positions of responsibility in the workplace? Frederick Hertzberg, professor of management at the University of Utah, proposed that 'job enrichment', that is, enlarging the job to give the employee greater self-authority, was one way forward. In his 1959 book *The Motivation to Work*, Hertzberg identified what we now understand to be the key drivers of satisfaction in the workplace – the factors that spurred individuals on to be motivated about their jobs – and how employers might get the most from their human assets by satisfying these key drivers.

Hertzberg's theory assumes that everyone is the same and is similarly motivated. Even Maslow recognised the simplistic nature of these categorisations. Later Maslow was to expand on these, saying that his thinking was based on key assumptions, including that humans prefer work over idleness and meaningful work over useless work.[5]

The question for today, and looking forward, is whether Maslow's approach is still valid for Gen Y (Gen X refers to those born between 1960 and 1980; Gen Y between 1981 and 2000). And how will his concepts apply to the post-2000 demographic that we know as Gen Z?

What will we name the group that comes after Gen Z? The jury seems to be out on that one, but the label *Gen Alpha* is getting some traction, if only because marketers like to have a system of categorisation and segmentation. Industry is increasingly moving to a so-called segment of one (i.e. dealing with consumers as individuals rather than as clusters or groups with similar behaviours). This is based on the ability of companies to understand the unique characteristics of individuals through access to big data. Will the need to categorise people into groups for the purpose of marketing, like many forms of work, simply start to die out as a result?

Equally important, as we consider the impact of technology on the nature of work and professions, and the approach to work more commonly being taken by a younger generation, is it perhaps time to rethink Maslow's hierarchy (see Figure 1)?

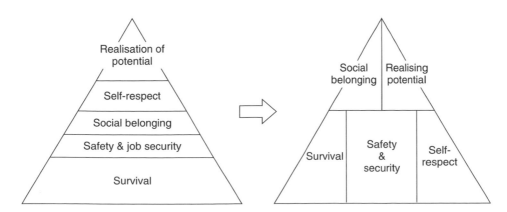

FIGURE 1   Maslow for a new age.

GEN Z AND THE FLAT WHITE SOCIETY

Gen Z, sometimes known as post-millennials or the iGeneration, are usually characterised by their access to a connected world. It is the first truly digital-native generation, communicating frequently (but not always) with words and still coming to terms with its cultural influences.

Its members will be an enormous factor in the economy of the future. By 2020 these young adults are likely to wield US$3 trillion of purchasing power in the United States alone. How they spend their time is different from what previous generations have experienced. In the 13-to-24-year-old bracket, 96% watched an average of 11 hours of online video per week, and 42% say that social media impacts their self-esteem.[6]

Even the way that they work is changing. The *flat white economy*, to recap, is a term applied to digital entrepreneurs chasing their fortunes with a winner-take-all mentality. Regular pay is minimal, but for those who hit the jackpot the benefits and rewards can be enormous. Only a few players are lucky enough to reach so-called unicorn status, named after the mythical horned horse. For this chance, they are prepared to trade economic safety and security for uncertainty, their extravagances often being confined to the latest high-tech kit: phone, laptop, and access to the latest apps.

The number of so-called flat whiters is growing globally, in locations as diverse as London, Paris, Moscow, Israel, Bangalore, and Beijing, to mention but a few. Like moths, they are attracted by the bright lights of a vibrant social scene, coupled with low-cost accommodation. In many cases, government help also provides a catalyst.[7]

It's impossible to question their commitment to seeking a fortune, even if their commitment to continuous employment is a little more dubious. Few seem prepared to work on the same project or with the same employer for more than a couple of years. In fact, continuous employment in the same place can even be seen as a bad thing.

They are constantly invited to break the mold and to be smarter about their relationship with the workplace. Writers such as Steven Levitt and Stephen Dubner ask their readers to 'think smarter about everything'. Their *Freakonomics* series of books, such as the one titled *Think Like a Freak*, challenges conventional workplace wisdom.

Levitt and Dubner also have asked what makes people truly happy, and have set out four key tenets:

1. Incentives are the cornerstone of modern life.
2. Knowing what to measure makes a complicated world less so.
3. Conventional wisdom is often wrong.
4. Correlation does not equate to causality.

They make the point that individuals often let their biases, such as political or economic bias, colour their world. The books seem to reflect the zeitgeist of the age, implying that the old way of thinking has become less relevant. Perhaps our historical approach to work is also changing, and the notion of the work ethic is diminishing equally in some way.

The members of Gen X and subsequent demographic groups are increasingly less likely to believe in God, at least in a traditional sense (see Table 2). If there is a link between work ethic and religion, indications are that if these trends continue, then religion will increasingly fall off the radar for members of these generations, perhaps to be replaced by some other form of spirituality.

TABLE 2   Religious belief by generational cohort.

Generational cohort	Belief in God
Younger millennial	50%
Older millennial	54%
Generation X	64%
Baby boomer	69%

Source: Pew Research Center (n.d.), *Religious Landscape Study.* http://www.pewforum.org/religious-landscape-study/generational-cohort (accessed 14 August 2017).

The idea of spirituality in the workplace isn't new. The notion of spirituality in the workplace, as distinct from religion, first emerged in the 1990s. It is characterised by an approach sometimes described as 'holistic thinking', whereby the worker has a heightened level of altruistic or unselfish awareness towards others.[8]

Buddhism, too, has an outlook on the concept of work. Originating sometime between the sixth and fourth centuries BCE, Buddhism has been described as 'a path of practice and spiritual development leading to insight into the true nature of reality'.[9] Buddhism also appears to have a view on the workplace. Tsunesaburo Makiguchi (1871–1944), a Japanese educational theorist, religious reformer, and founder of the largest lay Buddhist organisation in Japan, suggests in his theory of value that there are three kinds of value in the workplace: beauty, benefit, and good.

> *In the realm of employment, the value of* beauty *means to find a job you like; the value of* benefit *is to get a job that earns you a salary so that you are able to support your daily life; the value of* good *means to find a job that helps others and contributes to society.*[10]

Where does this leave us? As we start to look forward to a world of data-fuelled work, we are forced to leave behind some of the older notions of employment. Perhaps adopting a new spiritual approach might help to provide some form of template for the future world of work.

THE IMPACT OF UNEMPLOYMENT

It'll be easier for those who will actually be working in the future, however that work is fashioned, to be able to look forward more positively. After all, won't they be the ones to create the rules of work and invent new jobs? Perhaps all they will have to worry about is when, and not how, to pay the bills.

On the other hand, older generations will need to come to terms with the prospect of mass unemployment, as most routine tasks become automated and even many complex decisions become computer assisted. How will the older members of Generation X and those born later, who may become the victims of change, actually cope?

There is still uncertainty about the impact of automation. Kallum Pickering, senior economist at Berenberg, suggests that 'ever since the First Industrial Revolution we have been replacing humans with machine labor to raise the efficiency of production...' and that the key point is that 'most of the workers did not end up jobless and poorer. Instead such workers found other work and ways to generate supply'.[11]

As routine jobs become automated and disappear, it has been suggested that a whole new body of jobs will emerge, as human capital is freed up to do new things. 'As one job is destroyed', says Pickering, 'another can be created'.[12] That approach, together with lighter regulation and more informal work arrangements provided by so-called zero-hour contracts, may soak up some capacity in the labour market but is unlikely to be a panacea. Retraining will become increasingly critical, as will be the management of career expectations.

For those in mid-career, the fear of unemployment will not only continue as traditional routine roles and career paths disappear but is likely to create greater pressures and dominate their thinking. Finding work will become more and more difficult, especially for those with skills that can be replaced by automation. This phenomenon will not just be confined to low-skilled work. Even the work of a high-level financial advisor can be automated.[13]

Self-help books continually suggest that finding work needs to be dealt with as if the task is a job itself, albeit an unpaid and sometimes thankless one. It's no surprise therefore that many relate unemployment to depression. At the least, victims may suffer from unsettled sleep patterns coupled with the desire for comfort food – so-called binge eating. At the worst, problems of alcoholism, domestic violence, and an increased risk of suicide can result.[14]

Long-term unemployment makes the problem more acute. Only 1 in 10 of the long-term unemployed find work. Assuming the right skills and an active marketplace, about 3 in 10 people are able to find work in the first few weeks after losing their jobs. But after about a year of being out of work, the chances of landing a job fall to just 1 in 10 per month. Those who come from industries that are downsizing, or whose skills are outdated, can find it much more difficult.[15]

Aside from the issue of capability and economic opportunity, there is the issue of ageism. Unemployment levels of those over 55 are masked by rising retirement ages. Whilst some might argue that this aging demographic needs to stand aside for younger, perhaps more dynamic, employees, there are many in this group who believe that they still have much to give. In 2015 the UK government launched an older workers champion scheme aimed at over-55 job seekers, and suggested three key benefits of employing those in this demographic:[16]

1. *Economic improvement.* If the 1.2 million workless people over age 50 in the United Kingdom who wanted a job got back to work, this could add around £50 billion to the UK economy.
2. *Mentoring.* In workplaces that employ people aged 55–64 there is a positive effect on the performance of their younger counterparts.
3. *Stability.* Those aged 50–64 have an average job tenure of 13 years, compared with 7 years for those aged 25–49.

Loss of employment for the older generation is nothing new. The reengineering approach of the 1980s and 1990s often focused on those who were older and more expensive. This mentality has permeated into modern day recruitment, which (whilst constrained by legal remedies for age discrimination as well as gender) often shows itself through early deselection of those with a lengthy CV or evidence of qualifications in the 1970s and 1980s.

Few will have the luxury of simply doing nothing and resting on their laurels (or pension provisions). Whilst still remaining influenced by the work ethic, but also to supplement limited incomes and avoid boredom, many professionals at the end of their professional careers are increasingly adopting a two-pronged approach:

1. They are looking towards a portfolio approach to work and are prepared to undertake a variety of different, but perhaps complementary, roles.
2. The more entrepreneurial are prepared to align themselves with smaller companies and start-ups, perhaps for an equity share rather than salaried employment.

Some who are at the end of their traditional careers are deciding to invest in their own big ideas, pouring their own money into their development or marketing. Often this is to no avail, as they often hit a roadblock with respect to funding. Venture capitalists on the whole appear reluctant to support aging entrepreneurs.

According to the *Harvard Business Review*, which looked at the Billion Dollar Club (companies valued at US$1 billion by venture capitalists):

- The average age of those founding a start-up was just over 31.
- Founders under the age of 35 represent a significant proportion of founders in the Billion Dollar Club.
- CEOs and presidents are 42 years old on average, with a median age of 42.

Table 3 sets out the age of Silicon Valley's top founders. While these statistics are not suggesting that there isn't scope for the engagement of an older age group, they serve as a useful reminder that any involvement by this group in start-ups (at least for now) may be not much more than in a bit-part role.

In that sense, older workers and professionals may be no more than the embodiment of Shakespeare's quote:

> All the world's a stage,
> And all the men and women merely players;
> They have their exits and their entrances,
> And one man in his time plays many parts, ...
> *As You Like It,* Act II, Scene VII

TABLE 3   Founder age of US $1 billion VC-backed private companies.

Age of founder	% of companies
Under 20 years	2
20–24	23
25–29	19
30–34	23
35–39	14
40–44	14
45–49	4
50+	2

Source: Walter Frick, How old are Silicon Valley's top founders? Here's the data, *Harvard Business Review* (3 April 2014)

At least three key elements need to be in place for those at the end of their careers to remain engaged, especially in this increasingly threatening world of AI and technology:

1. *Retraining*. Individuals need to have a desire to be retrained, or at least need to ensure that they have an awareness of what is happening around them, as opposed to simply being victims, or passengers in a transformational journey. This retraining may be either formal or informal, and for optimum effect provided in such a way as to align to an individual's training style (i.e. verbal, visual, or tactile).
2. *Collaboration*. An environment for collaboration is important. Whilst this is often provided by innovation hubs, these hubs are frequently located in a city, requiring individuals to either travel (at their own expense) or miss out on the opportunity for sharing and learning. With respect to an aging yet experienced age group who find themselves on the market, perhaps there should be a new type of place (real or virtual) to get together and share ideas.
3. *Networking*. An effective network is critical. This goes beyond a social network, which is in itself important, and will provide a way to take good new ideas to market. The AI and cognitive landscape will gradually allow new business models to emerge that are fundamentally intended to be outsourced; the challenge will be how they can create value for the idea's originator.

Professional colleagues that I have spoken to on this topic also point to one other thing: the individual aging process itself. There will always be a small number of people who will be fit as a fiddle and capable of running a marathon at the age of 60, 70, or even over 80. We look to them as role models. Analysis by MarathonGuide.com indicated that in 2011 less than 1% of female runners and under 4% of male runners in US marathons were over the age of 60.[17]

But there is a harsh reality, which is that as we get older we invariably get more tired. Putting in a long, hard shift becomes increasingly difficult. For older employees who are still working, it is often momentum and habit that carries them through: they are stimulated by their work ethic, but their recovery time is longer. Employers and recruiters know that already. It's natural therefore that with age comes greater prioritisation – energy is saved to do things that are both important and valuable.

If earlier we suggested that the approach taken by Maslow in terms of his hierarchy of needs has been turned on its head by the new flat white culture of entrepreneurism, perhaps a different model might apply to Gen X entrepreneurs whose houses are paid for and whose kids have left home. They already have stability, but they still have a desire for self-fulfilment. Without self-fulfilment, will they perhaps run the risk of destabilisation? Do Maslow's ideas need yet again to be flipped on their heads with respect to Gen X survivors?

REPLACING THE NEED TO WORK

Perhaps there's no need to worry about working after all. Won't AI be the creator of such wealth and growth that the need to work just won't exist any longer? In such an environment, won't we increasingly become consumers rather than producers? Some economists say that the greatest benefits to the market come from what we consume, rather than what we make.

It's even been suggested that AI will be the trigger for a degree of growth that will generate sufficient taxes to meet all our needs. Taxation would then become the vehicle for redistributing massive private profits for the benefit of all.

We shouldn't hold our breath. In his book *Superintelligence*, Nick Bostrom, director of the Future of Humanity Institute and an Oxford professor, suggests that to provide the world's population of 7 billion people with an annual income of US$90,000 each would cost US$630 trillion a year. This is 10 times the current world GDP. Currently the global GDP stands at US$74 billion and is growing at 3% per year. Taking into account the maturing of markets, there has been a growth of global GDP of 19 times since 1900. If that trend not only continues but accelerates, with technology as a key catalyst, then (with the caveat that the population remains reasonably constant – albeit that it is currently growing about 3% annually) there might be enough in the pot to hit a US$90,000 payout for all of us within a couple of hundred years.[18]

Perhaps one day it will be possible to balance the books. If it does become possible – and it's a really big if – then the need for us to work, religious ethic aside, is likely to be a few generations away.

In the meantime it could be a rough ride, with fewer jobs, less personal income, reduced consumer spending power, less taxable income, and greater pressure on the public purse. Governments continue to create operational efficiencies as a result of e-commerce, but it's difficult not to feel that there is some form of crunch time ahead. How this will play out is anyone's guess at the moment, but public services are likely to be in the crosshairs of reduced spending targets, which will inevitably have a knock-on effect on public-sector workers.

Will advanced technology also somehow exacerbate class divisions rather than eradicate them? Wealthy workers are likely to be better placed to retrain and acquire new skills; retraining may not be available to lower-skilled workers, who may be left behind.

Those who are successful in this new age are likely to become very successful, but not everyone will be fortunate and society will need to come to terms with the consequences. The 1997 movie *The Full Monty* tells the story of six men from different backgrounds who fall on hard times as a result of a changing economy, revealing in painful detail how unemployment is unforgiving in terms of class distinctions. In the movie even the redundant executive loses his superior status at the end of the day, as he stands beside former steel workers and, also unemployed, all remove their clothes in front of a screaming audience.

CONCLUSION

The purpose of this chapter is to help place the world of work into context. By understanding why we need to work, we gain greater insight into our personal motivations. For sure, it is about paying the bills and in many cases survival, but beyond these incentives there seem to be deeper reasons.

We start to understand that different age groups have different drivers and attitudes towards work. The traditional motivators highlighted by Maslow seem increasingly turned on their heads as both young and old approach the work environment from new angles.

How we cope or even survive with this new age will be influenced not only by the way that we continue to communicate and collaborate with each other, but also by how we recognise the value of our abilities and how to monetise that value. Some will anticipate the future and prudently work towards it, either incrementally or radically. Others will need to be cognisant of what is happening around them and react accordingly. For both groups knowledge is critical, and it is for that reason that the next few chapters take us through some of the basics.

NOTES

1. Christopher Fyfe, Review of *Ancient Slavery and Modern Ideology*, by Moses I. Finley. *History Today* (1980). http://www.historytoday.com/christopher-fyfe/ancient-slavery-and-modern-ideology
2. Lorenz Diefenbach, Arbeit Macht Frei: Erzählung von Lorenz Diefenbach [in German] (J. Kühtmann's Buchhandlung, 1873).
3. Richard Donkin, *Blood Sweat and Tears: The Evolution of Work* (reprint edition) (Texere Publishing, September 2002).
4. Sandra Laville and Nils Pratley, Brothers who sit at Blair's right hand. *The Guardian* (14 June 2005). www.theguardian.com/uk/2005/jun/14/Whitehall.politics
5. Abraham H. Maslow, Maslow on management. London: John Wiley & Sons, 1998.
6. Caitlin Gibson, Who are these kids? *Washington Post* (25 May 2016). http://www.washingtonpost.com/sf/style/2016/05/25/inside-the-race-to-decipher-todays-teens-who-will-transform-society-as-we-know-it/?utm_term=.af4e2fef4a93
7. Douglas McWilliam, *The Flat White Economy* (London: Duckworth Overlook, 2015).
8. Spiritual England. Spirituality in the workplace. http://www.spiritualengland.org.uk/spirituality-workplace (accessed 14 August 2017).
9. Buddhist Centre (n.d.). Introduction. https://thebuddhistcentre.com/Buddhism (accessed 14 August 2017).
10. Ibid.
11. Kallum Pickering, Automatic response to fear rise of robots is flawed. *The Telegraph* (9 August 2017). http://www.telegraph.co.uk/business/2017/08/09/automatic-response-fear-rise-robots-isflawed
12. Ibid.
13. Jason Zweig, As automation spreads, new rivals stalk financial advisers. *Wall Street Journal* (26 July 2017). https://www.wsj.com/articles/talk-is-cheap-automation-takes-aim-at-financial-advisersand-their-fees-1501099600 (accessed 28 July 2017).
14. Elizabeth Landau, Unemployment takes tough mental toll. CNN (15 June 2012). http://edition.cnn.com/2012/06/14/health/mental-health/psychology-unemployment/index.html
15. Tami Luhby, Only 1 in 10 long-term unemployed find work. CNN Money (14 June 2012). http://money.cnn.com/2012/06/14/news/economy/long-term-unemployment/index.htm?iid=Lead
16. UK Department for Work and Pensions. Fundamental reform to fight ageism in the workplace: older workers' scheme to tackle age discrimination. Press release (22 December 2014). https://www.gov.uk/government/news/fundamental-reform-to-fight-ageism-in-the-workplace-older-workers-scheme-to-tackle-age-discrimination
17. MarathonGuide.com Staff (n.d.). USA marathoning: 2011 overview. http://www.marathonguide.com/features/Articles/2011RecapOverview.cfm (accessed 18 October 2017).
18. Nick Bostrom, *Superintelligence: Paths, Dangers, Strategies* (Oxford: Oxford University Press, 2014).

CHAPTER 1

Introduction to Analytics

SUMMARY

This chapter provides the reader with an introduction to analytics in its various forms, from relatively basic business intelligence (BI) to more advanced prescriptive and predictive analytics. It provides an introduction to cognitive analytics and artificial intelligence (AI). It concludes with the issue of machine infallibility.

INTRODUCTION

DAVE BOWMAN:	Hello, HAL. Do you read me, HAL?
HAL:	Affirmative, Dave. I read you.
DAVE BOWMAN:	Open the pod bay doors, HAL.
HAL:	I'm sorry, Dave. I'm afraid I can't do that.
DAVE BOWMAN:	What's the problem?
HAL:	I think you know what the problem is just as well as I do.
DAVE BOWMAN:	What are you talking about, HAL?
HAL:	This mission is too important for me to allow you to jeopardize it.

2001: A Space Odyssey

For many readers, the concept of AI is something that is seated in science fiction. The opening lines in this section recollect a fictional discussion in the Stanley Kubrick movie *2001: A Space Odyssey*, made in 1968 about a manned space trip to Jupiter.

The conversation is held between the captain of the space ship, Dave Bowman, and his on-board computer, HAL 9000 (known to the crew simply as HAL). The essence of the plot is that HAL knows more than the humans on the spaceship and attempts to take control, but is wrestled back by the remaining crew member, who pulls out HAL's plug. That's a hugely simplistic summary of the story. The full text in the Arthur C. Clarke book upon which the movie is based includes the suggestion that HAL has more information about the space mission than the crew itself, and therefore the computer is in some ways the superior being.

As a piece of cinematography, *2001: A Space Odyssey* received mixed reviews from science fiction writers, some of whom called the script 'banal'. On the other hand, it was also described by George Lucas of *Star Wars* fame as being 'the ultimate science fiction movie'. The story itself is loosely based on a short story written in 1948 and published in 1951 called 'The Sentinel of Eternity'. In it a kind of monolith is discovered on the moon, which is thought to have been left there as a warning beacon for future intelligent life forms.

The degree to which our perception of the future is influenced by the arts, such as science fiction stories and movies, is intriguing and curious. It is almost as if we are leaving it to others to create a vision that we will ultimately subscribe to, either as individuals or as humanity as a whole.

In its broadest sense, the concept of creating AI goes back to the ancient philosophers. The ancient myth of Pygmalion, a legendary figure of Cyprus, recalls him as a sculptor creating a beautiful figure from ivory that he attempts to breathe life into. In more recent times that same story replicates itself in Disney's *Pinocchio* and in the Broadway musical (and subsequent film) *My Fair Lady*.

The creation of intelligent beings has been a common theme through time. The Mary Shelly novel *Frankenstein* (also known as *The Modern Prometheus*) was published in 1820, when Shelly was only 20 years old. It tells the story of Doctor Victor Frankenstein, who creates a so-called monster. The creature itself is often referred to as Frankenstein, or more correctly, Frankenstein's Monster. In older movies it was most often portrayed by actors such as Boris Karloff and others from the silent film era as a humanoid assembled by a mad doctor. Nowadays we picture the monster's head as being fixed to its body by a large bolt assembly, the type that you can commonly buy in an everyday joke shop or fancy-dress shop. It's an enduring image, even if it's mainly misleading.

Shelley's story has its foundations in Gothic and Romantic narrative. Beyond this, it is specifically influenced by the modern (at that time) principle of galvanisation, which mainly described the ability to create apparent life in the legs of a dead frog by pushing an electrical impulse through the frog. 'What might happen', Mary Shelley might have mused, 'if a dead but reassembled humanoid was subject to a similar electrical impulse?' And so, as a result, we start with some preconceived ideas of artificial humanity lumbering through the forest in search of a similarly artificially created wife, the so-called bride of Frankenstein.

The Frankenstein concept has moved with the times. The movie *Westworld* was a 1973 science fiction thriller created by Michael Crichton of *Jurassic Park* fame about humanoid, extremely lifelike robots in an amusement park called Delos. The robots interact with (real) humans in a way that is virtually indistinguishable from the way real people interact and exist in a series of worlds, such as the Wild West period, and medieval and ancient Roman times.

The value proposition for paying visitors to Delos is that the robots give *absolute* satisfaction to the paying guests in whatever form that takes. However, a series of system failures start to result in the robots killing not only the paying guests but also each other. When asked to turn them off, the supervising scientist says, 'In some cases they have been designed by computers themselves. We don't know exactly how they work'.

The 2016 TV series *Westworld* adds a further novel angle. It deliberately becomes increasingly more difficult to identify who are the robots and who are the paying guests, as a result of the host robots developing a virus and distorting how they perceive their own existence. At the heart of this particular narrative is the unspoken question of what is better: a robot with a conscience or a real person who is nasty, and of these two types, who has the moral superiority?

So it is against this background of media-driven perception that we need to consider the realities and practicalities of the implementation and future use of advanced analytics and AI in business and professional life, and how their influence will affect the way that we conduct our day-to-day affairs. This approach will probably not entirely satisfy the curiosity of purist technologists, however, this book is aimed not at that audience but rather at the generalist and business practitioner, who will be on the front lines of decision-making, at least for the moment.

Our initial journey will take us from the very basics of BI, through the foothills of predictive and prescriptive analytics, and ultimately to the mountain peaks of cognitive analytics and AI. According to Deloitte, 'Cognitive analytics offers a way to bridge the gap between big data and the reality of practical decision making'.[1]

Whilst not strictly a proprietary terminology, cognitive analytics is often most associated with particular technology companies (such as IBM), which have used it to describe their own processes for gaining insights into big data usually through the use of so-called 'Intelligent API's' such as face, speech, and vision applications. (An API, or application programming interface, is a set of definitions, protocols, and tools that collectively provide the building blocks to help a programmer build a new programme.)

To start to set the scene, it might be helpful to try to explain the difference between cognitive analytics and AI. IBM's particular viewpoint is best expressed in its description of the use of each technology in a medical context: 'In an artificial intelligence system, the system would have told the doctor which course of action to take based on its analysis. In cognitive computing, the system provides information to help the doctor decide'.[2]

In the maturity curve of analytics, how this model works appears to be mainly a matter of degree. In time, a doctor who acts against the cognitive advice given might prove to be either brave or reckless; the model also opens the door to some very interesting future discussions on the topic of professional negligence. However, it is prudent to start with the basics and work our way through the evolution of analytics in order that the reader may have a firm understanding of the foundations.

BUSINESS INTELLIGENCE

Was there ever a time that those running businesses did not consider themselves to be intelligent? By the time that Adam Smith (1723–1790) had put pen to paper in 1776 to write *The Wealth of Nations*, it was already clear that industrialists had a pretty good idea about how the economy works and what makes businesses profitable and successful. 'High wages of labour and high profits of stock', wrote Smith, 'seldom go together ... except in the peculiar circumstances of new colonies'.[3] Perhaps the expression *disruptive technologies* could be substituted for the word *colonies* in this quotation?

Some of his ideas seem more obvious in hindsight. 'A great stock,' he said, 'though with small profits, generally increases faster than a small stock with great profits'. In those days, information would have been collected and stored in leather-bound ledgers more at home in a Charles Dickens novel. The advent of the modern computer created enormous stimulus for change, and it is sometimes argued that spreadsheets became one of the most important applications in their history.

Spreadsheet solutions such as VisiCalc, Lotus 123, Excel, and others have increasingly found their way into modern decision-making. For many accountants the work done by these tools (or their current replacements) is the backbone of their calculations. However, in a more complex and dynamic accounting environment, traditional spreadsheets are increasingly being viewed as dated, described by some as being limited in their ability to make substantial improvements in functionality (which seems to be mainly confined to better visualisations). It's a harsh verdict for tried and tested tools that remain the default way of carrying out calculations for many users. Even today, modern BI vendors still try to create a spreadsheet-type touch and feel to their more modern capabilities, paying homage to their software predecessors.

Nowadays, BI is increasingly becoming the cornerstone of enterprise decision-making. The pace of change has continued to accelerate as BI tools are increasingly becoming commoditised. There are multiple vendors in the marketplace and there is no shortage of advice provided by them. According to the analysts at Gartner, the BI market opportunity alone is projected to be valued at US$20.8 billion by 2018 (2014 sales were dominated by SAP, with a market share of 21.3%, followed by Oracle at 14% and IBM at 13%).[4]

In addition to these megavendors, there are many smaller specialist vendors. One of these recently issued its own views on the top 10 trends:[5]

1. Governance and self-service analytics becoming best friends
2. Visual analytics becoming a common language
3. The data product chain becoming democratized
4. Data integration getting exciting
5. Advanced analytics is no longer for analysts
6. Cloud data and cloud analytics taking off
7. The analytics centre of excellence becomes excellent
8. Mobile analytics stands on its own
9. People begin to dig into IoT (internet of things) data
10. New technologies rise to fill the gaps.

Stripping away the marketing hype and the possibility that data integration could *ever* be exciting, the summary appears to indicate that what started off a decade ago as being an enhanced replacement for spreadsheets has now become a fully blown industry in its own right, and an industry with ambition.

Standard BI software and systems, which some might suggest are no more than an enriched form of enhanced management information technology, are now increasingly overlapping with advanced analytics, cloud-based solutions, and mobile enablement. Consultative selling has become prevalent, with technology-enabled ex-accountants often operating in a quasi-sales capacity.

Not only are BI vendors suggesting the best technology for clients to use to resolve their business issues, they are also increasingly telling them how to internally restructure themselves to take optimum advantage of these new and enhanced capabilities.

For large and small vendors alike, there should be no real need to talk up the BI market. The economy has invariably created trading conditions of increasing complexity, and with that a need for greater granularity of data and more detailed insight. The speed of change in an increasingly volatile market forces practitioners to remain constantly on the lookout for change and to react accordingly. Where there are detrimental business results, it becomes essential to act quickly and decisively to stem the losses; where there are opportunities, to move equally quickly and take appropriate advantage. The ability to create a quarterly rolling forecast (or an even more frequent one) is sometimes described as one of the most important financial management planning tools of current times.

The detailed merits of financial performance management tools can be found elsewhere in many books about accounting practices, but the main point to be made here is that effective financial performance management is the cornerstone of enterprise analytics. Through this, it becomes much more straightforward for organisations to understand the impact of, for example:

- Deemphasising or sunsetting a product or solution
- Selling a business or growing thorough acquisition
- Changes in customer demand or supplier capacity
- Understanding the financial impact of organisational change, that is, headcount reduction
- Currency fluctuations and market volatility.

Despite these new capabilities there remain many companies who are at a very basic level of analytical maturity. Businesses in emerging markets, in particular, are at an early stage in their analytical journeys. With cognitive analytics and AI likely to be heavily influencing their business activities within a decade, it seems essential that emerging market players pick up the pace and start to implement new analytical ideas quickly.

Almost certainly, measuring the improvement in more advanced analytics and AI capabilities will rest on the effective use of BI tools.

It may be helpful to understand why some countries and markets haven't progressed as quickly as others. Part of the answer may well be in the strategies of the technology vendors themselves, who have tended to focus on the relatively low-hanging fruit of their local home markets, where there is still considerable growth to be obtained.

Other reasons may also be:

- Business partner strategies that also focus on home markets rather than emerging and growth markets.
- Absence of local evangelism.
- Soft or weak leadership.
- Ineffective marketing campaigns that focus on technical capability rather than business need.
- Geographical maturity.
- Sensitivity of smaller organisations to incurring the cost of new technologies.
- Inertia of small businesses – and some larger, more traditional businesses as well – with respect to change.

If there is concern about adopting and implementing even foundational analytics in the office of finance, then important questions might need to be asked about the ability of those businesses to embrace more advanced analytics, which will ultimately lead to cognitive insights and AI.

ADVANCED ANALYTICS

One of the leading analytics companies, Gartner, describes advanced analytics as follows: 'The analysis of all kinds of data using sophisticated quantitative methods (e.g., statistic, descriptive, and predictive data mining, simulation and optimisation) to produce insights that traditional approaches to business intelligence ... are unlikely to discover'.[6] It's as good a description as any, and better than most.

Advanced analytics, sometimes also known as predictive analytics, usually comprises the series of capabilities shown in Table 4.

Dr Colin Linsky, a leading analytics expert at IBM, helpfully clarifies the difference between advanced analytics and predictive analytics, saying:

Predictive analytics is a subset of all advanced analytics techniques. There are plenty more advanced analytics algorithms and routines that are not predictive.

Commonly, models that are built to describe when used again on fresh data would (also) be said to be predictive.

Some are, by design, looking at future time periods and would be thought of as predictive, whereas others just classify or segment. They only become predictive by being used on a later subsequent set of data to which the outcome of the business problem is unknown.

So, in effect, prediction depends not only on algorithms, calculations, and routines, but also on the nature of the data and the time frame. Put another way, *prediction* is a generic expression for a broader capability or function, not a tool.

At this stage the reader (perhaps like the author) might start to become confused, and even begin to feel that if advanced analytics is this complex, then how much more complex could cognitive analytics and AI be? And if it is so complex, then surely shouldn't it be left in the hands of other people – let's call them experts, for want of a better name – rather than the majority of us, who are relatively uninformed?

Doesn't a fear factor also start to emerge with respect to the technology itself as a result of not understanding the jargon? Isn't the individual fearful not only of the jargon and technology, but also of the impact of these on their jobs and livelihood?

This viewpoint is arguably no different than that taken by many people in business when they think they need technology to improve broader business results (as opposed to a day-to-day breakdown of the system or laptop) and they call on the IT department to give them a helping hand. Some will remember that for many, the relatively fractious nature of that relationship is typified by a difference in understanding of each party with respect to the needs of the other, with conversations often shrouded in jargon.

These new IT-led business solutions often have shown themselves ultimately to be technology solutions that are late and unduly expensive, and that usually don't solve the problem they were intended to solve. These kinds of problems are often also characterised by a silo approach to business problems, which is usually exacerbated by representatives of the IT department and the line of business each using different terminology.

Over time, this approach has been mitigated not only by a greater understanding of the role of IT in business (and vice versa) but also by the emergence of new roles and positions. Often these new roles carry relatively obscure titles, but overall we can generalise them colloquially as lobits: line-of-business IT professionals. In effect these

TABLE 4 Typical capabilities used in advanced analytics.

Capability	Function	Typical usage
Pareto analysis	Often known as the 80/20 rule, it is a form of analysis that identifies the top proportion of causes for the majority of problems. 80/20 implies that 80% of all problems arise due to 20% of causes, but this is not a hard and fast rule.	The application of Pareto's rule in risk management helps organisations focus on those causes which are likely to comprise the greatest risk.
Clustering/ k-means	Clustering is a way of grouping a set of objects together in some way, based on the fact that the objects in the cluster are more similar to each other than to those in a different cluster.	In biology, used to make spatial comparisons of communities. In market research, used to partition general groups of consumers. K-means clustering means to partition each group into a cluster based on the mean of that group; it is used in data mining to minimise intracluster variance.
Forecasting using Holt-Winters methodology	Also known as triple exponential smoothing, it's a process that can be used to forecast data points in a series, provided that the series is repetitive (or seasonal) over some period.	Used for making certain assumptions, such as calculating or recalling some data; for example, trending of house prices and inflation rates.
Decision-tree analysis	A decision support tool that uses a tree-like graph or model of decisions and their possible consequences.	Used in decision management to identify a strategy to reach a goal; often used in management science, healthcare, and operations management.
Rules of association	Rules-based learning method that identifies relationships between variables in large databases coupled with levels of confidence.	Promotional pricing, product placement, market-basket analysis.
Logistic regression	Also known as a logit model, it is a type of linear model that estimates the probability or dependency of a certain outcome.	Determines whether a customer will buy a product based on (for example) age, gender, geography.
Linear regression	An approach for modelling the relationship between a data set and one particular variable. Think of it in terms of finding a single line on a graph that represents a range of data points. Can show changes in data over time.	Used in creating trend lines (e.g. for GDP and oil prices). Capital asset pricing model.

(continued)

TABLE 4   (*Continued*)

Capability	Function	Typical usage
Correlation	A broad set of statistical relationships, although usually relating to two variables that appear to have a linear relationship with each other. Useful, as it can identify a predictive relationship with its members.	Correlation between electrical demand and weather. (This is a causal relationship, in that one is dependent on the other – but correlation is not necessarily causality.)
Bayes	Also known as Bayes Law, or Bayes Rule, it describes the probability of something happening based on prior knowledge that it may be related to an event.	Can be used in medical diagnosis or fraud detection, for example, but can be affected by false positives, which is, in effect, a statistical anomaly that shows positive when the answer should be negative and vice versa.

are roles – or, more usually, individuals – who sit between specific business functions (what we otherwise call the line of business) and the IT department. These individuals have at best an understanding – or, at least, a strong awareness – of the needs and language of each party. In many cases they will have an understanding of specific sector or business function as well as computer and system capability.

One question to be addressed is whether it is easier for a business person to learn technology, or a technologist to understand business issues. Both are equally complex, and the ideal lobit needs to be bidirectional in approach.

To become bidirectional in approach requires not only unique technical skills, but also an understanding of key business drivers or pain points. It also depends on having the right can-do attitude, coupled with agility of thought and flexibility of approach. These are as much about personal characteristics as about technical competence. Beyond this, the constantly shifting nature both of commerce and technology are such that technical and business skills need to be continually reinforced by training and experience. The mood of the moment is increasingly that of vertical (i.e. industry oriented or functional) solutions, which encourages individuals to create some degree of specialisation.

Inevitably, resourcing and bandwidth issues start to emerge. If there are not enough of these people around to meet the needs of the existing market, how then will the various industries cope with the massive expected increase in demand for advanced analytical services? And how will the emerging growth markets, such as Asia and Latin America, cope?

It seems inevitable that university and professional qualifications will have to quickly start to reflect these technological and business needs, through changes to curriculum. Employees, whose career paths have often focused solely on business or technology, will increasingly need to work in a learning environment that accommodates both.

One answer may well rest in the concept of 'analytics as a service', which is in effect an outsourced analytical capability, but this arrangement, too, is not without potential bandwidth problems. In any event, many organisations still remain nervous about data security, and the penalty for getting it wrong can be considerable in both financial terms and soft reputational terms. Outsourcing the analytical function is usually dependent on procurement experts becoming engaged in the selection process. It becomes critically important that the procurement team is aware of all the essential issues in order to advise properly on contracts and to manage the postcontract relationship effectively.

Employers increasingly need to look at the career development of their staff through a different lens. This impacts not only hard performance measures at the individual level, but a whole range of softer capabilities, such as awareness, flexibility, and agility.

At such a transformational time in business, there is also a sense that professionals within the human resources department may not yet have fully recognised the scale of the challenge in front of them. They, too, will need to change with the times.

Beyond these ideas, there is also a harsh reality about moving to the next stage of the analytics maturity curve. If organisations and technology companies are already struggling to support the individuals dealing solely with BI and advanced analytics, how can they possibly respond to the more complex needs of a world of cognitive analytics and AI?

Advanced analytics is an inevitable next step in the evolution of the analytics agenda. Most of the analytics companies and consultants are forecasting massive growth in this area, and predicting that companies will be using advanced or predictive analytics in multiple areas. One good example is the ability to predict equipment failure.[7] With this ability, manufacturers are able to plan for preventative maintenance, whilst dependent clients are saved the disruption of breakdowns, interruption to process, and costly downtime (see Table 5).

Advanced analytics will not only impact the way we work but will inevitably impact our social and private life as well, in terms of:

- The books we read and the music we listen to
- The TV shows we choose to watch (or more likely record for a later date – assuming, of course, that we have not reverted entirely to an on-demand form of viewing)
- The restaurants we visit and the nearest coffee shop
- The route home that we should take
- What we buy our partners for their birthdays
- Who might want to cause us harm, especially through online contact
- When our home freezer will break down, and what we should do about it
- Where we should go for our holidays.

The odd thing – if it is indeed odd – is that soon we will take this sort of information for granted. Of the eight relatively random items on the preceding list, only one of these is speculative: the issue of when the home freezer will break down. But that technical capability already exists and is used in commercial freezers, which are able to detect problems and make what's called a residual life prediction. Beyond this detection function, the system can also diagnose the problem and anticipate what work is needed to prolong the life of the equipment before breakdown. By being able to contrast the performance of the freezer (or other equipment) with competitive information obtained

TABLE 5 Uses of advanced analytics.

Function	Benefit	Industry affected	Industry imperative
Understand which customers might leave and offer them an incentive to stay	Optimised marketing expenditure, enhanced customer loyalty	Multiple; e.g. financial services	Cost reduction
Anticipate sales volumes of foodstuffs by considering weather conditions	Greater sales, more targeted sales promotions, optimised shelf life, customer loyalty	Consumer retail	Revenue improvement
Optimise delivery routes	Reduced fuel costs, reduces maintenance costs	Consumer retail	Cost reduction
Identify which machines are most likely to need maintenance	Reduced downtime, optimised cost through planned maintenance	Multiple; e.g. manufacturing, construction	Cost reduction
Anticipate which properties are most likely to be affected by hurricanes	Preventative action by insurers, homeowners, commercial businesses; more effective mobilisation of supply chain; better financial management	Insurance, construction, property development	Risk management, better profitability, cost reduction
Improve child protection	Social benefit, optimised services	Social services	Risk management, cost reduction
Clinical support systems	Better prioritisation, social benefit, optimised services; improved supply chain	Social services, healthcare, insurance	Risk management, cost reduction
Direct marketing	Reduced marketing cost, upsell, and cross-sell	Multiple; e.g. financial services	Cost reduction, improved revenue
Fraud detection	Improved granularity of pricing, better risk management	Insurance	Cost reduction
Underwriting	Improved granularity of pricing, better risk management	Insurance	Improved revenue, cost reduction
Collection analytics	Greater control over payment delinquency	Multiple; e.g. financial services	Risk management, cost reduction
Crime management	Social benefit, service optimisation	Police, crime prevention	Risk management, cost reduction

through external industry data, freezer manufacturers are not only able to manage their performance compared to industry benchmarks but also to use that information to ensure that they remain competitive.

Information and analysis in isolation is important, but perhaps more important is the use of that insight to allow comparisons to be made. Will this comparative process, in which information is placed in context (a process called contextual analytics) be one of the next waves of analytical development?

Turning back to the freezer question, how then might we feel if we received some form of individual e-contact forewarning us of a likely breakdown and recommending that action be taken to prevent this from occurring? Would we take action? How many reminders would be needed? Predictive analytics may provide a probabilistic insight into what might happen, but won't the action we actually take often depend on our own behavioural traits? Might our attitude change if we also received a message from our freezer insurance company saying that any claim for defrosted goods would be rejected because we had failed to take appropriate action? How might we feel if the supermarket refused to sell us more frozen goods at checkout because of the risk of not being able to store them?

In essence, therefore, this so-called new era of data, coupled with connectivity, predictability, and insight are not only likely to have an impact on the way we work but also on the way we live – in a way that is currently unimaginable. Should society wait for this to happen and then respond? Or is it better that we understand not only what is happening but why it is happening, in order that we all – as key stakeholders – can participate in the discussion and ultimately influence the outcome?

PRESCRIPTIVE ANALYTICS

Prescriptive analytics is generally thought of as being the third era of analytics (coming after BI and predictive analytics). If predictive analytics anticipates from the data what is likely to happen, then prescriptive analytics goes one step further by suggesting what should be done about it.

At the heart of prescriptive analytics is the question, why has this happened? By understanding this question, it becomes possible to identify a positive or a mitigating action to benefit from the prediction.

The term *prescriptive analytics* was first coined in a 2010 paper that appeared in *Analytics* magazine, in which it was described as 'a set of mathematical techniques that computationally determine a set of high-value alternative actions or decisions given a complex set of objectives, requirements, and constraints, with the goal of improving business performance'.[8]

The paper suggested that prescriptive analytics is the pursuit of two options, which the authors labelled 'optimisation' and 'stochastic optimisation'. They are:

1. How can we achieve the best outcome?
2. How can we achieve the best outcome and address uncertainty in the data to make better decisions?

The term *stochastic* is a form of probability model used to determine changes that evolve over time. More specifically, it is the mathematical model of a process whereby one of the variables is subject to the influence of another random variable. Examples of this might include:

- Analysis of how an investment portfolio might respond based on the results (probabilistic distribution) of individual stock returns.
- Modelling the survival of a rare species and how different strategies might impact that survival rate.

The expression *prescriptive analytics* was copyrighted by Texas-based Ayata, which was founded in 2003 and now focuses on the oil and gas production, insurance and renewables industries. It describes *prescriptive* as being '… a recipe. A series of time-dependent actions to improve future outcomes'.[9] Prescriptive analytics is described as a combination of the following items:

- *Models.* A way of organising data, often associated with a degree of standardisation.
- *Data.* The raw components of analysis, which comprise quantitative and qualitative values.
- *Business rules.* In this context, usually a piece of computer software that executes key business decisions in a production environment.

On the other hand, Ayata describes predictive analytics as comprising a series of key components or capabilities, which include:

- Machine learning
- Applied statistics
- Operational research
- Natural language processing
- Pattern recognition
- Computer vision (how computers gain understanding from digital images)
- Image processing
- Speech recognition.

If the casual reader was already confused by the difference between *predictive* and *prescriptive*, then this confusion might be worsened by reflecting on Ayata's description of *prescriptive*. After all, how many more capabilities might possibly be needed to provide cognitive analytics and therefore some form of AI?

Perhaps this is one of the issues of technological advancement? As professionals attempt to describe the different forms of analytics by giving them different titles, they create further confusion amongst lay readers, who are beaten down by jargon.

In time some analytical terminology will become obsolete. It's impossible to uninvent existing words, although it is quite natural for terms and expressions to fall from common use with the passage of time. (Who remembers the term *snoutfair* – a person with a delightful countenance – for example?) Perhaps the generic expression *management information* will eventualluy fall into that category – even if some colleges and universities still promote it as a course of study.

The term *management information* is usually taken to comprise the study of those systems that connect people, technology, and organisations – and how they relate to each other. Where does management information stop and BI start – and how do both of these morph into advanced and cognitive analytics? Maybe with time we will develop an entirely new and relevant lexicography, and new ways of expressing ourselves in these complex areas.

Figure 2 attempts to identify the relatively linear flow of progress of the subject of analytics.

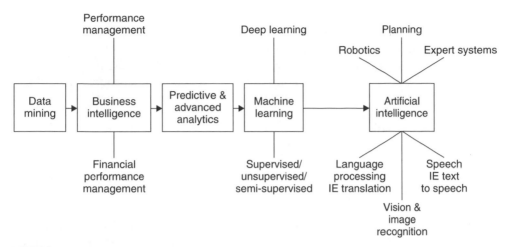

FIGURE 2   The road to artificial intelligence.

BUSINESS RULES

An essential difference between prediction and prescription is the application of business rules, usually through some form of business rules engine.

So-called business rules engines are often known as *operational decision management* and have been around since the early 1990s, when they were introduced by companies such as Pegasystems, Ilog (now part of IBM), and Fair Isaac. In effect, the rules adopted by a business (which might relate to operations, risk management, supply chain, or any other management policy) are put into operation through what is known as executional code in the system; that is, a directive to the system to carry out certain tasks according to coded instructions.

Business rules software may form part of a larger suite of business-rules management, which may include the following:

- Consistency and governance of key decisions
- Prioritisation for certain classes of customer
- Registration of rule changes.

Rules engines are often separate from the data system and allow users to make changes without involving the IT department. For example, in the case of insurance claim inspections, the claims department might be able to change the clip level – that is, the financial figure above which claims are always inspected – if there is a sudden surge of claims, such as in the case of a major weather incident.

Digging more deeply, the business rules process also generally comprises two elements:

1. Detection of some sort of business situation, which triggers a notification
2. Detection of an overload within the process, which may require some sort of change.

Underpinning both of these is the notion of workflow. Workflow is in effect the systemised sequence of activities that transform labour, materials, and other assets into consumable goods or services. With its foundation in time and motion studies, over time it has been seen in various guises, including Total Quality Management, Six Sigma, and more recently, Business Process Reengineering.

Looking forward, one of the potential weaknesses of these relatively traditional workflow processes is that they are linear in nature and are dependent on a linear sequence of events. It is entirely feasible that the traditional approach to relatively linear workflow will start to become outdated. In some cases existing workflows may already contain so-called loops, with the first step in the process being initiated by the last step in the process, but future workflows might prove to be much more random or complex in nature.

For example, the supply chain process has traditionally been thought of as a linear process: hence the term *chain*. One view of the supply chain of the future envisions a supplier ecosystem that is no longer linear in nature but depends holistically on bidirectional connectivity and collaboration.[10] In such a nonlinear model, intelligent systems continually assess multiple constraints and alternatives, and ultimately allow decision makers to simulate various courses of action.

The increased impact of the internet of things will certainly have an effect on traditional linear thinking. Analysts have already identified *interaction management* as being a critical success factor going forward. Interaction management comprises the ability to cope with multiple interactions and to orchestrate them. Gartner describes this as 'Thinking less about processes, more about interactions'.[11]

As with many parts of the technology sector, there are professional institutions and organisations for each aspect of a process. The US-based BPM Institute identifies a series of key skills and capabilities that are necessary to be successful in BPM, that is, Business Process Management (see Table 6).[12]

Whilst in many ways the preceding skills may seem to be relatively generic for the analytics industry, it might be argued that many of these could usefully form a framework for a broader Advanced Analytics/AI/Cognitive Analytics Institute were one to exist (or subsequently to be formed).

TABLE 6   Key skills and capabilities of BPM practitioners.

Key capabilities of BPM practitioners	Key skills of BPM practitioners
Aligning processes with business strategy	Systems thinking
Discovering and modelling processes	Process discovery and modelling
Measuring and improving processes	Facilitation skills
Harvesting policies and rules	Performance measurement
Managing the changing of culture	Process analysis and design
Governance and decision-making	Rules and decision management
Deployment of technology	Change management
	Project management
	Technical skills (requirements gathering, designing user experience, optimisation, and simulation)
	Governance and establishing centres of excellence

COGNITIVE ANALYTICS

According to Technopedia, 'Cognitive analytics can refer to a range of different analytical strategies that are used to learn about certain types of business related functions, such as customer outreach. Certain types of cognitive analytics also may be known as predictive analytics, where data mining and other cognitive uses of data can lead to predictions for business intelligence (BI).'[13]

Professional services company Deloitte has already trademarked the term *cognitive analytics*. A trademark is a distinguishing sign or expression that acts as to differentiate a product or service from competing companies. 'Cognitive analytics', Deloitte states, 'is a term used to describe how organisations apply analytics and cognitive computing technologies to help humans make smarter decisions.'[14]

These are relatively loose descriptions and arguably are more conceptual than definitive. At best, we need to understand cognitive analytics as representing a system that allows the user to interrogate both structured and unstructured data, both internal and external to the organisation, and from this data to

- Interact with the user in natural language
- Understand the issue that the user is trying to address
- Use a form of reasoning or basic intellect
- Learn from the answers and feedback.

One of the most-quoted representations of cognitive analytics is the much-heralded presence of IBM's Watson computer on the US game show *Jeopardy*, where a cognitive system outperformed previous champions. It follows IBM's previous and now legendary foray into games playing, when their Deep Blue computer beat the then world champion of chess, Garry Kasparov, in 1996.

In what should have been a clarion call for the power of technology, the incident unfortunately ended in a degree of acrimony. Kasparov (who many view as being the greatest chess champion of all time) accused Deep Blue's manufacturer of cheating, by using human intervention between the individual games in a series of six. Afterwards the officiator, Monty Newman, said, 'What Mr. Kasparov does have, that the computer doesn't, is a pulse'.[15] In retrospect, if that is the only distinguishing factor, then Deep Blue was a landmark invention.

The more recent IBM computer, Watson, is named after Thomas J. Watson (1874–1956), who was chairman and CEO of IBM. Watson provides cognitive intelligence through a series of connected APIs, which independently provide analytical capabilities. An API, as discussed previously, is a set of definitions, approaches, and tools to enable different capabilities to be bolted onto a system like a series of building blocks. APIs improve the ease, and therefore speed, of implementation.

In the case of Watson, the APIs that are available include such capabilities as

- Voice to text
- Text to voice
- Visual recognition
- Personality insights
- Tone analyser
- Various others.

An API is generally recognised as being the way in which disparate systems share information with each other. They underpin common web applications that are in everyday use. There's differing opinions about how hard it is to create – or write – an API. Experts describe it as anywhere from easy ('just writing a few lines of code') to painful, slow, and tedious.

This book has been written not for technocrats but rather for the layperson, whom the prospect of writing code will probably fill with horror. Simply, *code* is a series of instructions that are translated into binary messages to the computer using 0s and 1s that makes it carry out particular instructions.

The concept of binary coding goes back at least to the mid-1600s. Some suggest it might go as far back as the ninth century BCE and is even linked in some way to Chinese philosophical ideas. The ancient concept of yin and yang is described as a *duality*, in that each part represents an opposite force that is independent of the other, yet complementary and interconnected to the other, and which together interact to form a single dynamic system.

Microsoft's own cognitive solution, called Cortana, is rich in location and context awareness. It is marketed as having 'more personality' than its competitors. Developers have not only built gender into Cortana but even the ability to sing.[16]

This chapter opened with a quote from *2001: A Space Odyssey*; the closing parts of the movie show the computer HAL 9000 'dying' (if that is the right word for the decommissioning of a computer). As 'life' ebbs from HAL's system, the computer slowly sings the words to the old 1892 music hall song 'Daisy Bell' ('Daisy, Daisy / Give me your answer, do . . . '). The choice of that song by the film director Stanley Kubrick was not accidental. It recollects a historic, 1961 event, when one of the earliest and largest mainframe computers, an IBM 7094, warbled the first computer-generated song, which was (you guessed it) 'Daisy Bell'.

As an aside, it's often suggested that the name of the *Space Odyssey* computer, HAL, is a derivative of IBM, as the letters of the name (H-A-L) are one letter back in the alphabet from I-B-M. This has been denied by the writer Arthur C. Clarke and also by Kubrick, who both admitted some embarrassment over the apparently unplanned coincidence. In the follow-up *2010: Odyssey Two*, Clarke speaks through one of the characters, who says ' . . . I thought that by now every intelligent person knew that H-A-L is derived from Heuristic ALgorithm', a comment that Clarke subsequently reconfirmed in his novel *The Lost Worlds of 2001*.

Apple's Siri, its voice-driven personal assistant with an ability to interact with third-party apps, is said to have played a significant part in the development of the Apple Watch product. Similarly to Cortana, Siri seemingly has hidden depths of knowledge, including the ability to tell a bedtime story that allegedly ' . . . makes Siri seem so relatable. So delightful. So human.'[17]

The issue of 'personality' in computer systems is starting to get attention. As a result, we have begun to ask ourselves some slightly obscure questions. Typically these might include some of the following:

- How much does it matter whether a cognitive system interacts with a business user in a male or female voice? If it is important, are we subconsciously adding some element of gender to a computer system, and to what degree might this influence our personal relationship with the computer?
- Certainly scientific studies seem to indicate that people generally find a female voice more pleasing than a male voice. In his book *The Man Who Lied to His Laptop:*

What Machines Teach Us About Human Relationships, the author, Stanford University professor Clifford Nass, says, 'It's a well-established phenomenon that the human brain is developed to like female voices.' Because of this, many technology companies seemed to have steered clear of the male voice, so are we destined to a future of personal engagement with 'female computers'?

- What is the risk – if any – of users forming some type of personal relationship with their computer systems? *Her* is a romantic science-fiction drama about a man, Theodore Twombly, who develops a relationship with Samantha, the intelligent operating system of his computer, to the point that he even takes 'her' on holiday. The movie received generally positive reviews and received an Academy nomination for best picture in 2013.
- The story told in *Her* has its roots in an online article of the time that suggested that a user could potentially have an online, real-time conversation with an AI system. We now know that such capability is highly likely in the near future, if not actually here already.
- If we are concerned about the gender of and personal attachment to our cognitive systems, might this even extend to bereavement? Is the death of a computer system no more than some form of irreparable breakdown, or could it mean even more to us?
- We often say that our computer has 'died', and there are quite different thoughts about what we actually mean by 'death'. (The state of being dead? The permanent ending of vital systems? The permanent end of something?)

Is this thinking just nonsense? After all, we're just talking about machines, aren't we? But as we move forward – not only with technology, but also in the way the technology is adapted to create more attractive personas and as systems are adapted to better understand the user's personality – don't we somehow need to prime ourselves for some type of personal relationship with our machines different from our current one?

The classic movie *Blade Runner* from 1982 stars a young Harrison Ford and features Los Angeles in what seems now to be a not-so-futuristic 2019. In essence it is about beautifully made, smart humanoid robots that are built with a limited shelf life. Genius scientist Dr Tyrell not only creates a one-off robot called Rachael (which has embedded memories of a surrogate mother), but also teaches 'her' to love him, or at least to 'fool him into believing she would love him back'. The movie ends with Ford's character Rick Deckard and limited-life Rachael escaping to spend their limited time together.

Marcelo Gleiser's 2011 article 'Can Machines Fall in Love?' invites us (perhaps in a slightly tongue-in-cheek way) to reappraise the nature of the relationship between man and machine. In Japan, robots are already being created to keep the elderly company. As Gleiser puts it, 'If people in need are willing to compromise for less, while robots become more humanlike, there will be a joining of humans and machines. At what point then will machines stop being called machines?'[18]

THE ACCURACY OF ANALYTICAL OUTPUTS

Our journey so far has taken us from the proverbial valleys of management information to the lowlands of BI, predictive analytics, and prescriptive analytics, and ultimately to the peaks of cognitive analytics. In doing so, we have been lured into a technological trap that seems to suggest that the outcomes from the analysis are beyond doubt, but is that in fact the case?

In the case of BI, which we describe as being *descriptive*, one of the key tenets of the proposition is that there is a single version of the truth. In other words, time once spent in the boardroom discussing (and perhaps disagreeing about) who has the right set of figures is now potentially confined to history. Modern descriptive analytics embeds change controls and ensures that any alterations are fed through the entire set of figures.

Predictive and prescriptive analytics cannot be viewed in the same light. By definition, *prediction* is no more than a forecast about a set of events or circumstances. That forecast will have certain degrees of accuracy but should not be viewed as having absolute certainty. That is to say, if predictive analysis identifies a customer who is likely to change supplier, this prediction is nothing more than a hypothesis about a propensity to change, not an absolute guarantee.

Prediction is everywhere, from sports betting to the management of team performance and even to the political elections that determine our future. The accuracy of predictions can vary considerably, depending on which algorithms are used or the amount of data fed into the model. What is perhaps worrying is that, as individuals, we increasingly are relying heavily on predicted outcomes and using these predictions to drive our behaviour.

Prediction is often also associated with science fiction. Authors such as Philip K. Dick made fantastic guesses about what might happen in the future – for example, as with his literary creation of mutated humans (precogs) who can anticipate crimes in advance, as ultimately portrayed in the 2002 movie *Minority Report*. Such guesses are not, of course, real mathematical predictions, instead they exist in the realm of fantasy speculation.

The writer Isaac Asimov created the fictional concept of *psychohistory*, which combines history, sociology, and statistics to make fictional predictions about large groups of people and ultimately led to his 1951 *Foundation* series of books. His approach was to compare the behaviour of the human population to the behaviour of gases, in that it is impossible to predict the behaviour of one molecule of gas but possible to predict that of a larger volume of gas. This is known (in real life) as *kinetic theory*, which predicts the behaviour of a gas in motion by considering its pressure, temperature, conductivity, and other key attributes. Kinetic theory is not new. The Swiss mathematician and physicist Daniel Bernoulli was writing about it as far back as 1738, when he wrote *Hydrodynamica* (Latin for *hydrodynamics*), which set the ground rules for fluid mechanics.

It's tempting also to look at the accuracy of political opinion polls and how they affect individual behaviour. When there is a clear front-runner in the polls, it can often lead to reduced turnout or even so-called protest votes (when protesters want to make a point without affecting the likely outcome). When the poll results are ambiguous, members of the electorate may decide to vote in order to ensure that there is a clear majority for one side or the other, where otherwise they might have not bothered to do so. But polls have proven to be wrong in the past: sometimes badly wrong.

Increasingly, organisations rely on so-called polls of polls obtained from poll-aggregator specialists. These are companies that provide aggregated predictions that take into account multiple different algorithms and data sets. The concept of aggregated polls is not new. Meanwhile, in US political polling, one additional analytics element taken into account is the behaviour of so-called nearest-neighbour states (e.g. those with a disposition similar to the polled state), which is factored into the prediction in order to improve its accuracy.

The way in which a poll is carried out is also important, be it face-to-face, by email, or by landline. Much seems to depend on the nature of the poll, the age group being interviewed, and perhaps simply the impact of pressures exerted by the voting community, which may itself relate to specific local affairs. Aggregated polls smooth out different methodologies and variations in data sets.

And perhaps a prediction is not simply a matter of the statistical results of polls, but rather how it is interpreted and communicated. If data is the raw material and analytics are the methodology through which insight is obtained, then it is the purpose to which this insight is put that is the most critical. Few people who read blogs or articles will take care to check the results on which the conclusions of these blogs are based. In some cases, an item of published journalism may have been based on someone else's opinion and simply reworked, in effect creating an echo of an inaccuracy or misinterpretation.

Predictions about weather can be just as tricky. Even with the benefit of supercomputers, it can remain difficult to be certain about whether next June is a good time to schedule a wedding. Sometimes it can even be difficult to be sure whether or not to have a garden party in two weeks' time. Weather predictions often talk in terms of percentages of probability; for example, 'There is an 80% probability of rain tomorrow'. A proposed probability of 80% is certainly more helpful than one of 50% – in other words, a 50/50 chance of something happening – in which case you may as well just toss a coin. But an 80% probability of rain doesn't mean that 80% of the rain will fall on your garden in terms of volume, or even that it will rain on your garden for 80% of the time. Simply, it suggests that on 80% of days on which weather conditions (such as cloud cover and temperature) are similar to the one you are likely to get, you will get rain.[19]

The concept of *probability* is simply one way of expressing the chance of something happening: in this case, a rainy day. There is little or no certainty involved, unless a prediction proposes a 100% or a 0% likelihood.

In terms of predicting customer loyalty, it is also difficult to be absolutely certain regarding the degree of success. Many improvements in the probability of customer loyalty are underpinned by customer loyalty programmes, which are targeted, reward-based incentive schemes. According to Oracle, 'Airline frequent flyer programs enroll more than 200 million members worldwide; 76 percent of all U.S. grocery retailers with 50 or more stores now offer a frequent shopper program; 40 percent of all Visa and MasterCard issuers operate a rewards program'.[20]

Customer loyalty programmes help companies

- Analyse member data to view the demographics of various programme tiers and identify the factors that influence the buying patterns of different member segments
- Identify new enrollments and member growth rates over time
- Analyse member accruals and redemptions
- Understand the influence of different loyalty promotions on customer transactions and behaviour.

Through the use of analytics, companies are increasingly able to understand the overall performance of a loyalty programme, and measure its impact and the value it is bringing. Some might argue that measuring the impact and value of a loyalty programme is not truly predictive in nature, but it is the coming together of analytical and business processes that ultimately delivers results.

So how certain can we be about the accuracy of prediction and probabilistic modelling? At the end of the day, there are clearly at least three key, limiting factors:

1. Adequacy and accuracy of data
2. Quality and appropriateness of analytical work
3. Correctness of assumptions, especially that the future will be similar to the past.

The volatility of current markets, economies, and customer behaviour make decision-making even more difficult for managers and business leaders. The traditionally respected traits of experience and intuition retain value, but arguably at a reduced level. Increasingly, experience and intuition need to be supplemented by analytical insight.

Predictive modelling, be it through advanced or cognitive analytics, is still likely to bear an element of uncertainty, but there is sufficient evidence to indicate that it is better than the toss of a coin. In recognising this absence of infallibility, users need to appreciate that mistakes in prediction will still be made within systems and processes, at least in the short term. Will these mistakes be smaller or larger than failures of prediction due to human error?

Perhaps at the end of the day, some mistakes made by algorithms simply won't matter or will be less consequential. Doesn't it depend on whether the mistake involves the wrong choice of a birthday gift or the wrong coded instructions given to a pilotless aircraft?

As systems potentially displace human activity, one important question to consider is the degree of tolerance of mistakes we will be prepared to accept in even more advanced AI systems. Will more sophisticated systems inevitably demand greater accuracy? To what extent will mistakes ultimately undermine public and commercial confidence, and impair the implementation process?

CONCLUSION

This chapter has taken the reader through the foundational aspects of analytics, from the relatively basic theme of BI to the more advanced concept of cognitive analytics, challenging the accuracy of analytical outcomes along the way. Each subject on its own is capable of filling a textbook, but the intention here is primarily to provide an overview of the key components that ultimately lead to advanced intelligent systems, or forms of AI.

It's tempting to think that industries and professions will also follow the path of incremental improvement, but perhaps it is equally possible that they will leapfrog these foundational aspects and attempt to work directly with higher levels of AI.

This is entirely feasible, but it still remains important for organisations to be able to measure the financial benefit of such change. Therefore, the foundational tool of BI, financial performance management, remains an important part of the implementation process.

It's important also that we get over the potential stumbling block of poor data quality and avoid using that issue as a barrier to change. We are surrounded by poor information in our personal and business lives, yet cope with this by making judgements about the value, or veracity, of the information we get, weighting it accordingly. There's no reason why analytic and intelligent systems cannot take exactly the same approach.

In the next chapter, we will build on our knowledge of the foundational building blocks presented here, as we look forward to exploring the topic of AI in more detail.

NOTES

1. Bill Briggs, Cognitive analytics. *Tech Trends 2014*. Deloitte, 2014. https://www2.deloitte.com/uk/en/pages/technology/articles/cognitive-analytics.html (accessed 30 October 2016).
2. Steve Hoffenburg, IBM's Watson answers the question, 'What's the difference between artificial intelligence and cognitive computing?' VDC Research Group (24 May 2016). http://www.vdcresearch.com/News-events/iot-blog/IBM-Watson-Answers-Question-Artificial-Intelligence.html
3. Adam Smith, *An Inquiry into the Nature and Causes of the Wealth of Nations*. (Oxford University Press, 1776). Republished 1993.
4. Rita L. Sallam, Joao Tapadinhas, Josh Parenteau, et al. Magic quadrant for business intelligence and analytic platforms. Gartner report ID G00257740, 2014. https://www.gartner.com/doc/2668318/magic-quadrant-business-intelligence-analytics
5. Tableau Software (n.d.), Top 10 business intelligence trends for 2016. Tableau Software white paper. https://www.tableau.com/learn/whitepapers/top-10-business-intelligence-trends-2016 (accessed 31 October 2016).
6. Gartner. Magic quadrant for advanced analytics platforms. 19 February, 2014. https://www.gartner.com/doc/2667527/magic-quadrant-advanced-analytics-platforms
7. SKF (n.d.). Predictive and proactive reliability maintenance. http://www.skf.com/group/industry-solutions/oil-gas/services/mechanical-services/predictive-and-proactive-maintenance/index.html (accessed 31 October 2016).
8. Irv Lustig, Brenda Dietrich, Christer Johnson, and Christopher Dziekan, The analytics journey. *Analytics* (November/December 2010). http://www.analytics-magazine.org/november-december-2010/54-the-analytics-journey (accessed 18 October 2017).
9. http://ayata.com/software/ (accessed 10 January 2018).
10. Karen Butner, The smarter supply chain of the future. *Strategy & Leadership* 38, no. 1 (2010): 22–31.
11. Rob Dunie, W. Roy Schulte, Marc Kerremans, and Michele Cantara, Magic Quadrant for Intelligent Business Process Management Suites. Gartner report G00276892, 2016. http://www.integra-co.com/sites/default/files/Bizagi%20on%20Gartner%20Quadrant%20-%20Reprint.pdf
12. Gregg Rock and Andrew Spanyi, What skills are needed for BPM success? BPM Institute, 2014. http://www.bpminstitute.org/resources/articles/what-skills-are-needed-bpm-success (accessed 18 October 2017).
13. Techopedia (n.d.). Cognitive analytics. https://www.techopedia.com/definition/29437/cognitive-analytics (accessed 18 October 2017).
14. Cognitive analytics: the three-minute guide. https://www2.deloitte.com/us/en/pages/deloitte-analytics/articles/cognitive-analytics-the-three-minute-guide.html
15. Bruce Weber, Swift and slashing, computer topples Kasparov. *New York Times* (12 May 1997). http://www.nytimes.com/1997/05/12/nyregion/swift-and-slashing-computer-topples-kasparov.html
16. Damon Beres, Microsoft's Cortana is like Siri with a human personality. Huffington Post. 29 July 2015. http://www.huffingtonpost.co.uk/entry/microsofts-cortana-is-like-siri-with-a-human-personality_us_55b7be94e4b0a13f9d1a685a (accessed 10 January 2018).

17. Rene Ritchie, How to get Siri to tell you a bedtime story. iMore (26 October 2015). http://www.imore.com/how-get-siri-tell-you-bedtime-story
18. Marcelo Gleiser, Can machines fall in love? NPR website, Cosmos & Culture article (26 January2011). http://www.npr.org/sections/13.7/2011/01/26/133213460/can-machines-fall-in-love (accessed 21 March 2017).
19. Kevin McConway, The nature of probability. UK Met Office (9 October 2016). https://www.metoffice.gov.uk/about-us/who/accuracy/forecasts/probability (accessed 5 January 2017).
20. Oracle. Oracle loyalty analytics. Oracle data sheet, 2001. http://www.oracle.com/us/products/middleware/bus-int/064330.pdf

CHAPTER 2

Artificial Intelligence

SUMMARY

This chapter considers in more detail what is meant by AI and machine learning, covering the Turing test, the Dartmouth conference, and the factors that led to the so-called AI winter. Beyond this, it considers the concept of singularity and the key components of AI. Finally, it considers whether computers can be creative.

INTRODUCTION

The journey towards AI takes us from management information through predictive and prescriptive analytics, and towards cognitive analytics. Cognitive analytics and AI can be distinguished from each other by the function that each of them typically undertakes:

- Cognitive analytics acts as an informed advisor, giving greater insight to the decision maker.
- Artificial intelligence is the process whereby the system actually makes the decision.

There are numerous great and diverse articles about the topic, and a consensus of opinion is not always evident. Many, such as John McCarthy of Stanford University, start the journey by asking what we actually mean by the expression *intelligence*.[1]

McCarthy's definition of intelligence is 'the computational part of the ability to achieve goals in the world', but this is only one viewpoint. In fact the challenge of understanding what comprises intelligence goes back at least as far as ancient Greek philosophy, and probably before then.

The ancient Greeks felt that there were many facets to intelligence:[2]

- *Phronesis*, meaning *practical wisdom* (common sense)
- *Phrontis*, meaning *concern for fellow man*
- *Metis*, meaning *cunning*
- *Episteme*, meaning *understanding* or *knowledge* (as opposed to hearsay)
- *Gnome*, meaning *deep insight* (including emotional intelligence)
- *Techne*, meaning *technical skill*.

In *Republic*, written in about 360 BCE, the Greek philosopher Plato (c. 428–348 BCE) discusses a futuristic state where there is a 'higher education, intellectual as well as moral and religious, of science as well as of art, and not of youth only but of the whole of life'. It is a sort of John Lennon's 'Imagine', but written over two thousand years ago.

Republic includes an allegory about a cave, which Plato uses to represent Man's condition: chained in the darkness of a cave, perceiving the outside world only through shadows on the wall. Plato explores what might be the effect if Man was unchained. Would he be frightened or enlightened? And if he returned to the cave to explain what he had seen, would he then be mocked or thought mad?

An interesting extension of this thinking is how it applies to the concept of – and, equally importantly, the implementation of – AI. Should we be frightened, enlightened, or critical?

The next four sections will look in more detail at the development of the concept of AI over the past 50 years. If there is to be a period of rapid implementation, we will try to give some thought to how it will happen over the next 10 years and who will do it.

THE TURING TEST

The Alan Turing Institute was formed in 2015 and is the United Kingdom's national centre for data sciences. It is named after the inventor and pioneer Alan Turing (1912–1954), who was a pioneering British computer scientist who played a pivotal role in decrypting enemy signals. Indirectly (it is suggested), he played a part in reducing the duration of the World War II.

Decryption of enemy signals was done using a decryption device called a *bombe*. The expression comes from the name of a Polish invention, *bomba kryptologiczna*, which was also being used to decipher German messages. It is sometimes suggested that this *bomba* had been in use by the Polish for perhaps as long as six years before being shared with the Allied forces. As history is usually written by the victors, Turing and his team at Bletchley Park (about 50 miles north of London) are usually given the credit for breaking the Enigma coded messages used by the German forces.

Turing, portrayed by Benedict Cumberbatch in the 2014 movie *The Imitation Game*, spent the immediate postwar years on his design of the Automatic Computing Engine, under development at the National Physical Laboratory on the outskirts of London. In his 1950 paper 'Computing Machinery and Intelligence', he considered the question, 'Can machines think?' In the paper, Turing struggled with the concepts of *machines* and *thinking*, as he considered that there was uncertainty about what is meant by both expressions. Instead he replaced those words with what he called an *imitation game*. This term was based on a party game that involves three people: a man, a woman, and an independent party (called a judge) who cannot see either the man or the woman. The game, in effect, requires the independent judge (male or female) to identify which of the other individuals is male and which is female.[3]

In an extension of this approach, one of the humans (male or female) is replaced by a computer, and it becomes the task of the independent judge to identify which of the two is not human. If the judge cannot make a correct identification, then the computer wins the game. In this approach, the computer is not specifically trying to trick the judge, but rather prove that the computer is capable of cognitive operations.

As a next step, Turing asked the question, 'What might a computing device need by way of capability to be able to operate cognitively?' Turing expressed the rather democratic notion that 'all digital computers are in a sense equivalent'. By this he meant that all that distinguishes one from another is the system characteristics and storage power of each.

If we adopt the Oxford English Dictionary's definition of *democracy* as the 'the practice or principles of social equality', then the implication is that the definition can be extended to computer equality. How many of us are ready at the moment to even consider how the second principle of democracy – representation – might apply to computer systems, and how it might be adopted in an independent digital ecosystem?

Turing also explored some common objections to the possibility of a computer having intelligence:

- *Religious*. The religious objection suggests that the function of thinking is part of man's mortal soul, and the soul is the spiritual essence of a living being.
- *Head in the sand*. The head-in-the-sand objection suggests that, were AI ever to happen, the impact on humanity would be too terrible to consider. It is an emotional argument against undertaking system development, as opposed to a rational viewpoint as to whether or not AI is technically possible.
- *Mathematical*. The mathematical objection argues that AI is nothing more than a set of fallible algorithms. (Chapter 1 explored whether algorithms are merely calculations of probability, which inherently carry an element of error.)
- *Lack of consciousness*. The lack-of-consciousness objection argues that machines may not be able to have emotions – which Turing said is not proven.
- *Disability*. The disability objection refers to the technical limitations of a computer. Turing suggested that with enough computing power, anything is possible. This extends to self-awareness, suggesting that the computer can learn from its own mistakes.
- *Lack of continuity with a nervous system*. In effect, this argument holds that because the brain is not digital but rather analogue in nature, it cannot be replicated in a digital computer.
- *Absence of informality*. This argument holds that a true brain is capable of haphazard – that is, unpredictable – functions.
- *Inability to create and surprise*. This is the so-called Lady Lovelace Argument, which holds that the computer will only do what we order the machine to do.

The Lady Lovelace Argument is named after Lady Lovelace – Augusta Ada King-Noel, countess of Lovelace (née Byron; 1815–1852) – who was the daughter of the nineteenth-century Romantic poet Lord Byron. According to his peers, Byron was 'mad, bad and dangerous to know'.[4] Lovelace's work goes hand in hand with that of Charles Babbage (1791–1871), who invented the first mechanical computer in 1822. Babbage engaged Lovelace to translate a memoir written in French by the Italian engineer and mathematician Louis Menebrea. In addition to the translation, Lovelace added a series of detailed notes showing a depth of understanding of the work that even Babbage himself had not achieved.

She understood the punched-card method and how it could be used to design machines that could manipulate not only numbers but also symbols. Her translation notes include, in complete detail, a method for calculating a series of Bernoulli numbers (a sequence of rational numbers that are important in trigonometric functions) using an analytical engine. For this reason she is generally recognised as the first computer programmer.

Perhaps the list of objections explored by Turing could even form the basis of a type of checklist. Computer scientists might suggest that it is possible, for example, to program some randomness into analytical outcomes. Overcoming emotional or religious objections may perhaps be a little more difficult to cope with, however.

Even so, religious denominations are not turning an entirely blind eye to the topic. In 2016, the Pontifical Academy of Sciences at the Vatican held a two-day conference titled Power and Limits of Artificial Intelligence. The event drew multiple subject-matter experts from a wide range of disciplines, including Stephen Hawking, the prominent British professor at the University of Cambridge and a self-proclaimed atheist. Beyond technical issues, the conference also considered a wide range of ethical and social issues. At the conference, Stanislas Dehaene, a professor of cognitive neuroscience at the College de France and a member of the academy, commented that AI is 'an extremely important goal that has not been achieved yet … we don't [want to] create a system that is full of machines … that don't share our intuitions of what should be a better world.'[5]

Turing died in 1954, allegedly due to self-induced cyanide poisoning (although some dispute this finding and suggest that the poisoning was accidental in nature). His contribution is undoubtedly substantial, and he was listed in 1999 as one of *Time* magazine's Time 100: The Most Important People of the Century.

THE DARTMOUTH EVENT

For many, AI has its foundations in a 1956 conference at Dartmouth College in the state of New Hampshire in the United States. Called the Dartmouth Summer Research Project on Artificial Intelligence, the event was in effect a brainstorming session for a subject matter known variously as cybernetics, automata theory, and complex information processing.

It's worth dwelling for a moment on the topic of cybernetics. The science was defined in 1948 by Norbert Wiener (an American mathematician and philosopher at MIT) as 'the scientific study of control and communication in the animal and the machine'[6], but has been considered more recently as including the control of any system using technology. The systems included extend not only to mechanical, physical, biological, and cognitive systems, but also to social systems, such as the relationship between an individual and a group. According to Wiener 'Information is information, not matter or energy', which might be a useful demarcation. This notion of the interaction of science and social relationships inevitably will need to underpin much of our thinking going forward.

The Dartmouth conference was quite small in terms of numbers of attendees. In many ways it probably resembled the small groups that operate in a modern-day start-up environment. There were 47 attendees listed in total, but a nucleus of 10 (perhaps 11) stayed for the entire period of 8 weeks.

Fifty years on, there was a follow-up conference, AI@50. Five of the original 10 core members attended with which had been envisaged. The purpose of the follow-up was to not only contrast actual progress attained, but also look forward to the next 50 years. One of those attending was John McCarthy, who is credited with inventing the term *artificial intelligence*. The commemorative plaque of the event at the site says that the conference was the first time that the expression *artificial intelligence* had been used.

As you look at a photograph of those original five who attended AI@50, you cannot fail to be struck not only by the wisdom of their years but also by the grey hair and white beards. The resume of that reunion event is a good read, and, whilst the content seems to be more technical than practical (e.g. a discussion of the merits of logic-based AI versus probabilistic-based AI), those that attended did reflect on some broader issues. For example, Pat Langley argued the need for a return to 'psychological roots' if human-level AI is to be achieved. In essence, this implies that, to effectively achieve AI, we must understand our own brains better.

At AI@50, alumnus Ray Solomonoff said that AI 'was not that far off'. Ray Kurzweil, another veteran, claimed that we can 'be confident of the Turing test within a quarter century'. In terms of looking forward, McCarthy, who died in 2011, suggested that AI 'was likely but not assured' by 2056.[7] (In 1979 McCarthy had even originally suggested, perhaps outrageously to some, that 'Machines as simple as thermostats can be said to have beliefs, and having beliefs seems to be a characteristic of most machines capable of problem-solving performance'.)[8]

Does innovation in the classic Turing and McCarthy style mix experience and technical excellence with the attributes of being both outrageous and provocative?

POST-DARTMOUTH, THE AI WINTER, AND SINGULARITY

If the Dartmouth event was to set the ambition of the industry, then the proverbial bubble was burst by what is now generally known as the *AI winter*, a term that first arose at a conference held in 1984 by the American Association for Artificial Intelligence (now the Association for the Advancement of Artificial Intelligence).

The expression *AI winter* reflected the suggestion that enthusiasm for AI had spiraled out of control and that projects carrying an AI label were, in effect, tainted. The AI winter is generally taken to represent a period of underfunding and inactivity, brought on by a hype like that often accompanying technology initiatives (such as that leading to the dot-com bubble). There are usually considered to be two AI winters: the first during the years 1974–1980 (which predates the creation of the definition) and the second during the period 1987–1993.

Nowadays, AI, machine learning, and cognitive analytics have become sufficiently mainstream that many do not expect another AI winter, and moreover that it is 'long since over'.[9] The latter comment was made by the futurist writer Ray Kurzweil in his book *The Singularity Is Near*. In it he portrays a future world that reflects exponential growth in and advancement of AI technology.

The concept of *singularity* (sometimes known as *technical singularity*) was first conceived of by the mathematician John von Neumann, who said, 'The accelerating progress of technology and changes in the mode of human life give the appearance of approaching some essential *singularity* in the history of the race beyond which human affairs, as we know them, cannot continue'[10].

Put another way, singularity 'is the event or sequence of events likely to happen at the intersection of machine and human intelligence, that is, the period when AI at first matches and eventually surpasses our biological intelligence.'[11]

Singularity encompasses the notion that AI systems will not only develop but become self-improving. It's suggested that by 2045 there will be some sort of runaway reaction of self-improvement of technology, leading to an intelligence explosion and a superintelligence that would surpass human intelligence. Kurzweil also specifically says that 'there will be no distinction, post-singularity, between man and machine.'

The fundamental premise of Kurzweil's view is based on Moore's law, expressed over 50 years ago. This suggests that the number of transistors doubles every two years, leading to exponential growth. AI researcher Ray Solomonoff, who invented the concept of *algorithmic probability*, applied the same rule to self-learning machines (which double their speed every two years), and as a result he suggests that singularity will occur with a definite period.

Worried? A singularity symposium already exists, in the form of an informal community, which takes part in discussion 'about technology, AI and exponential growth'. Students of the subject should be careful not to mix prediction or speculation with science fiction, or to accept only one viewpoint as the definitive premonition of the future, as it may be wrong in terms of both nature and time frame. The history of technology is already sprinkled with so-called laws – some of which are more realistic than others.

Some of Arthur C. Clarke's favourite laws include:[12]

- When a distinguished but elderly scientist states that something is possible, he is almost certainly right. When he states that something is impossible, he is very probably wrong.
- The only way of discovering the limits of the possible is to venture a little way past them into the impossible.
- Any sufficiently advanced technology is indistinguishable from magic.
- For every expert, there is an equal and opposite expert.

Despite Kurzweil's reassurances that there is no likelihood of another AI winter, it's worth spending a moment to reflect on the causes of that period of stagnation and to consider whether they might occur again. If so, what mitigating action might be available to us?

The causes of an AI winter have been variously suggested as being due to the following factors:

- *Institutional factors.* Major institutions tend not to collaborate as budgets get tighter, resulting in less knowledge transfer and a reduced ability to leverage shared development.
- *Economic factors.* During a downturn in the economy, programmes that are viewed as being speculative and without hard benefit are at increased risk when cuts need to be made.
- *Empty research pipeline.* Unless organisations and institutions see tangible research output from a programme, it is at risk of being shelved.
- *Failure of existing systems to adapt.* Existing technology becomes redundant in the face of new systems and processes, and users of existing technology resist moving from tried-and-tested systems to new models.
- *Hype.* Extravagant and unrealistic promotions that exaggerate the benefits and possible outcomes of a technology lead to pessimism about its prospects.

The issue of exaggerated benefits is especially interesting. According to Gartner's *Hype Cycle for Emerging Technologies, 2016*, machine learning is at the top of the hype cycle. In that position on the cycle it is described as the 'peak of expected expectations'. The next step on the cycle is the 'trough of disillusionment', charac- terised by overpromising and underdelivering. Additionally, Gartner comments on many other subcapabilities of AI and cognitive intelligence, which it describes as being triggers for innovation.[13]

One major question to consider is whether there is likely to be another AI winter in the near or medium-term future. If so, how will this impact the use of AI in industry and by professionals?

In the same way that weather cycles run counter to each other in the northern and southern hemispheres, it is feasible that, were an AI winter to occur, it might happen at different times in different places rather than being a single global phenomenon. This is especially relevant when the economic characteristics of mature and emerging nations are considered independently, particularly in a market context.

The need for emerging nations to develop advanced analytical systems to support their rapidly growing financial services industries and to compensate for the relative lack of indigenous talent (in terms of numbers, not quality) may force the acceleration of AI development in those countries. Elsewhere, in markets suffering from relative stagnation, or excessive conservatism or cynicism, perhaps the platform is not burning intensely enough to force change.

SPRINGTIME FOR AI?

Despite the fear of singularity or an AI winter, it seems that there are still optimists out there. John Giannandrea, head of machine learning at Google, suggested in 2016 that, 'We're in a kinda AI spring'.[14] He was referencing the recent developments at that time in speech recognition and image understanding that were part of the machine-learning program. You don't need to be a weather expert to recognise that there's a very big difference between spring and summer. No one yet seems to be claiming that we are anywhere near an AI summer, but there are plenty of experts who think that we are close enough to start thinking about the practical aspects of a AI working environment.

In the 2015 open letter 'Research Priorities for Robust and Beneficial Artificial Intelligence', AI specialists set out three short-term and four long-term broad areas of impact:[15]

Short Term

1. Optimising AI's economic impact, which considers labour market impacts and also policies for managing adverse effects
2. Law and ethics research, including legal considerations relative to autonomous cars, autonomous weapons, and machine and professional ethics
3. Computer science research for robust AI in the areas of verification, validity, secu- rity, and control (as defined under long-term objectives).

Long Term

1. *Verification.* Did I build the system right?
2. *Validity.* Did I build the right system?
3. *Security.* How do I manage intentional manipulation?
4. *Control.* How do I retain meaningful control?

The leading signatories and authors of the open letter were Stuart Russell (professor of computer science at the University of California, Berkeley), Daniel Dewey (research fellow, machine superintelligence and the future of AI at Oxford's Future of Humanity Institute, Oxford Martin School), and Max Tegmark (professor and president of the Future of Life Institute, which supports research advancing robust and beneficial AI).

These academic heavyweights are probably amongst the current rock stars of the AI movement. As eminent as they are, perhaps their views should be either counterbalanced or supported by other, nonacademic stakeholders who may have slightly different, more commercial views.

Another individual who may fall into the category of industry rock star is Microsoft CEO Satya Nadella. In 2016 he postulated 10 of his own AI rules, which are that AI must:[16]

1. Be designed to assist humanity and to respect human autonomy, with a focus perhaps on machines doing dangerous work
2. Be transparent, which requires an understanding of how machines work and the ethical considerations involved
3. Maximise efficiencies without destroying the dignity of people, retaining culture and diversity
4. Be designed for intelligent privacy (an extension of the security argument)
5. Have algorithmic accountability 'so that humans can undo unintended harm'
6. Guard against bias, ensuring calculations are undertaken without discrimination
7. Provide for education, taking into account that innovation will require us to be educated in a different way
8. Recognise the creativity of the machine
9. Apply judgement and accountability – and understand that machines can make decisions but that humans must retain accountability
10. Have empathy – that is, humans and machines understanding each other's thoughts and feelings

The tenth rule implies that humans need to understand the thoughts and feelings of a machine. Do we think that the IBM Watson computer might have felt upset if it had been beaten by another competitor on *Jeopardy*?

There's a temptation to think that some of his comments, valid and valuable as they might be, verge on the obvious. However, other experts compare them to the Ten Commandments and comment that the difficulty is not in the statements themselves but rather in their implementation. Yet others suggest that these directives are based on our current knowledge and understanding of AI, but that the future may bring new issues and challenges.

Creating rules like these is akin to creating rules for driving, says Toby Walsh, Professor of AI at Australia's University of New South Wales. He suggests that, as in driving a car, it's impossible to have a set of rules that covers every contingency. Even so, having a set of driving rules does provide a yardstick against which action can be judged.

Perhaps rules might also differ from place to place and depend on market maturity? Would authoritarian regimes have a different view of what was acceptable and what was not, and place restrictions on AI systems that are free thinking and not aligned to the wider ethos of the society?

The creation of AI rules and so-called Ten Commandments should be taken with a pinch of salt. To have a bit of fun and to provoke thought, the following Ten Commandments of AI are suggested by the author:

1. Don't worship data as if it is some type of religion.
2. The definitions of cognitive analytics and AI are mainly in the eye of the user.
3. Cognitive computing is intended to supplement the human mind, not to replace it.
4. Do not believe the marketing hype, as technology solutions don't always do what they say on the packet.
5. Do not covet thy competitor's system, unless you are planning to acquire the system or the competitor.
6. Don't speak in jargon – it only reveals that you can't communicate properly using normal words.
7. Algorithms produce only approximate probabilities, so treat their results accordingly.
8. A computer needs to know its place in the pecking order.
9. There is no such thing as a 'good' computer – a computer is just a machine.
10. Honour thy science fiction writer – AI was probably his or her idea in the first place.

HOW DOES AI WORK?

In the lead-up to this chapter, we explored the evolution of analytics from management information through predictive and cognitive analytics to what we are now describing as AI. We explain it as if it was some form of natural progression. This would presuppose that the evolution of analytics is a Darwinian, linear process. But, as we have seen from science fiction writing and conferences held over 60 years ago, the concept of AI seems to have been thought of far in advance of more (relatively) basic forms, such as financial performance management and risk analytics. AI already appears to have its own ecosystem (see Figure 3).

When explanations are provided about AI, they seem to be about what it is rather than how it happens. In the spirit of trying to provide a basic guide to AI, here are the two main approaches to AI:

1. *Algorithm-based approach.* This approach comprises a series of capabilities found in advanced analytics, such as behaviour trees and statistical approaches, which are in effect stitched together to solve a particular problem or create a desired

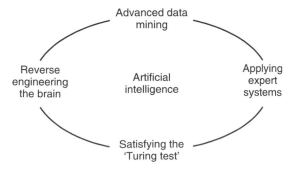

FIGURE 3   The AI ecosystem.

behaviour. This approach is usually seen in computational models that respond to particular tasks, such as voice or facial recognition.

Overall it's an approach similar to that of the human central nervous system, in which different layers of the brain examine different parts of a problem and combine to produce an answer.

2. *Machine learning approach (artificial neural networks)*. These networks are modelled on the way that the brain works. The networks have many neurons (as the brain has) that are connected with many others. Modern neural networks have a few thousand to a few million neurons, and millions of connections.

Machine learning is an expression used for a subsection of computer science, in which the computer has the ability to self-build analytical models and self-improve, without being explicitly programmed. The learning process is described as being operational rather than cognitive; that is to say, the learning occurs through a series of reiterative feedback loops, which fuel self-modifying algorithms.

Machine learning is used when it is difficult to create a specific algorithm or calculation to carry out a particular task, such as identifying cybercrime intrusion.

There are three types of machine learning tasks:

1. *Supervised*. The system is given data and a required outcome by a 'teacher' and is required to compute a set of rules.
2. *Unsupervised*. The system is tasked to find patterns in unlabelled data; for example, how neural networks are connected.
3. *Reinforcement learning*. The system learns in a dynamic environment, such as in the playing of a game, and the algorithm is modified depending on the level of success.

Purists might suggest yet another type: semi-supervised learning.

Whilst the ability to develop machine learning algorithms has been around for a long time, creating them has increased in popularity as a result of the increase in readily available data, such as data from social media. Such systems also feature in self-driving cars and online recommendations for purchases such as music and books.

Machine learning has an important part to play in a world with an increasing number of devices and expanded connectivity. 'With the right algorithms', says Mika Tanskanen, a manufacturing industry consultant in Finland, 'the system can be gradually taught to recognise any internal and external production-related factors, optimise the use and consumables, and improve the efficiency of the entire production process'.[17]

There are many different types of neural networks. Dynamic neural networks, for example, are able to create new connections and unlearn existing ones based on rules. By stacking neural network upon neural network, it starts to become possible to create a form of AI. Even if some information is missing, the ultimate decision made by the network isn't affected.

This type of approach indicates that we are, in effect. looking to create a technological replica of the brain, otherwise known as *whole brain emulation*. The reality is that we are not absolutely certain how the brain actually works, especially as it has developed organically over many centuries. Learning is complex, and seems to be based on a combination of neuroscience and psychology coupled with a form of feedback loop called *reinforcement learning*.

One of the main aims of computer scientists is to artificially reproduce this process of reinforcement learning, which they also call a Q-Network. Such discussions inevitably take us to the concept of memory. In a 2011 paper in the *Journal of Cognitive Psychology*, researchers suggested that there are three levels of memory:[18]

1. A core focusing on one active item
2. A surrounding area holding at least three more active items
3. A wider region containing passive items that have been tagged for later retrieval (put on the back burner).

Based on a series of tests involving colours and shapes, they discovered that the function of the core area is to direct attention to the correct item, which is affected by predictability of the input pattern. In other words, the brain seems to be carrying out a form of biological statistical data quality assessment.

Then, the brain retrieves the item, and subsequently, when needed, it updates it. As we are still learning about how the brain works, it is questionable as to whether the ultimate objective of machine learning is to replicate the working of the brain, or alternatively, to create a different form of brain. Any new type or model of a so-called thinking engine would somehow need to take into account the existing and future digital storage capabilities of computers.

Google's AlphaGo comprises neural networks, deep reinforcement learning that deals with the ability to plan, and the creation of a form of memory. Experts such as Demis Hassabis and his DeepMind team at Google are aiming to somehow combine these three at a metalevel.[19] Their work rests on the concept of artificial general intelligence (AGI), which is considered to be, and maybe is also defined as, the ability of a machine to do any work that a human can. AGI is also known as *strong AI* or *full AI*.

The concept of strong AI goes back over 30 years. At its roots is the philosophical question of whether a computer *has* a mind, *thinks* it has a mind, or just *acts* as if it thinks it has a mind. The third option seems to be mainly a matter of programming a particular behaviour.

Experts such as Hassabis suggest there are three layers within the human mind:

1. A perception layer, which can be simulated by statistical approaches
2. A concepts layer, which no one seems to have cracked yet
3. A symbolic logic layer, which is basically logical and mathematical.

Beyond technical capabilities, we also seem to be attracted to the concept of artificial emotion as it relates to machine learning. This comprises four key levels within the machine:

1. *Consciousness.* Consciousness is the state or quality of awareness and recognition of external objects and states within oneself.
2. *Self-awareness.* Self-awareness is the state through which one is aware of one's own traits and behaviours.
3. *Sentience.* Sentience is the ability to feel, perceive, and have emotion. In modern Western thinking, sentience is the ability to experience sensation. In Eastern thinking it is the characteristic that makes us care about others and to be attentive. Sentient thinking underpins moral considerations, such as those expressed by human and animal rights movements.
4. *Sapience.* Sapience is the ability of a system to have wisdom or discernment. The word, and thus the broader concept, has its roots in old French and from the Latin *sapere* (to be wise, to have taste).

Should a future computer be built with emotion? It has been argued that if a self-learning computer is to survive, it's critical that it has some emotional capability. Others suggest that it doesn't matter whether the computer has emotions or not, provided that the users (i.e. mankind) *think* that it has emotions.

Maybe the apparent authenticity of computer emotions will depend on how they reply to us, perhaps in terms of the type of language or intonation used. We shouldn't overlook the fact that most humans cannot be easily tricked when it comes to emotional cues. As a race we have evolved to be sensitive to small and subtle verbal and nonverbal signals, so we may be unforgiving in terms of artificially created sentiment.

These issues go far beyond the purely technical capabilities of computers to areas such as neuroscience and evolutionary psychology. Effective creation of AI systems increasingly recognises that we are looking at complex, adaptive, flexible, emotional, and vaguely humanlike forms of technology. Interdisciplinary cooperation becomes critical, but this is not an academic exercise. We continually need to be drawn back to the burning platform, that is, the need or reason to invent these AI systems in the first place. If the creation of AI is no more than an academic exercise, then research and development funding are bound to dry up. Finding the business value is a critical success factor.

The road to a deeper understanding of AI is littered with computer science jargon, yet as individuals and professionals we need to be able to cut through the mass of information to be able to extract the true value from the science and technology. It's tempting to add a compendium of frequently used terms to this book and provide some definitions, however, the complexity of the answers will not only provide a distraction but probably make effective implementation even more difficult. We can't afford to get caught in the weeds of technology jargon; AI is far too important for that.

We describe analytics as 'extracting' the value from both structured and unstructured data. Additionally, there is a need to constantly remind ourselves that analysis is not the destination, but rather that it is what is done with the analysis that counts – in terms of new processes, best practices, and customer strategies. In the same way, we need to recognise that the creation of AI systems, whilst important, is not the destination but rather is a vehicle for beneficial change.

CAN COMPUTERS BE CREATIVE?

Perhaps a computer cannot be truly intelligent until it has the ability to innovate and to be creative. The idea that computers cannot be artistic is increasingly being challenged. After all, what is *art*?

'Art', said Frank Lloyd Wright, 'is a discovery and development of elementary principles of nature into beautiful forms suitable for human use'[20]. Perhaps this statement might suggest that art is capable of becoming some form of process.

Oscar Wilde said that 'Art is the most intense mode of individualism that the world has known'. His comment was made in 1891 at the dawn of the industrial age, as he considered the concept in the 'Soul of Man Under Socialism', reflecting on issues of individualism and freedom in contrast to authoritarianism. He suggested art is that creative entity that 'disturbs ... the reduction of man to the level of a machine'.[21]

At that time, individuals were concerned with industrialisation reducing man to a machine. Nowadays our concern is whether the machine can ascend in some way to the level of man. Maybe there is some type of midway point, and if so, what is it?

If a distinguishing factor between man and machine (or computer) is the ability to be artistic, the question inevitably arises as to whether a computer can actually create art. In the context of this book, which considers the impact of AI on professions and industries, artists and designers are legitimately in scope, as they are part of the industry of design.

Beyond the pure design function, aesthetics (which is concerned with the nature and appreciation of beauty) also becomes an important part of the mix. How information is conveyed to users is a critical success factor. The strength (and implicitly, the beauty) of visualisations is paramount to our understanding, and therefore our acceptance of data. In its broadest terms, *beauty* is the appreciation of form, shape, and colour that please the senses, especially the eye. Could creative artists operating at the edge of design feasibly also help carve a path for greater acceptance of an AI era?

Beyond purely functional aspects, it might also be argued that if a work of art created by a computer is indistinguishable from that created by a human, either in terms of style or content, then it satisfies the Turing test. And what if the computer designs the artwork but the human implements it (in effect, the human is serving the computer)?

In 2016 computer experts worked with the New York fashion house Marchesa to create a 'cognitive dress'. The dress, or more accurately a ball gown, comprised embedded LED lights that were connected to social media. The colours changed depending on social media sentiment as captured by Twitter feeds.[22] Described as a fusion of design and technology, the colours of the dress were able to reflect the social-media mood of attendees. The 'system' chose the colours based on Marchesa's previous designs to reflect the five human emotions that they wanted to convey. For example, red represented confidence and grey represented futurism. This is unmistakably technology, but is it really art? Where is the real creativity in the machine?

As to whether computers can actually create art: in 2015 Google introduced software that took existing photographs and converted them into psychedelic images. Algorithms were used to both enhance and reengineer the images to make them more vivid. The 'revitalised' images were subsequently sold at a 2016 charity auction in San Francisco, with the most expensive one selling for US$8,000.[23]

The images were reengineered using four approaches:

1. *DeepDream*. The running of a process multiple times (numbered in the thousands) to create a new but recognisable image.
2. *Fractal DeepDream*. The same process, but with different sized versions that create fractal images. (A fractal is a form of geometric expanding symmetry. It's probably the technological equivalent of a kaleidoscope.)
3. *Class visualisation*. The ability to focus in on a single image of a particular class, for example, a face.
4. *Style transfer*. The creation of new images based on a particular style, for example, Vincent van Gogh's *The Starry Night*.

It will be interesting whether these images will still be considered works of art in the future, although at the moment that certainly appears to be the case.

Computerised music also has made inroads into the arts. Iamus is a computer cluster and the brainchild of scientists at the University of Málaga in Spain. The compositions of Iamus are entirely computer generated and have been favourably compared to French classical music of the early twentieth century. The music has even been played by the London Philharmonic Orchestra. Iamus appears to satisfy the Turing test, in that it is impossible to tell whether the music has been composed by a computer or by a human being.

Iamus also has a younger sibling called Melomics 109, whose music is described as being more populist in nature. Similarly to some elements of art, the musical process comprises a combination of randomness and repetition within the framework of an established formula. There's a sense of the 1970s German electronic group Kraftwerk about the works of Melomics 109.

The composition of this AI-created music is fundamentally methodical. For example, in a fugue, firstly a short melodic phrase or theme is taken. Then it is overlapped, and the composer applies variations to that theme, which build it into a sophisticated and ultimately pleasing mesh. Sonatas and concertos are also structured by clear musical rules, which are capable of being digitally captured. If that is the case, then why should music not be capable of being created artificially, that is, without human intervention?

The question really has to do with uniqueness. Is it more reasonable to describe music based on the work of previous composers as original than that based 'just' on algorithmic repetition? Again the question arises: What is originality? And why can't computers possess it?

We shouldn't be too snobbish about this. The UK-based rock band Status Quo has been a legend since 1962 for its ability to create an entire repertoire of modern rock music based on a 'three-chord-trick'. But could computers ever create the excitement of the Rolling Stones or Led Zeppelin in their heyday – and besides, wouldn't the concerts be, in comparison, pretty dull?

CONCLUSION

This chapter aimed to provide an introduction to the topic of intelligent systems and AI, referencing the early work of Turing, amongst others, and conversations on the topic that took place over 60 years ago at Dartmouth.

Technological purists will undoubtedly recognise the brevity with which the topic of how AI actually works has been dealt with. The intention here has not been to provide a nuts-and-bolts description of how such highly complex systems work, but rather to provide a degree of awareness not only of the components, but also of the potential, by considering issues of creativity.

In raising awareness, the proverbial door is now opened to considering in more detail what the impact of these systems on industries and professions might be. There is no certainty as to the extent of the influence of these intelligent systems. Because of this, going forward, readers should not feel any degree of constraint in using their imaginations. The indications are that the capabilities of intelligent systems are unlikely to be limited by the technology alone, but rather by speed of their application to business and societal needs.

The essence of this book is also to place the concept of intelligent systems in the context of specific industries and professions. In Chapter 3 we will consider the impact of these new technologies on what are described as the leading-edge industries: financial services, amongst others.

NOTES

1. John McCarthy, What is artificial intelligence? Stanford University, 2007. http://www-formal.stanford.edu/jmc/whatisai (accessed 1 December 2016).
2. Steve Theodore, How did the ancient Greeks define intelligence? Quora (1 February 2015). https://www.quora.com/How-did-the-Ancient-Greeks-define-intelligence
3. Alan Turing, Computing machinery and intelligence. *Mind* LIX 236 (October 1950): 433–460.
4. Terry Castle, Mad, bad and dangerous to know. *New York Times* book review (13 April 1997). http://www.nytimes.com/books/97/04/13/reviews/970413.13castlet.html.
5. Elise Harris, Vatican ponders power, limits of artificial intelligence. Catholic News Agency, *Crux* (4 December 2016). https://cruxnow.com/vatican/2016/12/04/vatican-ponders-power-limits-artificial-intelligence (accessed 23 March 2017).
6. Norbert Wiener, *Cybernetics: Or control and communication in the animal and the machine* (Cambridge, MA: MIT Press, 1948).
7. James Moor, The Dartmouth College artificial intelligence conference: the next fifty years. *AI Magazine* 27, no. 4 (2006): 87–91. http://www.aaai.org/ojs/index.php/aimagazine/article/view/1911/1809 (accessed 1 December 2016).
8. J. McCarthy, Ascribing mental qualities to machines. In M. Ringle, ed., *Philosophical Perspectives in Artificial Intelligence* (Atlantic Highlands, NJ: Humanities Press, 1979).
9. Ray Kurzweil, *The Singularity Is Near* (Viking Press, 2005).
10. Nikola Danaylov, 17 definitions of the technological singularity. Singularity weblog, 18 April 2012. https://www.singularityweblog.com/17-definitions-of-the-technological-singularity/ (accessed 6 June 2017).
11. Singularity Symposium (n.d.). What is the technological singularity? www.singularitysymposium.com (accessed 18 October 2017).
12. Geoff Holder, *101 Things to Do with a Stone Circle*. Holder offers as his source Arthur C. Clarke's 1999 *Profiles of the Future* (Millennium Edition) (History Press, 2009), p. 143.
13. Gartner's 2016 hype cycle for emerging technologies identifies three key trends that organizations must track to gain competitive advantage. Gartner press release (16 August 2016). http://www.gartner.com/newsroom/id/3412017 (accessed 23 March 2017).
14. Christina Warren, Google's artificial intelligence chief says 'we're in an AI spring'. *Yahoo News* (20 May 2016). https://uk.news.yahoo.com/googles-artificial-intelligence-chief-says-191328375.html.
15. Stuart Russell, Daniel Dewey, and Max Tegmark, Research priorities for robust and beneficial artificial intelligence. *AI Magazine* 38, no. 4 (2015): 105–114.
16. Hope Reece, AI experts weigh in on Microsoft CEO's 10 new rules for artificial intelligence. TechRepublic (30 June 2016). http://www.techrepublic.com/article/ai-experts-weigh-in-on-microsoft-ceos-10-new-rules-for-artificial-intelligence (accessed 21 March 2017).
17. Machine learning: what it is and why it matters. SAS. https://www.sas.com/en_us/insights/analytics/machine-learning.html (accessed January 6, 2018).
18. Chandramallika Basak and Paul Verhaeghen, Three layers of working memory: focus-switch costs and retrieval dynamics as revealed by the N-count task. *Journal of Cognitive Psychology* 23, no. 2 (2011): 204–219.

19. Clemency Burton-Hill, The superhero of artificial intelligence. *The Guardian* (16 February 2016). https://www.theguardian.com/technology/2016/feb/16/demis-hassabis-artificial-intelligence-deepmind-alphago

20. Maria Popova, What is art? Favourite famous definitions, from antiquity to today. Brain-Picking, 22 June 2012. https://www.brainpickings.org/2012/06/22/what-is-art/ (accessed 13 January 2018).

21. Oscar Wilde, *The Complete Works of Oscar Wilde*. Collins, 2016.

22. Brian Mastroianni, Marchesa, IBM Watson design 'cognitive dress' for Met gala. CBS News (2 May 2016). http://www.cbsnews.com/news/marchesa-ibm-watson-to-debut-cognitive-dress-at-mondays-met-gala.

23. Georgia Wells, Google's computers paint like Van Gogh, and the art sells for thousands. *Wall Street Journal* (29 February 2016). http://blogs.wsj.com/digits/2016/02/29/googles-computers-paint-like-van-gogh-and-the-art-sells-for-thousands

CHAPTER 3

The Impact of AI on Leading-Edge Industries

SUMMARY

This chapter deals with the impact of machine learning and artificial intelligence on some of the key leading-edge industries, as distinct from individual professions, although there is invariably an overlap in places. These key industries comprise the financial services, automotive/assembly, and high-tech/telecom industries.

Our current fast-moving environment makes it impossible to provide a comprehensive summary in terms of the total marketplace or with respect to individual industries. Future publications might comprise entire editions for specific industries. The intent of this chapter is to provide a strong indicator as to the breadth and depth of the AI initiative in the front-runner industries and some of the wider impacts that it will have on commerce as a whole.

INTRODUCTION

Industries will inevitably change as we increasingly move towards the era of cognitive analytics and AI. This change is nothing new – industries have been evolving from the time of the Industrial Revolution. Today the dynamics of and imperatives for change would likely be mainly unrecognisable to our forefathers, although perhaps many of the great entrepreneurs, such as Ford and Carnegie, would not find it too difficult to get up to speed.

Almost all industries are currently being increasingly affected by what are now described as the megatrends of technology: the *cloud*, *mobile*, *social*, and *analytics*. The FinTech movement, which consistently stimulates disruptive forms of innovation in the financial sector, is also increasingly being seen as a megatrend. Additionally, we are on the wave of a completely new cycle of major influences. Soon all industries will be affected by what we are coming to know as the *new megatrends*.

In his book *New Mega Trends: Implications for our Future Lives*, Sarwant Singh lays out the issues that he believes will dominate the agenda going forward.[1] They are defined not in hard terms, but rather in terms of their characteristics:

- Megatrends are global
- They are sustainable
- They are transformational.

Singh suggests that whilst there are 200 potential megatrends across all industries, they can be condensed down to 12 key possibilities. This book has further condensed them down to 6, for the sake of brevity:

1. *Smartness.* The connected nature of the future and how it will impact energy consumption.
2. *Travel.* So-called e-mobility, the movement of transport from reliance on hydrocarbons to reliance on electricity, improvements in high-speed travel, and even how rail will replace flight as the principal mode of transport.
3. *Process change.* Impact of new business models, including how these will change work from the traditional linear model to a more collaborative approach, and the concept of *innovating to zero.*
4. *Social interaction.* The impact of transformational social trends, including the importance of geolocation, which will lead inter alia to geosocialisation (systems understanding where individuals are located physically and pushing offers to them based on those locations, for example, shopping malls and airports).
5. *Healthcare and well-being.* How megatrends will help with the challenge of increasing healthcare costs and an aging population.
6. *Data congestion and security.* The issue of infrastructure challenges and how security and privacy can be maintained.

None of these potential future megatrends sits in isolation. They are all interdependent and industry agnostic. Furthermore, to some degree they are all speculative. Who can really be sure that there will be a shift from air travel to high-tech rail travel? If that were to happen, it may take decades to be achieved because of the need to create appropriate infrastructure and to manage the politics and vested interests.

This book is about analytics, machine learning, and AI. Despite uncertainty regarding implementation timetables, these three areas are likely to have a much earlier and much quicker impact on our lives than the broader megatrends mentioned above. Initially, change in the AI space will probably occur in key areas, such as process improvement and management. In these two areas implementation will probably be speedy, as their impacts are likely to be relatively nonpolitical in nature and mainly driven by commercial considerations, such as cost reduction.

But their influence *will* have massive impact on industries and the way we work. To a certain extent, perhaps there is a political angle to explore. After all, isn't politics a debate about how a country or a society is going to be run? Individual resistance to these changes is probably futile (although this book will explore some coping strategies). Overall it's critical that industries, professions, and individuals have some insight into the changes that are coming, so as to allow them at the very least to guide the direction of change and avoid being victims or targets.

Where might this guidance of change come from? Perhaps it will come from professional institutions, but this is doubtful. These institutions are places of learning and qualification, but they are not quasi unions whose role is to represent their members' interests in the workplace. In fact, relatively few professionals overall are members of trade unions. Institutions might reasonably say that it is not within their scope to take on such political arguments. However, these types of organisations do provide an effective environment, which is relatively free of politics, to discuss these potentially confrontational issues, especially as regards the ethical dimension.

Professional institutions also have a vested financial interest in this debate. If their members are going to be displaced by machines, don't the organisations themselves run the risk of fewer subscriptions and ultimately less revenue? And in any event, with AI, who really needs professional institutions anyway?

Not everyone will agree that change is needed. Those who resist change are often referred to as Luddites. The Luddites were a group who in 1812 were named after a Nottingham apprentice called Ned Ludd (possibly born Edward Ludlam). Ludd smashed his knitting machine (called a stocking frame) when he was threatened with being whipped for not working hard enough. It was a revolt against the industrialisation of the textiles industry that spread into the north of England, where weavers set fire to their mills.

The main argument of the Luddites did not relate to the equipment itself but to the resistance of employers to allowing new employment terms and working conditions. In more recent times, this resistance has given rise to the neo-Luddite movement, which in essence is an anti-technology movement that describes itself as 'a leaderless movement of passive resistance to consumerism and the increasingly bizarre and frightening technologies of the Computer Age'.[2]

Just over 200 years after the first Luddites, another group is following a similar line of thinking . The Luddites200 Organising Forum has a number of questions about issues resulting from technological change (see Table 7).[3]

TABLE 7   The Luddites200 Organising Forum's objections to technological change.

General issues	▪ Who benefits, who loses? ▪ Who is in charge: the human or the machine? ▪ What kind of a world is implied by the new technology?
Labour issues	▪ Creating unemployment? ▪ Control and surveillance of workers
Socioeconomic impacts	▪ Is there a genuine need? ▪ Concentration of market power ▪ De-skilling, creation of dependency
Social issues	▪ General effect on equality ▪ High price of technology excludes access for poor people ▪ Concentrating power or democratising it? ▪ Speeding up or slowing down the pace of life?
Environmental issues	▪ Energy/resource consumption/carbon footprint
Ethical issues	▪ Acceptable manipulation of nature? ▪ Turning human bodies into commodities?
Health issues	▪ Prevention or cure?

Source: Adapted from Luddites200 Organising Forum (n.d.). 21st century technology debates & politics. Luddites200 Organising Forum website. http://www.luddites200.org.uk/TechnologyPoliticsNow.html

The Forum's members are not alone. The group Breaking the Frame references Ed Ludd's smashing of the stocking frame, and its members describe themselves as follows: 'We believe there is an underlying politics of technology which connects various political issues – from how our food is produced, to the freedom of the internet, to nuclear power and many other concerns. These debates are currently *framed* as if they are completely separate and unrelated. *Our aim is to change this.*'[4]

In 2014 Breaking the Frame claimed to have 200 supporting organisations, but it is difficult sometimes to imagine this collection of well-meaning parties as representing anything more than a niche viewpoint. Perhaps this description does them a disservice, as they seem to have some well-established supporters, at least in principle.

The well-known scientist Stephen Hawking has already personally expressed some concern independently:

> *If machines produce everything we need, the outcome will depend on how things are distributed. Everyone can enjoy a life of luxurious leisure if the machine-produced wealth is shared, or most people can end up miserably poor if the machine-owners successfully lobby against wealth redistribution. So far, the trend seems to be toward the second option, with technology driving ever-increasing inequality.*[5]

Hawking's comments are not a statement against technology but about the distribution of wealth and the impact of capitalism. His comments appear to restate the apparent interlock between technology, capitalism, and politics.

Resistance to, and nervousness about, technological change is not confined solely to niche pressure groups whose members have linked themselves to events in English history, however. In the same way that Ludd was not against technological change itself, but concerned about the rights of the workers affected, neo-Luddism could prove to be a Trojan horse in a wider public reaction to the increasing impact of technology.

For example, in 2001 at the American Association for the Advancement of Sciences, Francis Collins (at the time head of the Human Genome Project) claimed: 'Major anti-technology movements will be active in the U.S. and elsewhere by 2030'. In a 2014 article referencing the event, writer Caroline Gregoire also cites the Amish and reform Luddites as other evidence of resistance to change (she explains that reform Luddites are critical of technology but do not reject it outright).[6]

There is something both exciting and disturbing about these examples of resistence to technological change. Clearly, for some there is both curiosity and fear about a technological future that will inevitably incorporate forms of AI into our lifestyle. As a society, we seem to increasingly value our creativity and decry automation, whilst at the same time accepting automatically generated recommendations about what we should be watching on TV and the quickest way home.

Have the major technology companies missed a trick by focusing on the technology and not thinking hard enough about its effect on key stakeholders: that is, ourselves? By understanding the implications of technology and by being able to express these implications in a layperson's terms (including laypeople who are qualified professionals in a nontech fields), through greater engagement commercial organisations can help in the management of stakeholder expectations.

Don't even the most basic of programme management approaches recognise that effective stakeholder management is one of the critical success factors in successful change management?

As technology increasingly integrates itself with business, it becomes possible to narrow or even remove the gap between AI and business decision makers by greater understanding of business issues and more effectively aligning AI's solutions with them. If the essential step of businessmen understanding AI isn't taken, isn't the historic gulf that emerged between technology and business in the early part of the twenty-first century likely to occur again?

It is in this spirit that we will attempt to consider individual industries in the context of AI. Our forecasts are, by definition, nothing more than predictions. But they are predictions made with the benefit of understanding the present and anticipating the future based on that understanding.

In a 2017 report, McKinsey stated that 20% of AI-aware firms were concentrated in the financial services, automotive/assembly, and high-tech/telecom industries.[7] We will chiefly consider these three industries, with the aim of understanding what we might learn from them.

FINANCIAL SERVICES

Financial services are at the vanguard of progress in the use of advanced analytics, cognitive analytics, and AI. In this section we will consider three sectors: banking (retail, commercial, and investment), wealth management, and insurance.

Retail Banking

According to a 2017 Accenture survey of 600 top bankers and experts, AI will become 'the primary way that banks will interact with their customers within the next three years'.[8]

Advocating a move in banking from 'mobile first' to 'AI first', the resultant findings place AI alongside other key technological capabilities as being critical developments:

- Embedded AI solutions (40% of respondents)
- Computer vision (40%)
- Machine learning (38%)
- Natural language processing (37%)
- Robotic process automation (34%).

Seventy-nine percent of respondents to the survey said that they believed AI would create a more 'human-like' customer experience. Says Alan McIntyre, head of the Accenture's banking practice and co-author of the report, 'The big paradox here is that people think technology will lead to banking becoming more and more automated and less and less personalised, but what we've seen coming through here is the view that technology will actually help banking become a lot more personalized.'

The report points out that whilst the number of human interactions in bank branches or over the phone has fallen and is likely to continue to do so, the customer still wants some form of branch contact. Even so, surveys seem to indicate continued reduction in branch usage by customers. For example, in the UK HSBC announced the closure of 62 more branches in 2017 as a result of a 40% fall in customer usage.[9] Cynics might suggest that the fall in customer usage in retail banks is partly associated with the falling quality of front-office service.

In a Finextra survey that asked affluent users (defined as the top 10–15% of earners) about their banking habits, the results were relatively evenly split into four groups:[10]

1. Prefer to bank via an app (24%)
2. Favour using a website (29%)
3. Prefer personal contact over the phone (21%)
4. Prefer to visit a branch, especially for complex or high-value transactions (26%).

The retail banking market appears ripe to apply AI-type capabilities directly in the first three of these front-office functions, and some form of AI advisor could certainly be used to support the fourth.

It's no surprise that over three-quarters of the respondents to the Finextra survey also anticipate that 'the majority of organisations in the banking industry will deploy AI interfaces as their primary point for interacting with customers', and that 71% believe 'that AI is capable of becoming the face of their organization or brand'.

It appears that one of the main intentions of banks is to move employees to 'more judgement-based and higher value-added roles'. It's inevitable that fewer employees will be needed and it's no surprise that Mark Carney, governor of the Bank of England, has warned that up to 15 million UK banking jobs could be replaced by robots.[11]

Where robotics are already being used, savings for banks have been significant. In a 2015 report from Cognizant

- The percentage of banks that claimed a savings of more than 15% was 26%
- The percentage expecting similar levels of savings in the next 3–5 years was 55%.

Beyond savings on direct costs, business users were also experiencing:

- Reduced error rates
- Better management of repeatable tasks
- Improved standardisation of workflow
- Reduced reliance on multiple screens to complete a process
- Reduced process friction.[12]

So, are front-office staff in retail banks becoming an endangered species? Bank of Tokyo-Mitsubishi UFJ is already piloting a robotic humanoid bank teller in its flagship Tokyo branch. The robot, named Nao, is the result of a collaboration between SoftBank and IBM. It can potentially operate in 19 languages and has the ability to 'remember' details about 5.5 million customers and 100 products.

Its bigger brother/sister, Pepper, stands about 1.2 metres tall and currently retails at roughly US$1600 plus software costs. Pepper has a so-called emotion engine that can recognise human feelings and simulate them, which is a mechanism that is also used in the healthcare industry. The developers say that Pepper can 'learn new skills from the cloud as it communicates with thousands of other Peppers'.[13]

So, what does the future look like for retail banking? Perhaps the branch will remain in some form, although probably not as we know it. Already we are seeing the emergence of café-banks, which provide informal workspaces and merge the apparently equally important functions of banking, working, and drinking coffee. This seems to mirror how FinTech start-ups seem to operate, through small groups collaboratively working in public spaces. Some of the smarter café-banks even allow the ordering of coffee online at a discounted price to ensure that those unnecessary and pesky queues are avoided. What's really to stop there being some form of robot banking advisor in the same location?

Commercial Banking

Commercial banks are defined as banks, or a division of large banks, that provide banking services to corporations and large or mid-sized businesses, as opposed to a retail bank, which generally deals with individuals.

Earlier considerations have focused on retail banking, but what is the future of AI in a commercial bank setting? In many ways, the issue to resolve remains the same: How does a bank extract all the relevant information from critical data and then provide a commercial client with the best advice? Beyond this, how might that advice be most effectively communicated in a digital environment?

All of the major banks are currently looking at digital platforms and are increasingly looking at applications in the commercial banking sector. Even so, initial activity in the AI space seems to be mainly on the retail side, with commercial banking coming in a relatively poor second.

Although we have divided the banking industry into a retail and a commercial segment, we need to also understand that within commercial banking there is further segmentation, principally between larger, incorporated banks and small and medium-sized enterprises that offer specialised services. In the same way that insurers split their business between retail insurance and commercial insurance, there is also a segmentation between retail and commercial business that predominates in the banking industry. Figure 4 gives some indication of the complexity and breadth of the banking industry, although some countries, such as India, have quite different industry characteristics.

Although banks are currently focusing on AI in the retail sector, it appears clear that AI-type capabilities could readily lend themselves to the commercial sector, especially in the relatively simple marketplace for small and medium enterprises (SMEs). It's a big market that could benefit from innovation. In the United Kingdom, for example, there are 5.2 million businesses, 99% of which are classified as SMEs (fewer than 250 employees).[14] In Canada there are over a million SMEs. (It's a difficult market for SMEs: half of UK start-up SMEs fail within five years, citing the UK tax system and poor bank lending as the main causes. Nearly two-thirds don't have the confidence to project three years of consecutive growth).[15]

With so much emphasis on innovation through FinTech, these statistics don't seem to bode well for start-ups. Perhaps commercial banks could add more value for their customer bases by using AI-fuelled add-ons? Some questions to ask follow:

- To what degree can commercial banks learn from retail banks in terms of the use of AI?
- Can AI contribute to helping the 'Flat White Economy' by helping commercial customers create more sustainable products that are closer to the needs of their target markets?
- Can commercial banks also support their larger, commercial customers by adding value to their financial offerings, such as providing contextual advice with financial data?
- Can commercial banks continue to reinvent themselves as trusted partners to major organisations, perhaps by providing embedded AaaS (Analytics as a Service) with their existing financial products?

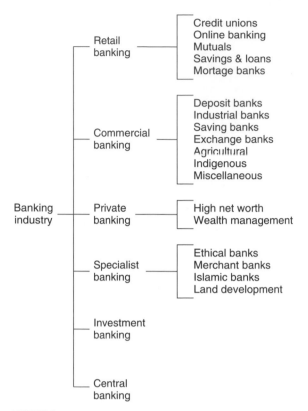

FIGURE 4   Segmentation of the banking industry.

Like many industries, commercial banks operate in a fiercely competitive environment. Some will inevitably see the journey towards AI as being the best route to competitive advantage going forward.

According to David Lynch at Standard Chartered, 'In the old days, it was the war for talent and to convince everyone that your organisation was the best place to work. We may get to a point where the most intelligent brain becomes a major source of competitive advantage. It's hard to know where that's going to land.'[16]

It's not difficult to imagine that the 'most intelligent brain' will not necessarily be a human one.

Investment Banking

How likely are people to trust their investments to a robot? After all, the value of investments can fall as well increase, as we are often reminded. Despite this, investment banking, which provides financial services to individuals, businesses, and governments, is perhaps one of the industry sectors that is best suited to an environment of advanced analytics, even if AI is perhaps a step too far for some at the current time.

Investment banks help their clients raise capital for expansions, mergers, and acquisitions, and usually comprise two distinct operations, known as the *sell side* and the *buy side*.

The sell side trades securities for cash or other securities. A security has tangible (or *fungible*) value that can be traded. It can represent part ownership in a publically traded company (known as stock), a creditor relationship with a government or corporation, or a right to ownership (known as an option).

The buy side provides advice to institutions that buy investment services, such as insurers, hedge funds, pensions, and mutuals.

These are both complex entities. The point of the buy side is to identify investments that can make money for investors. Secrecy is essential, as any suggestion of market activity can influence value. Buy-side analysts are usually engaged in researching market movements and providing advice, often for the money managers of the commercial bank.

One of the key activities of investment banks is portfolio management, that is, management of a group of assets and liabilities that will result in optimisation of the portfolio, or collection of funds. Investment banking is a highly regulated industry whose analysts consider exposure limits, risk weights, and returns from each category of assets. The job is analytical in nature, often using genetic algorithms to search for exact or approximate solutions to meet portfolio-optimisation targets. Genetic algorithms are a particular class of evolutionary algorithms that use sophisticated techniques inspired by evolutionary biology, such as inheritance, mutation, selection, and crossover.[17]

Investment banking is also a potentially risky area of commerce, which is heavily affected by individual behaviours. It particularly lends itself to advanced analytics, especially given the volatility of marketplaces. It plays an extremely important role in how our pensions are funded.

In such an analytically fuelled business environment, is there a role for intuition? In their 2010 paper, 'Intuitive Decision Making in Banking and Finance', authors Ann Hensman and Eugene Sadler-Wells reviewed the banking industry and recognised that:

- [In] uncertain and time-pressured decision environments where information about alternatives may be unavailable, incomplete, or overwhelming, rational decision making is bounded both by the complexity of the task and by the information processing capacities of decision-makers
- In business settings, formal techniques of rational choice may sometimes be difficult or impossible to apply.[18]

In our pressurised world, made worse by constant accessibility through mobile connectivity, isn't it becoming harder to make decisions due to market volatility and uncertainty? Equally, might some think that it's better to make an irrational decision (which we describe as being intuitive), rather than no decision at all? In a fully automated environment, would intuitive decisions ever be made?

Banking and finance are vitally important sectors, and have impacts that dwarf other sectors. The consequences of a poor decision can have a major knock-on effect, as has been seen with the Royal Bank of Scotland (RBS) situation, where following their acquisition of ABN Amro Bank, the UK Government had to step in and acquire 58% of RBS shares, spending £37 billion or £617 for every UK citizen, to avert wider financial sector meltdown. Financial institutions increasingly appear to be models of analytical insight, yet even now still rely to some degree on intuition – and this is still probably constrained by the experience of individuals.

Intuition is affected by:

- The nature of the task (e.g. factors of time and uncertainty)
- Individual factors (e.g. participants, their experience, and confidence)
- Organisational contextual factors (e.g. constraints and conventions, accountability and hierarchy, team dynamics and organisational culture).

The findings of the Hensman and Sadler-Wells paper coincide with those of one of the pioneers of management theory (especially as regards intuition), Chester Barnard. This former AT&T executive drew a distinction between two types of thinking in management:

1. Logical thinking, that is, conscious thinking that can be expressed in words and other symbols (that is, reasoning)
2. Illogical thinking, that is, thinking that is 'not capable of being expressed in words or as reasoning' underpinned by processes that are unconscious and 'so complex and rapid that they could not be analyzed by the person within whose brain they take place'.[19]

If we accept that illogical thought is part of the overall decision-making process in a human, then isn't it necessary to consider how this might be reproduced (if it is necessary to the process) in an AI environment? Is there room for illogical thought in an AI system? Wouldn't illogical thought *crash* the programme?

Alternatively, are we conceding that all decisions need to be logical in nature? There is an element of *Star Trek*'s Spock coming into the discussion. Spock, as you may remember, sought logic in every decision. Although he was a fictional character, the precedent for using fiction to foreshadow the future or reflect reality (or merely to provoke further thought) was introduced when we considered another fictional creation, HAL 9000, earlier (see Chapter 1).

If we can accept that the best decisions are completely rational and therefore in effect emotionless, then personal bias would inevitably be avoided. Isn't that a good thing in major financial decisions, especially in a highly regulated environment? And wouldn't an AI approach lend itself especially well to such circumstances?

Wealth Management

Personal wealth management can be considered to be close to investment management in its approach, although it is more relevant at an individual level. Analytics already form part of the wealth management tool kit. In making investment decisions for individuals, the starting point is to establish the risk appetite of the investor, which is usually done through a simple questionnaire. Surely this rather basic approach is capable of significant improvement by using (with consent) other relevant information, such as social media profiles?

Personal financial profiling recognises that different people are comfortable with different levels of risk. Comfort levels can change depending on individual circumstances. As a result, an individual's risk appetite is dynamic in nature, even if current profiling seems to suggest it is relatively static. The creators of FinaMetrica, who have designed (with the School of Psychology at the University of New South Wales) what they describe as a 'risk tolerance test', also say that there is 'no absolute measurement' of risk tolerance, only a relative scale 'much in the same way that IQ is measured'.[20]

If we accept that risk appetite changes with individual circumstances, then we also should recognise that our investment needs may also change over time. The most effective fund managers constantly measure investment benefits and make regular recommendations applicable to the individual. Increasingly the market is seeing the emergence of *cognitive wealth advisors*, which are in effect automated systems that provide support to the human advisor sitting across the table.

At what point does the automated advisory system become more important than the human advisor? Put another way, how much value does the human advisor actually add to the decision-making? Might the human be nothing more than window dressing for the computer's recommendations? If the computer were more humanoid, might we consider the real human to be obsolete?

The other side of the coin may well be the degree of confidence that the individual investor might have in dealing solely with a machine, even if many (or most) of the back-office decisions are already analytically driven. Doesn't the moment that we place our investment and pension decisions entirely in the hands of a machine evoke a moment that we place our whole future in 'their' hands?

Beyond emotions, there are commercial aspects to consider as well. Financial advice is a profitable business, with advisors earning around 1% of invested assets in annual fees. Increasingly, the ability to source that advice online or over the phone using automated methods opens the door to lower-cost – and perhaps even zero-cost – advice.

Automation not only has the ability to reduce costs for consumers but also can open the door to a much larger marketplace. What impact might this have on the 4,000+ investment advisory firms in the United States that each has over US$100 million in assets under management, totalling US$5 trillion in aggregate?[21]

So here is the rub. Would individuals rather trust a logical machine or an intuitive and emotional human being with their money? Frankly, in a volatile and uncertain environment doesn't the machine increasingly look as if it could be the better option?

And in any event, won't it soon be possible to teach the system how to be both emotional and irrational – within agreed limits – so that at the end of the day we might not notice any difference between man and machine?

Insurance

As with banking, insurance is both broad and wide in terms of what it represents as an industry. The two principal subsets are commercial insurance and retail insurance. Additionally, there are many other subsets, including reinsurance, captive insurance, and the specialist market, which provides insurance for specialty areas, such as marine and aviation. Figure 5 gives an indication of the breadth and complexity of the insurance industry.

Much of the insurance action to date in terms of AI has focused on the retail marketplace. That makes sense to most business users, as the retail sector is the easiest to understand and digest, if only because these users can do so through personal experience. However, some might argue that AI's greatest value in the insurance sector could emerge from the other three major insurance categories: commercial insurance, reinsurance, and specialist risk.

There's clearly a lot of activity in this space. Accenture found that the combined number of UK deals in insurance across AI and IoT technology increased by 79%

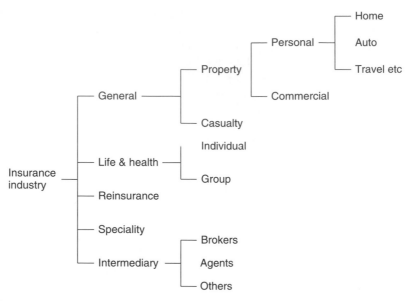

FIGURE 5   Segmentation of the insurance industry.

in 2016 and accounted for 44% of global *insurtech* (the use of emerging technology by insurance companies) deals. Roy Jubraj, digital and innovation lead in Accenture's UK financial team, says: 'We've seen a rapid acceleration of investment into, and deal activity around, intelligent automation and IoT start-ups over the last 12 months.'[22]

To fully understand the AI opportunities, insurers need to look at the three key drivers of activity in their industry, which are:

1. Management of risk
2. Improved customer retention and loyalty
3. Operational optimisation.

Management of Risk   For insurers, the optimum situation is for them not only to have a complete understanding of the nature of the risk but also to price the risk accurately. The risk may be predominantly material, as in the case of the likelihood of flood or earthquake, but may extend to other types of risk, such as losses arising through legal liability (product liability, negligence, nuisance, and professional mistakes). Insurers must also ensure that the cost of the insurance (known as the *premium*) has been correctly calculated.

The calculation of an insurance premium is predominantly an actuarial function and it is primarily statistically based. Analytical systems not only allow for structured and unstructured information to be converged to provide a much more granular view of the risk involved but also allow the risk to be much more accurately rated.

There are, of course, some more complex risks that perhaps do not readily allow themselves to be automated, for example, the smile of Julia Roberts (US$30 million) or the legs of Maria Carey (US$1 billion), but these are exceptions rather than the rule. It remains to be seen how an automated system would cope with such nonstandard policies.[23]

Improved Customer Retention   Improved customer retention is predominantly an issue for the reatil sector of insurance, as it is for banking's retail sector. It is becoming increasingly possible to gain a better understanding of likely customer behaviour at a more granular level. This helps insurers improve customer loyalty by anticipating any intention to switch insurers and allowing the current insurer to make a more attractive and timely offer.

To some degree, predictive analytical tools already provide this capability, but the objective is for insurers to use better intelligence to improve their messaging and accuracy. There are additionally other niche opportunities. One Spanish start-up, for example, proposes the use of AI to offer collaborative and one-time insurance for people attending public or private entertainment events.

Increasingly insurers are also likely to turn to the use of chatbots to engage directly with customers. Such digital technologies create new portals and (with consent) allow for the analysis of unstructured content, such as that held on mobile devices. Sentiment analysis then potentially allows insurers to create more personalised offerings.

Operational Optimisation   Many insurance activities are back-office functions that lend themselves to increased automation. One of the key areas is fraud prevention, either at the point of claim or in terms of misdescription at the time of initiation or renewal of the policy. Whilst individual cases of fraud might be small in real terms, the aggregate cost to the industry is high and is said to represent 10% of the cost of all claims.

The following findings are from a report from Insurance Europe called *The Impact of Insurance Fraud*:[24]

- A study conducted by the German Insurance Association concluded that more than half of all claims arising from loss or damage to smartphones and tablet PCs could not have actually happened and therefore must have been fraudulent.
- A 2012 Finnish study of 1,000 adults conducted by Finance Finland, an industry group, found that 27% said they knew a person who has deceived his/her insurance company.
- In the United Kingdom, the Association of British Insurers estimates that fraud adds, on average, an extra £50 (approximately €58) a year to the annual insurance bill for every policyholder.

Misdescription is defined as individuals or businesses misdescribing themselves with respect to elements that an insurance company might use to assess the correct premium to be paid. These elements might relate to age, gender, profession, claims history, medical condition, or multiple other factors. With regard to fraud by misdescription, it seems entirely possible to compare social media activity with a policyholder's declaration, assuming issues of privacy are overcome (which may simply be a matter of making such disclosures a condition of entry for obtaining insurance coverage). Beyond social media activity, in certain classes of insurance it could be possible to source additional information to gain insight about policyholders' behaviour, for example, with respect to their driving records or lifestyles. Even so, insurers are on difficult ground because of issues of privacy, unless permission is explicitly given to access information.

Increasingly, advanced analytics is being used by insurers in the area of fraud management. Some insurers are already indicating that this is an area of low-hanging fruit for AI, especially as the business benefit is so strong.

One question to address is when (if ever) insurers will be prepared to deny a claim without any human intervention whatsoever, but rather based on the facts of the matter, which have been automatically gathered and sorted. In most cases of fraud investigation we are likely to see, at least for the moment, a combination of human and analytical analysis. To that extent the technology might be described as cognitive, *augmenting* human decision-making rather than replacing it. However, the profession of fraud investigation is likely to continue to mature in terms of technical ability.

One major potential impact in the use of smarter insurance methods may well be in the area of setting insurance reserves. *Reserves* are the amounts set aside by insurers against their potential liabilities, both short term (e.g. in the case of a major weather incident) and long term (such as in the case of life and pension provisions).

The calculation of reserves is critical, in that such calculations help to establish correct profit margin forecasting for insurers and the success (or otherwise) of their book of business. When major short-term liabilities arise from a major claim, for example, much can often depend on the experience of individual experts in carrying out and subsequently ratifying or correcting their initial assessments of likely cost. It is feasible to try to create more sophisticated AI practices to create greater accuracy. Actuarial models, which traditionally have been used for longer-term calculations, can be incorporated into more sophisticated loss evaluations.

For insurers, increasingly the mood is to become proactive rather than reactive. This relates not only to lifestyle management (or at least lifestyle 'advice') but also to material risk management. By the latter we are referring to, for example, the prediction of major weather events and what mitigating actions might take place to avoid or reduce the degree of damage. It is implicit within an insurance policy, and consequently embedded in insurance contract law, that policyholders are obliged to take action to prevent, or *mitigate*, loss or damage that could potentially occur. Failure to do so invalidates the insurance coverage.

In time, not only will systems be able to identify particular incidents that are likely to occur, such as a major storm, but also to recommend what action should be taken at an individual policyholder level. The next level of intelligence will allow machines to recognise whether or not appropriate mitigating action has actually been taken. Future smart systems will automatically activate remote systems to reduce or avoid damage.

In the domestic sphere, the notion of the *smart home* is increasingly gaining attraction. Innovative processes are starting to embed new workflows, such as automatically turning off the water supply in a house when there has been a sudden loss of pressure.

Smart factories are likely to follow. Many commercial policies already have conditions known as *warranties*, which oblige the commercial customer to take certain actions, such as keeping stock at a certain height above floor level to avoid water damage. Remote devices with spatial awareness can readily detect the location of objects and can either send a warning, invalidate an insurance policy or claim, or automatically instruct a storage device.

And if we are concerned with smart homes and smart factories, then why not with *smart employees*? With employer liability and workers' compensation coverage being major insurance exposures, the ability of an employer to be able to not only record activity but also specifically direct an employee's actions cannot be ruled out. More dangerous activities might be undertaken by a robotic device, as in dangerous inspections being carried out by drones.

Implementation is key. To gain widespread use of smart systems, insurers must incentivise their customers, penalise them for not using them, or use a combination of incentives and penalties. Insurance marketers (or their systems) will need to consider whether the carrot or the stick is likely to have the greatest impact.

It's not difficult to see that 90% of the retail and life insurance industries has the capability to become automated. This will leave only complex and nonstandard decisions as requiring some degree of human intervention. The big debate is over *augmentation* versus *automation*. It's a debate that is not confined to the insurance sector.

Major commercial and specialist insurers will probably lag behind in terms of automation, not least because of the nature of the client base and the speed at which the clients themselves become automated. Notwithstanding, commercial and specialist insurers will still be affected by the application of AI systems to the regulatory environment, for example, capital requirement or the alignment of an underwriting decision to the risk appetite of the insurance carrier.

It's also likely that new categories, or classes, of insurance risk will start to emerge. At the current time the focus is on cybersecurity, especially with regard to the risk of loss of data and its consequences. As we increasingly enter a data-fuelled age across all industries, new risks will be discovered and their consequences are likely to increase exponentially. There will be not only operational issues but significant long-term reputational impacts.

Insurers will increasingly also need to specifically consider risk attached to the automated decisions made in an AI environment. What type of insurance coverage needs to be in place for, say, a self-driving car, for example, and where will responsibility and liability rest in the case of an accident? Although conceiving of these new types of insurance, if requiring creativity, could well remain with humans, to what degree will we rely on machines as helpers? Will an automated system be able to accurately assess the risk of failure of another automated system? And if such an assessment is possible, then couldn't one system interact with another in some way to reduce the likelihood of failure?

AI has the potential to transform a 300-year-old industry. This will especially help in growth areas, such as the Asia-Pacific region and Latin America, where insurance penetration is at a relatively low level compared to the more mature markets of Europe and North America, and where there is likely to be a shortage of talent.

For insurers, AI will inevitably open up new markets and the likelihood of significant market growth. Costs will be lower than they have been traditionally and digital distribution will be more effective. There may be some clouds of uncertainty, but for the insurance industry an AI future is almost unquestionably likely to have a silver lining.

AUTOMOBILES

In 1964 Isaac Asimov (1920–1992), the American science fiction writer and professor of biochemistry at Boston University, predicted, 'Much effort will be put into the design of vehicles with "robot brains" that can be set for particular destinations and that will then proceed there without interference by the slow reflexes of a human driver'.[25]

Continued investment by vehicle manufacturers and their partnership with key technology vendors make the infusion of cognitive analytics and AI into mobile vehicles highly likely. The main obstacles seem to be issues of law, culture, confidence, and insurance. Technology is increasingly unlikely to present a barrier.

AI Implementation Timeline

The UK-based Thatcham Research Centre, an auto research institute, has already described a five-stage process of implementation (see Table 8).

Experts suggest that implementation is currently at the intersection of stage 2 (automated steering, braking, and/or acceleration, but driver otherwise in control) and stage 3 (automated steering and braking, but with some limited driver intervention). However, they say that the step between stage 3 and stage 4 (vehicle can complete sections of journey but driver is given/can take control) will represent a *step change* in our engagement with the car.

The timeline being considered is already within sight, with predictions that stage 4 will be reached by perhaps 2020 and stage 5 (vehicle completes the journey with no human intervention) by 2040.

These timeline predictions do not simply apply to vehicles for personal use, but also extend to commercial haulage vehicles, including trucking. In 2015 Daimler unveiled its self-driving truck, Inspiration. Already, the Rio Tinto mining group is operating 50 self-driving trucks, which haul up to 500 tons of iron ore apiece on its private mining sites in Western Australia.[26]

TABLE 8   The five-stage process of implementing AI in autos.

Stage 1	Stage 2	Stage 3	Stage 4	Stage 5
Driver control	Assisted driving	Partial autonomy	High autonomy	Full autonomy
Driver is completely in control but with some automated systems	Automated steering, braking, and/or acceleration, but driver otherwise in control	Automated steering and braking, but with some limited driver intervention	Vehicle can complete sections of journey, but driver is given/can take control	Vehicle completes the journey with no human intervention
Cruise control	Autonomous braking	Keeping in full lane	Road following	Technical and public confidence
Automated braking	Adaptive cruise control	Traffic jam assistance	Junction decisioning	
Electronic stability control	Parking and lane assistance		Hazard detection and evasive decisioning	
			Ethical decisioning	
			Interaction between vehicles	

Source: Andrew Miller, The road to autonomy: driverless cars and the implications for insurance. *Thinkpiece* 118 (July 2015). Chartered Insurance Institute. http://www.cii.co.uk/media/6321203/tp118_miller_thatcham_driverless_cars_vf_july2015.pdf

Motor manufacturers increasingly believe that drivers want their cars and mobile devices to be interconnected. The Open Automobile Alliance, which was formed in 2014, comprises an alliance of auto manufacturers and tech companies aimed at using the Android system in cars. Most major car manufacturers are members. (*Android* is a mobile operating system developed by Google and usually seen in smartphones and tablets. It's considered by most to be a competitor to Apple.) The commercial model for the auto industry seems to follow that of the Open Handset Alliance, which is a consortium of hardware, software, and telecom companies.

We've come a long way since the invention of the automobile. The year 1886 is recognised as the year the modern car – invented by Karl Benz, who created the Benz Patent-Motorwagen – was born. The twentieth century saw the emergence of the car as a means of transit for the masses, and the history of vehicle development over the past 50 years can be mapped by the dates technological advances were introduced. In many cases the dates can be disputed, as the capabilities are known by various names and often there are multiple claims to ownership and development, but the following dates reflect the general progression:

- Electronic fuel injection (1958)
- Airbag (1953)
- Antilock braking system (1969)
- Navigation (1981)
- Electronic stability program (1995)
- Braking assistance (1996)
- Passive night vision assistance (2002).

The car has now become a mobile computer. Experts estimate that the modern car has over 100 million lines of code, compared to the 44 million lines of code in Microsoft Office 2013.[27] The analytics company Gartner predicted in 2009 that 30% of the cost of a car will comprise electronic components by 2018. The creators of Statista, an advanced analytics software package, suggest a cost percentage of 35% by 2020 and 50% by 2030.[28]

Key Developments

Gartner's 2015 report covering auto-electronic trends identified key auto developments. (Gartner uses the term *hype cycle* in place of *trends*; its Hype Cycle is a branded graphical illustration that represents the maturity, adoption, and use of modern technologies. Although it provides a useful indicator, some critics suggest that what is being represented is not a cycle, in that it is not a natural flow of technological change, but rather a point of view. Even so, the Hype Cycle provides a good indicator as to what is hot and what is not.)[29]

Table 9, taken from Gartner's *Hype Cycle for Automotive Electronics, 2015*, focuses on those components that have a cognitive/AI element, as opposed to the power train and the battery, for example.

Underpinning the future of the automobile is the issue of connectivity. This extends not only to the use of satellite navigation and smartphones on the move, but additionally to the relationship between vehicles, drivers, other drivers, and road infrastructure. Better connectivity will affect not only traffic congestion but also road safety and the driving environment.

TABLE 9   AI extract, Gartner Hype Cycle report.

Hype cycle	Description	Explanation
On the rise	Driver monitoring system	Measuring driver attention through monitoring eye movement
	Neuromorphic hardware	Deep-learning capability embedding analytics into hardware
	802.11p (an amendment to a standard used in vehicular communication systems)	Information to be wirelessly communicated to other vehicles with roadside sensors
	ISO 26262	Codes of practice relating to the functional safety of devices and systems in cars
	Autonomous vehicles	
	IoT	
	Embedded hypervisor	A so-called virtual machine manager ensures that no conflicts arise in the activity of each of the operating systems
	Gaze control	Car recognises your gaze in order to select a specific action, such as radio controls
	Biometric driver identification	Automatically identifies the driver based on physiological features
	Lane assist	Vehicle uses cameras to recognise whether the car is drifting
	Genivi alliance	Alliance that focuses on in-car entertainment technology platforms
	(a) Near field communications	Improvement of connectivity between handsets and vehicles
Climbing the slope	Electric vehicles	
	Gesture control	Controls activated with a wave of the hand
	Haptics in automobiles	Touch screens
	Night vision enhancement systems	Increase the distance drivers can see in the dark and in poor weather

Source: James F. Hines, Hype cycle for automotive electronics. Gartner report ID G00277793 (29 July 2015). https://www.gartner.com/doc/3102919/hype-cycle-automotive-electronics

Congestion remains a major and increasing problem. The challenge is one of optimising the entire process of travelling. Do we really need to travel to work? Is working at home a better alternative?

Travelling by car is likely to remain with us, as is almost certainly the problem of traffic congestion. Working at home supposedly brings with it increases in productivity and improvements in work–life balance, but its benefits can be offset by the psychological issues of feeling remote, lonely, or depressed. Some employers are already also beginning to reverse the trend towards working at home in favour of office-based work.

Car ownership will continue to feature in society, but perhaps more as a symbol of status rather than exercise in practicality. A survey by Progenium in 2011 created a pecking order of the status of various vehicles. Unsurprisingly, it clearly reaffirmed the status of prestige vehicles over more basic cars. Using a score of 1 for high status through 4 for very low status, Porsche and Mercedes featured at 1.8 and 2.0, respectively, whereas an Opel came in at a lowly 3.5, which was apparently slightly lower than a washing machine.

Their survey also went on to identify the characteristics that created status in vehicle ownership. These were:

- Manufacturer's brand
- Performance
- Design
- Expression of financial resources
- Expression of personality.[30]

Not all age groups are moving at the same pace. China, for example, has the youngest premium-car buyers in the world. Their tech-savvy demand for connected cars has led to rapid growth in the usage of onboard systems, already outstripping Western Europe and the United States. Research indicates that as many as 60% of Chinese drivers (compared to only 20% of German drivers, for example) would switch car brands solely in order to have complete access to data and applications inside their vehicles.[31]

Innovating to Zero

In Sarwant Singh's book *New Mega Trends: Implications for Our Future Lives*[32] (mentioned in the introduction to this chapter), the author lays out a series of megatrends, one of which he describes as 'innovating to zero'. As part of this broad concept he suggests a trend towards a 'zero' mentality, which ultimately will lead to:

- *Zero hours contracts*, in which there is no commitment to minimum hours for employees on the part of the employer
- *Zero waste*, or civilisation operating in a green environment, which extends to carbon-neutral cities
- *Zero friction* in existing processes, meaning functions (and people, presumably) not adding value are stripped out of the system
- *Zero accidents*, especially in the workplace.

It becomes easy to extend the concept of innovating to zero to an automobile environment, as did Thomas Koehler and Dirk Wollschlaeger in their book *The Digital Transformation of the Automobile*. They suggest a world in the year 2025 in which there are:

- Zero traffic accidents
- Zero congestion
- Zero failure, that is, no breakdowns.[33]

As the concept of cognitive analytics and AI is explored in the auto industry, it may be worthwhile considering each of these in more detail.

Zero Traffic Accidents   According to the World Health Organisation, traffic accidents kill 1.27 million globally on an annual basis. Nearly half of all victims are pedestrians, cyclists, and motorcyclists.[34] Road traffic injuries are predicted to become the third leading contributor to the global burden of disease and injury by 2020.[35] Beyond the obvious impact on individuals, a zero-accident environment would clearly have major implications for the healthcare and insurance industries.

The answer is not only in the development of smarter vehicles. Reduction in accident levels must arise through a combination of factors, including:

- Planning and designing roads for safety
- Setting road and safety rules
- Securing greater compliance
- Improving transport policy.

Zero Congestion Whilst car sharing, transport planning, and optimised travel will all have a part to play, economists suggest congestion arises due to a combination of wider economic factors, such as:

- A reduction in the cost of driving, because the costs of cars and fuel have fallen in real terms, even taking inflation into account
- Perceptions that public transport is an inferior way to travel, and people naturally switch from inferior goods
- There are few restrictions on the use of roads, and tolls are only a mild deterrent
- The fixed cost of motoring encourages drivers to use their cars as often as possible
- Drivers operate in isolation and don't really understand the full impact they individually have on others.[36]

AI alone is unlikely to be a panacea for reducing congestion, but it may help. Future thinking must take into account elements of reduced dependence, changes in working rules, better collaboration and cooperation, and a rethink about the status of the auto.

Zero Breakdowns A visit to an auto factory seems to indicate that it is a haven of automation with minimal manual intervention. Shouldn't manufacturing in the car industry be a shop window for the benefits of automation? But even with high levels of automation and so-called intelligence, cars are still unreliable. Some are worse than others. Why should that be? Certainly autos are getting ever more complex, with computer controls replacing manual functions. Perhaps there isn't one single cause for unreliability but many, including design flaws, material quality, and process and engineering failures.

Maybe the concept of zero breakdowns is within our control, and can be improved in an AI environment. The next section looks more specifically at the topic of motor manufacture.

AI and Motor Manufacturing

According to experts, the manufacture of autos, as well as the entire auto ecosystem, will be transformed by AI in the future. These changes typically will apply to the manufacturing and repair processes.

Manufacturing Process The manufacturing process will become increasingly robotised and increasingly adopt new technologies and business models. The use of technologically rich methods, such as the use of vision-guided vehicles (VGVs), will have an even greater impact on workflow. These VGVs (which are, in effect, mobile sensors) will measure all key data points not only in terms of actual performance, but also with respect to the anticipated breakdown of a vehicle. Parts will be continually tracked through intelligent supply chains.[37]

KPMG's 2016 survey of 800 automobile executives[38] revealed that 80% believe that digitalisation will strongly disrupt their industry by the end of this decade. The report is especially interesting in that it reflects a year-on-year change showing the fast-moving pace of this particular industry. 'Connectivity and digitalization has finally outpaced "growth in emerging markets" and "alternative drivetrain technologies" as the key trend dominating the executive's strategic agenda until 2025', they say.

The KPMG survey also reveals concern amongst manufacturers relative to their own historical domination of the consumer marketplace, suggesting that their position may well be eroded by ICT companies (information and computing technology companies). One in five respondents to the survey were concerned that vehicle manufacturers could simply turn into external suppliers for tech companies.

With the anticipated cost of electrical components in a car reaching 50% of the total by 2030, this seems a distinct possibility. In effect, this would signal a repositioning, from vehicles having high-tech functionality to computers having passenger-and-goods-carrying capabilities. If this is the case, then the consumer should anticipate a much more technology-led marketplace for the auto industry, which is currently worth US$800 million per year.

The 2015 *MIT Technology Review* article 'How Might Apple Manufacture a Car?' also points to the ability of companies such as Apple to simply reproduce its existing technology business model in auto manufacturing. The article's author suggests that this would occur by outsourcing the production of cars to third parties, allowing Apple to focus on the software.[39] The *Wall Street Journal* has also published an article suggesting that an Apple vehicle could well be on the market within four years.[40] It's hardly surprising that established auto manufacturers cannot afford to rest on their laurels.

Accenture also take a similar viewpoint. Its report based on the results of a survey identifies six key trends that they believe motor manufacturers need to embrace:

1. Greater automation, especially in terms of extending asset life
2. More flexibility, not only in terms of business models but also in terms of movement of work among sites
3. Operational excellence, including productivity increase and reduced downtime
4. Visibility, with 38% of respondents to the survey recognising that performance management is a 'leading initiative'
5. Contract manufacturing, which adds capacity and flexibility without increasing capital cost
6. Skill management, including the use of predictive modelling, Six Sigma, and talent analytics.[41]

Reading between the lines, what are the implications? Three ideas stand out:

1. *Increase in manufacturing analytics.* Firstly, there will need to be an increase in the use of manufacturing analytics. Many motor vehicle manufacturers are still at the first and second levels of analytics (which we described as descriptive and predictive, respectively), although they are stretching these capabilities into asset and talent management.

2. *Outsourcing rather than capital investment.* Jobs may not be lost in the automotive industry, but they most certainly will be moved. For the workforce that remains, a higher degree of flexibility will be needed.
3. *Increased importance of supply chain entities.* With contract work and outsourcing becoming more important, supplier management will take a greater role in the value chain. Suppliers will also need to increase their analytical capabilities, and more 'super suppliers' will undoubtedly emerge.

As the auto industry moves towards self-drive cars and greater autonomous automation, its own use of analytics to inform the manufacturing process still appears to remain at a relatively basic level. If it is still focusing on performance management in its own processes, which some might consider to be a relatively elementary level of analytics, how long will it be before it uses a much higher level of analytics (such as AI) to inform its own operational decision-making?

At the very least, automated systems should modify their approach to supply chain management by adapting automated Six Sigma thinking to workflow and component supply.

Industry 4.0 is an expression used to refer to an extremely lean manufacturing environment. *Lean manufacturing* is not a new concept and initially was developed in the motor industry, deriving originally from the Toyota Production System. In summary, it comprises five key elements or principles:

1. *Value.* Understand clearly what the customer wants
2. *Value stream.* Management of the entire flow of the process, otherwise known as the value stream, from ingestion of raw materials through to final completion
3. *Flow.* If it is not moving, then it is creating waste
4. *Pull.* Do not make anything until the customer wants it
5. *Perfection.* Systematic removal of the causes of poor quality from the production process.

Six Sigma is one set of tools for process improvement. It comes from statistical process control aimed at the creation of manufacturing processes. It aims to produce a high proportion of output within agreed specification standards, for example, 3.4 defects per million opportunities.

Lean Six Sigma (LSS) is a systematic approach that combines lean manufacturing and Six Sigma to reduce waste, specifically in terms of:

- Overproduction
- Waiting time
- Transport
- Inappropriate processing
- Excess inventory
- Unnecessary movement
- Defects.

LSS relies heavily on a data-driven analytical approach, and lends itself to increased automation. Some companies have embraced LSS to such a degree, incorporating it into their day-to-day business processes, that they claim that separate LSS programs are no longer deemed necessary.[42]

Instead of the original spreadsheet form of recording, there are now software tools that help implement a Six Sigma approach, typically:

- Tools that test and measure the implementation process
- Quality control monitoring packages
- DMAIC (design, measure, analyse, improve, control) Six Sigma process-improvement tools
- Product management tools that model the process
- Project optimisation and simulation.

Many of these tools are already underpinned by advanced analytics. It seems feasible to infuse a higher level of AI and advanced automation into them. With AI intended to imitate the thought process of a human, the possibility of modelling and optimising complex processes seems distinctly in the cards.

It's not that Six Sigma practitioners haven't been aware of the potential of AI. Thomas Pyzdek, author of *The Six Sigma Handbook*, already regards AI as one of the potential tools at the disposal of the Six Sigma expert, although to date it has been considered expensive and complex, and with other viable options available.[43] With the cost of AI coming down and the availability of cloud-based solutions, it is only a matter of time before we start to see AI-infused LSS integrated into the manufacturing process.

Repair Process   The repair process is also due for transformation. Fewer and fewer body shops will be able to repair the more sophisticated vehicles. This will also impact distribution channels for manufacturers, who will only be able to sell where there are adequate support facilities. Already problems with vehicles are being diagnosed by plugging it into a diagnostic laptop tool. ('Problem with your automated gearbox? You probably need to download the most up-to-date software.')

The impact on the auto insurance industry is unquestionably important. It will not only need to rethink the insurance proposition but also will need to recognise the likelihood of fewer accidents, albeit at a probably greater cost for each.

How will this affect not only the need for insurance but also the insurance claims process? The need for less insurance could result in lower income from premiums, resulting in further overcapacity in the insurance sector. Coupled with increased automation of its own industry, what will be the effect of these changes on jobs in the auto insurance market? In a nutshell, could advances in auto design ultimately decimate the auto insurance industry?

The auto insurance industry will also inevitably see the emergence of a new profession of automotive insurance appraisers who will necessarily acquire the skill of mobile computer repairers. Even the appraisals might be done remotely. Where once the damage to an auto body was obvious, now the greatest effect of an impact or accident will lie hidden amongst the wiring, gadgets, and systems. Auto damage assessment is already a changing profession, and one that is set to either evolve or to disappear completely.

In summary, all the experts suggest that auto manufacturing is an industry set for continued transformation, and in many cases it has already moved substantially towards total automation. It's difficult to be clear about how many traditional manufacturing jobs in the auto industry have been lost to automation to date and how many more jobs will go. It's an industry that is extremely sensitive to the impact of the economy in terms of new car sales.

However, it's impossible to overlook the impact of increased technology on the spending power of consumers and the knock-on effect of unemployment in that sector. It's thought that 10% of the US workforce is directly or indirectly employed in the auto industry.[44]

Despite the degree of current automation, the auto industry is still mostly a people industry, although their skills and capabilities have changed over the years. The nature of job changes in the auto industry is a good indicator of the ability of a workforce to transform itself and adopt roles that are more technologically oriented.

For example, in a survey of 100,000 (nonduplicated) job descriptions from 11 major US automakers posted from January 2016 to January 2017, nearly 10% were for 3 job titles: design engineers, software engineers, and systems engineers.[45] The top 10 jobs were, in order:

1. Design engineer
2. Software engineer
3. Systems engineer
4. Quality engineer
5. Project manager
6. Research specialist
7. Business analyst
8. Control engineer
9. Process engineer
10. Sales manager.

There is still a need for what the survey describes as hard skills (versus technological), but even those capabilities have undergone change. The top six hard-skill roles advertised by automakers were in power train (the engine and transmission elements), followed by those in design failure analysis, and only then jobs in engineering. Only after 3-D design (known as CATIA, an acronym for *computer aided three-dimensional interactive application*) and manufacturing does stamping or traditional metalworking, appear on the list:

1. Power train
2. Design failure analysis
3. Engineering
4. 3-D design (CATIA)
5. Manufacturing
6. Metalwork.

In the same survey, researchers identified 134500 workers who could be categorised as working in one of these five specific hard skills. However, these workers were found not only at other auto manufacturers, but also in other manufacturing operations (such as at Boeing, Cummins, and thousands of other companies). The point is that most of these nonautomotive companies use the same job titles as the automakers, suggesting a degree of job mobility.

Like the stonemasons of old who travelled across Europe to build cathedrals, mobility will be a key requirement in this new technological environment, which is suffering from talent shortages. And if this is so, isn't it true not only for those with advanced IT skills but also for those with more traditional hard skills?

MEDIA, ENTERTAINMENT, AND TELECOM

The third area that is described as leading edge is the high-tech and telecom industries. One way of demonstrating change for these is in the media and entertainment sectors.

We increasingly live in an environment of media on demand. Traditional broadcasters are facing growing pressure from subscription services that promise better programmes funded by larger budgets and supported by more effective marketing. As with other industries, the media industry is increasingly being divided into haves and have-nots. The haves are those who can afford better-quality viewing, including the best sports action; the have-nots will have to struggle along with catching the results later.

What do we mean by *media*? When we consider the meaning of a *medium* we think in terms of a channel of communication in either a traditional – that is, paper – form, or an electronic form. The expression *mass media* refers to the manner in which communication is transferred to the masses, which has come to mean a one-to-many model.

Mass media is distinguished from the personal communication of individuals by being:

- Omnidirectional, in that it is conveyed from the producers to the consumer, usually over distance
- Technologically based, in that some form of equipment is needed to convey and receive the message
- It involves scale
- It is a quasi commodity, in that it comes at a price.[46]

Increasingly we now live in a many-to-many environment, in which information flows through social media, where there is less distinction between producers and consumers. It's an environment that Vin Crosby, managing director of Digital Deliverance, also defines as being:

- Personalised, despite the fact that the message is being delivered to large numbers of people
- Collectively controlled, in that each consumer has the opportunity to shape the content.[47]

Today, users of online news content almost take this for granted. They are provided with the key headlines and have the chance to select those topics in general terms that are of most interest to them. The content provider also prompts the reader with news items that they might also be interested in. This is a model similar to what we experience in the selection of reading material, music, and consumer goods. The system gives us choice, but helps, or augments, our decision-making.

Media, marketing, and advertising are inevitably interlinked. Advertising not only helps consumers to better understand a product, but more importantly places the product into context. In the business, this is called *affective conditioning*. Affective conditioning enhances the product by putting it alongside other things that the consumer likes. (Think in terms of toilet paper and puppies.) Similarly, prestige brands that sell for prices far above the cost of production are meant to make the user feel better, and use techniques to:

- Create fashionistas, by the individual wearing what's in and not what's out
- Build attachment to halo individuals, whom the consumer aspires to be like
- Add value, that is, provide some sort of ability to look behind the scenes
- Enhance visualisations to appeal to the emotional limbic brain, aimed at those of us who are trying to rationalise a purchase in terms beyond a purely emotional decision.[48]

The ability to link these concepts to entertainment media is not new. In James Bond's outing in *Dr. No* in 1962, whilst some will remember Ursula Andress emerging from the blue waters of the Caribbean, wristwatch experts will have recognised Sean Connery's Rolex Submariner. Connery wore this watch throughout his seven Bond screen appearances, as did all the other Bonds through to 1989. This is not a coincidence. The author Ian Fleming says of James Bond in his 1953 book *Casino Royale*, 'He could not just wear a watch. It had to be a Rolex'.[49] But in 1995, Omega won the bid to become Bond's new watch, signifying a new look.

The application of AI to the advertising and media industries is likely to be one of the great areas of progress. The business model is mainly B2C (business to consumer), and the addressable market is very large compared to other industries. It is likely to have the greatest impact in two particular areas: apps and advertising. We should expect increasingly personalised advertising.

Elsewhere, AI is likely to have a deep impact in interactive gaming, but this is viewed as a particularly challenging area. Gaming is viewed as being one of the first environments that tested the fundamentals of how intelligent systems can satisfy the entertainment needs of humans. Key development issues in gaming include:

- The ability to create believable opponents and companions
- Interactive storytelling, which is a form of storytelling in which the storyline is not predetermined
- Procedural content generation
- Player modelling
- Path planning
- Developing tools and representations that empower designers to bring their visions to life.[50]

The effectiveness of media and advertising will also ultimately be heavily dependent on effective telecommunications. Telecom in itself is an industry that has relied on automation from the outset. The American inventor Almon Strowger created the Strowger switch, which was an automated switching device for telephones to prevent the operator from misdirecting the call. Whilst an early example of automation, it is the demand for growth that has led to ever-increasing automation in the telecom industry, one that is now primed for the benefits of an AI-infused world.

Automation increases reliability, gives greater security, and proves the ability to scale. In the back office, automated systems that connect calls, calculate costs, and send out invoices are simply replications of human effort. As the industry grows, so do the problems of scaling up these solutions.

The telecom market is rapidly advancing and so are the demands on the system. Next-generation mobile networks are already looking to use AI-infused capabilities to ensure that consumers are continually provided with reliable service. Known as a self-organising (or self-optimising) network, this greater automation is required to make the planning, configuration, management, optimisation, and self-healing of mobile networks simpler and faster. These networks are designed by users in terms of performance requirements and limits, and the system is left to automatically structure the network itself to meet these requirements.

Experts are already suggesting that with the advent of the IoT, network requirements will need to multiply by 10,000 times or more, to a point that human management simply won't be able to cope.[51]

With customer satisfaction at the core of retention, the ability of artificial systems to deal directly with the customer in terms of meeting their needs and responding to their complaints starts to become paramount. The ambition of the industry is to use AI to create a dynamic mobile network that provides an effective conduit for data and information, aligned at the same time to customer needs and service demands.

It's a tall order, but perhaps one of the most critical of all. Without effective networks, the entire concept of the IoT, automation, and AI starts to fall apart. It's a critical success factor in the overall context of progress.

RETAIL

Although the topic of retailing is covered in Chapter 5, it would be incorrect to consider analytical first-movers without considering the retail industry.

Retail is a complex and multifaceted business, aligned closely with other industries and professions such as sales, marketing, production, supply chain management, and asset management, and with significant dependence on others, such as financial services.

It is an industry defined by, or perhaps obsessed with, the topic of consumption and consumers. In its original meaning, *consume* was a bad thing, originally meaning *squander* or *destroy*. It once was even used to describe a respiratory illness (pulmonary tuberculosis). In more recent times the word has been redefined as relating to the utilisation of goods manufactured by (at that time) human labour – although increasingly its goods are a product of automation.

The whole topic of consumption is the linchpin in much of the political and economic discourse by people such as Adam Smith and Karl Marx, stimulating debate as to whether consumption was more important than production, or vice versa. In the *Wealth of Nations*, Adam Smith argued that increased production stimulated the economy and led us to consume more, and for this reason it made sense for nations to invest in infrastructure.

It's still an area of great debate. People refer to the consumer society and the rise of consumerism as if they are bad things. Even the way we eat, in franchised outlets such as McDonalds, seems to reduce one of the bare necessities of survival to that of a consumer activity. As Thomas Hine put it 'we are now all shoppers' and our species could be defined as 'one that shops'.[52]

In considering the retail industry, it's useful to try to understand consumer behaviour a little better. In his 1997 article for the *New Yorker* magazine[53] the writer Malcolm Gladwell tried to define what we mean by *cool* and how the retail industry itself identifies emerging trends. He said that there are 'three rules of cool':

1. Cool cannot be defined, only felt
2. Cool can only be observed by those who are themselves cool
3. Cool cannot be manufactured.

He indicated that cool consumers cannot be told what to wear by advertisers, but set the trends themselves. As a result it's important that 'cool marketers' visit the 'right places' to understand what's going on. Marketers talk in terms of the conventional diffusion of innovation (DoI) model – that is to say, how an idea catches on and diffuses through society, and how the market needs to focus on early and late movers.

Beyond the need to be cool, the retail industry also focuses on human *desire* for things. Partly aided by the influence of marketing, we are continually invited to transform our lives through the acquisition of objects. Through acquisition we are led to believe that we will attain new or enhanced social, professional, and personal characteristics. How we mentally do this is by giving the objects a value that is greater than their actual usefulness or price. In other words, it's the creation of some form of perceived value that helps us personally on our journey towards Maslow's target of self-actualisation.

If, as we have considered elsewhere, however, Maslow's now historic hierarchy of needs is less relevant to younger and older members of the community, then doesn't this also impact on their desire for acquisition? Doesn't the marketing message inevitably need to be different, and if so, then how?

Beyond this complexity sits the impacts not only of the major technology trends such as mobile and cloud, but also the increasing influence of what we have described earlier in this chapter as the new megatrends, such as urbanisation and geosocialisation.

We also need to think about the geography and seasonality of consumption as part of the wider matrix. The use of public spaces, such as streets and shopping malls, still provides a natural environment for consumption, building on the traditional model of the marketplace. In fact, in many cases the shopping mall seeks to replicate that traditional format, as well as offering other locational attributes (such as eating and gathering places), to add value and create a shopping experience. Increasingly, the future of shopping malls is likely to be experience based. When added to external aspects such as the seasonal nature of some goods and products, coupled with the festive demands of events such as Christmas, an extremely complicated industry in which to work results.

The management of such multivariable factors is difficult. Done properly, it lends itself to automated and intelligent methods. What is the right product to place before the right purchaser at the right time, and where is the right place to do it? And what is the right price? Old thinking for new times.

The advent of the digital consumer helps that process rather than hinders it by creating data points where information can be collected. Increasing the number of online purchases potentially allows retailers and intermediaries to track what is being done, by whom, where, and when. In turn this provides greater insight into the requirements of the supply chain and logistics (e.g. what to put on the real or virtual shelf), with a cost/price that reflects factors such as price elasticity.

Taken to its ultimate level, effective use of data and analytics not only helps retailers to understand issues of cost and service, but potentially also to optimise the offering to the consumer. Optimisation in itself is an interesting topic, depending on the perspective that you see it from. It doesn't necessarily mean that the item is provided at the lowest price to the consumer, but rather that it is provided at a highest cost which the consumer is prepared to pay, everything else being taken into account.

Improved profitability for suppliers and lowest cost to the consumer are not mutually exclusive. Both can exist in tandem if properly managed. This might extend to second-level supply chain management, in which not only suppliers but also *their* suppliers are part of the equation. The entire supply chain can gain greater understanding into market need and prepare accordingly.

But there is a risk, and that is one of passing cost reductions/price optimisation all the way down the food chain to the lowest denominator, who in turn tries to make its profit by compromising on quality. At the end of the day, don't we always get what we pay for? Many purchasers wait to make a final decision until they have checked customer feedback on social media.

It's increasingly seen that supply chain and commodity managers overseeing the procurement process (often seen as the bullies of the buying process) also have a key role to play. We have not considered procurement in detail in Chapter 5, but there is an interdependency that cannot and should not be overlooked. How this is set to manifest itself in a world of advanced analytics and intelligent systems has yet to fully reveal itself, but the need for procurers to not only understand but operate within such intelligent systems is critical.

Rolling the clock forward, perhaps the procurement role as we know it might even disappear. Buying and selling of commodities as part of the supply chain process could be increasingly replaced by quasi-auction processes.

As part of new supply chain methodologies, increased automation of, for example, the manufacturing process, might more fully integrate with predicted end-consumer behaviour, ensuring that supply–demand imbalances could become a thing of the past. Cynics might alternatively suggest that one way of maintaining or increasing the cost of a commodity may be to artificially limit production, and that is entirely possible. In doing so, we start to slip into issues of ethics and can only hope that regulation provides some type of solution for that kind of problem.

There's a lot to think about. Advanced analytics, intelligent systems, and AI will increasingly affect our shopping experience.

Will systems increasingly understand our proximity to a store and push offers to us by way of inducement, or are they likely to be more sophisticated than that? To some degree, the pushing of offerings is already happening. We are willing participants in that process by agreeing to share our personal and location information through loyalty card and other similar reward programmes. Attitudes towards sharing information differ considerably among age groups, but there is an increasing tendency for individuals to be prepared to share personal and location data if they get something valuable from that sharing process, for example, a tangible discount.

Looking forward, we also need to consider the impact of AI not on the shopping experience itself, but on the disposable income of purchasers who may be faced with either unemployment or changed working conditions. Elsewhere we have suggested that traditionally routine jobs will disappear as a result of robotic intervention, but these jobs might be replaced by new leisure-related positions. Will retailing become more dominant, primarily as a leisure activity, and if so what will these new roles look like?

Some might argue that shopping is already a form of leisure. Shopping malls contain fashion and high-end stores that are nothing more that showrooms, with consumers checking out the goods and then buying online. Are we likely to see that as a continuing trend?

One question to ask is about speed of implementation. In 2011 Gartner predicted that 'by 2020 customers will manage 85% of their relationship with the enterprise without interacting with a human.'[54] Here we are, 7 years on, and it doesn't yet seem like that (although it's easy to be cynical about predictions). After all, what do we really mean by our *relationship* with an enterprise in any event?

That relationship might simply exist as a form of online dialogue or feedback. In such a model it becomes increasingly important that the retailer is not passive and responds in such a way as to create a two-way dialogue. Many hotels seem particularly good at responding to customer comments, for example.

Shoppers who interact by posting online reviews, or what is called consumer-generated content, are 97% more likely to convert with a retailer than customers who do not.[55]

Beyond this:

- The percentage of US shoppers who read online reviews before making an e-commerce purchase is 54%.
- The percentage of shoppers who read online reviews *before* buying in-store is 39%.
- The percentage of shoppers who read reviews *while inside* a store, immediately before making a purchase, is 82%.
- The most-read reviews are for electronics, with 58% of shoppers performing research before buying anything in this product category in-store.[56]

Retailing is clearly at the vanguard of understanding consumers and is increasingly taking advantage of their emerging digital behaviour. But perhaps it's difficult to immediately accept this as being AI in its purest form, as opposed to predictive or advanced analytics. Even so, the degree of knowledge and advancement of retailers is sufficient to make other industries envious, and for them to look for retail talent to migrate to other industries. After all, industries may differ, but the behaviour of an individual consumer remains consistent.

In retailing, the AI opportunity is so much greater than clever selling. Fully exploited, it potentially extends throughout the supply chain and into the distribution function. In a 2016 survey, 47% of supply chain managers recognised AI as having the potential to be disruptive to existing supply chain business models.[57] Effective use of analytics and intelligence through tagging is also likely to increasingly improve inventory control, reducing stock redundancy and improving efficiency.

According to Guy Chiswick, managing director of Webloyalty, Northern Europe, 'The various AI initiatives show how retailers are working hard to evolve customer journey. They are thinking outside the box and coming up with new ways to answer customer demand for convenience and immediacy, as well as looking for solutions to improve every step of the supply chain.'[58]

With retail being so important not only to commerce, but seemingly to the way we live and perceive ourselves, this is clearly a story that will run and run.

CONCLUSION

This chapter focused on the leading-edge industries that are concentrating on advanced analytics and moving more quickly towards the use of AI. It's a difficult call to be prescriptive in identifying these industries, and some might argue differently for one industry over another. For example, is predictive analytics more advanced in policing, than, say, education?

In reality, there isn't direct competition between these industries, and no Grand Prix of analytics or AI. But there are, however, cross-over areas and knock-on effects. The behaviour of a consumer when buying financial services is unlikely to be substantially different from when that same consumer buys his or her utilities, for example.

It follows that, in a labour market suffering from talent shortages that may get even worse, there is the potential for migration of people with key skills from one leading-edge industry to another. Migration can also happen between leading-edge companies and organisations to second-movers, with a resultant levelling effect. Perhaps second-mover advantage may occur precisely because those with first-mover knowledge have taken their experience elsewhere, determined not to reproduce any failure that they have seen.

Whilst it is difficult not to fail to recognise the financial services sector as being at the head of the analytical pack, on the other hand, the inclusion of the retail sector on the list of leading-edge industries might be a little more controversial. In this particular context, retailers have been included as a leading-edge industry for their widespread usage of predictive and other forms of advanced analytics (which are often misdescribed as AI.)

What we see also is the issue of different uses. Financial services may use AI and analytics to help with risk management, which is an area less important to retailers (although risk of a kind does rest with retailers), whereas retailers are more focused on the customer reaction. Cross-over naturally occurs where retailers need to think about supply chain and regulatory risks, for example, whilst at the same time both retailers and financial services need a better understanding of the digital customer.

We should explore the issue of cross-over a little more. Does cross-over suggest the potential for *convergence of industries*? As we look harder at insurance, for example, we recognise distribution as a key function within the value chain. Could distribution of financial services be done more effectively by, say, a retailer?

At the beginning of the chapter we also considered the new megatrends of urbanisation and geosocialisation, for example. Will traditional business models remain suitable for these new trends, or will progress force change to happen, as in the case of the use of advanced analytics to relieve the burden on overworked doctors in Chinese cities?

We have argued that advanced analytics and AI is not the destination, but rather what we do with that knowledge is what counts. The use of insight to create new business models indicates that not only is defragmentation (breaking up) of traditional models possible, but that new converged business models will inevitably take place. Will the first signs of convergence occur within the first-mover group?

We already know that first-mover advantage normally comes from three conditions:

1. Learning/cost curves that provide a barrier to second-movers trying to follow, as second-movers are prevented from being able to catch up with the original developers' investment and ability to scale
2. Scarceness of resources, especially, but not specifically, confined to talent
3. High switching costs, where first-movers lock in their customers.[59]

With these thoughts in mind, maybe there are common characteristics that link all these first-movers, either as an industry or at the level of individual organisations? Is it possible that these commonalities might lead to the evolution of new converged business models, or new forms of technologically driven merger and acquisition? (Business models are considered later in this book.)

Overall there has always been some degree of common ground between auto manufacturing, financial services, and insurance, for example. Will advanced analytics and AI become the catalyst for greater change and become the cement that starts to bond industries together? Will new industries start to emerge, and if so, what form will they take? With more time on our hands, perhaps these new industries will be leisure oriented. And finally, will it be for humans to work out the possibilities for change through converged data and systems, or at some time in the future will the computer figure these out for itself?

In Chapter 4 we look at what we describe as the impact of technological change on second-tier, or following, industries (without the intent to demean).

NOTES

1. Sarwant Singh, *New Mega Trends: Implications for Our Future Lives* (London: Palgrave Macmillan, 2012).
2. Kirkpatrick Sale, America's new Luddites. *La Monde Diplomatique* (February 1997).
3. Luddites200 Organising Forum (n.d.), 21st century technology debates & politics. http://www.luddites200.org.uk/TechnologyPoliticsNow.html (accessed 8 November 2016).
4. Breaking the Frame (n.d.). About us. http://breakingtheframe.org.uk/about (accessed 8 November 2016).
5. Alexander Kaufman, Stephen Hawking says we should really be scared of capitalism, not robots, Huffington Post (8 October 2016). http://www.huffingtonpost.com/entry/stephen-hawking-capitalism-robots_us_5616c20ce4b0dbb8000d9f15
6. Caroline Gregoire, A field guide to ant-technology movements, past and present. Huffington Post (17 January 2014). http://www.huffingtonpost.com/2014/01/17/life-without-technology-t_n_4561571.html
7. Jacque Bughin, Eric Hazan, Sree Ramaswamy, Sree, et al. (2017). How Artificial Intelligence Can Deliver Real Value to Companies. McKinsey Global Institute report.
8. Accenture (n.d.). Banking Technology Vision 2017. Accenture report. https://www.accenture.com/us-en/insight-banking-technology-vision-2017
9. Jill Treanor and Patrick Collinson, HSBC to close 62 more branches this year, blaming online banking. *Guardian* (24 January 2017). https://www.theguardian.com/business/2017/jan/24/hsbc-close-branches-online-banking-unions-jobs
10. Christopher Evans, Face-to-face banking has been given a lifeline, but what does it mean for loyalty? Finextra.com (7 February 2017). https://www.finextra.com/blogposting/13663/face-to-face-banking-has-been-given-a-lifeline-but-what-does-it-mean-for-loyalty

11. George Bowden, Mark Carney speech sees Bank Of England governor warn over robot job takeover. Huffington Post UK (6 December 2016). http://www.huffingtonpost.co.uk/entry/mark-carney-speech-robots_uk_584675e1e4b07ac724498813

12. Cognizant, The Robot and I: How New Digital Technologies Are Making Smart People and Businesses Smarter by Automating Rote Work. Cognizant report (January 2015). https://www.cognizant.com/InsightsWhitepapers/the-robot-and-I-how-new-digital-technologies-are-making-smart-people-and-businesses-smarter-codex1193.pdf

13. Jim Marous, Robots and AI invade banking. *Financial Brand* (July 2015). https://thefinancialbrand.com/52735/robots-artificial-intelligence-ai-banking

14. FSB, UK Small Business Statistics (details taken from UK Department for Business, Innovation & Skills). https://www.fsb.org.uk/media-centre/small-business-statistics (accessed 14 January 2018).

15. Elizabeth Anderson, Half of UK start-ups fail within five years. *The Telegraph* (21 October 2014). http://www.telegraph.co.uk/finance/businessclub/11174584/Half-of-UK-start-ups-fail-within-five-years.html

16. Future Banking, Artificial intelligence: clever design. Future Banking (14 November 2012). http://www.banking-gateway.com/features/featurefba-standard-chartered-artifical-intelligence

17. A. K. Misra and V. J. Sebastian, Portfolio optimization of commercial banks – an application of genetic algorithm. *European Journal of Business and Management* 5, no. 6 (2013): 120–129. www.iiste.org

18. Ann Hensman and Eugene Sadler-Wells, Intuitive decision making in banking and finance. *European Management Journal* 29, no. 1 (2011): 51–66.

19. Chester Barnard, *The Functions of the Executive*, 30th ed. (Harvard University Press, 1968).

20. Finmetrica, Personal Financial Profiling. Copyright © FinaMetrica Pty Limited. http://www.dsfinancial.org.uk/FinaMetrica%20Questionnaire_UK[1].pdf

21. Jason Zweig, Talk is cheap: As automation spreads, new rivals stalk financial advisors (26 July 2017). http://jasonzweig.com/talk-is-cheap-automation-takes-aim-at-financial-advisers-and-their-fees/

22. Rosie Quigley, Half of insurtech investment is in artificial intelligence and IoT. *Post* (30 March 2017). http://www.postonline.co.uk/insurer/3151306/half-of-insurtech-investment-is-in-artificial-intelligence-and-iot

23. Kriti Saraswat, Famous celebrities who've insured their body parts. HealthSite (13 September 2013). http://www.thehealthsite.com/beauty/famous-celebrities-whove-insured-their-body-parts

24. Insurance Europe, The impact of insurance fraud. 2013. https://www.insuranceeurope.eu/sites/default/files/attachments/The%20impact%20of%20insurance%20fraud.pdf

25. Isaac Asimov, Visit to the world's fair of 2014. *New York Times* (16 August 1964). http://www.nytimes.com/books/97/03/23/lifetimes/asi-v-fair.html

26. Aviva Rutkin, Autonomous truck cleared to drive on US roads for the first time. *New Scientist* (8 May 2015). https://www.newscientist.com/article/dn27485-autonomous-truck-cleared-to-drive-on-us-roads-for-the-first-time

27. Information Is Beautiful (n.d.). Codebases. InformationIsBeautiful.net. http://www.informationisbeautiful.net/visualizations/million-lines-of-code (accessed 28 August 2017).

28. Statistica (n.d.). Automotive electronics cost as a percentage of total car cost worldwide from 1950 to 2030. https://www.statista.com/statistics/277931/automotive-electronics-cost-as-a-share-of-total-car-cost-worldwide (accessed 18 October 2017).

29. James F. Hines, Hype Cycle for Automotive Electronics, 2015. Gartner report ID G00277793 (29 July 2015). https://www.gartner.com/doc/3102919/hype-cycle-automotive-electronics

30. Michael Mandat, Der Status des automobils [in German]. Progenium (2011). http://www.progenium.com/wp-content/uploads/2016/04/PROGENIUM-Auto-nicht-mehr-Wunschobjekt-der-Deutschen.pdf

31. Julien Girault, Technology drive sees 'connected car' link-ups in China. Phys.org (27 April 2016). http://phys.org/news/2016-04-technology-car-link-ups-china.html

32. Singh, *New Mega Trends*.

33. Thomas R. Koehler, and Dirk Wollschlaeger, *The Digital Transformation of the Automobile* (Media-Manufaktur, 2014).

34. Betsy McKay, Traffic accidents kill 1.27 million globally, WHO says. *Wall Street Journal* (16 June 2009). https://www.wsj.com/articles/SB124509433747116067

35. Worley, Heidi, Road traffic accidents increase dramatically worldwide. Population Reference Bureau (March 2006). http://www.prb.org/Publications/Articles/2006/RoadTrafficAccidentsIncreaseDramaticallyWorldwide.aspx

36. Road congestion. Economics Online. http://economicsonline.co.uk/Market_failures/Road_congestion.html (accessed 14 January 2018).

37. Chris Visnic, Disruption ahead: automotive manufacturers look to the future. SeeGrid blog. https://seegrid.com/blog/disruption_ahead_automotive_manufacturers_look_to_the_future (accessed 28 August 2017).

38. KPMG (n.d.). Global Automotive Executive Survey 2016. KPMG. https://assets.kpmg.com/content/dam/kpmg/pdf/2016/01/gaes-2016.pdf

39. Will Knight, How might Apple manufacture a car? *MIT Technology Review* (9 October 2015). https://www.technologyreview.com/s/542111/how-might-apple-manufacture-a-car

40. Daisuke Wakabayashi, Apple targets electric-car shipping date for 2019. *Wall Street Journal* (21 September 2015). https://www.wsj.com/articles/apple-speeds-up-electric-car-work-1442857105

41. Accenture (n.d.). Getting More Out of Existing Operations. https://www.accenture.com/t20150523T023640__w__/us-en/_acnmedia/Accenture/Conversion-Assets/DotCom/Documents/Global/PDF/Dualpub_11/Accenture-Getting-More-Out-Of-Existing-Operations-Automotive-Infographic-v2.pdf (accessed 18 October 2017).

42. Matthew Daneman, Xerox cutting back on Lean Six Sigma program, jobs. *Democrat and Chronicle* (13 October 2014).

43. Thomas Pyzdek, *The Six Sigma Handbook*, 3rd ed. (McGraw-Hill Professional, 2009).

44. Catherine Rampell, How many jobs depend on the Big Three? *New York Times* (17 November 2008). https://economix.blogs.nytimes.com/2008/11/17/how-many-jobs-depend-on-the-big-three

45. Joshua Wright, Workforce supply and demand in the automotive industry. EMSI (6 March 2017). http://www.economicmodeling.com/2017/03/06/workforce-supply-and-demand-in-the-automotive-industry

46. Brian Dutton, Tim O'Sullivan, and Phillip Rayne, *Studying the Media*, 3rd ed. (Bloomsbury Academic, 2003).

47. Vin Crosbie, What is new media? *Digital Deliverance* blog (1998 and 2006). http://www.digitaldeliverance.com/signature-writings/what-is-new-media

48. Jeff Bullas, How 5 prestige brands innovate and market on Facebook. JeffBullas.com. http://www.jeffbullas.com/2012/09/07/how-5-prestige-brands-innovate-and-market-on-facebook (accessed 28 August 2017).

49. Ian Fleming, *Casino Royale*, first Vintage ed. (Vintage Classics, 2012).

50. Nathan Sturtevant and Brian Magerko, eds., '*Proceedings of the Twelfth Artificial Intelligence and Interactive Digital Entertainment International Conference*. (AIIDE 2016). Association for the Advancement of Artificial Intelligence (2016). http://www.aaai.org/Press/Proceedings/aiide16.php

51. Wedge Greene and Trevor Hayes, The promise of artificial intelligence in telecom. *Pipeline* 12, no. 12 (2016). https://pipelinepub.com/telecom_innovation/AI-in-telecom

52. Thomas Hine, *I Want That! How We All Became Shoppers* (HarperCollins, 2002).

53. Malcolm Gladwell, The coolhunt. *New Yorker* (17 March 1997). https://www.newyorker.com/magazine/1997/03/17/the-coolhunt

54. Gartner customer 360 summit 2011. Gartner prospectus. https://www.gartner.com/imagesrv/summits/docs/na/customer-360/C360_2011_brochure_FINAL.pdf

55. BI Intelligence, Consumer-generated content helps drive online sales. *Business Insider* (4 May 2016). http://www.businessinsider.com/consumer-generated-content-helps-drive-online-sales-2016-5?IR=T

56. Sandra Guy, More online shoppers read reviews before buying, *Internet Retailer* (11 March 2016). https://www.digitalcommerce360.com/2016/03/11/more-online-shoppers-read-reviews-buying

57. Pierfrancesco Manenti, Artificial intelligence and future supply chains, *SCM World* (31 January 2017). http://www.scmworld.com/artificial-intelligence-future-supply-chains

58. Paul Keldon, Artificial intelligence fuels innovation in retail industry, *InternetRetailing* (7 July 2017). http://internetretailing.net/2017/07/artificial-intelligence-fuels-innovation-retail-industry

59. Tony Boobier, *Analytics for Insurance: The Real Business of Big Data* (London: Wiley, 2016).

The Impact of AI on Second-Mover Industries

SUMMARY

Chapter 3 considered the use of advanced analytics and AI in what we consider to be leading-edge industries, notably financial services, the automotive sector, and tech/media. Chapter 4 considers what might be loosely described as trailing-edge, or second-mover, industries.

In Appendix B we identify over 700 different roles spread across multiple industries that potentially will be affected by AI. In this chapter, we will focus specifically on eight industries: construction, education, agriculture, utilities, technology, public services, police, and healthcare.

All of these appear to be at different stages of technological progress, and this chapter will explore how some innovative technologies might be usefully stitched together and re-presented under an AI wrapper.

INTRODUCTION

The term *second-mover* is possibly a misnomer. Some might even describe it as unfair, but all industries inevitably move at a pace that best suits the dynamics of their own marketplaces.

For many, being a follower is not necessarily a disadvantage, especially in a business sector that is volatile, with risks and uncertainty. The commercial world is full of organisations that did not consider themselves to be innovators and rather took advantage of the experience of others, and in doing so obtained a so-called second-mover advantage.

On the topic of AI, there is much to be learned from other industries. Customer service for one industry is much the same as that for another, even if the product bundle is different. Because of this it becomes crucially important for industries to have open minds and a 360-degree view of their business environments, and not to simply consider the progress of their peers.

One issue to be aware of is the potential shortage of skilled people, either technical practitioners or those able to understand systems and put them to the best use. In the same way that potential migration of staff with hard skills from one industry to another is feasible in the auto industry, so too should the marketplace be prepared for migration of AI staff from one sector to another despite their lack of knowledge bespoke to that particular industry.

In the industries that are discussed in the sections that follow, there are mixed levels of technological advancement. Some, but not all, of their issues are bespoke to their particular industry needs. All have one thing in common, however, and that is an increased emphasis on data and analytics. The issue for these industries is to understand how these new capabilities can best play to the particular imperatives and market demands of their sectors.

CONSTRUCTION

We are surrounded by examples of civil and structural engineering, and the construction industry is omnipresent. The profession of civil engineering is the basis of our infrastructure, ranging from roads to railways, and structural engineers design the skeletons of our buildings. These professions are relatively modern compared to those of antiquity, such as stonemasons, yet are well established. The Institution of Civil Engineers, based in London, was formed in 1818 and was the world's first professional engineering body; currently it represents 88,000 members. Their vision for the organisation is:

- 'To qualify civil engineering professionals and give them the tools they need to continue to develop
- To help the industry learn more and share our knowledge so we can maintain the natural and built environment
- To promote the contribution that civil engineers make to society worldwide'.[1]

The American Society of Civil Engineers is a little younger, but not too much so. It was founded in New York in 1852, and in 1999 compiled a list of the greatest civil engineering monuments of modern times, which include:

- The Hoover Dam on the Colorado River in the United States
- The Golden Gate Bridge in San Francisco, as an example of long-span construction
- The Eurotunnel that connects the United Kingdom and France
- The Panama Canal, as an example of water engineering.[2]

The earlier vision of the Institution of Civil Engineers is in keeping with the Victorian age that it grew up in. It says that 'Civil Engineers are those who harness the power of nature for the benefit of mankind'. At that time, the powers of nature that were being harnessed by engineers were primarily material, and usually comprised gravity, hydraulics, and natural materials.[3] As a result, the institution's members were the creators of roads, railways, canals, and dams around the world, adding significant value to a country's or region's economy.

Engineering and politics were never far apart. In fact, the headquarters of the institution was deliberately placed close to the seat of the UK Parliament at Westminster so that leading engineering representatives could cross the road and offer advice to elected members on how best to develop UK infrastructure.

The advent of the era of data and analytics has not replaced the institution's members' desire to 'harness the power of nature', but rather supplemented it. Civil engineering, like many other forms of so-called traditional engineering, has increasingly found a need to reinvent itself in order to reflect the needs of the profession and its membership.

It's a challenging marketplace. In this digital age, the profession of engineering is having a hard time. In a recent survey, 44% of engineering firms said they find it hard to recruit experienced recruits. This threatens their target of an additional 2.56 million engineering recruits by 2022, especially taking into account the current shortfall (as of 2016) of engineers in the United Kingdom alone of 66,000.[4]

This is an industry on the road to reinvention, suggesting that 'in addition to technical skills, there are three obvious needs: technology skills, social skills, and commercial skills', and that technology is the big one. One particular risk, says intelligent transport consultant Zipabout, is that 'many engineers who think they are technologically aware are in fact some way off the pace'.[5]

The civil engineering profession is at the beginning of its transformation journey. One of the most prevalent areas of technology that seems to feature is that of building information management (BIM). This digitally integrates location details into the design of roads, railways, and other infrastructure. It's linked in many ways to the core activities of the civil engineers themselves, but there is a view in the profession that a broader input may be needed in this new technological age.

Senior members suggest that the Institution should be a more open house, to the point that psychologists and anthropologists should also be welcome. It's a reflection of the increased blurring of traditional boundaries among professions and within industries.

The following section looks at some particular uses of technology (such as augmented reality, and drones and remote imagery) by the construction industry in several applications, including preventive maintenance. These have the so-called golden thread of location analytics that ties them together. Can some or part of these emerging capabilities solve specific industry problems, such as threats to employee safety, or are there deeper cultural issues that need to be addressed? And as the construction industry enters a period of transformation, what new skills might be needed and what does it have to do in the competition for technologically savvy talent?

Augmented Reality

Whilst not quite under the rubric of AI, civil engineers are increasingly using augmented reality capabilities. *Augmented reality (AR)* was coined as an expression in 1990 by Thomas Caudwell at Boeing, but the idea goes back much further than that. The author L. Frank Baum (of *The Wizard of Oz* fame) suggested as far back as 1901 that it may be possible to overlay data onto real life. AR is a technology that allows images of a future structure to be overlaid onto existing locations, allowing engineers to gain a better understanding of productivity and health and safety.

AR comprises four key elements:

1. The display, either on a tablet, computer, Android, or AR glasses
2. A visual rendering engine, which creates the AR
3. A content management system, which delivers the AR to the device
4. Location tracking capability, which positions the AR relative to the real world. This includes interaction with BIM, and image recognition.

Engineers have already been testing AR on site, but acceptance is at a relatively low level, with civil engineering being recognised generally as a trailing industry in terms of innovation.[6] Barriers to usage by engineers include:

- Poor connectivity
- Quality of visualisation – at one site users preferred more simple visualisations in so-called blocks to full reality visualisations
- Site practicality; for example, the need to handle electronic devices whilst wearing safety gloves and safety goggles
- Positional accuracy and GIS interface
- Cost versus benefit.

Drones and Remote Imagery

According to a PriceWaterhouseCoopers (PWC) report, the market for drones was estimated in 2015 to be US$127 billion: not bad for what many still consider to be just a plaything (see Table 10).

Drones have many different characteristics, and their specifications need to be carefully assessed when making decisions for usage. Typical criteria might include:

- Coverage in terms of square kilometres covered (1–$20km^2$)
- Height/autonomy (often ranging up to 50m, or 100m)
- Flight conditions (typically, wind and rain)
- Accuracy (usually at 100m, on the order of 1–3cm)
- Quality of data/modelling input
- Time to result, measured in hours
- Complexity (including expertise of the user, ranging from trained to expert)
- Price (the most expensive being upwards of €75,000).

The regulatory environment for usage is also complex and varies from place to place. Most require a flying license, and some countries permit flying below the line of vision, that is, out of sight of the operator.

TABLE 10 2015 market for commercial drones in US$ billion.

Industry	2015 market in $US billion
Infrastructure	45.2
Transport	13.0
Insurance	6.8
Media	8.8
Telecommunications	6.3
Agriculture	32.4
Security	10.5
Mining	4.3
Total	**127.3**

Source: PriceWaterhouseCoopers, Global market for commercial applications of drone technology valued at over $127 bn (9 May 2016), https://press.pwc.com/News-releases/global-market-for-commercial-applications-of-drone-technology-valued-at-over--127-bn/s/AC04349E-C40D-4767-9F92-A4D219860CD2

Komatsu's Smart Construction uses drone technology to survey construction sites, create 3-D maps, extract blueprints, and simulate construction plans. The company says that processes that formerly took weeks are now only taking days, and sometimes just hours.[7]

Contractor Plant and Equipment

Increasingly there is a recognition that AI-type processes can assist in the construction process by improving operational efficiency on site. In July 2013, Komatsu released its Intelligent Machine Control bulldozers, and in 2015 it launched its Smart Construction process in Japan.

The Smart Construction principle 'connects all jobsite information concerning not only construction equipment but also people, machines and the ground that are involved in construction in all phases from pre-construction to completion'.

Their branded offering (KomConnect) is a cloud-based software service with a single technology platform connecting all the information. Storing all information concerning construction activities in one place allows key construction stakeholders to analyse, simulate, and make proposals, with access for all concerned via the Internet, anywhere, anytime. By analysing the site using drones and transferring the data to the Intelligent earthmoving machines, the site can be earth-worked efficiently, that is, more cheaply and quickly. More importantly, the work can be done without the traditional human intervention of *setting out*, that is, the hammering of wooden stakes or pegs into the ground to determine the height and/or slope of the ground.

The Smart Construction methodology also allows less experienced employees to work on site. Komatsu has already benchmarked its system against work done in a traditional way, where construction employees bring their experience to the table and know where and in which direction to start work. Currently Komatsu is looking to 'accumulate such veterans' expertise in KomConnect and provide it to all operators'.

In this data-driven environment, design changes can be quickly incorporated and communicated to the site for implementation by Intelligent machines. The cost of changes can also be tracked, resulting in a more precise cost analysis.

One of the advantages of KomConnect, say the manufacturers, is the ability to retain information about sites into the future, to allow for maintenance and intervening events, such as natural catastrophes. Flying drones over a damaged site and comparing the post-event conditions to those before the damage allows equipment to be more quickly and efficiently deployed.

The ability to integrate such a construction approach with preventive maintenance and self-driving technology seems to start to create an integrated approach to a more analytically orientated construction process. One important question to consider is whether such an approach is both scalable and economically viable.

Employee Behaviour

The use of digital devices to track employee position is increasingly becoming a key tool in the armory for the prevention of construction workplace accidents. The construction site is a hazardous place.

- One in 10 US construction workers are injured every year.
- Over the course of a 45-year career, a construction worker has a 1 in 200 chance of dying.

- Falling is the greatest cause of fatal construction injuries.
- The most-violated OSHA safety standard is fall protection/sufficient barriers.
- The job with the highest injury rates in the construction industry is structural steel erectors.
- The construction industry is second in the United States for fatal injuries in workers younger than 18.
- Sixty percent of US construction workplace injuries occur within the employee's first year of employment.
- Between 2002 and 2012, 19.5% of all US workplace deaths happened in the construction industry.[8]

The UK position is not much better in terms of construction accidents when relative size is taken into account. Whilst there has been improvement over the past 20 years, construction is still viewed as a high-risk industry. Construction workplace injuries account for 22% of all fatalities in the UK workplace. This is very high when it is recognised that construction employees only make up 5% of the UK workforce.

The worker fatal injury rate in the UK construction sector (1.62 per 100,000 workers) is over 3.5 times the average rate across all industries (0.46 per 100,000 workers).

The UK Health and Safety Executive (HSE) recorded 80,000 cases of work-related construction industry injury and illness during 2016–2017 in the United Kingdom,[9] allocated as:

- 26,000 were to workers in the Construction of Buildings sector
- 47,000 were to workers in the Specialized Construction Activities sector
- 7,000 were to workers in the Civil Engineering sector.

According to UK Government statistics from the HSE for 2015/2016, the cost to Britain of workplace fatalities and self-reported injuries and ill health is £1,481 million per year (see Table 11). These figures are a combination of human costs (the impact on the individual's quality of life, and for fatal injuries, loss of life), together with financial costs (such as loss of production to due absence from work and health-care costs).

Increasingly there are calls for construction employees to be better monitored in terms of location to help in understanding their precise locations and in identifying whether they are in a potentially hazardous position. But given the number of smaller contractors and the relatively high cost of technology, the use of such devices in the construction industry in significant numbers might be some distance off.

Perhaps it will be for insurers to drive the usage of such devices in order to reduce accidents and therefore reduce compensation payouts, rather than waiting for the industry to take action of its own accord.

It is tempting to suggest that these statistics only reflect conditions in the United Kingdom and United States, but this is not the case. According to the HSE, the United Kingdom consistently has one of the lowest rates of fatal injury across the EU. In 2013 the standardised rate of injury in the United Kingdom was 0.51 per 100,000 employees, which compares favourably with other large economies, such as France (2.94 per 100,000 employees), Germany (0.81 per 100,000 employees), Italy (1.24 per 100,000 employees), and Spain (1.55 per 100,000 employees).[10]

TABLE 11   Costs to Britain of workplace injury and new cases of work-related ill health by industry, 2015/16.

Industry	Estimated cost £m (2015 prices)
Agriculture, forestry and fishing	245
Mining and quarrying, electricity, gas, steam and air conditioning supply, water supply; sewerage, waste management and remediation activities	257
Manufacturing	1,002
Construction	1,024
Wholesale and retail, repair of vehicles	1,478
Transportation and storage	880
Accommodation and food services	459
Professional, technical, financial and admin services	1,834
Public administration / defence	1,027
Education	1,557
Human health / Social work	2,625
Arts, entertainment, recreation and other services.	653
Industry not known	1,809
Total	14,851

Source: UK Health and Safety Executive, Health and safety statistics: key figures for Great Britain, 2015/16. http://www.hse.gov.uk/statistics/cost.htm

Cultural Change in Construction

Perhaps one of the fundamental barriers to change and adoption of new technology is the insular nature of the construction sector. The Centre for Digital Built Britain has identified as a key goal 'the creation of relationships outside the traditional construction industry to create a holistic, outwards looking and inclusive industry'.[11]

This recognises the need for essential disruption from a new order of engineering and requires the profession itself to reinvent itself not only in terms of skills but also in terms of its wider relationships.

The focus on digital engineering by the Institution of Civil Engineers is reinforced in its 2017 *State of the Nation* report, which concentrates on smart cities, integrated services, and new financial models, such as total, or whole-life, cost (totex) rather than capital expenditure (capex) or operational expenditure (opex).

In the *New Civil Engineer* article 'Smart Skills', Margo Cole argues that 'Traditional roles and skills are no longer enough: This changing infrastructure environment needs people who can collect, interpret and manage data; understand systems' thinking; and make our infrastructure smarter.'[12]

She references Sharon Kindleysides, managing director of an intelligent transportation system specialist company, who is a fellow of the Chartered Institute of Highways and Transportation (fellowship being its highest recognition), 'despite', in Kindleysides' words, 'having none of the qualifications to be a member'.

In the article Kindleysides expands her thinking on why the traditional role of the engineer is not what it used to be, saying, 'There's a blurring of boundaries and you can't cubbyhole things anymore. You've got roads talking to vehicles, and traffic lights talking to cars. When we start looking at autonomous vehicles, we will have to change the rulebook, and stop having divisions between civil engineering, mechanical engineering, architecture, et cetera'.

Echoes of a conversation allegedly held between the famous lightbulb inventor Thomas Edison and a famous chemist, Martin Rosanoff, perhaps?

M.A. ROSANOFF:　Mr Edison, please tell me what rules you want me to observe.
THOMAS EDISON:　There ain't no rules around here. We're trying to accomplish something!

Such thinking starts to become critical as the engineering industry, which is already focusing on infrastructure, is placed under increased pressure as a result of climate change.

A report issued in October 2016 by Princeton University predicts that a repeat of Hurricane Sandy (which caused US$53 billion of damage to the East Coast in the United States) is now between 3 and 17 times more likely due to changing climate and increased sea levels. Not only did Sandy kill 117 people, but it left a further 8 million people without power and destroyed or damaged 650,000 homes. Conservative estimates are that global sea levels will increase by between 200 millimetres and 2 metres by 2100, and that 444 million people (or 6% of the global population) will by then live within a range of a 10-metre rise in sea levels.[13]

The mood of the engineering industry is not one of resisting change but rather of preparing itself for resilience. In other words, how can the industry design and construct itself for the future rather than for the present? This extends not only to constructing new property assets but also to utilities and telecommunications. Beyond this, there seems to be a desire for increased collaboration so that decisions are made for the common good rather than simply to accommodate vested interests.

By way of an example of collaboration, the Hurricane Sandy Rebuilding Force aimed to come up with innovative solutions to respond to similar disasters. Its members recognised that the answer may not necessarily be an entirely technological or engineering solution; the way that the community responds to the event, interacts with the technical solution, and ultimately mobilises itself is important as well. Collaboration also includes the interaction between the private and public sectors.

The Rebuilding Force also ran a competition to converge practical civil engineering solutions with enhancement of the local community. Perhaps the best known of these is the Big U. Its name reflects the fact that it comprises a U-shaped shield around Manhattan that not only guards against flooding through its use of berms and levees but takes the form of parkland and art installations.[14]

There is also the challenge of the public–private sector funding balance. Clearly private investors will not want to incur unnecessary cost for an event that may – or may not – occur at some time in the future. But there is a need to incentivise them to do so. This will not only avoid the creation of high-risk areas, but also climate-change migrants – those people who cannot live or work in a particular place because of risk of flooding.

Utilities and Infrastructure Resilience

In its broadest meaning, civil engineering also extends to the installation and management of utilities such as gas, water, and drainage, all of which are increasingly becoming instrumented. *Instrumentation* in this context is often also described as *industrial control systems*.

Control system engineers sit at the crossover between engineers and technologists; civil or mechanical engineers install (and often maintain) systems that are then handed over to control system engineers to operate. There is often a layer of expertise that sits above the control system engineer that analyses data and directs resources through the utilities. The control system engineer role is defined as being responsible for something tangible in the utility, such as a sensor on a pipe or a pump, or a valve on a gas system.

These are systems that are vulnerable to cybersecurity issues and it is therefore no surprise that major engineering firms also seek to ensure that their systems are cyber-resilient, with utility systems being built with cybersecurity in mind. Whereas traditionally the urban terrorist might consider introducing poison into the water system (perhaps to a reservoir), the modern-day urban terrorist might equally want to focus on hacking the system of controls and flow management to cause disruption of usage.

In the United Kingdom, the government has set up the National Cyber Security Centre at GCHQ – the secretive Government Communications Headquarters, based in Cheltenham – which aims to be a source of advice and support, working 'together with UK organisations, businesses, and individuals to provide authoritative and coherent cybersecurity advice and cyber-incident management'.[15]

The issue of physical resilience is also important with respect to terrorist activities, especially in the form of a bomb attack. The Centre for the Protection of National Infrastructure advises that 95% of all injuries are due to the effects of flying or falling glass, with the emphasis increasingly being on precautionary measures, such as lamination or bomb-blast net curtains. Intelligent systems become all the more essential in design and construction to safeguard buildings, the infrastructure, and citizens.

Construction Industry Summary

The construction industry is slow but not averse to change. In this section we have considered a number of technological developments, all of which appear to be building towards a more 'intelligent' and integrated construction industry (see Figure 6).

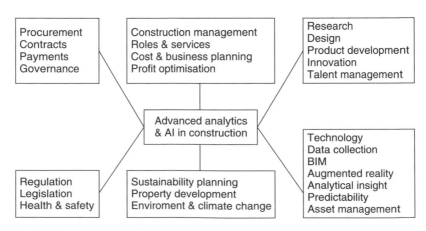

FIGURE 6   Intelligent and integrated construction industry.

Overall, as we consider the impact of AI on construction, is this simply a question of a new technology trying to find a use case? There are certainly some significant hurdles to cross operationally and economically before there is mainstream adoption. Traditionally construction has been complex – both in major and less major works – but increasingly, both constraints on cost and demand for speed seem to be leading to a more sophisticated set of answers.

Construction isn't glamorous from a technological point of view and is likely to struggle to attract talent, despite the apparent encouragement of the professional institutions. Universities also have a role to play in starting to reinvent an old but important industry. Perhaps also there are issues of leadership to consider? Who will be the early movers in this diverse and international marketplace, and where will they be? For those who approach the market with a mentality of the glass being half full, there are clearly opportunities to be identified and pursued.

UTILITIES

Although we have partly considered the topic of utilities under the construction section, we also need specifically to turn our heads to the impact of an AI environment on the use of utilities. This is linked also to agricultural sector (covered later), which is heavily dependent on one of the key utilities: water.

By *utilities*, we mean organisations and private companies that are involved in the manufacturing and distribution of natural assets, such as water and gas, but the term can also extend to include other public services such as sewerage, telephone, and electricity.

Each area of utilities has its own set of issues, but there are common themes that appear to emerge:

- Balancing supply against demand
- Satisfying regulatory requirements
- Managing population growth, including increased urbanisation
- Increased dependence
- Working with climate change, and accommodating a renewable energy agenda
- Dealing with a long lead time for infrastructure development (measured in years and sometimes decades).

There are also very different issues in so-called First World and Third World nations. In this section we will look at four key utilities: electrical power, gas, water, and the disposal of wastewater.

Electrical Power

The UK-based Royal Society for Engineering in 2013 gave warning of potential power cuts if there was a severe winter, as a result of the closure of older electricity plants coupled with the slow rate of construction of new plants.[16] Elsewhere in the world the notion of power cuts and outages are commonplace, as electricity companies undertake *load shedding*. This term refers to the practice of energy companies turning off the power supply to avoid overloading of the system, especially on extremely hot days when the demand for air conditioning is at its highest. Whilst often it is possible to rely on natural energy sources, such as wind turbines, these are also dependent on appropriate windy conditions that are not reliable.[17]

At its best, load shedding can last a couple of hours in selected places. At its worst, entire regions of a country might be involved, such as the statewide blackout of South Australia in 2016. In that case the incident was not due to extremely hot weather but as a result of storms taking down power cables and distribution towers. It's a fine and problematic balance.

Gas

Gas also suffers from issues of supply and demand. The United States generates 80 billion cubic feet of gas per day, yet extreme cold in 2014 led to gas shortages. Gas providers such as Southern California Gas asked its consumers to reduce usage, Montana State University cancelled classes, and Texas and Wisconsin called a state of emergency.[18]

The problem, say experts, is primarily a combination of extreme temperatures coupled with a shift towards the use of cleaner gas and away from coal-fired installations. The additional impact of environmental protection agencies has also resulted in less coal-fired generation of electricity and a consequent loss of jobs in the US coal mining industry.

In Europe, shortages of gas supply are of a quite different nature. With heavy dependence on international gas pipelines, the sensitivity of the relationship between the east and the west is as critical as ever. As a result of disagreements over Ukraine, in 2009 Russia cut off the gas supply and six European countries were affected. Gas shortage in Europe seems predominantly to be of a geopolitical nature but beyond this, the commercial relationships between gas suppliers and distributors can make access to gas at affordable prices very difficult, and some say impairs competition and transparency.[19]

Water

In 2005, the United Nations launched the Water for Life International Decade for Action. The purpose of this initiative was to recognise that water scarcity is one of the main problems facing the globe. Water usage has been growing at twice the rate of population growth. By 2025, the United Nations says, '1800 million could be living in areas of water scarcity and two thirds of the world's population could be living under stress conditions'. It also makes the point that there is enough fresh water available globally, but that it is poorly distributed, contaminated from pollution and wastage, and suffers from poor management.[20]

Not all the problems are man-made. Changing precipitation and climate change are affecting natural hydrological systems, leading to water shortages and emerging political tensions. Some might argue that climate change is man-made, but there are others who disagree on that point. Whatever the reality, it's a major problem. According to Jean Chrétien, former Canadian Prime Minister and co-chair of the InterAction Council, a prestigious group of world leaders: 'The future political impact of water scarcity may be devastating … Using water the way we have in the past simply will not sustain humanity in future.'[21]

Wastewater

Although not quite in the same realm as fresh water or electrical power, the effective management of the wastewater and sewerage infrastructure is also a critical success factor for humanity. In Western Europe, much of the sewerage infrastructure was built over 100 years ago and is not able to meet today's needs in terms of volume and the trend towards increased urbanisation.

In the United States alone it is estimated that over US$400 billion will need to be spent over the next decade to fix the problem. The future will need to take into account changing needs, weather patterns, and traffic. It will be a complex solution, combining analytics and asset management, aimed at providing a more reliable service at a lower operational cost.

In Sacramento, the 35th largest city in the United States and capital city of the US state of California, two key agencies (the Sacramento Area Sewer District and the Sacramento Regional County Sanitation District) are already using advanced analytics for more than 400,000 assets in the system. This includes 98 pump stations, 3,000 miles of main lines, and 279,000 service connections, which treat 165 million gallons of wastewater every day.[22]

On other continents, the problem is acute in a different way. According to Coalition Eau, a network of French nongovernmental organisations (NGOs), 40% of the world's population (or around 3 billion people) lack access to toilets. All seven continents are affected, although South Asia and sub-Saharan Africa are the worst off. Access to drinking water and access to safe sanitation go hand in hand. According to a UNICEF report, 240,00 young people die every day as a result of drinking contaminated and unclean water.[23]

Smart Homes, Smart Infrastructure?

At the moment, the focus on developing AI for utilities seems to be mainly concentrated in mature markets. The promotion of so-called smart homes increasingly encourages the consumer to install Wi-Fi–enabled devices at the point of delivery of the utility, be it gas, water, or electricity.

These devices allow utility providers to gain a greater understanding of the consumption patterns of users and also have the incidental benefit of reducing the cost of manually checking individual metres on a property-by-property basis. They also help the consumer to be aware of and engaged in the amount of the utility being consumed, perhaps also encouraging them to change behaviours.

Beyond this, some providers are able to include seasonal tariffs, which help in demand management. Put another way, such tariffs dissuade users from watering their lawns at the time of least rainfall in the summer.

The intention is not, at least for the moment, to regulate the use of domestic sanitation by using metered measurements of wastewater. Even so, it should be remembered that according to the US Environmental Protection Agency, more water is used in flushing the toilet on a daily basis than in any other activity. In California alone, an estimated 203 million gallons of treated municipal drinking water are used every day in flushing toilets. The average flush volume is 2.7 gallons, compared to ultralow flush toilets, which use 1.6 gallons. In the meantime, experts suggest just wrapping a brick in a plastic bag and placing it in the cistern, which reduces the volume of water used by half a gallon.

Looking to the future, we are increasingly likely to live in a superconnected home, with sensors on heating, ventilation, water, electricity, and all other services. Beyond this, we will see remote security sensors, lighting controls, and the control of domestic appliances. The ability of systems to not only detect our work but also observe our recreational patterns will result in recommendations being pushed to consumers. Perhaps they will even be automatically triggered unless we override them. The home environment in mature markets will be one that, more than anywhere, will be measured, interconnected, and intelligent.

In the factory, the correlation between just-in-time supply chain management and lower-cost utility tariffs will increasingly help to further reduce costs. Energy management and storage will become more integral to the manufacturing process.

An example of energy management is hydroelectric power storage, such as Dinorwic in Wales, which is used predominantly as a power-surge storage facility. Water is stored high in the mountains in the Marchlyn Mawr reservoir and discharged through turbines at times of peak demand to the lower Llyn Peris reservoir. At times of low demand, water is pumped back up the mountain. Although the system uses electricity to pump this water back uphill, the cost of this is lower when it is done at times of low demand, and therefore it is a cost-efficient approach to storage.

Increasingly, there is likely to be linkage between the location – or relocation – of factories relative to available energy and utility provisions. Location optimisation in manufacturing will become yet another component in manufacturing cost reduction. With labour costs historically being one of the key business drivers for cost, won't replacement of labour by automation invariably place greater emphasis on the cost and dependability of power and utilities?

Interconnectivity, Poverty, and Famine

In 2009 the UN secretary-general Ban Ki-moon instituted a data programme called Global Pulse. This aimed to create an innovation laboratory tasked with raising awareness amongst key stakeholders as to the use of data in managing poverty. The use of shared data by NGOs is not a new idea but many still operate in a vacuum, not having fully appreciated the value of sharing data to provide a universal view of a particular problem in a region of location.

In *Poor Economics: A Radical Rethinking of the Way to Fight Global Poverty*, the authors showed from a review of 18 countries that people were not starving from hunger (i.e. they had enough food) but rather that they were suffering from a lack of nutrition. The authors proposed that governments need not provide more food such as noodles or rice but rather to provide more nutrients. They asked whether somehow combining data from multiple utilities could give us a different viewpoint about the world. 'Why would a man in Morocco who doesn't have enough to eat buy a television?' they asked.[24]

We need to be realistic. It's beyond the scope of this book to provide a panacea that will cure world ills. But we perhaps start to see potential for some sort of broader advanced analytical model that will help us to have an understanding of the key drivers of change. This involves collecting and sharing multiple data sets and somehow making better sense of them. The number of variables involved make this beyond being a human task, and surely AI has a role to play.

At a more local level, the essence of an interconnected, instrumented, and intelligent world is that we strive to optimise the limited utilities and services that we have, and to act responsibility. Perhaps the greatest risk is that of managing geopolitical and commercial pressures. Even the best AI technological systems are unlikely to be able to help us in that regard without effective regulation.

At the end of the day it may ultimately just come down to a desire, in a relatively closed environment of people and resources, to somehow manage our natural resources for the common good. Invariably we will need to delegate those responsibilities. Effective management by those whom we choose to assume these responsibilities will ultimately rest with the ability to persuade those with resources to participate and collaborate. Their decisions and responses are bound to be influenced by accurate data and information.

Those who suggest that data is the new fuel of the age are not entirely correct. Will the traditional fuels of water and power not still dominate our world?

The open question is the degree to which better data and AI will help us in balancing supply and demand of those traditional fuels, if at all.

PUBLIC SERVICES

Perhaps it would be slightly irresponsible to consider commercial industries without taking into account public services, also known as the public sector. Rather than being concerned with people as consumers, public services are concerned with people as citizens, either on a direct basis at individual level, or indirectly through their relationship with businesses. The composition of the public sector differs from country to country and may comprise military, police, infrastructure, public education, elected officials, and even the management of utilities when they are not privately owned. The public sector is a significant employer, and in the United Kingdom employs approximately 20% of the workforce.[25]

But the pressure is on the public sector. Like the private sector, our public sector 'servants of the people' are also living with the challenges of the drive for cost efficiency, improved productivity, and better service. In cities, individual public servants have the same challenges as their counterparts in the private sector, such as commuting, stress, and performance management.

The public sector is a market that is ripe for the initiation of automation and AI. Large numbers of civil servants spend time checking applications and responding to multiple simple e-mails whose answers can probably already be found somewhere on the Frequently Asked Questions section of overcomplicated websites (if the questioner had either the time or the patience to look harder). Or maybe it is just that answers to frequently asked questions are couched in such complex terms as to be virtually unintelligible, or so vague as to be of limited use to individuals with specific problems.

Systems that respond effectively to simple requests and allow more complex ones to be escalated up the line through a form of triage appear to be an ideal solution to speed up replies to simple queries. Such systems could provide more rapid access for complex enquiries, improve consistency, and reduce cost. But on the whole, governments do not appear to have the most successful track record in terms of technological advancement. They are not alone. The commercial sector is also littered with failed IT implementations – a few of the worst in both sectors are listed below:

- Failure of the UK National Health Service (NHS) IT system, which was to be the world's largest, initially estimated at a cost of £4.6 billion but abandoned after an expenditure of £10 billion due to data management issues, patient confidentiality, and missed deadlines.
- The Ministry of Defence's failed IT programme to recruit soldiers to front-line duty cost £150 million and ran over by two years at an additional cost of £1 million per month, or over £50 million in total.
- Royal Bank of Scotland's software glitch prevented customers from accessing their accounts for over two weeks in June 2012 and cost RBS £125 million to resolve.[26]

Recent publications summarized the top AI failures of 2016; examples follow:

- Results from an AI system designed to identify the likelihood of a person's carrying out repeat crime were viewed as not only incorrect but also racist, as the system wrongly predicted black offenders were more likely to recommit crimes.
- A fatality of an auto-drive pilot, when the driver was killed in a collision whilst the vehicle was in autopilot, or self-drive, mode.
- A robotic chatbot that engaged in homophobic and racist responses.[27]

In all cases, the manufacturers/designers pointed to the problem being one of incorrect algorithms and that the problem (if not the consequence of the failure) was capable of being corrected.

There's plenty of literature and advice on why IT implementations fail. In simple terms, they appear to be summarised as follows:

- Poor procurement policies
- Inadequate project management skills
- Lack of understanding of the requirement by the supplier
- Insufficient checking of references/proof points by the purchaser
- Too much learning on the job by clients who overstated their own capabilities
- Overambitious scope management, including a big bang approach rather than incremental improvement
- Weak quality management.

One issue to consider is whether these more complex AI projects will be prone to the same potential weaknesses as mainstream technology or whether a new set of failure symptoms may emerge. These new causes of failure of AI implementations could include:

- Incorrect algorithms
- Lack of understanding of the business problem that AI is trying to address
- Overambitious implementation in terms of scope and timing
- Incorrect self-learning/deep-learning processes
- Overpromising and underdelivery by technology vendors
- Misalignment of cultures in client–vendor partnerships.

Many failures are often put down to the human element, but in an environment of more advanced analytics, perhaps the system itself (or its designers/managers) will increasingly need to take the blame? Important questions will start to be asked about where the thresholds of responsibility rest, regardless of whether these are funded publicly or privately, or in some way are covered by insurance.

Whilst we appear to have focused on failure rather than success, this is because of the greater consequences of failure in the public sector in terms of the scale, importance, cost to the public purse, and impact on public confidence. Failure can also be used as a political tool. For these reasons, is the consequence of failing in the public sector more critical than in the private sector?

One of the key drivers of change in the public sector is that of cost control or cost reduction. It might be worth considering what one of those main protectors of employment, the union movement, might have to say about technological change.

The union movement is not oblivious to changing work environments. After all, change in the workplace isn't a new phenomenon, and the effect of automation has been on the agenda now for a few decades. In their report *Labor and Technology: Union Response to Changing Environments*, presented at a conference on labour and technology held at Pennsylvania State University way back in 1981, the authors reported that 'by 1990 65–75% of factory jobs could be replaced by automation and that 25 million jobs would be eliminated'.

What is interesting about that 35-year-old paper is that, in effect, the problems of technological change are the same. The difference is that now the technology has matured. A visitor to an auto manufacturing, bottling, or consumer goods site would be unlikely to see very many people on the production line. The writers of the paper suggested, even then, 'Unionists cannot be concerned only with events in their own industry, nor can labor educators communicate only with other labor educators. If they do, labor's progressive voice becomes fragmented and ineffective'.

In what might be a prediction of the AI future, they also said, 'For workers who keep their jobs or are displaced by machines but find new work, the impact of technology may well be that their jobs become de-skilled, simplified, devalued, and less fulfilling: in other words, more machine-like'.

To what degree should unions have a say in this wider AI debate? Union membership has shrunk and politicians may also argue that the labour movement, if not in decline, certainly does not have the support that it previously enjoyed. Perhaps the time is right for a swing of the pendulum in the opposite direction?

Back then the authors suggested a series of key union responses to the changing technological environment, which probably still hold true. They include:

- The need for unions to understand the impact of technological changes on collective bargaining, including an agreement among union negotiators on what they consider to be a threat – requiring them to be imaginative and to redefine some bargaining units
- The need for unions to organise themselves properly both at a local and national level, and to understand the impact both of deregulation and industrial relocation
- The need for unions to understand and influence political strategies, ranging from narrow self-interest to a broader approach.[28]

Nearly 40 years on, don't the unions again need to consider what their response should be to an AI-infused industrial environment? Back then it was expected that women and disadvantaged minorities would be the most adversely affected, and that workers would be more active in protecting their jobs, maintaining their wages, and protecting their self-respect and dignity. One way to counter the current effects of techological change would have been through a resurgence of union power, but this hasn't happened.

Today, many (but not all) people most likely to be affected by AI are from blue- and white-collar industries, and for these people the principle of unionisation does not come naturally. Many will also be children of a more industrial age for whom union action was not the most positive of experiences.

It seems that nowadays we do not see the unions as the protectors of society, but rather as pariahs who prevent the trains from running, our planes from leaving, the post from being delivered, and rubbish from being collected – in other words, nuisances who generally get in the way of our smoothly running society. Not only do our politicians protest, but also the man in the street increasingly calls for legislation to ensure that so-called essential services are not disrupted by strike action. But doesn't strike action embody our freedom to withdraw labour, and isn't it still one of the main tools in the union's armory? If AI is to play such a large part in the running of society in terms of the operation of public services, isn't there still a need for workers to be adequately and collectively represented in that discussion?

Like the Luddites of old whose foremost aim was to improve working conditions rather than destroy equipment, doesn't the union movement need to get more engaged in the AI debate?

There's no real doubt that the public sector will be impacted by AI. According to the 'think tank' Reform, in the United Kingdom alone 'Automation will replace up to nine in 10 of the Whitehall's 140,000 administrative roles in the next decade, saving £2.7 billion a year. Similar changes in the NHS could save a further £1.7 billion. When the national debt remains twice as high as its level before the financial crisis – and still rising – these efficiencies are essential'.[29]

With public services being at the heart of a smooth-running society, the intro- duction of new intelligent methods in an environment of flawed implementation and worker reaction is bound to create some ripples. It's going to be an interesting journey for all of us.

Education

Where does teaching stop and learning begin? Some would quite reasonably argue that the two go hand in hand. There appears to have been a shift in the process of education away from a teaching-based or teacher-centred approach to one of a learner-centred approach. College and university students with a limited amount of lecturer face time will immediately recognise this, as will those taking professional examinations, such as accountants. The changed model also seems increasingly to find its way to the earliest stages in the classroom, such as first grade or in the primary school.

Learning-based education, also known as competency-based education or person- alised learning, allows students to progress at their own pace based on their ability to master a skill or capability, regardless of the circumstances in which they are learn- ing. The target is to allow students to obtain the best outcomes given their different learning abilities.

The key principles for developing a competency-based education programme follow:

■ The programme reflects robust and valid competences and that they should align to professional or academic targets that are explicit and transparent.

- Students can learn at a variable pace and are supported in their learning. In effect this adds the attribute of personalisation to a generic teaching process and reflects the concept that people have different leaning styles, speeds, and abilities.
- Effective learning resources are available at any time, so learning resources need to be continually accessible.
- The process for mapping progress is clear, with a series of key targets and independent checks.
- Assessments are secure and reliable, are beyond manipulation, and pass the test of objectivity.[30]

Competency-based education seems to be especially attractive where the cost of education is rising, much in the same way as healthcare. It also responds to the need for a more customised education profile, especially in higher education, where a generalised approach may not be sufficient.

Many if not all of these key criteria pass the test for some form of automated or semi-automated approach. An inevitable question to consider going forward therefore is that of the role of the teacher or lecturer in this new model.

In the summer of 2016, Georgia Tech, a university in Atlanta in the United States, employed a teaching assistant called Jill Watson for a postgraduate course to help students and to respond in an online forum. Students discovered that Jill Watson answered questions and gave feedback more quickly than other teaching assistants. In fact, Jill Watson was not a human but rather a prototype teaching robot. 'She' was related to IBM's Watson computer of *Jeopardy* game show fame, and was being used by the Pearson global education group in an experimental project. The fact that the students could not tell that this was a robotic helper recalls the Turing test covered earlier in Chapter 2, one of the tests of computer intelligence.

There are pro and counter arguments to such usage. If AI can be used in financial services, manufacturing, and retailing, then why should a profession such as teaching be immune? Alternatively, how can a student who is entrepreneurial or innovative be adequately recognised by an algorithm?

In her paper 'AI and Education: Celebrating 30 Years of Marriage', Beverly Park Woolf of the University of Massachusetts refers to the need for new 'intelligent systems' – AI by another name – not only to personalise teaching but also to be able to provide mechanisms that react and respond to the student's emotions. She reminds us that learning is often linked to a student's emotional state – something that seasoned teachers will also recognise. Intelligent tutoring systems can not only identify student mood but also can customise the instruction to match that mood. (In a slightly different approach, human teachers tend to employ tactics to change the mood of the student, and in doing so get the student in the right mind-set for learning.)

She also suggests that twenty-first-century systems are particularly well placed to teach twenty-first-century capabilities, both soft and hard capabilities, making the point that many teaching establishments 'look like nineteenth century establishments' and that 'teachers lecture; students are passive'. Her remarks imply a mismatch between nineteenth-century educational processes and twenty-first-century (or later) educational needs.[31]

Elsewhere, experts also propose that AI in education can provide:

- *Virtual mentors for every learner.* Giving omnipresent support that integrates user modelling, social simulation, and knowledge representation.

- *Analysis of interaction data.* Bringing together the vast amounts of data about individual learning, social contexts, learning contexts, and personal interests.
- *Opportunities for global classrooms.* Increasing the interconnectedness and accessibility of classrooms worldwide.
- *Lifelong and life-wide technologies.* Taking learning outside of the classroom and into the learner's life outside of school.[32]

One question to consider is whether AI in education will create a divided educational society between the haves and have-nots. Some might argue that such a society already exists, an example being the British public school system – which is not *public* at all, but rather a form of private education. (The term *public school* originates from the notion that it is funded by the public (i.e. fee paying), rather than funded by the government.) According to UK government reports, 1 in 20 eligible public school students went on to study at Oxford or Cambridge, compared to 1 in 100 from state schools.[33]

Based on a survey by the Sutton Trust charity, students of Oxford and Cambridge (institutions known collectively as Oxbridge) represented one-third of the United Kingdom's professional elite; students from the 10 top independent boys' schools (Eton, Winchester, Charterhouse, Rugby, Westminster, Marlborough, Dulwich, Harrow, St Paul's, and Wellington) represented 12% of the country's elite. Eton College alone educated 4% of the UK elite, among whom were 19 Prime Ministers.[34]

Alternatively, will the use of AI in education serve to level the playing field? By tailoring the teaching to the needs of the individual at a pace to suit that individual, providing that the learning objectives in the long term can be reached, there could be better equality of opportunity.

Is automated education suitable for the very young or the old student? And at what age might a child be able to benefit from either a semi- or fully automated robotic learning system without human presence? One clue might be in the accepted age at which a child might generally be left home alone unsupervised, and there seem to be different rules across the globe. One commonly agreed benchmark seems to be around the age of 11 or 12 years old. By comparison, many young children are technologically competent – at some level – well before that age. One issue to contend with is, without some form of supervision, whether children will be able to focus on the task of learning rather than playing unrelated games or being on social media instead.

By 2012, 84 million iPads had been sold, and some were being used by children not much over the age of 2 years. Retailer PC World in the United Kingdom named the Apple iPad as the toy of the year in 2010.

Elsewhere, in a two-week study involving children ages three to seven and conducted by the Public Broadcasting Service (a broadcaster and web provider of, among other offerings, children's content, which describes itself as America's largest classroom), it was found that educational apps can improve a child's vocabulary by as much as 31% in two weeks. PBS's SuperVision app allows the parent to have insight not only into their child's online activity but also the development of key competencies, such as literacy, knowledge of science, and emotional interest. The app offers, for example, learning activities such as thank-you goals aimed at the two-to-five-year-old and intended to help with expressions of appreciation, creativity, dexterity, and literacy.

What also is becoming clear is a need to create educational processes for the very young that prepare them better for later life. The expression 'Give me the child until he is seven and I will show you the man' is often associated with the Jesuit religious order but actually has its origins in the Greek philosophy of Aristotle. It makes the point that the foundations of future essential capabilities are laid at a young age, and at an early stage in the education process.

On a global basis, the ability to customise the learning process could increasingly have the effect of creating a more level educational playing field. Teaching and learning may start to be constrained only by access to technology. For some, however, the impracticalities of access and the cost of the technology will be prohibitive, and this could cause issues going forward. Maybe a role for traditional teaching might still exist amongst the have-nots?

Where will all this leave teachers and lecturers? An intelligent system clearly has the capability to create personal learning dependent on student age, ability, and perhaps even on affordability. Computerised teaching assistants also appear feasible and replicate the robotic financial advisor assistant of the wealth management industry.

The future will increasingly require teachers at all levels to become more conversant with enabling technology. In the early phases of transformation, hybrid roles will start to emerge. These changes will almost certainly place additional pressures on existing teaching staff, many of whom already are under pressure to satisfy the challenges of external audit in the face of larger class sizes; funding constraints; changes in syllabi, curriculum, and delivery requirements; greater administrative loads; and disruptive pupils. For some teachers from older generations, this additional burden could well push them over the edge, and experience could be lost from the sector.

As in other professions, younger teachers will increasingly need to be trained in these new teaching methods. Most may be more willing to embrace change. Dependent on the quality and nature of change and the individual teacher's personal relationship with technology, as well as with the pupil, it may also create additional attractions to join the sector. However, a more passive role, such as monitoring student–machine interactions, may prove to be less appealing.

Policing

Already new intelligent policing methods are emerging that identify crime hot spots and route police cars more effectively. Higher and timelier visibility is optimising the use of costly policing resources, by using a combination of advanced and geospatial analytics. But perhaps *intelligent policing* is about to reach a whole new level.

Dubai deployed the first robot police officer in 2017 and is set to have its first fully automated police station by 2030. That is, a station that doesn't require humans. Already Dubai police are planning to use it alongside automated payment processing, virtual assistants, and algorithms to anticipate and prevent crime. Robot police will be multilingual and will be put into service predominantly in tourist areas as deterrents to crime. Additionally, it will be possible to pay fines through this modern robocop. Brigadier Abdullah Bin Sultan, who is director of the police force's Future Shaping Centre, has said he wants robots to make up around a quarter of the police force by 2030.[35]

In the United Kingdom, Durham police are also planning to use AI to score criminals, in order to assess the future likelihood of their committing crimes. Their assessment tool is called HART (the Harm Risk Assessment Tool). It operates on a scoring basis and has been found to be 98% accurate in the case of low risk and 88% accurate in the case of high risk. The apparent lower accuracy with respect to high risk is said to be as a result of a bias within the system to place a 'cautious' weighting on those more likely to recommit.[36] Whilst described as AI, technology purists might reasonably suggest that this approach is more a matter of predictive analysis, much the same as that used by marketers to identify propensity to buy.

Crime prevention in an AI environment might not entirely be plain sailing. In 2016 ProPublica wrote about the use of similar evidence-based software in the United States, suggesting that it could contain bias. ProPublica checked the records of 7,000 individuals arrested in 2013 and 2014 and ran their details through the predictive tool, discovering that of those judged likely to offend, only 61% did so. They described this as a better analytical outcome than a toss of the coin. In the cases reviewed, the algorithm used was proprietary and took into account education, employment, and previous criminal record.

Predictions regarding individual propensity to commit crime have been used since the 1970s and have come in for some criticism. The argument is that if an intelligent system can anticipate who is likely to commit a crime in the future, couldn't decisions about who to lock up be made more effective? Wouldn't the use of already overcrowded jails and custody therefore be optimised? Equally, couldn't other services, such as probation, be more effectively employed as a deterrent?

At best, scoring systems are only meant to be indicators, but some judges have used them in a more prescriptive way when sentencing. In August 2013, a Wisconsin judge declared that the defendant had been 'identified, through the (scoring) assessment, as an individual who is at high risk to the community' and imposed a sentence of eight years and six months in prison.[37]

Healthcare

Increasingly, tech firms are looking at the healthcare sector. Tech investment firms are investing in AI start-ups that are focusing on the following areas:

- *Biopharma.* Principally, the creation of medicines that are extracted or semisynthesised from biological sources. It's a highly regulated industry, and one that often involves clinical trials over many years.
- *Diagnosis.* This applies to both routine medical conditions and more complex conditions, such as cancer.

Automated diagnosis comprises intelligent patient triage and first-level care. Like all of AI, it is heavily dependent on data, and with the consequences of failure being so serious, the road to implementation is potentially strewn with difficulty.[38]

As with all technological implementation, there usually need to be burning platforms to encourage progress. In healthcare, these burning platforms comprise issues such as aging populations, shortage of skilled staff, stress-related illness amongst healthcare employees, and the need for better cost management. There is an increasing mood to direct more simple medical issues away from doctors towards better equipped nurses and more knowledgeable pharmacists. Beyond this, the impacts of urbanisation are also placing great pressure on healthcare services.

In China, where there are only 1.5 physicians available for every 1,000 people (compared with 2.4 in the United States and 2.8 in the United Kingdom), intelligent diagnosis tools are expected to replace half of the workload of doctors within a decade. According to the consultancy Frost & Sullivan, in addition to relieving the burden on doctors, intelligent systems have the potential to improve outcomes of medical treatment by 30–40% and to reduce costs by as much as 50%.[39]

Increasingly, new technologies are being used for automated image analysis, which is an established area for machine learning. Automated tissue analysis uses computation to improve the measurement of cells, such as cancer cells. In doing so, subjective decisions by human inspection are removed and there are benefits both in time and cost.

Elsewhere, early tests indicate that intelligent automated methods can even be used in the treatment of depression, as the 'Woebot' has demonstrated. A pilot study involved US college students who described themselves as being depressed. It concluded that fully automated conversation apps can deliver easily accessed, engaging, and effective cognitive-behavioural therapies to the patient.[40]

Treatment of an aging population will also be transformed. On a worldwide basis, there will be over 1.5 billion people over the age of 65 by 2050. In the United Kingdom, children born today are likely to live into their 90s. Japan, which has the world's oldest population, is one of the countries in the forefront of researching robotic companions for the elderly. These 'social companion robots' not only can assist with diet and nutrition advice but also will be able to enter into conversation; one such robot being developed at Stanford is called the 'Carebot P37S65'.[41] Experts suggest that these new technologies should not be a replacement for human contact but rather supplement it. Perhaps with the number of job losses as a result of AI, there will be more people with time on their hands to look after elderly neighbors and relatives.

The topic of healthcare will be covered in more detail in Chapter 5, but as with other industries, many in the healthcare sector are likely to be increasingly affected by emerging intelligence methods.

AGRICULTURE

We are potentially faced with a forthcoming food shortage. Global demand for food is likely to double within 50 years as the population of the world increases from 6 billion today to 9 billion by 2040.

Already:

- 1 billion people in the world go to bed hungry every single night.
- Somewhere in the world, someone starves to death every 3.6 seconds, and three-quarters of these individuals are children under the age of five.
- Approximately a third of all children in the world under the age of five suffer from serious malnutrition.

Beyond this, 25% of potential farmland suffers from environmental degradation. In India, 75% of the water is contaminated by industrial and agricultural waste (where, according to UN data, there are more people who own mobile phones than have access to a toilet).[42]

There's no shortage of worrying information. Perhaps this most critical and humanitarian area is one in which experts could best put substantial leverage and resources into the application of AI to begin solving this problem? The agriculture industry has multiple dimensions and traditionally has relied on intuition and experience, but the time seems to have now come for a more scientifically based approach to the challenge.

The agricultural market is already increasingly being affected by devices such as driverless tractors, milking robots, and automated harvesting machines. Smaller robotic segments include seeding robots, mowing robots, and pruning robots.

There is, however, considerable scope for further activity in the AI space:

- Greater accuracy in the understanding of the optimum time for planting and fertilizer treatment to ensure increased yields, taking into account climate and weather, harvesting and baling, and soil fertility
- Management of crop stress using sensors and applying intervening techniques in a timely and cost-effective manner
- Alignment of growth with market demand and supply chain availability and capacity
- Automation of farm activities to replace manual labour – especially given that farming is not the career of choice for many young people
- Robotic harvesting
- Pest and disease management
- Automated irrigation, including just-in-time watering
- Measuring and management of crop quality, including inventory and risk management.

Elsewhere we have discussed the issue of megatrends, one of which is urbanisation. The movement of people from the field to the city, coupled with the loss of agricultural labour, seems at face value to be a slippery slope towards lower agricultural production at a time that the world's population is growing.

So what will the 'farmers' of tomorrow look like? In a profession historically based on intuition and uncertainty, farmers are increasingly looking to analytical methods to gain greater understanding of the best time to plant, where to use fertilizers, when best to harvest, and how to track the quality of their crop.

Beyond more effective measurement, the harvest itself is increasingly becoming more technically orientated. Expensive 'plant' and equipment are becoming automated. The harvester and the adjacent tractor collecting the harvest are wirelessly connected and totally in sync. The driver of the harvester only exists to ensure that no one has left an old bicycle in the field, and in any event a cowcatcher type of device can readily stop the machine in its tracks if an obstacle is found. Both harvester and tractor can be remotely controlled.

The use of geographical information systems ensures not only that the entire field is optimally harvested, but checks on the harvest can help farmers understand the best quality and quantity of yield.

For many traditional farmers, such an approach doesn't come completely comfortably. Increasingly they need to rely on effective partnerships with equipment manufacturers and suppliers. Elsewhere, farmers increasingly liaise with specialist agricultural data analysts to collect and interpret the data and to recommend optimal courses of action, in a process that is increasingly known as *precision agriculture.*

In addition to crop management, dairy farmers are able to better understand and manage their herds. Automated milking machines require minimal human intervention and track both the quality of milk and any diseases or infections.

Beyond this, agricultural insurers are able to better understand and quantify crop losses due to severe weather conditions. Traditionally, farmers haven't bought crop insurance, either because it didn't cover the crops they grew or because the paperwork was simply too onerous. New data-driven approaches are allowing new insurance models to be created for 'whole farm revenue protection'.[43]

Farming, perhaps once considered (maybe unfairly) a profession for those who left school without qualifications, is increasingly assuming a role as one of the professions of choice for the brightest students in the class. It's a great example of an industry successfully reacting to change.

Finally, let us return to the issue of global food shortages. Data and analytics alone, even when coupled with automated and intelligent systems, cannot be the panacea for world problems, but they can help.

In India, scientists from the International Crops Research Institute for the Semi-Arid Tropics and engineers at Microsoft have worked together to use cloud-based predictive analytics to arrive at a precise date for sowing. Early results are encouraging, with record increases in yields of up to 40% being measured on the 175 farms piloted, with a further 2,000 to be brought into the pilot programme.[44]

TECHNOLOGY INDUSTRY

In considering the impact of technology, AI, and cognitive analytics on other industries, we run the risk of overlooking the impact that it will have on the technology industry itself. Possibly we simplistically assume that the tech sector will influence everyone else's life but that its own environment will remain relatively unscathed. This is unlikely to be the case, and in fairness it's only reasonable that the technology industry itself should also be affected.

The IT industry, like many others, comprises multiple professions, from developers to sales to marketing. Most of these (perhaps all) will be affected in some way by the AI revolution.

The biggest issue is probably that of resources and recruitment. The march towards AI is such that there is a major drain on specialist resources. Corporations are look-ing to the academic sector for talented people, but arguably academics don't have sufficient commercial awareness. Professional migration is inevitable. It's an obvious move for many relatively low-paid academics to move to higher-paid commercial roles. Many major tech developers are already replicating research facilities, but with better funding, especially as the stakes are so high.

For those individuals who are thinking of making the move from academia to commerce, there is the inevitable ethical issue of how they feel about sacrificing their personal ideals about benefiting mankind in favour of benefiting individual businesses and stockholders. Fortunately the two are not mutually exclusive.

Big companies such Google, Baidu, and others are not without a dollar or two. With the march towards AI, it seems that there is likely to be continued investment either internally or in external academic organisations. In 2016 Google announced that it had made a CAD$4.5-million donation to support AI research in Montreal. The University of Montreal and the city's McGill University now claims 150 researchers working in this booming field, a concentration of talent now said to be greater than anywhere else in the world (at least for the moment).[45]

Beyond this, tech companies are also oiling the wheels of innovation hubs that incubate and accelerate new ideas, often with in-kind rather than financial assistance. They do this by providing support and low-cost/no-cost technology. IBM, for example, through its Smartcamp programme, provides coaching, mentoring, and networks, and ultimately a competition in which the winner gains investment funding. The company's Global Entrepreneur programme provides qualified start-ups with up to US$120,000 of cloud credits, which allow access to its suite of apps. The current (as of 2018) criteria require the start-up to be less than five years old, have an income of less than US$1 million per annum, and be working with an approved entrepreneurial organisation, such as an innovation hub or venture capitalist.[46]

IBM is not alone in this approach. Oracle's Startup Cloud Accelerator programme also provides similar capabilities, for example. In 2016 Baidu also earmarked a US$60 million allocation for a programme called Easterly Ventures to support start-ups in Brazil. This was the first time that the Chinese tech giant had set up a fund outside China. For that programme, Baidu requires that the start-ups are already in the growth phase and that their products are both defined and validated. In return, it offers technical support, mobile traffic, and international experience, and facilitates access to the Chinese market.[47]

All these schemes and others offer support and advice in the areas of sales and marketing. They are the lifeblood of the start-up tech sector, especially when progress in both start-ups and major corporations alike (and all in between) is measured by revenue growth. Revenue is critical, of course, if only to pay the bills, even if many start-up organisations are measured by their value rather than by their turnover.

The *value* of a company is simply what someone is prepared to pay for it. There's no single way to measure it. It can be based on the assets of the company, its potential cash stream, its profitability, or even just a hunch about its future prospects.[48]

The technology sector in particular is often valued on what is called *coming technology*, that is, technology with capability, even if there is no obvious way of monetising its value at present. Facebook struggled to monetise its customer base until it started to use customer data for advertising. Also, profit may not necessarily be the key to understanding value, as often start-ups plough any surplus money back into sales, marketing, and development.

The general rules of value appear to be something like this:

- One or two times revenue for moderate-growth companies
- Three or four times revenue for high-growth companies
- Up to ten times revenue for really high-growth companies.

It is even possible to value a company with no revenue whatsoever, but this might be more in the realm of crystal ball gazing. Consideration of investment in the company's research and development programme, or comparison to other peers, may provide some sort of an indicator.

As in other industries, sales and marketing in the tech sector will be transformed by AI. There will be greater alignment between demand and supply, speedier time to market, more customisation, and different revenue models.

Client buyers will be more aware of vendor capabilities. It's likely that the emphasis will move away from service or product to a new experience-based relationship with tech vendors. That experience will increasingly depend on the culture of that organisation, and performance of individuals will increasingly be measured against culture through sophisticated talent management systems.

In the early 1940s, Thomas Watson, who founded IBM, famously said that the world only needs five computers. That statement is often ridiculed, but the reality seems to be that some are even suggesting that five computers may be too many. Companies such as Google, Amazon, and Deutsche Telekom are already building powerful computing grids that can serve 'thousands or millions of individual servers and PCs'.[49] Perhaps the reality is that as AI becomes more pervasive and is developed not only by companies but also by their network of external innovators and start-ups, that Watson will be proven right.

There are some interesting ethical issues that emerge, which relate to the concept of work and the value of the individual. The concern goes along these lines: as individuals, we all are able to influence the direction of change when we act collectively. Cab drivers, for example, can withdraw their services en masse if they are unhappy with the creation and development of new business models such as Uber. Roll on the calendar 10 or 20 years to an environment of self-driving taxis controlled by the algorithms of a small number of technology companies. Where then might the muscle to resist change actually lie?

In an AI environment, tech companies seem to have the potential to wield enormous power. Perhaps it is due to fears such as this that they not only should embrace such concerns, but actively encourage discussion.

As pivotal players, shouldn't tech companies actively encourage debate rather than leaving moral and ethical issues for others to discuss in isolation (and possible ignorance)? Won't a failure to do so only lead to suspicion? Isn't effective stakeholder management one of the key success factors in effective project delivery?

CONCLUSION

Some might suggest that, in a book such as this, dividing industries into first tier and second tier is a risky approach. After all, it's possible to identify different degrees of innovation in both tiers. Money talks, as they say, and those industries with the greatest spending power, such as financial services, might find it easier to not only identify opportunities for progress, but also to find the funding for implementation. Invariably these industries also have the greatest need for change, especially in saturated marketplaces in which there is greater competition and a need to differentiate.

On the other hand, there seem to be plenty of opportunities for niche innovation in individual second-tier industries, especially when evaluated against specific industry problems. In these cases, innovation may involve no more than taking a first-tier idea and customising it for a second-tier industry. For example, how might consumer behaviour analytics apply to, say, dentistry? Or what is the analytical overlap, if any, between media and education? As the media industry increasingly customises what individuals want to be entertained by, can the same thinking be applied to how we learn?

We should not be constrained by an apparent hierarchy. Perhaps there are ideas and approaches submerged within second-tier industries that might comprise the salvation of some first-tier commerce?

It would be interesting to see what a Venn diagram might throw up in an exercise like this. Perhaps systems themselves might create their own equivalents of Venn diagrams, in the same way that they seem to have created the Interlingua language code to design a common language.

Won't second-tier players want to step up to the big league? Inevitably there will be movement of talent from first-tier innovators to second-tier. Perhaps this will result in some sort of levelling process in terms of innovation, implementation, and application. When compared to the maelstrom of first-tier expectations, won't second-tier industries, with less organisational politics, be more attractive to some forward-looking individuals?

Elsewhere we have considered first- and second-mover advantage. Perhaps migration of talent will result in second-tier industries moving up the ladder or even leapfrogging so-called market leaders in terms of thought leadership.

Naturally it hasn't been possible to cover all industries in this book, which perhaps only pays lip service to the wide spectrum of industries, professions, and jobs. But who would have dared or been able to write about all the consequences of the Industrial Revolution before the event?

It shouldn't be assumed that the industries that haven't been covered are third tier; their omission has simply been a matter of bandwidth. Similarly, although some industries are covered in more detail than others, this shouldn't be taken as indicative of the scale of innovation in each. Innovation seems to be happening everywhere, all the time, and in different measures.

Chapter 5 considers the issue of professions. We define professions as those jobs having recognisable qualifications. From the outset, readers are invited to consider capabilities rather than qualifications and experience, and should try to recognise that, like industries, almost all professions will be affected.

NOTES

1. Institution of Civil Engineers, Our mission and work. https://www.ice.org.uk/about-ice/who-runs-ice/our-mission-and-work (accessed 15 January 2018).
2. American Society of Civil Engineers, Historic landmarks. http://www.asce.org/Landmarks/#/e6ea0cd2d528ba2f3cdec3a624404fef (accessed 15 January 2018).
3. Institution of Civil Engineers (Great Britain), Minutes of Proceedings of the Institution of Civil Engineers. The Institution (1870), p. 215 note 1.
4. Engineering Professors Council, State of Engineering 2016 (2016). http://epc.ac.uk/state-of-engineering-2016
5. Mark Hansford, Time to evolve. *New Civil Engineer* (November 2016), pp. 22–24.
6. Stephen Smith, Will augmented reality in construction deliver on its promise? Institution of Civil Engineers(19 August 2016). https://www.ice.org.uk/disciplines-and-resources/briefing-sheet/augmented-reality-in-construction
7. Komatsu embarks on SMARTCONSTRUCTION: ICT solutions to construction job sites. Komatsu. Press release (20 January 2015). http://www.komatsu.com/CompanyInfo/press/2015012012283202481.html
8. Rachel Burger, 13 shocking construction injury statistics'. Capterra Construction Management blog. Previously published 4 November 2014 in *Construction Management*. http://blog.capterra.com/13-shocking-construction-injury-statistics
9. Health and Safety Statistics for the Construction Sector in Great Britain, 2017. UK Health and Safety Executive (November 2017). http://www.hse.gov.uk/statistics/industry/construction/construction.pdf
10. European comparisons. UK Health and Safety Executive. http://www.hse.gov.uk/statistics/european

11. Centre for Digital Built Britain, Welcome. Centre for Digital Built Britain, University of Cambridge. http://digital-built-britain.com
12. Margo Cole, Smarter skills. *New Civil Engineer* (2016), p. 30.
13. Robert Henson, Ready for anything. *New Civil Engineer* (December 2016), pp. 18–23.
14. Steve Nolan, The 'Big U' plan for flood protection in New York made to look like art installations. *Mail* Online (29 October 2013). http://www.dailymail.co.uk/news/article-2478834/The-Big-U-plan-flood-protection-New-York-look-like-art-installations.html
15. UK National Cyber Security Centre (n.d.), About us. https://www.ncsc.gov.uk/about-us
16. BBC, Warning of future UK power shortages. BBC.co.uk (17 October 2013). http://www.bbc.co.uk/news/business-24560196
17. Nick Harmsen, SA power: What is load shedding and why is it happening? ABC News (10 February 2017). http://www.abc.net.au/news/2017-02-09/sa-power-what-is-load-shedding-and-why-is-it-happening/8254508.
18. Helman, Christopher (2014). How can a nation awash in natural gas have shortages? And what to do about it. Forbes (8 February). https://www.forbes.com/sites/christopherhelman/2014/02/08/how-can-a-nation-awash-in-natural-gas-have-shortages-and-what-to-do-about-it/2/#5800ddcc77df
19. Michael Harrison, UK blames Europe for gas shortages. Independent.co.uk (22 November 2015). http://www.independent.co.uk/news/business/news/uk-blames-europe-for-gas-shortages-516358.html
20. Coping with Water Scarcity: Challenge of the Twenty-First Century. UN-Water, FAO (2007). http://www.fao.org/3/a-aq444e.pdf
21. Robert McKie, Why fresh water shortages will cause the next great global crisis. *The Observer* (8 March 2015). https://www.theguardian.com/environment/2015/mar/08/how-water-shortages-lead-food-crises-conflicts
22. Bill Sawyer, Modernising water infrastructure with asset management and analytics. Waterworld.com. http://www.waterworld.com/articles/uwm/articles/print/volume-4/issue-20/features/modernizing-water.html (accessed 18 October 2017).
23. Ruby Pratka, Water and sanitation in Africa. Worldpress.org (26 March 2012) http://www.worldpress.org/Africa/3897.cfm
24. Abhijit V. Banerjee and Esther Duflo, *Poor Economics: A Radical Rethinking of the Way to Fight Global* Poverty'. PublicAffairs; reprint edition (27 March 2012).
25. Heather Stewart, Public sector workforce 'will shrink to record low by 2017'. *The Guardian* (25 March 2012) https://www.theguardian.com/society/2012/mar/25/public-sector-workforce-shrink-record-low-2017
26. Claire Vanner, 5 of the worst IT system failures. Computer Business Review (14 January 2014). http://www.cbronline.com/news/verticals/cio-agenda/5-of-the-worst-it-system-failures-4159576/3
27. Hope Reece, Top 10 AI failures of 2016. TechRepublic.com (2 December 2016). http://www.techrepublic.com/article/top-10-ai-failures-of-2016
28. Donald Kennedy, Charles Craypo, and Mary Lehman, eds., Labor and Technology: Union Response to Changing Environments. Report (January 1982). https://www.researchgate.net/publication/234734199_Labor_and_Technology_Union_Response_to_Changing_Environments
29. Andrew Haldenby, AI will soon replace hundreds of thousands of public sector workers – and that's a good thing. *The Telegraph* (5 February 2017). http://www.telegraph.co.uk/news/2017/02/05/ai-will-soon-replace-hundreds-thousands-public-sector-workers
30. Sally M. Johnstone and Louis Soares, Principles for developing competency-based education programs. *Change* 46, no. 2 (2014): 12–19.
31. Beverly Park Woolf, AI and education: celebrating 30 years of marriage. College of Information and Computer Sciences, University of Massachusetts Amherst. *AIED 2015 Workshop Proceedings: Vol. 4.*

32. Barbara Kurshan, The future of artificial intelligence in education. *Forbes* (10 March 2016). https://www.forbes.com/sites/barbarakurshan/2016/03/10/the-future-of-artificial-intelligence-in-education/#2dfa068b2e4d

33. UK Department of Education, Destinations of key stage 4 and key stage 5 pupils: 2012. Official statistics. Gov.UK (November 2014).

34. Hannah Richardson, Oxbridge dominates list of leading UK people. BBC News (20 November 2012).

35. Mark Molloy, Real-life robocops will soon replace human police. *The Telegraph* (20 March 2017). http://www.telegraph.co.uk/technology/2017/03/20/real-life-robocops-will-soon-replace-human-police

36. Chris Baraniuk, Durham police AI to help with custody decisions. BBC.co.uk (10 May 2017). http://www.bbc.co.uk/news/technology-39857645

37. Julia Angwin, Jeff Larson, Surya Mattu, and Lauren Kirchner, Machine bias. ProPublica (23 May 2016). https://www.propublica.org/article/machine-bias-risk-assessments-in-criminal-sentencing

38. Rajib Ghosh, Taming the challenges in healthcare with artificial intelligence: a pragmatic approach. *Analytics*. http://analytics-magazine.org/taming-challenges-healthcare-artificial-intelligence-pragmatic-approach (accessed 28 August 2017).

39. Celine Ge, Alibaba, Tencent see AI as solution to China's acute shortage of doctors. *South China Post* (12 July 2017). http://www.scmp.com/business/china-business/article/2102371/alibaba-tencent-see-ai-solution-chinas-acute-shortage

40. Kathleen Kara Fitzpatrick, Alison Darcy, and Molly Vierhile, Delivering cognitive behavior therapy to young adults with symptoms of depression and anxiety using a fully automated conversational agent. *JMIR Mental Health* 42, no. 2 (2017): e19.

41. Alex Hudson, 'A robot is my friend': Can machines care for elderly? BBC.co.UK (16 November 2013). http://www.bbc.co.uk/news/technology-24949081

42. The coming global food shortage. EmergencyFoodSupply.com (20 April 2010). http://theemergencyfoodsupply.com/archives/the-coming-global-food-shortage

43. Joshua D. Woodard, Whole farm revenue protection (WFRP). Ag-Analytics (14 March 2017). https://www.ag-analytics.org/AgRiskManagement/Blog/WFRPBlog

44. Shreya Nair, What are some applications of AI in the field of agriculture? Quora.com (2 May 2017). https://www.quora.com/What-are-some-applications-of-AI-in-the-field-of-agriculture

45. Richard Waters, AI academic warns on brain drain to tech groups. *Financial Times* (22 November 2016).

46. IBM Developerworks, Global Entrepreneur. https://developer.ibm.com/startups/ (accessed 15 January 2018).

47. Chinese group Baidu supports start-ups in Brazil. MacauHub (29 September 2016). https://macauhub.com.mo/2016/09/29/chinese-group-baidu-supports-start-ups-in-brazil

48. UK Individual Shareholders Society (n.d.). 'Unprofitable companies – valuing unprofitable companies and companies not valued on profits'. Sharesoc.

49. Nick Carr, How many computers does the world need? Fewer than you think. *The Guardian* online (21 February 2008). https://www.theguardian.com/technology/2008/feb/21/computing.supercomputers

The Impact of AI on Professions

SUMMARY

In this chapter we will look more specifically at the impact of advanced analytics and AI on the professions. A profession is an occupation that requires a lengthy period of training and usually some form of qualification. It's sometimes also described as a vocation or a work-oriented commitment. The implication is that the function goes beyond work for simple remuneration and plays a part in sharing knowledge and information for the common good, such as through professional bodies, for example.

Often power and status are accorded to a profession. Prestige, elements of being elite, and especially the ability for self-direction are critical components. It's difficult to be certain about how many professions there are in the world; it certainly ranges in the hundreds. This chapter simply cannot cover all of them, but has sought to identify a few key ones, such as management, finance, law, and sales, amongst others, in an attempt to give examples of what the future might hold for all professions.

Readers who are members of a covered profession may wish to add to or edit the capabilities we've suggested will be needed for them. The main purpose of this chapter is that they should think about how changes will require them to reinvent themselves going forward. Hopefully those readers whose professions have not been included will discover some generic trends.

INTRODUCTION

Artificial intelligence and the use of cognitive analytics will not only change industries and professions, but will also affect the way that we all live. Some of these changes will be more dramatic than others. They may be sudden and relatively traumatic, as traditionally secure jobs are lost (which, in turn, may affect corporate careers and personal ambition). Other changes will be more gradual, and individuals will look backward and perhaps say, 'How did that happen?'

One thing that will be necessary to reappraise is the concept of *work*. It's an idea that's been around for a long time, and many of us define ourselves by the work we do, or perhaps used to do. It is natural, therefore, as we consider the impact of AI on professionals, that we also further consider the concept of work and how it has also changed. To some degree this has already been covered earlier in the text, so we'll try to avoid unnecessary repetition.

There's a danger that we view all work as being the same. Work can be manual, professional, or both. It can be paid or unpaid, but even without payment, isn't it still work? How might AI impact on unpaid (i.e. volunteer) work? As permanent paid work increasingly evaporates due to the pervasive impact of AI, won't volunteer work have more of an impact on our daily lives? Our own contribution to the community and how we look after our neighbors may also carry the label of work.

Many already describe this period of big data and analytics to be as significant an industrial shift as that that took place in the eras of steam, electricity, and hydrocarbons. Each of these eras created a paradigm shift in the way that work is undertaken. There's no reason to think that robotics and AI will not have as big an impact, if not bigger.

One question that we need to address is whether we will become victims of that change or if there are things that can be done to influence the direction of innovation. If we view ourselves as victims, then it's likely that we will look at AI in a negative light, rather than as a power for good. And if we simply take a back seat and bury our heads in the sand, allowing progress to happen to us, then won't we probably deserve what we might end up with?

On the other hand, if we see positive potential for AI and increased automation, and engage effectively in that debate, then don't we have the potential to become custodians of change? By gaining greater understanding not only into what it means to work but also what AI really means in the context of work, aren't we more likely to work more effectively with the new system?

WORK AND PROFESSIONS

'If it was fun, they would call it fun. It's not fun, so they call it work', as the saying goes. The nature of work has changed throughout the history of mankind. Things have always needed to be done to stay alive, and to feed and to protect ourselves from predators. But what do we mean by *work* in the context of our current understanding? Is there a distinction between doing things we want to do and things that we don't want to do? Craftspeople or artists who create a thing of beauty and sometimes usefulness are doing a particular kind of work. They take pleasure in their creativity, yet at the same time are able to benefit either in terms of barter or direct remuneration.

Some functions transcend work. Works of art by famous artists such as Caravaggio, Rembrandt, and Michelangelo are examples of the use of great skill and dexterity. Their works are creative in nature and have provided humanity with a lasting legacy, but in their time were often commissioned, that is to say, painted or created on demand, by their usually wealthy clients. They were originally items of work.

But it wasn't always like this. Manual labour has always sat alongside creativity. The ability to *create* has remained the domain of the wealthy, the gifted, and the exceptionally able. Who amongst a civilised population would prefer the plough to the paintbrush, the whip to the writing implement? And as conquest between nations and civilisations became increasingly the norm, the phenomenon of even talented people being committed to some degree of slavery, which normally comprised physical work, became progressively more common.

Even so, some skills remained important. More than that, they were critical. Individuals brought with them special abilities that were seldom shared except among a chosen few. The word *mystery* derives from the word *misterium*. It comes from the Latin word for *secrecy*, which typified the behaviour of the enigmatic guilds of tradesmen that dominated the city of London commercially, as elsewhere.[1] Such tradesmen, often with the title *freemen*, had a privileged status and were allowed to travel in safety. At the other end of the scale was the *villein*, the common villager, *a person of uncouth mind and manners*, which developed, over time, into the word *villain*. The *villein* was often also viewed as a sort of criminal who would carry out work of the lowest nature.

Work was not without politics and this overflowed into religion. The eventual emergence of Catholicism saw a future life that was predestined as a result of good deeds. On the other hand, Protestants saw their afterlife as being influenced by the amount of effort that they put into their chores. This is the core of many areas that have divided these two religions over many centuries, leading to great pain and persecution.

It now becomes important to roll the clock right up to modern (or at least comparatively modern) times. We conveniently bypass the Industrial Revolution, which, through steam, changed workers' status from cottage workers, who worked on a needs-must basis, to components of the industrial manufacturing process. In the new industrial age, clocking on became an essential component of the worker's life.

The Victorian work ethic exemplified by Andrew Carnegie and described in books such as *Up the Ladder*, amongst others, reassured the worker that fame and fortune could come to all those who were prepared to put in the effort.

Quotes by Carnegie such as 'Teamwork is the ability to work together toward a common vision. It is the fuel that allows common people to attain uncommon results' and 'The first man gets the oyster, the second man gets the shell',[2] feel as if they come more from modern-day self-learning books rather than from over a century ago. The Bill Gates of his day, Carnegie had amassed a fortune by the time of his death in 1919, and donated US$350 million (a massive amount by standards of those days) to funding libraries, education, and hospitals.

For those at the other end of the food chain, such as employees of the Pullman railway carriage factory, the impact of industrialisation led to worsening wages and, for many, ultimately strike action and dismissal.

It was a time of strife. The growing power of the unions increasingly led to a fragility of relationship between the employers and the employed. To add to this, the use of scientific approaches to the function of work continued to develop between the two world wars. The worker was being progressively viewed as a temperamental asset in the process, one to be nurtured and cared for, as indeed were the machines that they worked with.

Manufacturing became a complex and subtle interaction of material and human assets, and the role of management comprised the ability to get the most from both parts of the equation.

More detailed insights into the management of cost and productivity led to a greater understanding of the value of material and human assets. Manufacturers were anxious to offload their most expensive and least productive assets in the pursuit of additional profit. The use of modern analytics, such as financial performance-management tools, increasingly enabled employers to make such decisions with greater certainty.

At the helm of many of the companies undertaking reorganisation were so-called giants of industry, such as Jack Welch of GE. Their reputations and fortunes were built on their ability to identify what needed to be done to restore a business to profit, to guarantee the survival of a company, or to get it in good shape for acquisition. How might these leaders have operated in an AI environment? Might they defend change by saying, 'It has to be done, because the analytics tell us so!'?

One thing for certain is that the leaders of tomorrow will have no experience in managing industry in any of its forms in an AI/cognitive analytics era. One question to consider, however, is whether experience of this type will actually matter in the future.

It is becoming more common for executives to leave employees to run the company whilst they set the vision and strategy, avoiding the relative dirtiness of micromanagement. In his book *The Grand Strategist*, Mike Davison suggests that the main role of management is to 'manage the mission' by providing shared values and shared purposes.[3] By doing this and providing a framework for success, executives can, in effect, leave their employees to run the business themselves.

Henry Mintzberg offers a different viewpoint, suggesting that 'walking the floor' is a critical success factor for executives. In what is sometimes known as the paradox of Mintzberg, he says, 'Effective strategists are not people who abstract themselves from the daily detail, but who immerse themselves in it while being able to abstract the relevant messages from it.'[4]

Walking the floor becomes more difficult when the employee is a teleworker based at home and fitting his or her workday around other tasks. With the challenge of managing the individual, the technology, or both, managers have increasingly moved their focus to managing outcomes. As Richard Donkin puts it:

> If old style management becomes extinct, management itself will flourish, because it remains an organizational foundation of human society. Management wasn't invented. It has remained from the earliest times. Only the definition changes periodically. Work will remain in tomorrow's enterprise and will still need to be managed. But people will increasingly manage themselves.[5]

How will that apply to individual professions in a new era of AI? Perhaps self-management is the new big thing? Is management of oneself more and more likely to be one of the guiding principles of the portfolio worker, who instead of having a single loyalty to an organisation has a series of relationships with many potential employers?

The role of the interim manager or interim worker will be a more attractive one. These interim individuals normally have the ability to bring certain levels of knowledge or insight to the table beyond what is available from intelligent systems. These will be the true knowledge workers, as described by Peter Drucker. In an age of analytics and measurement, the paradox will be how it is realistically possible to measure their performance and contribution through normal performance management tools, other than as a broad contributor to output?

If, however, we then roll the clock forward and recognise that simple tasks can be done by robotics and automation, and that the role of the knowledge worker can be replaced by the cognitive features of true AI, what then is left?

- Is it really feasible for a system to be able to make decisions based on the experience of others rather than its own?

- Can experience be learned from gigabytes rather than through an apprenticeship or the school of hard knocks?
- What is the incentive for knowledge workers to willingly share their ideas and experience with the corporation or system if the corporation or society will ultimately repay them through job cuts?

Competition even in an AI era will inevitably remain, and knowledge will increasingly represent power. Commercial entities are already able to control sharing of knowledge as a result of restrictions and conditions placed on an employee's terms of employment. Despite these employment terms and conditions, knowledge sharing will still prevail. Is sharing likely to increasingly become unintentional, occurring through the impact of continuous mobility of staff, the effect of social media and the desire of individuals for media attention, or the ubiquitous impact of the Internet?

In his 1996 book *The Jobless Economy*, Michael Dunkerley considers the impact of technology on work of the future, questioning whether this will bring a future of 'opportunity and leisure, or misery and decline'.[6] It is curious to think that these issues were already being anticipated two decades ago – and perhaps half a decade or more before AI reared its head in regular practical use.

Dunkerley also refers to Pavlina's idea of *social drag*.[7] This is the inertia that attaches to all of us when we have undergone some sort of change but are still perceived by our peers as continuing to do what we always used to do.

In the context of the new era of AI, will we as individuals still be perceived as doing the same thing as before, but within a different operating framework? Perhaps the new, changed way of working will have rendered our old jobs, as we currently know them, as being obsolete. Of course, some functions will remain important – medicine, accountancy, engineering – but will the manner in which they are undertaken become unrecognisable to today's professionals?

In their report *The Future of Employment: How Susceptible are Jobs to Computerisation?*, the authors reviewed 702 jobs listed in the US federal government's Standard Occupational Classification system that they viewed as vulnerable. From this they concluded that '43% of US jobs are at risk'.[8]

They also identify a direct correlation between those at risk, the educational standards needed, and the wages paid for those roles. Additionally, they identify a 'hollowing out' of the job market, in which mid-market roles disappear but there is an increase in low-level manual work and high-end cognitive jobs.

Using probabilistic theory and algorithms, they map the likelihood of the propensity to computerise a role by adopting three variables:

1. The ability to perceive and manipulate (typically involving dexterity and the ability to work in cramped spaces)
2. Creative intelligence, including art and originality
3. Social intelligence, including the ability to negotiate.

A table of the most vulnerable professions (jobs, really) is included in Appendix B. The table reminds us, unsurprisingly, that the job of being a *dancer* is not one that is imaginably vulnerable to computerisation. It would be an especially hard job to persuade a ballerina, for example, that her profession was likely to be threatened by technology, but where do we draw the line? The news that a humanoid robot, YuMi, has conducted the Lucca Philharmonic and performed a concert of opera highlights with the world-famous classical singer Andrea Bocelli seems to be pushing some of the limits of both technology and creativity.[9]

How safe is any role or profession in the future? Perhaps that in itself is an idea worthy of further consideration, and which we will look at later in this book. Equally, who would fail to lose sleep at the thought of a robotic dentist?

THE IMPORTANCE OF COMPETENCES

Competences are often viewed as the capabilities that an individual brings to a particular job. They are the required personal attributes that an employee might need to utilise in a particular role to fulfil the job function.

In their book *The Value-Added Employee*, authors Cripe and Mansfield set out what they describe as being 31 'core competences', which overall can be grouped, or clustered, together to give common skill sets (see Table 12).

These competences, whilst valuable, are relatively generic. Individual professions usually will have to look for specific competences relative to their job outputs. For example, accountancy looks for numerical competence in particular.

As we consider employment in a new AI age, it's important to look at these in more detail with specific reference to job roles. The approach that has been taken is to consider existing competences or capabilities, and then to suggest what might be potential future needs of role holders.

In doing so, an assumption has been made that the role or profession as we currently know it will exist in the future. It rather depends on whether automation augments existing job functions or replaces them. For the purpose of this exercise, the former assumption – that of augmentation – has been adopted. This is the most likely, at least in the short-to-medium term.

THE MOREVEC PARADOX AND WHY IT THREATENS PROFESSIONALS

Hans Morevec was known not only for his work on robotics, AI, and futurism, but particularly for the fact that he was a transhumanist. Transhumanism (often abbreviated as h+, or H+) is described as an intellectual movement that focuses on the ability to transform the human condition through the use of advanced technologies.

The concept of transhumanism relates to both the ethical and realistic issues affecting the use of technology in the human environment. One of its leading lights was Iranian philosopher Fereidoun M. Esfandiary (1930–2000). He decided to rename himself RM-2030, firstly because he thought that he would live to be 100 years old (in fact he didn't make it, by a considerable margin) and secondly to break a naming convention that he viewed as a reflection of mankind's tribalistic past.

He seems to have been an intriguing character. An atheist and vegetarian, he said about his adopted name, '2030 will reflect a magical time. In 2030 we will be ageless and have the chance to live forever'. Rather than being buried or cremated, he was vitrified, which is a form of cryopreservation using rapidly cooling water. Will it be possible to discuss his ideas with him again later, personally, sometime in the future?[10]

TABLE 12 Core competences in the workplace.

Internal or external to business	Cluster	Competence
Internal to business	Dealing with people cluster	Leading others
		Providing motivational support
		Fostering teamwork
		Empowerment
		Management of change
		Developing others
		Managing performance
Internal to business	Communication and influencing cluster	Attention to communication
		Oral communication
		Written communication
		Persuasive communication
		Interpersonal
		Influencing others
		Building collaborative relationships
		Customer orientation
External to business	Preventing and solving problems cluster	Diagnostic and information gathering
		Analytical thinking
		Forward thinking
		Conceptual thinking
		Strategic thinking
		Technical expertise
External	Achieving results cluster	Initiative
		Entrepreneurism
		Foster innovation
		Results orientation
		Thoroughness
		Decisiveness
Self-management	Self-management cluster	Self-confidence
		Stress management
		Personal credibility
		Flexibility

Source: Edward J. Cripe and Robert S. Mansfield, *The Value-Added Employee*, 2nd ed. (Routledge, 2001). https://books.google.co.uk/books/about/The_Value_Added_Employee.html?id=z02znlfi4Y0C&redir_esc=y

Transhumanism is excitingly controversial. It considers the concept of the advanced super being who is somewhere between AI and normality. Within this difficult area are concepts such as:

- *Democratic transhumanisation.* How we apply transhumanism to the political structure.
- *Immortalisation.* Considering issues such as lifespan and how it can be extended.
- *Postgenderisation.* The breaking down of male/female segregation through technological advances.
- *Technogaianism.* How technology might become the solution to the problem of ecological imbalance.

These notions are not shared with readers with any intention of trying to influence them, but rather to draw attention to the very considerable degree of thought and discussion that has already taken place. Beyond these particular ideas we also shouldn't overlook the concept of technopaganism, which focuses on the spiritual side of technology.

The essence of the Morevec paradox is the discovery that, contrary to popular assumption, high-level thinking in the human brain actually requires relatively little computation. On the other hand, low-level skills, such as those of mobility and perception, which we carry out unconsciously, apparently require greater brain resources. This is explained by the idea that the brain's processes, or sensorimotors, that control unconscious actions have taken millions of years to evolve. As a result, they are much more complex in nature.

For scientists, this implies that what appears simple in humans may be very difficult to replicate in a machine.

The corollary is that actions that appear complex for a human may be easier for the computer to undertake. This has led to one roboticist, Rodney Brooks, to pursue a new line of thinking, which is that of building robots with the same level of intelligence as insects possess. His mantra is one of 'No cognition. Just sensing and action'.[11] It's an idea which has come to be known as *nouvelle AI*.

But we aren't insects. So, we now need to consider those tasks and professions that we personally consider to be complex by nature and how intelligent systems might change them and us. Naturally we can't cover every single profession in this compendium, but hopefully some generic issues and indicators will emerge.

MANAGEMENT

It's tempting to consider management a function rather than a profession, but those who study business would undoubtedly view it as a profession. After all, isn't the study of business models, strategy, and operations every bit as complex as finance or the law?

In the *Harvard Business Review* report 'How Artificial Intelligence Will Redefine Management', taken from a survey of 1,770 managers, the authors identified five likely key practices in the use of AI:

1. *Leave administration to AI.* This extends to the creation of management reports and systems for monitoring.
2. *Focus on management judgement.* They say the essence of good management is the application of organisational understanding and experience.

3. *Treat intelligent machines as colleagues.* This involves the ability to trust the output of the system.
4. *Work like a designer.* The manager should apply creativity and that of others to create integrated solutions.
5. *Develop social skill.* As the system frees managers up from time-consuming tasks that add little value, managers now have the time to develop their social skills.[12]

The Harvard report is bullish in its recommendations for implementation of AI systems. It suggests:

- The use of *exploration* in the early stages to help better understand how managers should work with AI
- Development of *new performance indicators* to drive adoption
- Building *new training and recruitment strategies.*

Immediately it appears that there are at least three other professions or functions that start to be drawn into the equation:

1. The analyst or creator of performance indicators and their systems, who will need to think about what might be the most appropriate indicators for usage.
2. The trainer or enablement team, who will need to understand how the individual will interact with the system and devise training schemes accordingly. This might be especially difficult in the early stages, as the trainers themselves will have either limited or no experience to rely on.
3. The recruiters (normally in the human resources department but possibly at intermediaries, such as recruitment agencies), who similarly will have no experience, and who may perhaps be looking for prospective candidates or recruits who equally may have limited or no experience.

A new set of management capabilities will need to emerge, even if built on traditional requirements. Overall, the role of management has always been difficult, as it continually balances the operational requirements of the business against the expectations of key stakeholders. This new paradigm inevitability will take difficulty to a new level. Management in the future will not be for the fainthearted (see Table 13).[13]

OFFICE OF FINANCE

The role of the chief finance officer (CFO) and his or her team has undergone significant change over the past two decades, transforming from being the accounting gatekeeper of the organisation to being the strategic financial advisor to the CEO. The CFO has even been described as being the copilot of the organisation.

In the future, typical business objectives that we recognise from today's working environment are likely to remain the same. Key objectives are unlikely to change:

- Make a profit
- Beat the competition
- Delight customers
- Satisfy stockholders.

Leading-edge companies no longer focus just on the cost of products. Rather, they need greater financial granularity, and they need to understand the cost of

TABLE 13 The new role of the manager.

Existing required competences	Additional competences required going forward
Proficiency in use of communication skills	Capable of being communicative, creative, transparent, and imaginative
Capable of understanding multioperational workforce trends	Ability to effectively understand the use of advanced analytical systems to measure performance, and to use intelligent systems to anticipate competing and threatening internal and external forces
Ability to produce high-level impact	Possessor of a strong personal brand that is reinforced by technology
Ability to focus on career development of employees	Ability to empower individuals and systems; capable of effective alignment of employee career development with intelligent systems
Ability to maximise leadership strengths	Collaborative leader with both humans and intelligent systems; able to work in a fast-moving and volatile business environment without personal emotional insecurity
Ability to advocate for organisational change	Entrepreneurial in nature, flexible, and able to deal with continual uncertainty and operational fluidity

process, products, geographies, segments, customers, and channels. Through micro-management CFOs are able to create macro-certainty within the business enterprise.

In addition to this, they need to create forecasts with increasing frequency and accuracy. In doing so, they ensure that the performance of the organisation remains aligned to strategy and, where necessary, that corrective action can be taken.

Much of the work done by the office of finance remains relatively straightforward, with a routine application of sets of rules in order to develop processes and create output. Beyond this, the office may identify outliers from available data and fix them if possible, or refer them to a human expert who perhaps has greater qualifications or experience.

As AI develops, the need for human intervention is likely to decrease. However, there are still going to be roles for those with relational, or interactive, skills that so far only humans seem to be able to undertake.[14]

Typical responsibilities of the CFO's office, and where automatic systems and AI might assist, are in the areas of:

- Financial accounting, where AI can help in the classification and measurement of financial instruments
- Calculation of loan loss allowances, for example, to optimise taxation
- Budgeting and planning, managing and reconciling the top-down, middle-out, bottom-up business processes
- Debtor follow-up, including sales outstanding and debt collection
- Reconciliation, or the use of advanced analytics and RegTech to help with regulatory risk requirements such as Basel, Solvency II, IFRS, and CoRep/FinRep.[15]

Part of the domain of the office of finance is the need to arrange for the auditing of publicly traded companies. These audits not only assure the accuracy of financial statements, but also identify insights into the performance of the company.

In its 2015 report *Audit of the Future*, reported in a CFO.com article 'Future Audits Must Do More: Survey', Deloitte identified the need for the use of advanced analytics to provide greater insight, and a need for the profession 'to expand outside the domain of historical financial statements'. The report also pointed out that 'whilst 70% of audit committee members ... say that the audit's adoption of innovative technology and process improvement keeps pace with their industries, only 45% of statement users agreed.'[16]

With Oxford researchers suggesting that nearly half of US jobs are open to automation within the next two decades, it is suggested that change will happen in two waves:

1. Firstly, vulnerable fields, such as administration, product manufacture and transportation (and also possibly some jobs in sales, services, and construction)
2. Secondly, management, science, engineering, and the arts.[17]

In the case of the former, the Oxford report suggests that 'low skill workers will reallocate to tasks that are non-susceptible to computerisation – i.e. tasks that require creative and social intelligence'.

This rather optimistic statement presupposes that there are enough creative and 'social' jobs around to compensate, and that those in vulnerable roles have both the ability and desire to change themselves as well as the nature of their work. In the office of finance, where administrative tasks are anything but creative (with creative accountancy being frowned on), this might seem like a tall order. We will consider personal reinvention later in this book.

With respect to whether finance can be completely automated, one need only look at the transformed behaviour of the trading floor, which once required humans to shout to gain attention. This has now become a workplace where ultrafast computers using advanced algorithms are the norm. In that environment, the speed of electronic communication has become a critical success factor, and milliseconds can mean the difference between profit and greater profit.

As one replaces human assets with computer assets, particularly those with learning abilities, CFOs will also need to figure out a way of valuing those computer assets on the books. Operational efficiencies may inevitably arise by sharing technologies with others, but as industries increasingly move towards a coexistence of machine and human, won't the metrics of valuation also start to change?

In the words of Professor John Boudreau of the Marshall School for Business, it will be necessary to look at the current and future spectrum of work and to 'deconstruct, automate, and reconstruct'.[18]

The impact of all these factors is beginning to further reinvent the role of the CFO; it is being made into one that places more emphasis on the CFO's expertise as subject matter expert (see Table 14).

LEGAL PROFESSION

Of the professions that are likely to be affected by the impact of AI, many might imagine that lawyers, judges, and the legal profession are probably right down at the bottom of the list – perhaps somewhere with dentists and ballet dancers.

This might not be the case. Computer experts at University College London (UCL) and the University of Sheffield think that already they can automatically identify the outcome of judgements in the European Court of Human Rights with 79% accuracy.

TABLE 14   The new role of the CFO.

Existing required competences	Additional competences required going forward
Ability to be an effective financial manager for the organisation	Able to act as an internal business partner to the organisation with particular expertise in financial and capital management
Capable of acting as financial gatekeeper in terms of cost control	Capable of being creative and entrepreneurial, using predictive and other advanced analytics to anticipate adverse operational costs that arise; promotes and manages mitigating actions
Capable of following business and regulatory rules and requirements; values compliance by nature; rules driven	Able to be a challenging agent provocateur and advocate of new relevant technologies (such as RegTech) that improve financial efficiencies and reduce risks at a lower cost
Ability to be an effective team leader, providing guidance and acting as a role model	Ability to personally partner with intelligent systems that are operating as robotic financial advisors

The European Court is an international court established in 1959 that focuses on whether one of the 47 states or countries that are party to the court have breached human rights in terms of civil or political rights. It was set up after World War II; its scope includes mistreatment of prisoners, discrimination, and abuse of civil rights. Consisting of 47 judges, one from each member country, over 13,000 cases have been referred to it. In a sample of 584 human-rights cases which invloved torture, the right to a fair trial, and privacy, an algorithm was able to establish the likely outcome of the trial with a 79% success rate.[19]

Some UK-based lawyers have already embraced this sort of technology by applying probability analysis as to whether they should take a case on or not. Certainly there's no reason why a decision to take a case, especially one funded through contingency fees (payment on success) should not be impacted by some sort of probability analysis. If lawyers reasonably think that there is no money to be made from pursuing an action on a contingency fee basis, it makes commercial sense for them to decline the case.

Similarly, parties to a legal action might also want to think harder about the strength of their commitment to pursuing the matter if an automated system gives an accurate indication of likely success or failure.

Perhaps the use of AI technology will increasingly take us down the route of lawyerless courts? The benefits of lawyerless courts are argued to be trials that will be paperless, speedier, and an extension of the existing virtual videoconference system. Those against the idea suggest (perhaps not unreasonably) that an automated legal system will only disadvantage the weakest.[20]

This approach opens the door for some fairly radical thinking. Certainly there might be advantages in terms of speed, but is that a reasonable exchange for justice? Will automation inevitably reduce cost, especially at the lower end, and, as a result, won't the legal system become more accessible for the poor? Perhaps computerisation is a fair trade-off if it improves accessibility, reduces costs, and avoids delays.

An automated legal system could have the capacity for some sort of appeals process. Equally interesting, could an automated or virtual lawyer gain greater insight into the attitude of plaintiffs through their online personalities and behaviour?

What does this mean for the trainee lawyer? There is an unattributed quote from a divorce lawyer involved in a case about the custody of a parrot who said, more or less, 'And I spent seven years in law school for this?' Whilst automated systems might increase the total amount of low-value, relatively low-importance litigations, does this matter if it frees up time for the more important cases?

Dr Nikolaos Aletras of UCL told UK newspaper the *Mirror*, 'We don't see AI replacing judges or lawyers, but we think they'd find it useful for rapidly identifying patterns in cases that lead to certain outcomes'.[21]

The timing of decisions also appears important. A 2011 article in the *Proceedings of the National Academy of Sciences* stated that 'experienced Israeli judges are substantially more generous in their rulings following a lunch break', suggesting that there is a good case for the use of AI to ensure impartial decisions.[22]

The downside is the issue of training. Don't junior lawyers need to whet their teeth on the small stuff? Isn't part of the training of any profession to be the bag carrier and to be left to deal with the simpler issues? Isn't it there that we all hone our styles, recognise our strengths and weaknesses, and ultimately become better professionals? Where do we start to draw the line? The UCL algorithm that predicts legal outcomes already appears to take into account moral considerations. Can morality be coded? Maybe it always has been, in some very subtle, nontechnological way.

In his 2008 blog post 'Core Competence: 6 new skills Now Required of Lawyers', Jordan Furlong, who describes himself as a legal futurist, introduces six additional competences for the 'new age'.[23] A decade later, these are worth revisiting. What we see is a profession that is not invulnerable to the impact of AI and augmentation. Why should they be any different from everyone else? (See Table 15.)

TABLE 15   The new role of the lawyer.

Existing required competences	Additional competences required going forward
Ability to have attention to detail	Ability to gather facts from big data ecosystem and to gain additional insights that would direct further lines of questioning
Ability to undertake logical reasoning	Capable of allowing robotic legal advisors to test the logical reasoning process or present alternative forms of reasoning
Capable of being persuasive at a personal level and able to effectively communicate in writing	Capable of understanding and effectively using omnichannel media methods
Capable of having sound judgement	Possessor of emotional intelligence used to augment robotic logical decision-making, and where appropriate to overrule it
Having knowledge of the law and analytical ability	Understanding and effectively using new relevant technologies, such as robotic legal advisors, which replace the need of the human to have full knowledge of the law, who will only need to know the basic principles
Holder of courtroom presence and high integrity	Open-minded approach to the use of data-driven insights and high ethical stance on the use of information

SALES AND MARKETING

The process of sales rests at the heart of commerce. Without sales there would be no business. Even if many view salespeople as 'coin operated', especially where commission is involved, it is still a noble profession of sorts. Distinct from sales but closely aligned, marketing is the process of promoting services or products, including market research and advertising.

The function of the salesperson is fundamentally to transfer ownership on terms that are satisfactory to both buyer and seller. At its best, the sales function collectively operates hand in hand with the marketing department to generate leads and then to convert them. Often organisations also use specialist third-party companies to generate leads.

Lead generation occurs through the use of databases, computer software systems, and Internet research to identify individuals, companies, and institutions. Increasingly, analytics are being used both to manage individual performance and also to create gamification models that provide some internal competition between employees. The lead-generation business claims to be ethically oriented, in that it frowns on the use of spyware, or trojans, to identify contact details. Mass blanket e-mailing is also usually viewed as being a blunt instrument and can even result in organisations being blacklisted.

The compensation of salespeople is often heavily commission driven. Their targets are usually aligned to the business revenue targets of the company, the division, the department, or all three. Traditionally, salespeople have been asked to create a pipeline of potential revenue with a multiplier of perhaps five times, a standard that assumes only one-in-five leads will eventually result in a sale. The process of sales qualification is used to ensure that there is a match between the needs of the client and the sales opportunity. Effective sales qualification avoids time-wasting and misleading internal information about what might be signed by the end of the accounting period, for example.

It follows that effective marketing, lead generation, and sales qualification are critical success factors in the sales process. It is, however, a changing world. With over 40% of sales already being conducted online without human intervention, the opportunity for face-to-face intervention is increasingly reduced. Beyond this, purchasers are becoming much more knowledgeable in understanding what they want, and usually how and when they want it. They also know the pressures that salespeople are under to hit revenue targets by key dates and use this information to secure the lowest possible price. Sales is not for the fainthearted.

Technology is increasingly helping the sales process. Many organisations are relatively public in their strategic comments, and often state their strategic or tactical objectives. These objectives might include the level of customer growth or the extent of branch closures. Intelligent software that analyses these public statements is already being used to align customer need with vendor capability. In doing so, the lead qualification process is improved by creating what are described as warm leads for the sales team.

Whilst some technology vendors describe this as adding AI to the process, this is more a matter of the use of advanced analytics, and is yet again an example of the use of a misnomer or buzzword. A decade ago, every new service was being described as a solution. Nowadays, advanced analytics is often being described as AI, which manifestly it isn't.

TABLE 16   The new role of sales.

Existing required competences	Additional competences required going forward
Ability to effectively communicate	Ability to develop a personal brand that adequately distinguishes the human salesperson from the intelligent sales system
Respond efficiently to the role's reward system (e.g., the sales commission structure)	Ability to cowork effectively with intelligent systems, helping the system to self-learn and be capable of closing small deals, whilst the human salesperson focuses on large, complex, and high-value transactions
Ability to act fairly towards the customer	Ability to increasingly be the customer's friend, whilst working in a highly regulated environment
Capable of acting opportunistically	Ability to work not only in a systematic way with robot-generated hot leads, but also bringing creativity to the sales process (when this cannot be done by the intelligent system itself)

The sales process is, however, still firmly rooted in services and products. In his book *Re-Imagine!*, Tom Peters invites us to reinvent selling as the creation of experiences. He suggests that companies such as Starbucks no longer simply sell coffee, but rather create a coffee experience. He also restates the importance of brand association as a wrapper for such experiences, which yet again is a reminder of the close association between sales and marketing.[24]

What, then, will be the impact of AI on the sales process? At the very least, the salesperson increasingly needs to become the trusted advisor to the purchaser instead of being just the beneficiary of commission payments. This will require greater understanding and empathy, but how will AI influence this process?

Chris Engman suggests at least in three ways:

1. More effective lead generation
2. Better alignment between opportunity and talent management
3. Improvement of trust (coupled with reduction of risk).[25]

The summary considers new capability sets that will be needed going forward by salespeople (see Table 16).

Similarly, marketing experts, as the other side of the coin, will need to develop new capabilities that are even more technologically oriented, especially as they are likely to be more greatly affected by the AI agenda.

The marketing role is also likely to be increasingly affected by working conditions and also by the progression of the marketing industry towards technological (in the case of marketing, digital) management of the customer. Above all, this is an area that must firmly recognise its own importance in the value chain of success, in particularly challenging times, and rise to it (see Table 17).

RETAILERS

The retail industry has close associations with the sales and marketing roles. The future of retailing is likely to be gradually transformed by artificial systems coming

TABLE 17   The new role of marketing.

Existing required competences	Additional competences required going forward
Effectively use interpersonal skills and operate collaboratively as part of a wider human team	Able to work with an intelligent system that is their closest operational business partner within the enterprise
Able to apply creativity and innovation in marketing campaigns	Capable of effectively applying advanced digital marketing techniques in creative and innovative ways
Ability to use mainly basic technologies, but able to work with other experts, such as programmers and data analysts	Ability to have technology as a core competence, using advanced systems to help customise and personalise marketing offers in an automated environment
Commercial awareness of the products being marketed, the marketplace, and the competitive environment	Capable of understanding and optimising the new role of marketing, which comprises human and robotic interaction, within the overall value chain of the business

to understand human emotions. Apple's research paper on studying human expressions considers the use of 'emotient technology' to help advertisers assess the reactions of viewers to their advertisements and to check the reactions of buyers on the products in its stores. The technology helps retailers understand the emotion or sentiment of a consumer by using a head-mounted camera to understand how the customer is reacting and to tailor their sales techniques accordingly.[26]

> *It is aimed at identifying and tracking the seven expressions of primary emotion ... such as joy, surprise, sadness, anger, fear, disgust, and contempt, as well as overall sentiments like positive, negative, and neutral.*[27]

The use of this technology inevitably stretches beyond retail into patient care (to help doctors to understand the pain of patients who cannot communicate), into law enforcement, and perhaps even into marital fidelity. In being able to understand and interpret emotions from both verbal intonation and facial expression, it also allows experts to get one step closer to replicating these functions in a machine environment.

Beyond such emotional alignment, the future of the retail space or shopping mall is inevitably being drawn into question. Over the past few decades, the shopping mall has been extended from a place of shopping into a place of experiences (aka the shopping experience). Experts such as McKinsey suggest the future of the shopping mall will be defined by the following factors:

- Differentiating the consumer offering, with a focus on experience and convenience. This includes the integration of new activities, such as recreation, local produce, and fine dining, into the traditional shopping environment, as well as creating a 'sense of the unexpected'.
- Transforming mall activity by leveraging technology, especially by digitally engaging with customers before, during, and after the customer visit.
- Exploration of new formats of the physical space, for example, by creating new ambient environments such as trees and gardens, and managing the site more like content and media rather than a collection of shops.

The implication for retailers is that of the arising necessity to develop and extend digital capabilities, including the creation of 'customer experience teams'. Managers of retail malls need to consider themselves not as retail brokers, but rather 'customer-facing providers of shoppable entertainment'.[28]

Artificial intelligence's pervasive influence will infuse retail site design and management by tapping into customer data, gaining better understanding into how the customer interacts with the retailer, and predicting consumer behaviour to help better manage stock inventory. The mood is increasingly one of delivering a highly personalised service to the consumer in a more enjoyable shopping place.

In a 2017 survey of UK retailers, nearly half surveyed said that they were already using a form of AI to understand customer behaviour and to predict demand. (Purists would again suggest that this is not AI but rather advanced analytics, with little evidence of actual machine learning.) The survey by analysts Qubit showed it used in:

- Driving of sales and anticipation of demand (50%)
- Understanding of consumer behaviour (46%)
- Targeting offers and promotions (46%)
- Targeting on customer segments (46%)
- Assessing competition (46%).[29]

At a more domestic level, the escalation in digital shopping is disrupting the traditional shopping experience in the area of groceries and essentials. People are already asking whether or not the traditional grocery store will die. The reality is that, at least at the moment, consumers are using online purchasing as a matter of convenience. This seems to suggest that online grocery providers haven't really got their heads around the ability to create adequately focused promotions to individuals and segments, and haven't figured out that their real ambition should be one of creating 'total household satisfaction.'[30]

The intelligent refrigerator may already exist in practice and is perhaps one of the closest things we have to AI in the kitchen. Smart fridges scan food barcodes, add content by voice recognition, and monitor content and reorder online when stocks are down, but to date they haven't really taken off in terms of usage. It's clear that the technology is available but that effective distribution partnerships may not yet have been created and that the consumer hasn't been converted. Smart fridges seem to be the ultimate in consumer convenience, and for the food retailer they seem to give a virtually guaranteed distribution channel to a household. What is there not to love in such a concept? But as some people might say, 'Who wants to talk to the fridge anyway?'[31]

With the focus remaining on maintaining and increasing sales, many of the key imperatives of the retailing profession will remain but will become increasingly digitalised going forward (see Table 18).

COMMERCIAL MEDIA

Elsewhere we have emphasised the likely importance of advanced analytics and AI to create better interlock with the customer through more focused marketing. Much of this will be online.

TABLE 18   The new role of the retailer.

Existing required competences	Additional competences required going forward
Ability to gain share of real growth by understanding where the growth opportunity is	Able to use advanced analytics to improve understanding of existing and new markets and proactively take action using intelligent systems to improve growth
Ability to gain a share of the customer's decision-making – how to get the customer into the store?	Able to support the growth of providing customised, highly personalised offerings, coupled with better online virtualisation of the shopping experience and increased expertise in store location optimisation
Ability to gain a share of customers' wallets – how to get them to spend money?	Improved alignment of retail opportunity with predicted consumer disposable income through use of contextual analytics, greater use of unstructured data, and behavioural manipulation
Ability to gain a share of the solution by broadening the depth and value of the relationship with the customer	Continually implement brand reinvention or brand reinforcement through trusted brand extensions and creation of new digital strategies
Ability to gain greater customer engagement – how to get the customer to care more about the retailer's business?	Able to promote an increased ethical orientation of brand, including greater active social awareness and interaction through empathy, gaming, and other digital interaction

Creative Arts

It is intriguing to try to place the creative arts within a competence framework. This has been done in a project called Training Requirements and Key Skills for Artists and Creative Practitioners to Work in Participatory Settings. Key competences were suggested within a framework of creativity of children and young people by the International Foundation for Creative Learning – an organisation that focuses on unlocking the creativity of children in and out of education. It's probable that these competences can also be potentially stretched into the commercial creative environment.

Key competences were identified as:

- Artistic and creative practice
- Organisational ability
- Working with others
- Face-to-face delivery and facilitation
- Reflection and evaluation.[32]

Artistic producers have a role in bringing together individuals and institutions, but what of the artists themselves? In the book *Training Artists for Innovation: Competencies for New Contexts*, the authors suggest that artists 'offer contradiction, as well as confrontation and friction, and they provoke new ideas'.[33] Doesn't this seem to be the right thinking for our disruptive age? Certainly there is evidence that computers have the ability to be creative, but can they also be provocative? To what degree can a robotic solution create such a provocative environment?

TABLE 19 The new role of the creative artist.

Existing required competences	Additional competences required going forward
Understanding of the needs of commercial organisations in terms of the need for creativity in the context of innovation and business growth	Possessing deeper understanding of the added value of creative media, including the use of creative intelligent systems in the commercial environment, by identifying and applying key metrics and then measuring improvement
Understanding and recognition of societal changes and how these impact on customer behaviour	Use of social media, sentiment, and contextual analytics to create a composite understanding of the customers at a granular level, and from this optimising the impact of creative arts in a commercial setting
Able to design new spaces of relationship beyond traditional interactions	Personalise the relationship by aligning creative marketing and selling with behavioural traits of consumers, and by using intelligent systems to understand and apply spatial and dimensional analytics, gaming concepts, and improvements to the creative innovation process
Capable of matching organisations with creative artists in order to optimise creative value	Ability to implement intelligent talent management processes as far as they apply to creative arts by aligning skill with commercial client need, and to further leverage the creative capabilities of intelligent systems

Source: Adapted with changes from Anna Grzelec, Artists in Organisations – Mapping of European Producers of Artistic Interventions in Organisations. *Creative Clash* (March 2013). http://www.nck.pl/upload/attachments/302579/Creative_Clash_Mapping_2013_GrzelecPrata4.pdf (accessed 12 January 2018).

At a time when creativity will become all the more critical in capturing mindshare through the use of innovation, Table 19 considers the roles and capabilities of the creative profession. Existing required competences are based on existing text by 'Creative Clash' (referenced in Table 19).

Publishing

In the context of media, it is important also to consider the role of the publisher, whose primary function is as a sort of gatekeeper or curator of knowledge. Extending this, if AI is going to depend on sources of information, then the publishing industry is likely to provide some of that input, which may be in an either digital or hard copy form.

We shouldn't underestimate the importance of the publishing industry in this context going forward. Although there is a natural tendency to suggest that everything will become digital, humans at least still appreciate the familiarity of the printed medium, even if artificial systems do not.

The role of the publisher is to commission or create quality content for technical, scientific, and educational reasons across multiple industries. The process by which this is done usually requires specific industry insights. Publishing, as all sectors of business are, is a commercial activity, and publishers need to understand their marketplaces and the financial opportunity that exists. Electronic books appear to provide an opportunity for the publishing industry to revitalise itself, but there is always a need to create content.

Whilst different from the book industry, newspaper publishers are also working hard to understand the relevance of the published word in a digital age. There seems to be a cannibalisation effect between the printed word and the digital version. In any event, many online newspapers still depend on the printed version for content. Although online newspapers have increased in popularity, there's evidence to suggest that if readers need to pay for news, they are more likely to prefer the printed version.

In terms of publishing in an AI future, the question is really whether digital versions of publications exist to complement the printed version or to replace them. Sceptics may suggest that, at the end of the day, digital versions are just a way of reducing cost and therefore maximising publishers' profits. On the other hand, digitalisation of information allows much greater customisation of information. Elsewhere, under the topic of education, we considered how in the future education will also become more personalised, and there is no reason why the publishing industry should not follow some sort of similar trend.

With questions arising as to whether production is still a core competence of the publishing industry,[34] there's a possibility that publishers will increasingly need to rework their business models (see Figure 7) and focus solely on providing vision, values, and financial management. It's a model that is likely to be replicated in other industries (see Table 20).

In what traditionally seems a linear process, the alternative of a new defragmented model appears not only likely but also probable as we approach the AI age. As the notion of personalisation becomes more prominent, a more automated approach may also start to emerge.

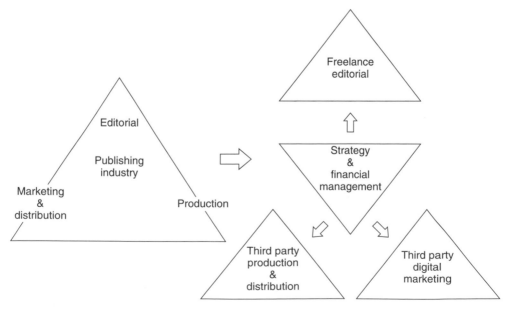

FIGURE 7   Defragmentation of publishing.

TABLE 20　The new role of the publisher.

Existing required competences	Additional competences required going forward
Ability to effectively undertake the editorial function, comprising commissioning, creating quality content, and author liaison, for example	Ability to provide greater customisation of editorial content, focusing on customer needs and through increased automation of commissioning and author liaison processes; use of advanced analytics and intelligent systems to predict trends and burning platforms for timely content creation, and to align content to personal needs of consumers
Capable of carrying out the function of media production, including formatting and specification of work, for example	Able to create multichannel media, providing information on demand through use of higher levels of automation; effectively use of intelligent apps to translate text to voice and vice versa, for example
Effectively carry out the marketing function, including promotion, publicity, sales, and distribution	Able to develop an increasingly personalised and customised approach to marketing, including the use of digitally targeted marketing strategies; ability to create new publishing business models that optimise the advantages of intelligent systems

TRANSPORTATION

As we consider this new era of AI and data, and perhaps get excited or worried about change, we often overlook a major transformation that is already happening beneath our noses: that of transportation. We have considered autonomous cars elsewhere and this can also be readily extended to autonomous trucks. In this sector we will also think about other autonomous means of transport.

The Digital Railway

Earlier we considered the possible emergence of the railway system as a viable alternative to air carriers in terms of cost, reliability, and also proximity to key locations, such as city centres. The digital railway, and more particularly, digital signaling, are already being viewed as key catalysts in the improvement of the railway system's reliability, timetabling, and efficiency – all without building new track. In the United Kingdom, the capacity increase in the South West corridor from allowing trains to travel closer together is estimated at a 40% improvement.[35]

The technology is already proven. The European Train Control System (ETCS) already allows trains to run closer together and operate at the best speed. This requirement, which deals with the standardisation of in-cabin train controls, arose following recognition in the mid 1980s that there were 14 national train standards across Europe. There was a need to provide a capability that would allow inter-European trains to pick up track information electronically, rather than relying on visual trackside signals. In fact, the coordinating body European Railway Traffic Management System says that the systems are safer, as traditional signals involving lighting cannot be accurately interpreted at speeds of greater than 350 kilometres per hour.

ETCS is part of a wider European train framework that forms part of the European Train Management System (ETMS), which in addition to ETCS also includes GSM-R, the Global System for Mobile Communication standard for railways. ETMS equipment can be categorised into onboard equipment, and trackside/infrastructure equipment.

Although the key imperative for change has been that of allowing trains to travel across boundaries without stopping, it also aims to improve energy consumption and reduce noise levels, and make the rail sector more competitive when compared to roads.

Beyond these tools, train drivers also have the Connected Driver Advisory System. This collects real-time data from a huge range of sources to calculate the ideal speed of the train to help ensure it arrives exactly on time. Automatic Train Operation, linked to Automatic Train Control and Automatic Train Protection, jointly ensure that trains operate within their timetables. Most systems elect to have a human operator as a fail-safe in case of emergencies.

The rail industry in its many forms is undergoing a significant revolution. Aging tram systems in cities are being replaced with modern tramway and metro systems. These are potentially contentious areas for the railway industry. As other industries increasingly will need to come to terms with automation, including autonomous trucking and remote passenger flights, it will be increasingly difficult for the heavily unionised rail industry to maintain its traditional stance by resisting robotic train management. Their only bargaining card seems to be one of safety, but this is perhaps becoming of limited value, especially because manned trams have been found to be subject to human error. When a manned tram allows the driver to fall asleep at a speed of 40 miles per hour, resulting in seven deaths and multiple injuries (as in the case in Croydon in 2016), this argument no longer holds water.[36] According to UK Network rail head of digital railways David Waboso, 'You've got to be understanding of what makes people nervous. This involves some changes to the industry – to the roles and to the skills.... Let's build a new skillset, a new digital skillset'.[37]

Futurists such as Sarwant Singh herald a new era of high-speed rail,[38] reminding us of the march towards continental and intercontinental rail travel now evident in many countries, such as TGV in France, HS2 in the United Kingdom, and the so-called bullet train in Japan, as well as the rapid expansion of high-speed Chinese railways, which is seen as an important contributor to Chinese GDP. Some suggest that China is set to become the world leader in rail construction. By comparison, despite being one of the world's most influential countries, US high-speed trains seem to be well behind the curve in terms of development.

With robotics already being contemplated for the design and construction of rolling stock by companies such as ABB, it seems only a matter of time before we also have driverless trains. Robotic customer service advisors will also be created, who will be able to tell you on which platform and at what time your train will leave. Perhaps union pressures will continue to exert resistance to change, but will they succeed? One guess is that the guard is likely to remain on some services, alongside the human-managed buffet car, at least for the foreseeable future.

Autonomous Flight and Virtual Pilots

Whilst we often think in terms of drones, or unmanned aerial devices, when we think of unmanned flight comprising, these devices are often remotely controlled and are not autonomous in their true nature. Yet today, many planes are of such complexity as to be virtually autonomous, or very close to it. The use of robotic assistants, such as ALIAS (Aircrew Labour In-Cockpit Automation System), are being tested in planes and helicopters, especially in the area of human–system interaction.[39]

TABLE 21 Future competences for pilots.

Existing required competences	Additional competences required going forward
Able to effectively manage manual and automatic flight systems (i.e. to fly the plane)	Ability to operate as human backup to mainly automated and robotic systems, from either inside or outside the plane
Able to demonstrate leadership and team building	Capable of regaining or retaining control or perceived control of aircraft (in the eyes of the passengers), even if acting in a virtual capacity and not actually inside the aircraft itself
Ability to have situational awareness, solve problems, and be an effective decision maker	Able to have appropriate experience, obtained through regular training and scenario modelling in simulated conditions, and to be able to apply mitigating actions where there are problems
Ability to correctly apply procedures	Ability to cowork with robotic pilots so that both of them comply with greater levels of regulations, including ethical protocols, taking into account the impact of new regulations that will inevitably need to be created

Source: Adapted with changes from Viktor Robeck, IATA Training and Qualification Initiative (ITQI) – a total system approach to training. European Airline Training Symposium, Berlin. 2012. https://www.halldale.com/files/halldale/attachments/Robeck.pdf

How will this affect pilots? Table 21 considers the competences needed to be a pilot in the future. Existing required competences are loosely taken from the International Air Transport Association's Training and Qualification Initiative, referenced in Table 21.

Will there be significant differences in competence levels needed for pilots of passenger aircraft, commercial aircraft, and miltary aircraft? Pilots are expensive: the cost of training can be £100,000 and the annual salary of a short-haul pilot can be as much as £100,000. With analytics and AI increasingly focusing on the business drivers of change, alternatives to the human cost of piloting a plane look commercially attractive for airlines.

The reality, though, is how confident would we be as fare-paying passengers in knowing that there was nobody sitting at the front of the plane holding the controls? What if the pilot wasn't actually sitting in the plane itself, but somewhere completely different?

Air Traffic Controller

Perhaps our confidence towards robotic pilots might also be affected by our confidence in air traffic control. After all, aren't the takeoff and landing processes potentially the most hazardous activities in the process of flight?

With regard to air traffic controllers, there is increasingly a move towards virtual management, even if some degree of human intervention remains. For example, in 2019 London City Airport is to become the UK's first airport without a manned control tower, as eagle-eyed, locally based controllers are replaced with a mast with sensors and cameras.

By agreement with the National Air Traffic Control Services (NATS), London City will capture 360-degree information 'in a level of detail greater than the human eye', which will be relayed to a national control centre in Swanage over 130 miles away. The intention overall is to use the UK's pool of over 2,000 controllers to manage movement in multiple airports using virtual images. In doing so, the costs of managing air traffic will be reduced by 20–30%.

Many countries are already testing these technologies. At the time of print, trials are under way in Australia, Hungary, France, Ireland, Germany, Switzerland, France, and the United States. The pioneers of this approach were in Scandinavia, where remote airports with only one or two flights per day could not justify full-time air traffic controllers. The first use of virtual control was at Örnsköldsvik airport in April 2015, followed by Sundsvall in 2016. Take-up since then appears to have been rapid, despite the view that this is a technology for small airports only.

As Steve Anderson, head of airport transformation at NATS puts it:

Yes there are clear benefits for smaller airfields, absolutely. Economies of scale, the ability to control multiple airports from one location, that's all true, but I think it's a total misconception that digital towers are only suitable for airports of low complexity and low ATM [air traffic management] volume. Frankly, that's just lazy thinking.[40]

Whilst virtual air traffic control is still dependent on humans, these humans are located some distance away from the point of action, and their services are heavily supported by technology. It seems quite plausible for intelligent systems to directly interact with aircraft and to perform with increasingly less human intervention.

ENGINEERS AND THE BUILT ENVIRONMENT

Elsewhere we have considered the construction industry and the likely AI-infused changes that will take place, but what do these mean for the engineer at a personal level? The term *engineer* is wide ranging, and there are many subsectors of the profession, such as civil engineers, mechanical engineers, chemical engineers, and even software engineers. It's likely that some generic change requirements for the future might apply to this wide-ranging community, estimated to range between three and five million professionals worldwide. All engineers seem to have relatively common competences, typically:

- Applying engineering knowledge, methods, and techniques
- Using engineering tools, equipment, and technology
- Protecting the public interest
- Managing engineering activities
- Communicating engineering information
- Working collaboratively in the environment
- Maintaining and enhancing engineering skills and knowledge.[41]

Building Engineers

Looking specifically at the profession of building engineers, who focus on construction and the built environment, industry bodies can start to apply these generic requirements

TABLE 22 Future competences for building engineers.

Existing required competences	Additional competences required going forward
Ability to apply general and specific knowledge of engineering techniques	Acquisition of specific knowledge of data-driven solutions to solve construction problems, for example, using predictive analytics to anticipate machine breakdown
Able to understand and apply theoretical and practical methods of design and construction	Ability to identify where intelligent data-driven solutions can be used, including the use of robotics in hazardous work, intelligent site control, and predictive weather data
Demonstration of technical and organisational skills	Effective engagement with robotic systems that augment traditional technical skills, such as the design of steelwork; work with employee management systems to improve productivity, reduce downtime, and avoid accidents
Ability to exhibit a personal commitment to maintaining professional standards	Skilled industry ambassador, effective communicator, and upholder of data ethics

Source: Adapted with changes from Engineers Canada, Core engineering competencies. Engineers Canada (27 November 2012). https://engineerscanada.ca/sites/default/files/w_Competencies_and_Feedback.pdf

with a more functional lens (see Table 22). Existing required competences are loosely taken from Engineers Canada, referenced in Table 22.

Building Planners

Beyond the specific role of construction, there are many professionals who sit in the relative background and whose jobs will also be transformed going forward. As we retain our focus on construction, let's look at the profession of building planners. Building planners play a critical role in the design and development of places that we live and work in. The work they do not only needs to align to national and local policies, but also to create places that inspire. Additionally, they create spaces that support economic prosperity, reduce crime, and tackle climate change.

Not only do they need to think about the existing environment, but from time to time they even have the chance to create new towns and cities on a white piece of paper. The design of the city of the future is likely to rest in their hands to a large extent.

Increasingly, the move towards urbanisation will put bigger strains on resources. Cities today are notoriously inefficient and it will be a mammoth task to improve that situation. The future of cities will bring a complex interlock of:

- More effective infrastructure
- Better management of transportation and congestion
- Better management of energy, pollution, and waste
- Utilities management
- Improved crime and policing
- Other factors.

Underpinning all these will be effective financial management of the city, from controlling cost to collecting money from the citizen. Independently, these are all tricky

TABLE 23   Future competences for building planners.

Existing required competences	Additional competences required going forward
Ability to undertake core planning and plan making, and using evidential and evaluation skills.	Able to work with systems which integrate structured and unstructured information, and from these to obtain actionable insight for planning and plan making.
Capable of planning for sustainable development, environment and climate change, with communities and neighborhoods, services and infrastructure.	Understand, apply and be an advocate for new relevant technologies such as predictive analysis to anticipate future climate changes, for example; effective user of advanced visualisation tools such as augmented reality to improve communication with key stakeholders.
Ability to have effective communication and engagement skills.	Ability to gain insight from, and to leverage, social media and sentiment analytics, and apply multichannel engagement strategies with key stakeholders.
Able to apply of specialist personal skills such as archaeological or rural expertise.	Able to work collaboratively with intelligent systems where specific data is domained, such as in specialist archeological records, and to operate at a cross-industry level.

Source: Adapted with changes from Local Government Association, The national competency framework for planners. Local Government Association. https://www.local.gov.uk/national-competency-framework-planners (accessed 15 January 2018).

operations. Collectively, they comprise a level of complexity that not only is beyond human management but lends itself to more intelligent systems. The notion of the *smart city* has been around for a while, but in reality we have only touched the surface of the problem. In many cases only point solutions have been provided, rather than an integrated viewpoint.

The need for smart cities will inevitably result in entirely new professions emerging, in which individuals are able to personally integrate with advanced systems for maximum effectiveness. It's uncertain where these new professions will emerge from, but perhaps the planning industry may be one option. Table 23 builds on the current capabilities of building planners and looks forward to the future. Existing required competences are loosely based on the references shown in Table 23.

MEDICAL PROFESSION

In Chapter 4, the healthcare industry was considered. Like many industries there are many parts to the equation. Whilst general practitioners, dentists, and health specialists are viewed as being at the tip of the spear, the medical profession as a whole is an industry that comprises a huge ecosystem.

Healthcare is already one of the industries that is at the forefront of the use of advanced analytical systems, sometimes loosely described as AI, as a result of industry imperatives to provide effective patient support at a time of rising cost.

Let's look at three examples of professions in the healthcare system and speculate what the future might look like for them in an AI-infused healthcare environment.

General Practitioners

The general practitioner, or GP, provides a wide range of services including advice on health problems, vaccinations, examinations and treatment, prescriptions for medicines, referrals to other health services, and social services.[42] It's a demanding task, especially when they are faced with perfectly healthy people insisting that they need to see their doctors along with those who are unwell and suffering. These pressures can lead doctors to experience both personal stress and burnout.[43]

The problem becomes more acute as a result of the aging population and urbanisation, and increasingly the profession is turning to robotic assistance to help with triage and medical decision-making. Based on the Royal College of General Practicioner's assessment of essential competences, what might the required competences of a GP in the future look like? Will there be different considerations and capabilities needed for private versus public-sector patients? (See Table 24.) Existing required competences are loosely based on the reference shown in Table 24.

Part of the solution may rest in better healthcare, where AI and robotics may have impact in our day-to-day living. A talking robot called ElliQ, designed by Intuition Robotics, is described as being one of the most advanced companion robots. ElliQ conveys emotion through different speech tones, lights, and body language. The robot chats with the elderly and suggests activities such as reading, walking, playing games, and phoning friends and family. The aim is to prevent older people from feeling socially isolated and to keep them connected to friends and family.[44]

Dentists

The idea of robotic dentists will send a shiver down the spine of most people. Whilst this is a profession amongst those less likely to be affected by automation, they will, however, not go entirely unscathed in terms of the analytics era. Based on current assessment of competence by the American Dental Education Association, what might future competences need to be? (See Table 25.) Existing required competences are loosely based on the reference shown in Table 25.

Is it possible that analytics will lead to greater intervention in dietary advice, a move from reactive dentistry to proactive dentistry? For example, the use of dental sealants or coatings as a preventive measure has been seen to significantly reduce the degree of tooth decay. There is a strong link between dentistry and medical (or dental) insurance. Analytical advances by insurers will invariably start to influence dental practices.

Neurosurgeons

At the other end of the medical spectrum, the highly complex profession of neurosurgery, or surgery of the brain, is also in the frame. As we consider how to replicate the human brain in machines, it may be that machines themselves can help neuroscientists gain a better understanding of the brain itself. The functional MRI (fMRI) scan has only been around for about 25 years and is still regarded by many as being at an

TABLE 24   Future competences for general practitioners.

Existing required competences	Additional competences required going forward
Ability to be focused on patient care	Able to more accurately understand and calculate patient lifetime value (in terms of age, condition, for example) relative to cost of treatment, taking into account all appropriate ethical considerations
Possession of depth of medical knowledge	Ability to access and apply insights from medical records, including global data, and use intelligent systems to augment individual decision-making in terms of the most appropriate treatment; willingness to share patient information and clinical insights with self-learning systems
Able to demonstrate professionalism and high ethical values; possess interpersonal and communication skills	Ability to communicate complex issues to patients and trust an intelligent system to deal with less serious issues that are easier to remedy
Capable of learning and improving through practice-based learning and improvement	Ability to personally learn new medical practices through increased use of simulation through computer-based training
Able to work with systems-based practices (the processes in the system that provide cost-effective care to individual patients and to populations, including appointments, referrals, and governmental impact)	Ability to effectively integrate traditional and new working practices, such as the use of robotic health advisors, into system-based practices, to apply automation to these practices, and, where appropriate, to create new model systems of treatment

Source: Adapted with changes from Royal College of General Practitioners, WPBA Competences (Workplace Based Assessment). http://www.rcgp.org.uk/training-exams/mrcgp-workplace-based-assessment-wpba/wpba-competence-framework.aspx (accessed 16 February 2018).

early stage of development. This advanced technology helps detect what are known as voxels, which in size are less than 1 millimetre cubed. Within each voxel are perhaps 100,000 neurons.

Traditional fMRI is used to identify where the brain lights up to show levels of increased activity, but even neuroscientists still aren't certain about what actually happens in these illuminated areas, or how they connect with each other.

Language, for example, is thought to take place in the left hemisphere of the brain, specifically in two areas known as Broca's area and Wernicke's area. Scientists know that if these areas of the brain are damaged, speech is impaired, but they are wondering whether the whole brain is involved in language comprehension. The complexity of this problem is such that if scientists could tap into the brain and somehow decode the messages of brain activity, then this would give us a greater understanding of how the brain actually works. From this they could better treat mental and brain disorders, and apply more appropriate treatments.

TABLE 25 Future competences for dentists.

Existing required competences	Additional competences required going forward
Able to exercise effective communication and interpersonal skills, including health promotion	Ability to be increasingly proactive in terms of treatment by anticipating problems, including effectively modifying and intervening in patient behaviour as far as dental health is concerned
Capable of effectively managing the dental practice, using appropriate informatics	Create new financial models for the dental value chain, mirroring the use of analytics in the medical insurance sector, and use advanced financial performance management effectively to reduce cost and improve profitability; use digital marketing and social media to support practice growth strategies
Able to undertake patient care, including assessment, diagnosis, and treatment, and establishing and maintaining oral health	Provide customised added-value services, such as dietary advice and personal dental management; use advanced analytics to reduce misdiagnosis or treatment error, improve certainty of outcome, and reduce practitioner stress levels

Source: Adapted with changes from American Dental Association, Competencies for the new general dentist, *as approved by the ADEA House of Delegates on April 2, 2008.* http://www.adea.org/about_adea/governance/Pages/Competencies-for-the-New-General-Dentist.aspx

It has been suggested that one way to better understand the brain would be to transform neuroscience into a specific form of big data science.[45] There is a reciprocal benefit, in that by better understanding the way that the brain operates, perhaps we will become closer to understanding how to reproduce the human brain in a machine.

With the primary skills expected of a neuroscientist to be those of mathematics and science, together with an aptitude for cellular research, perhaps the infusion of analytics into neurosurgery might be a relatively small step professionally.

DATA CENTRES

Some would suggest that work carried out in data centres does not legitimately comprise a profession, but is rather a function of the business value chain. Those managers who have worked in data centres throughout their professional lives might wish to disagree. Others might even suggest that data centres are an industry in their own right.

Data centres store, manage, process, receive, and transmit digital data at scale within secure, specialist, resilient buildings. In terms of the AI agenda, they are likely to be the hidden force or key enabler, without which the overall plan may not be able to operate. In the United Kingdom there are approximately 500 data centres, split approximately equally between those that provide colocation facilities, those that support information communications technology service providers, and those that directly support in-house commercial enterprises.[46]

Data centres underpin the economy and will underprop the AI generation. In the United Kingdom, data centres already apparently contribute 10% of GDP, with a rate of growth of 10% annually, and add £225 billion to the UK economy.

Elsewhere data centres are equally important. According to Boston Consulting Group, the size of the opportunity for the IoT in the G20 Nations (the 20 largest economies) is estimated at US\$4.2 trillion, and data centres clearly have a major role to play.[47] Seventy percent of FTSE 100 companies and 75% of Fortune 500 companies are located in London, so it is perhaps natural to think about the influence of AI on data centres there specifically.

Technological developments will invariably take place against a background of heightened security and regulation. If the lifeblood of artificial systems is data, and data centres are accepted as being the key enablers of an advanced analytics environment, then the ability to effectively and securely operate such centres becomes critical. This invariably includes data security, including the EU General Data Protection Regulation and the lesser-known EU–US Privacy Shield Framework, which allows for the free movement of data between the United States and the EU.

The EU–US Privacy Shield builds on the International Safe Harbor Privacy Principles, which are, in effect, a self-certification process for US companies relating to the storage of customer data. The Privacy Shield was considered invalid by the European Court of Justice in 2015, however. It was claimed that Facebook's processing of data between its Irish subsidiary and its US servers constituted a breach of appropriate protections for the individual citizen.

This issue reinforces the impact of regulation on the topic of data flows, especially those between jurisdictions, and also the impact of personal security. If, as we speculate, an era of AI is one that exists in an environment of data exchange, then regulation and data centres are inevitably at the heart of the conversation. Regardless of the impact of AI, data protection and privacy will remain at the core of many discussions going forward.

Whilst we have specifically considered the impact of data on the AI environment, we haven't really covered the influence of AI on the data centre environment itself. The first area to consider is that of skills and talent. If governments are intent on focusing on STEM (science, technology, engineering, and mathematics) principles and on increasing the level of competence in this area, then we may have a problem.

The latest surveys suggest that in the United Kingdom 68% of employers are concerned that the educational system is struggling to keep up with the skills required for technological change. In the same survey, the Institution of Engineering and Technology discovered that the traditional skills of engineering and technology are being increasingly replaced by more *data-specific* roles.[48]

According to Peter Hannaford, chairman of Datacenter People, 'The data centre is now the home of the cloud and simply relying on power and cooling expertise is not enough'.[49] As we are seeing in the emergence of new IT-savvy line-of-business professionals, resulting in new roles and job descriptions, a similar situation seems also to be occurring in what some call the *engine room* of AI.

If we consider that, as in emerging nations, there will be a skills shortage in this engine room, then what will be the solution? Progress cannot be inhibited by a lack of talent or by an absence of technological talent.

AI solutions will increasingly need to be created to avoid a slowdown in the rate of progress. Already Google is using AI to reduce energy consumption, and other companies will surely follow their lead. Google claims that the use of its DeepMind algorithms has 'cut the cost of cooling by 40% and the overall energy consumption by 15%'.[50] In a sign of the times, IBM also recently announced AI-infused data centres.[51]

ENTREPRENEURS

In this chapter we have looked at a selected number of professions and tried to draw a distinction between those competences currently needed and what might be necessary in the future. In doing so, we mainly considered recognised professions that require an accepted qualification, but we will conclude the chapter with something slightly different: the loosely defined profession of entrepreneurism.

One doesn't often see *entrepreneur* described as a profession, but certainly there is some evidence of there being serial entrepreneurs. As AI and cognitive analytics increasingly reduce the workforce and permit new ways of working and new approaches to work, could entrepreneurism emerge as a new profession? If so, what will it look like, especially in this new working environment?

It's already expected that increased use of advanced analytics, automation, and artificial systems will result in job losses. On the other hand, some suggest that this will give rise to new roles and types of work. Will unemployment of the so-called thinking classes spawn a new wave of entrepreneurism?

An entrepreneur is simply a person who takes on business risk in the hope of making a profit. Entrepreneurs are often seen as being business leaders rather than business managers.

There appear to be two popular views with respect to the entrepreneur:

1. Entrepreneurs are those who run their own companies and are self-sufficient, often replicating others. In many cases these are small companies, perhaps even a company of only one person.
2. Entrepreneurs are those who are genuine innovators and have identified a market opportunity to exploit with a product or service. They have an eye on scale from the outset, and in doing so, search for the capability to overtake other small competing companies.

These are two quite different models. If the dynamism of an economy is measured by the number of start-ups, isn't the real measure of success that of how many of these are successful, sustainable, and realistically make a significant contribution to the GDP of a country or marketplace?

There is a demographic element to entrepreneurism. Increasingly, we see this particular breed coming from a well-educated background, often with some experience in the family of running a business (although this is not always the case).

Nowadays, 45% of American self-made entrepreneurs have advanced degrees; compare this statistic with Henry Ford, who dropped out of school to 'tinker' around. For those who might suggest that Ford was supported by parental wealth: his father and mother were Irish and Belgian immigrants, respectively. He entered into industry because he 'despised' farm work and the obligations thrust upon him. Henry Ford was quite genuinely a self-made man. After his promotion to being the chief engineer of the Edison Illuminating Company, he found that he had the time to think about gasoline engines. The Henry Ford Company was founded in 1901, with Ford as chief engineer at the age of 38.

Is entrepreneurship a question of nature or nurture? In Ford's case, it seems to have been embedded in his DNA to some degree. After all, his parents were prepared to cross the Atlantic in search of a new life. He was dissatisfied with the status quo and was ambitious and opportunistic. There was an element of luck involved as well, both in terms of timing and in the people that he met.

Ford not only had a global vision of large-scale manufacturing and the production line, but must also have had *entrepreneurism* in his nature.

In reality, from the outset he didn't have all the know-how to set up and manage a business. In starting up the Detroit Automotive Company in 1899, he was financially backed by lumber baron William H. Murphy. Later on (as Ford and Malcomson, trading as the Ford Motor Company) he was backed by Alexander Malcomson, who was a Detroit coal dealer. Malcomson even installed his clerk James Couzens to keep tabs on Ford.

The alternative to having entrepreneurism in the DNA (i.e. nature) is nurture: here, the concept that it is possible to teach individuals or organisations to be entrepreneurial in style or capability. Certainly there is much greater emphasis on entrepreneurism in higher education than ever before. Students travel globally to find the secret of success that they can take back to their homelands. Universities provide institutes for innovation and innovation management. It is as if doing work without innovation is no longer good enough.

The downside of this approach is that executives are constantly challenged to drive innovation and change (sometimes for the sake of change). They are measured in terms of how much change has occurred, even if the results of the changes haven't been properly evaluated. In fairness, it may not matter too much. Despite a volatile marketplace, the average tenure of the senior executive is still about 10 years, which is nearly twice that of their employees.[52]

The question remains, is it really possible to nurture entrepreneurism? Can we create an entrepreneurial tool kit that helps start-ups, especially one for mature professionals, away from the relatively cosseted environment of innovation hubs?

If so, perhaps an entrepreneurial tool kit for mature candidates might comprise:

- Legal and tax advice
- Financial advice
- Technological advice
- Sociological advice, including how to collaborate.

All of these could be supplied on demand as outsourced activities. The problem is that there is usually a charge for such services, and spending money, which may be difficult to replace, is probably the last thing that start-ups want to do.

If the AI era is to lead to unemployment or redistribution of employment, isn't there a need for government to support start-ups, especially amongst the older workforce? That requirement is likely to accelerate in the coming years. Whether this is just a mechanism to keep professional people from the brink of boredom remains to be seen, but it appears that solutions should not necessarily come from the private sector alone.

There is also a distinct national issue to take into account. The Chinese economy, for example, is currently recognised as one of the engine rooms of innovation, creating new low-cost products and increasing the pace of supply chains. To support this, the Chinese government has introduced tax incentives for small tech firms, but these presuppose that these small firms are already on their own two feet rather than operating as a group of independent sole traders.[53]

Traditional characteristics of an entrepreneur are described as follows:

- *Aptitude.* Having natural talents, tendencies, or capabilities.
- *Vision.* Having the ability to visualise end goals.
- *Risk tolerance.* As distinct from recklessness.
- *Confidence.* A belief by the entrepreneur in his or her own abilities.
- *Creativity.* The ability to link things together in an imaginative way.
- *Perseverance.* The ability to cope with setbacks.
- *Initiative.* The willingness to take on a new venture.
- *Integrity.* A personal commitment to keep promises, which inspires confidence.
- *Passion.* A desire not only for success, but beyond this, a genuine love of what you are doing sufficient to seize a business opportunity.

These soft characteristics, whilst credible in their own right, are not a substitute for technical business skills. Hard capabilities for an entrepreneur include knowing how to:

- Structure an organisation, perhaps as a sole trader, partnership, limited company, or other legal combination
- Manage income and expenditure, including the raising of venture capital
- Comply with regulations
- Bring a product to market and support it post sale
- Manage resources, including relationships and supply chains.[54]

Advanced analytics and AI are likely to provide a catalyst for change by making many of these technical elements easier to implement. They potentially allow entrepreneurs to bring ideas to market more quickly and to sunset them more rapidly as well. In many ways, this might herald the formation of a new entrepreneurially infused *postindustrial era*.

A postindustrial era is just another step along the journey of work. If we consider the preindustrial era, this comprised many individual workers, often operating from their homes, usually cottages. The industrial era brought about restructuring of the workforce and mass movement away from a home-based working system into one that was factory based. At that time the idea of working at home was not that of a glamorous existence but one in which the focus was on generating enough income to keep one alive.

Whilst some might frown at the cost of industrialisation in terms of working conditions, few would argue that, despite austere factory conditions, the certainty of income was preferable to starvation. In *The Rise and Fall of King Cotton*, Anthony Burton suggests that 'industrialization is an essential stage through which man must pass if he is to enjoy a decent life'.[55]

Is it possible that an AI-oriented, postindustrial world might look very much like the preindustrial era? Might we somehow go full circle in our approach to work?

Perhaps what may occur is a different approach to the support of the mature entrepreneur. Innovation hubs could become more automated or virtual, with better access to online help and support. But if entrepreneurs could rely on automated advice about how to generate wealth, could the systems themselves ever be able to generate wealth or value without human intervention? Realistically, this is probably unlikely, but as ultimately we allow ourselves to be guided by intelligent systems with respect to

TABLE 26   Future competences for entrepreneurs.

Existing required competences	Additional competences required going forward
Ability to have aptitude to recognise opportunity	Awareness of cutting-edge skills and competences that provide unique solutions to specific business issues; predictor of future trends, rather than responder of existing trends
Ability to have vision	Preparedness to be radical and unconfined by previous business models, product histories, and consumer behaviours
Capable of tolerating risk	Willingness to be risk seeking where appropriate, albeit within the agreed risk framework or risk appetite of external funders
Possessor of confidence	Possessing boldness; having a clear view of the likelihood of success
Able to be creative	Capable of being unconstrained by existing or previous business rules or products; able to recognise and utilise creative capabilities of intelligent systems
Possessor of perseverance	Ability to have a realistic approach to progress, including a preparedness to walk away from a project or idea
Capable of using own initiative	Self-motivated, with clear understanding of the benefit case, both in terms of hard and soft benefits
Possessor of integrity	Capable of maintaining high moral standards, recognising that those standards might be impacted by volatile market conditions and consumer behaviours
Able to be passionate about the venture	Ability to be realistic about the venture

wealth management and medical advice, would we ever find ourselves working with systems that have entrepreneurial capability in themselves?

In his book *Re-Imagine!*, Tom Peters comments on entrepreneurship and suggests that we are entering a new phase. He describes:

- 1962 as being the era of conglomerates and management
- 1982 as the era of corporate entrepreneurship
- 2002 as the era of outsourcing and network management
- 2022 as probably being the era of 'transience', that is, the state of only lasting a short time.

Peters argues that the next phase, in 2022, will be one where 'new ideas will follow new ideas with reckless abandon, total disregard and disrespect for today's regnant geniuses, and at unprecedented speed'.[56] This will inevitably demand some new capabilities (see Table 26).

CONCLUSION

Predicting the future is difficult. In Chapters 3 and 4 we considered the impact of advanced analytics and AI on a number of industries, and in this chapter we have looked at the impact on some professions. The latter range from the highly technical, such as engineering, to one that is on the periphery of the term *profession*: entrepreneurship.

There are other professions that equally could merit detailed attention. For example, education and teaching are critical, and the future will increasingly bring automated, customised methods of learning. Although these professions haven't been covered in this chapter, they were touched upon in Chapters 3 and 4. For professions not covered specifically, the burden falls on readers to look at industries that may employ them and not only to apply their imaginations but share their ideas.

Like work itself, the nature of professions is set to change, in the same way that old roles have always disappeared and new ones emerged. If there are any consistent trends, they include the following:

- The need for data and software experts to be able to actually create and manage the systems. Potential shortfalls of skill in terms of capability and numbers will increasingly force the development of machines with self-learning capabilities.
- The need for humans to increasingly change the way they work with intelligent systems, perhaps as colleagues or partners, as opposed to adopting a master–servant relationship.
- Recognition that this new industrial revolution will bring benefits, but potentially also detrimental effects to the workforce.
- That intelligent systems may create a more level playing field in terms of industry knowledge as a result of knowledge sharing, and in doing so will contribute to a more global society.

If we were to focus on two professionals alone – management and entrepreneurship – we might see two common threads: *opportunity* matched with *uncertainty*. The manager will be obliged to steer his ship through uncharted territory, with no experience of such waters and with a worried (and potentially mutinous) crew. The entrepreneur is perhaps less worried about the crew, or even himself or herself personally, but sees uncertainty as an opportunity.

Future success for managers, entrepreneurs, and all other professions rests to a great extent in their hands. If we accept that there inevitably will be changes going forward, it will be for those at an organisational, institutional, or individual level to be proactive about these matters. They can either be victims of future changes or collaborators with the future – their future.

In the same way that the Luddites faced change and reacted to it, modern professionals will face change of a similar, or even greater, magnitude. The tactics of riot and resistance used by the Luddites are not likely to provide an effective response. For that reason, it's important that we embrace inevitable change, regardless of the vagueness of the timescale, and to shape the future into an image that we find acceptable. To do so requires us to move forward without fear, and in an enlightened way. More than ever before, we all need to wake up to the future.

NOTES

1. Livery companies/guilds. Technical Education Matters (6 January 2011). http://technicaleducationmatters.org/2011/01/06/livery-companiesguilds (accessed 6 November 2016).

2. Joel Brown, 30 motivational Andrew Carnegie quotes. Addict2Success, 2016. https://addicted2success.com/quotes/30-motivational-andrew-carnegie-quotes/ (accessed 15 January 2018).

3. Mike Davison, *The Grand Strategist* (Palgrave Macmillan, 1995).

4. Management Mania, Paradox of Minzberg. https://managementmania.com/en/paradox-of-mintzberg (accessed 15 January 2018).

5. Richard Donkin, *Blood Sweat and Tears: The Evolution of Work* (Texere Publishing, 2002).

6. Michael Dunkerley, *The Jobless Economy* (London: Wiley, 1996).

7. Steve Pavlina, Social drag. Steve Pavlina blog, 2006. http://www.stevepavlina.com/blog/2006/03/social-drag

8. Carl Benedikt Frey and Michael Osborne, *The Future of Employment: How Susceptible Are Jobs to Computerization?* (Oxford Martin School, University of Oxford, 2013). http://www.oxfordmartin.ox.ac.uk/downloads/academic/future-of-employment.pdf

9. Angus McPherson, Robot conductor to lead Italian orchestra in Bochelli concert. *Limelight* (8 August 2017). http://www.limelightmagazine.com.au/news/robot-conductor-lead-italian-orchestra-opera-highlights

10. Singularity Weblog, Are you a transhuman? Larry King interviews futurist FM-2030 (23 November 2012). https://www.singularityweblog.com/are-you-a-transhuman-larry-king-interviews-futurist-fm-2030/ (accessed 15 January 2018).

11. Rodney Brooks, *Flesh and Machines* (Pantheon Books, 2002). As quoted in Pamela McCorduck, *Machines Who Think*, 2nd ed. (Natick, MA: A.K. Peters, 2004).

12. Vegard Kolbjornsrud, Richard Amico, and Robert J. Thomas, How artificial intelligence will redefine management. *Harvard Business Review*, 2016.

13. Alisa Blum, 6 key competencies of effective managers. *Training* (24 March 2014). https://trainingmag.com/6-key-competencies-effective-managers

14. John Parkinson, Will machines take over finance? CFO.com, 2016.

15. Sridhar Srinivasan, Artificial intelligence and the banking CFO: the endless possibilities. Tata Consultancy Services, 2016.

16. Katie Kuehner-Hebert, Future audits must do more: Survey. CFO.com, 2015.

17. Aviva Hope Rutkin, Report suggests nearly half of US jobs are vulnerable to computerization. *MIT Technology Review*, 2013.

18. John Boudeau, Smart machines: The new human capital. CFO.com, 2014.

19. Katie King, There's a computer judge . . . . Legal Cheek, 2016. http://www.legalcheek.com/2016/10/theres-a-computer-judge-that-can-predict-then-verdicts-of-the-european-court-of-human rights/?utm_source=twitter&utm_medium=social&utm_campaign=SocialWarfare

20. Katie King, Top judge calls for lawyerless courts. Legal Cheek, 2016.

21. Sophie Curtis, Artificially intelligent 'judge' could help deliver verdicts in human rights trials. *Mirror* (24 October 2016) http://www.mirror.co.uk/tech/artificially-intelligent-judge-could-help-9114133

22. S. Danziger, J. Levav, and L. Avnaim-Pesso, Extraneous factors in judicial decisions. *Proceedings of the National Academy of Sciences* 108, no. 17 (2011): 6889–6892.

23. Jordan Furlong, Core competence: 6 new skills now required of lawyers. Law21.ca (4 July 2008). https://www.law21.ca/2008/07/core-competence-6-new-skills-now-required-of-lawyers

24. Tom Peters, *Re-Imagine! Business Excellence in a Disruptive Age* (DK Publishing, 2003).

25. https://www.linkedin.com/pulse/artificial-intelligence-companies-doing-large-deals-sales-engman- (accessed 16 November 2016).

26. Tim Hinchcliffe, Is Apple's research paper on AI a blueprint for mapping human emotions? *The Sociable* (27 December 2016). http://sociable.co/technology/apples-research-mapping-human-emotions

27. Ingrid Lunden, Emotient raises $6m for facial expression recognition tech, debuts google glass sentiment analysis app. TechCrunch.com (5 March 2014). https://techcrunch.com/2014/03/06/emotient-raises-6m-for-its-facial-expression-recognition-tech-debuts-sentiment-analysis-app-for-google-glass

28. Roberto Fantoni, Fernanda Hoefel, and Marina Mazzarolo, The future of the shopping mall. McKinsey.com (November 2014). http://www.mckinsey.com/business-functions/marketing-and-sales/our-insights/the-future-of-the-shopping-mall

29. Deborah Weinswig, Deep dive: artificial intelligence in retail – offering data-driven personalization and customer service. Fung Global Retail and Tech. https://www.fungglobalretailtech.com/research/deep-dive-artificial-intelligence-retail-offering-data-driven-personalization-customer-service

30. Hartman Group. What's the future for online grocery shopping? *Forbes* (accessed 28 August 2017). https://www.forbes.com/sites/thehartmangroup/2015/06/17/whats-the-future-for-online-grocery-shopping/#33f128c0230e

31. Susan Steiner, Smart fridge? Idiot fridge, more like. *The Guardian* online (11 January 2012). https://www.theguardian.com/lifeandstyle/2012/jan/11/homes-fooddrinks

32. *Case Studies Exploring the Competencies of Artists and Creative Practitioners Who Work in Participatory Settings to Develop the Creativity of Children and Young People.* Training Requirements and Key Skills for Artists and Creative Practitioners to Work in Participatory Settings project. International Foundation for Creative Learning. http://www.creativitycultureeducation.org/wp-content/uploads/Case-studies-exploring-the-competencies-of-artists-and-creative-practitioners.pdf (accessed 29 August 2017).

33. Kai Lehikoinen, and Joost Heinsius eds., *Training Artists for Innovation: Competencies for New Contexts* (Helsinki: Theatre Academy of the University of the Arts, 2013). https://firstindigoandlifestyle.com/2014/01/07/training-artists-for-innovation-competencies-for-new-contexts (accessed 18 October 2017).

34. *Is Production a Core Competence of a Publisher?* (Dublin: Deanta Global Publishing Services, 2015).

35. Mark Hansford, Why engineers should be excited by the digital railway. *New Civil Engineer* (June 2017).

36. Peter J. Walker, Croydon tram driver suspended after video of man 'asleep' at controls. *The Guardian* (19 November 2016).

37. Mark Hansford, Interview: Waboso pushes digital rail. *New Civil Engineer* (9 May 2017).

38. Sarwant Singh, *New Mega Trends: Implications for Our Future Lives* (London: Palgrave MacMillan, 2012).

39. Stacey Liberatore, DARPA's autonomous flight program steps closer to reality after successful tests with 'robot pilot' in planes and a helicopter. *Mail* online (29 December 2016). http://www.dailymail.co.uk/sciencetech/article-4074200/DARPA-s-autonomous-flight-program-steps-closer-reality-successful-tests-robot-pilot-planes-helicopter.html

40. Control without bounds: the rise of the digital 'remote' tower. NATS. http://www.nats.aero/discover/control-without-bounds (accessed 19 May 2017).

41. Engineers Canada. Core engineering competencies (27 November 2012). https://engineerscanada.ca/sites/default/files/w_Competencies_and_Feedback.pdf

42. What your GP does. NHS. http://www.choosewellmanchester.org.uk/in-your-area/what-your-gp-does (accessed 2 August 2017).

43. Nigel Praities, Pulse launches major survey of GP burnout. Pulse.co.uk (30 April 2013). http://www.pulsetoday.co.uk/home/burnout/pulse-launches-major-survey-of-gp-burnout/20002805.article

44. Sarah Knapton, A robot 'friend' to keep elderly active. *The Telegraph* (12 January 2017).

45. Brian Resnick, Brain activity is too complicated for humans to decipher. Machines can decode it for us. Why we need artificial intelligence to study our natural intelligence. Vox.com (3 January 2017). http://www.vox.com/science-and-health/2016/12/29/13967966/machine-learning-neuroscience
46. Silver linings: The implications of Brexit for the UK data centre sector. Tech UK (October 2016).
47. BCG Perspectives, The Internet economy in the G-20 (March 19, 2012). https://www.bcgperspectives.com/content/articles/media_entertainment_strategic_planning_4_2_trillion_opportunity_internet_economy_g20/ (accessed 16 January 2018).
48. Institution of Engineering and Technology, Skills and Demand in Industry, 2013 Survey.
49. Peter Hannaford, From rock star to sage: 'The time for change is now'. Data-Economy (30 September 2016). https://data-economy.com/rock-star-sage-time-change-now
50. Jane Wakefield, Google uses AI to save on electricity from data centres. BBC (20 June 2016). http://www.bbc.co.uk/news/technology-36845978
51. Ambrose McNevin, IBM plans four new UK AI based cloud data centres. *Computer Business Review* online (22 November 2016). http://www.cbronline.com/news/verticals/ebanking/ibm-plans-four-new-uk-ai-based-cloud-data-centres
52. Adams, CEOs staying in their jobs longer. *Forbes* (11 April 2014). https://www.forbes.com/sites/susanadams/2014/04/11/ceos-staying-in-their-jobs-longer/#4498c13a67d6
53. Linda Darragh, How to foster entrepreneurship in emerging markets: A Q&A with four entrepreneurs about the global startup landscape – and what governments can do to help. *Kellogg Insight* (30 March 2016). https://insight.kellogg.northwestern.edu/article/how-to-foster-entrepreneurship-in-emerging-markets?utm_source=subscriber&utm_campaign=BoomtrainMailer042017&utm_medium=email&bt_alias=eyJ1c2VySWQiOiAiNmE4M2MzMjctNmU0MC00NjI2LThjNWEtYmNmYzc4ZjUyNGUyIn0%3D
54. Thomas Haney Business, Characteristics and skills of entrepreneurs. thssbusiness.com. http://thssbusiness.com/business-10/chapter-13.pdf
55. Anthony Burton, *The Rise and Fall of King Cotton* (Andre Deutsch, 1984).
56. Peters, *ReImagine!*

CHAPTER 6

Risk and Regulation

SUMMARY

The road forward in terms of advanced analytics, machine learning, and AI is shrouded in uncertainty. When there is the possibility that uncertainty will bring a detrimental result, we call that uncertainty *risk*. In this chapter we will focus specifically on operational risk, such as failures of systems and data security, reputational impacts, and external events. We will be considering not only how AI may cause risk, but also how its effective use may mitigate risk. Beyond this, we'll consider the aspect of regulation and compliance, both in terms of general principles and also with respect to the professional functions, such as risk managers and compliance officers, involved.

INTRODUCTION

The topic of *risk* in the context of AI has the potential to ring alarm bells for some readers. After all, when we think about risk as a topic, we invariably focus on the downside, that is, the risks that AI can bring to us as individuals and also to society as a whole. This isn't, however, the focus of this chapter. Its purpose is rather to consider the wider topic of risk, and how AI can not only create new risks, but also provide solutions for existing, new, and future ones.

To do this we will first consider what we mean by *risk* and then address the sorts of risks that might apply to an AI environment. Finally, we will consider how AI can help with the management of risks.

In October 2016, the American Institute of Artificial Intelligence released what it described as the 'world's first and most comprehensive Artificial Intelligence Governance Model and Product'.[1] It was labelled as a prototype and addressed thousands of data points through multidimensional analysis aimed at addressing human safety, creating transparency, achieving social good, and providing regulatory compliance.

It's a welcome addition to the topic of risk and governance from an organisation that sits beside many other AI-oriented professional organisations, such as the US-based Association for the Advancement of Artificial Intelligence. (Other professional AI organisations are listed in Appendix C.)

There's no doubt about it – if businesses and the public were already concerned about the concept of big data and analytics, then their nervousness will increase in the era of AI. As we have considered elsewhere, successful implementation of an AI environment will depend on key drivers such as:

- Technology
- Culture
- Leadership
- Enablement.

However, underpinning all of these will also be issues of ethics, privacy, and security. These could be reasonably described as hygiene factors, in that they do not necessarily encourage implementation, but without them progress would be inhibited. Without managing these three additional aspects, arguably the above four key drivers become irrelevant.

WHAT IS RISK?

To understand the real issues and benefits of AI effectively requires us briefly to describe what we mean by risk.

In general terms, we understand risk to comprise the threat of loss, damage, injury, liability, or another injurious occurrence that is caused by internal or external actions and that might otherwise have been avoided by prevention.[2] Loss may also extend to meaning *loss of value*. Risk may also include financial risk, that is, risks involving financial transactions.

Risks are all around us, but in the context of business they can be either industry specific or generic. Generic risk is usually described as operational risk, that is, losses arising through:

- Technology and systems failures
- Employee errors, including fraud and other criminal activity
- Inadequate or failed procedures, systems, or policies
- Reputational risk
- External operational risk, such as weather and legal risks.

Whilst not all of these operational risks can be managed out of a business, organisations can decide to take certain levels or types of risk dependent on their *risk appetite*. A company's approach to uncertainty is usually expressed in some form of risk-appetite statement, which helps guide its risk management strategies. Often risk is managed through a risk assessment framework which is an effective way of communicating risk management throughout the business in a way that nontechnical people can understand.

Risk management is an established profession, which increasingly relies on analytical assessment to quantify and manage the hazards attaching to a business. Risk managers usually (although not always) report to the finance line of business or directly to the CFO. It is unusual for risk managers to sit on the board or to progress through the ranks to board level, as they are viewed as gatekeepers rather than value creators, although such promotions are not unprecedented.

TECHNOLOGY AND SYSTEM FAILURES

Technology risk is usually associated with data security and cyberattack and is often extended to include the terms *information security* and *information assurance*.

Because of the volatile and fiercely competitive marketplace, many organisations are more readily placing their bets on progress through the use of advanced analytics, cognitive analytics, and AI technologies. With such relatively unproven capabilities, these strategies might ultimately be seen as either extremely shrewd, or as high risk. With all the hype, there may also be an element of 'me too' in order to keep up with the competition. Unfortunately, failure in systems and development are not entirely unheard of, and not only leads to massive financial loss but also affects the business's credibility.

What would have been the world's largest civilian computer system was abandoned in September 2013 by the UK National Health Service (NHS) despite having already cost taxpayers £10 billion. The eventual report provides a very helpful review into the causes of failure, and even defines *failure* itself; *failure*, it said, occurs in cases in which implementation of the process:

1. Goes over budget
2. Has significant delay in terms of years
3. Does not do what it was meant to do in terms of the contracted specifications, or
4. Does not fit in the organisational structure or work processes.

In the case of the NHS system, the prime causes of failure were described as problems in project management, engineering principles, organisational change, and change management. Specific other topics mentioned in the report, which seem to be recurring themes, include 'accountability, professionalism, formal training, research, good communications, leadership, risk management and ownership'.

In the report, investigators identify three principal periods of failure:

1. Pre-implementation
   a. Lack of research, risk management, and long-term commitment
   b. The 'acceptability' of failures
   c. Lack of user buy-in and ownership
   d. Inappropriate use of technology
2. During implementation
   a. Poor communications
   b. Lack of a powerful guiding coalition
   c. Lack of change management
   d. Lack of short-term wins
3. Post-implementation
   a. Declaring victory too soon
   b. Failure to learn from previous mistakes.[3]

There is no shortage of papers and reports that diagnose the failure of other projects. These have given rise to what is known as Cobb's paradox. It is named after Martin Cobb, who, when CIO for the Secretariat of the Treasury Board of Canada in

1995, asked the simple question: 'We know why projects fail, we know how to prevent their failure, so why do they still fail?'[4]

A Project Management Institute survey on project and programme management highlights a stark difference between high-performing organisations (better than 80% success rate), and low-performing organisations (greater than 40% fail rate). It indicates that the processes typically used by the high-performing organisations and ignored by low-performing organisations are straightforward to implement and use. They include:

- Using standardised project management processes
- Establishing a process to use mature project, programme, and portfolio management practices
- Using a process to increase project management competency
- Employing qualified project managers.[5]

DATA SECURITY AND PRIVACY

Data privacy and security are at the heart of analytic systems that merge structured and unstructured data, commonly held data, and personal data. System and technology failure often manifest themselves in data security issues.

Many are already considering the ethical question with respect to the availability of data. Already partially immersed in an AI environment, some might reasonably suggest that the whole notion of big data is old hat and yesterday's news. Yet at the same time, some of the work on ethics also done in the big data space helps provide us with a form of moral compass.

Neil Richards and Jonathan King address these issues, amongst others, in their paper 'Big Data Ethics'. They argue against the expression *big data* and suggest that even small amounts of data that are collectively and intelligently assembled can provide new insights, which in turn require an ethical viewpoint. At the heart of their discussion is the topic of privacy, which is described as one of the rules that 'govern the use of information'.

> *Critically … if we fail to balance the human values that we care about, like privacy, confidentiality, transparency, identity, and free choice, with the compelling uses of big data, our big data society risks abandoning these values for the sake of innovation and expediency.*

Four points are argued:

1. That the need to recognise privacy as one of the key rules of information, suggesting that the maxim 'privacy is dead' is not true and that our weakness is that of inadequate self-management
2. That there is a right to shared information (e.g. between a patient and doctor) remaining confidential, and that it can remain private
3. That transparency in big data is critical, especially to avoid the abuse of institutional power
4. That data can compromise individual identity, with identity defined as the 'ability of an individual to define who we are'.[6]

This opens up a very interesting discussion in the context of personal liberties, civil defense, and anti-terrorism. Increasingly, the use of data, insight, and advanced algorithms is helping police and government authorities identify both existing and prospective terrorists. Some might suggest that, used properly, this is a reasonable trade-off for our safety. Inevitably, this will not only require closer cooperation among organisations that collect and store data, but also approval by the citizen/customer and/or legal permission to access and use this data.

Much of this information gathering, analysis, and sharing is shrouded in secrecy. The lack of transparency adds to our concerns. How do we know that the data is being used for the right reasons and not for commercial advantage?

John Whittaker of Dell also comments about the emerging topic of data ethics, advising:

- 'Practise ethics at every turn … and adopt a 'better safe than sorry' approach
- Don't rely on regulations alone, and don't assume that your clients won't be upset by ethical breaches, provided that laws weren't broken
- Practise data gathering and analytics, and taking an ethical stance will drive analytical excellence.'[7]

Douglas Patterson, in a *Forbes* article by Howard Wen called 'The Ethics of Big Data', suggests: 'One useful definition of big data – for those who, like us, don't think it's best to tie it to particular technologies – is that big data is data big enough to raise practical rather than merely theoretical concerns about the effectiveness of anonymization.'

In the same article, Kord Davis, a former Cap Gemini consultant, also spoke on the topic of big data ethics, saying that having 'a common set of values' can actually increase the pace of innovation. Says Davis, 'It turns questions from "Should we do this?" to "How *can* we do this?"'.[8]

Increasingly, regulators are focusing their attention on consumer privacy. In Europe, the General Data Protection Regulation (GDPR) has replaced the Data Protection Act, which had been around since the 1990s. Under GDPR, penalties for noncompliance are punitive, and can be as much as 4% of a company's annual turnover. These fines apply not only to data controllers but also to data processors. It seems that everyone in the data chain is affected. The GDPR not only applies to data processing carried out by organisations operating within the EU, but also applies to those outside the EU that offer goods or services to individuals in the EU.

Such regulatory attention is a response to the epidemic of cybercrime. In its 2014 report *Net Losses: Estimating the Global Cost of Cybercrime*, the Center for Strategic and International Studies, together with security experts McAfee, estimates the global cost of cybercrime to be in the order of $400 billion annually. They state, 'The returns are great, and the risks are low. We estimate that the likely annual cost to the global economy from cybercrime is more than $400 billion. A conservative estimate would be $375 billion in losses, while the maximum could be as much as $575 billion'.

They paint a gloomy picture going forward, saying 'We do not see a credible scenario in which cybercrime losses diminish'.[9]

The degree to which the analytics era will be affected by cybercrime has yet to be fully understood. It's unlikely to be a showstopper, but it has the potential to become a significant inhibitor to progress. In the 2017 article 'AI and Cybercrime: Good and

Bad News', Ann Johnson, Microsoft's vice president of enterprise and cybersecurity suggests, 'We have AI, but so do the bad guys'.

Johnson further sees a time when machine learning will make cybersecurity 'a lot more intelligent', even predictive. She asks us to imagine a security environment that warns us of problems in advance, for example, if '10 computers in a data center are going to go down, or a network connection can potentially be compromised.'[10]

EMPLOYEE ERROR AND FRAUD

How important is human error in the problem of risk management? Certainly in the NHS case study mentioned earlier many of the problems were put down to human failings, but we should explore these in a little more depth.

Let's start with the topic of *honesty*. In her paper 'Lying in Everyday Life', published in the *Journal of Personality and Social Psychology*, psychiatrist Bella DePaulo remarks that we lie in one in five of our daily interactions.[11] Pamela Meyer, author of *Liespotting*, claims that we're lied to from 10 to 200 times a day.[12]

The reason that people lie is complex, and may arise through omission, exaggeration, or issues of self-security – especially where there is insecurity in the workplace. Detecting lies often involves clues from body language gestures and other nonverbal clues. In their book *Frogs into Princes: Neuro Linguistic Programming*, Richard Bandler and John Grinder even determined that the eyes of those lying often move in a particular way or direction.[13]

Of course, not all human errors are deliberate in nature. We are an error-prone race. Errors in our behaviour and decision-making often occur as a result of:

- *Environmental factors*: physical, organisational, personal
- *Intrinsic factors*: selection of individuals, training, lack of experience
- *Stress factors*: personal, circumstantial.

In his book *Reliability, Maintainability, and Risk*, which is a course textbook on the topic of *reliability engineering*, Dr David J. Smith, lists average human failure rates across industries collected during the latter half of the twentieth century. Error rates are calculated for particular functions and assigned a number.[14]

Even entering data in a routine way is error prone. Putting 10 consecutive numbers into a calculator carries an error rate of 0.005%. That is to say, in every 1,000 activities there will be 5 incorrectly entered sequences of numbers. The figure increases considerably when an individual carries out a complex operation in a highly stressed environment, in which case the error rate increases to 0.25%, or 25 times per thousand.[15]

From research, especially into the aircraft industry, it seems clear that the human element and the human factor are the most error-prone of all, from the boardroom to the shop floor. Reliability management is a form of engineering that emphasises the ability to manage out or remove defects, and is a subdiscipline of systems engineering.

AI and robotics are more and more frequently seen as being the panaceas for avoiding mistakes, especially in routine tasks. One of the main arguments for robotic systems is that they automate error-prone activities in large-volume, repetitive tasks. As a result, there are fewer mistakes, greater consistency of decision-making, scale efficiencies, and ultimately greater customer satisfaction.

In the more complex area of project and programme management, automated tools that manage the project have become more common. These tools not only automatically notify key stakeholders of progress, but also manage workflow and automatic messaging to provide a 'prompt' on key activities.

Beyond this, US news station NPR carried out an assessment of work that might be replaced by AI, suggesting that umpires and referees have a 98.3% chance of being replaced by robots.[16] Whatever will sport become if there are no mistakes in referees' decisions?

Not all employee error is innocent in nature. Employee fraud can comprise expenses fraud, procurement fraud, and payment fraud. Employee fraud may not be the subject that keeps CFOs awake at night, but it can still have a damaging effect on the bottom line and on business reputations. According to a 2014 report by the Association of Certified Fraud Examiners, companies leak 5% of their revenue to fraudulent behaviour.[17]

The complexities of sales commission payments are also a prime area for fraudulent behaviour, usually where there are poor controls and minimal management oversight. Sales commission fraud usually relates to:

a. Sales that did not occur
b. Overinflated sales
c. Sales that are returned by the customer
d. Prebooked sales.

There is also scope for fraud in many parts of the supply cycle, including:

- Distribution fraud – goods lost in transit, or general leakage
- Quality assurance fraud – where faulty goods are fast-tracked as being of good quality
- Stock inventory fraud
- Invoice fraud.

INADEQUATE OR FAILED PROCEDURES, SYSTEMS, AND POLICIES

Inadequate or failed procedures, systems, and policies are extremely varied in nature and often focus on fraudulent behaviour by the consumer. One particular area of interest is that of so-called card not present (CNP) transactions, where organisations seek to balance the smoothness of customer service during the sales process with the risk of fraud. During the 2017 US holiday season, fraudulent card usage increased by 22%.[18]

Merchants that accept CNP transactions are turning regularly to forms of AI to help them out by reducing the number of false positive results, improving friction-free trading, and reducing fraud. Their focus is turning towards adaptive behavioural analysis to better understand their customers and peer groups through building a normal pattern of behaviour in real time so that they can spot when behaviours fall outside that which is expected.

According to experts, merchants using adaptive behavioural analysis coupled with machine learning are enjoying the benefits of:

- Speedier and more accurate fraud decision-making and acceptance to increase revenue

- Up to a 70% reduction in genuine transactions declined, including in fraud target areas
- Reduced manual intervention and a smoother ordering process
- Reduced card authentication friction.[19]

Similarly, the insurance industry is turning to advanced analytics in its own fight against insurance claims fraud. It's a lucrative area for attention, with fraud said to be costing insurance companies up to 10% of their profits. In France, start-up firm Shift Technology says it has already processed over 77 million claims and boasts a 75% accuracy rate for detecting fraudulent insurance claims.[20]

According to reports, Tokyo-based Fukoku Mutual Life Insurance intends to reduce its claims-payment department staff by 30% in favour of an AI system that will help manage over 130,000 insurance claims annually. The cognitive learning system can think like a human, with the ability to understand speech and gather, research, analyse, and interpret both unstructured documents, images, and videos, and preformatted, machine-ready structured data.[21]

REPUTATIONAL RISK

Reputational risk is loss arising from damage to a firm's reputation as a result of issues such as trust, ethics, security, behaviour, and management culture. It's often very difficult to quantify the loss in real terms. In this context we will consider the use of AI in the management of reputational risk. Two specific areas in which AI might be used in the area of reputational risk are in wealth and investment management, and in marketing management.

The banking industry is especially keen to ensure that the right advice is provided when decisions are being made about wealth management. Incorrect advice and investment decision-making are critical in terms of the reputation of the bank. Reputation in this context refers to the credibility and confidence that an institution or individual might have in an organisation.

Effective real-time reputation management provides a methodology by which investment results are constantly compared to those promised in the original investment decision. It can also help to assess the advisors' behaviour and reliability in order to distinguish trusted from unreliable advisors.

In marketing management, artificial intelligence marketing is a methodology that combines direct marketing with machine learning. The main difference between it and predictive analytics is that the marketing algorithms are created by the computer itself rather than by a human. In essence, this is meant to comprise an improvement in targeted marketing. It is considered under reputational issues, as in many cases direct marketing companies impair their reputations as a result of inappropriate and incorrect direct marketing.

Beyond these examples, the reputation of an organisation can be affected by issues such as culture, leadership, and its general ability to implement innovation. All three are interconnected insofar as those organisations that choose to adopt and implement an analytical or AI pathway are dependent on the quality and vision of leadership, and the ability of the leaders to reorganise the business to take advantage of these technological changes. The importance of this ability should not be understated, as for many employees change will bring with it uncertainty and perhaps personal risk.

For leaders themselves, this is also a risky journey. They are leading their companies or corporations into territory that they personally have no experience of, which may carry considerable risk to them as individuals and to their stakeholders. To lead effectively in these circumstances requires openness to coping with uncertainty and a willingness to engage impartial and knowledgeable advice.

EXTERNAL RISK

The final area of operational risk is that of the impact of external factors on a business. These are often industry specific and can extend to problems as diverse as supply chain breakdown, extreme weather conditions, and political volatility. In the case of insurers, for example, their business model is almost entirely dependent on an ability to predict locations of extreme weather and calculate the maximum probable losses. From this they can manage their exposure according to their risk appetite, obtain reinsurance, modify their pricing, or simply withdraw from business in high-risk areas.

With unstructured data (typically from video, text, and voice) comprising 80% of the data universe, the opportunity increasingly exists to tap into this source of information and gain competitive advantage. Automated systems will ease the burden of making sense from such fragmented data.

Information in context, or contextual analytics, is a potential growth area. Whilst businesses are keen not only to know the results of historical and real-time performance, and to anticipate what is likely to happen, by the same measure they also need to understand what is happening in the context of the wider environment. How is my competitor doing? Why are my customers behaving that way? Contextual analytics is part of the solution that will help organisations manage their external operational risks in a more effective way.

One source of data that is likely to rise in importance is that of location information. Everything and everyone is somewhere, so the ability to geocode data provides a golden thread that ties together apparently disparate data sources. Beyond this, robots also need to understand where they are physically and geographically, so geo-awareness will become more of a critical success factor.

Similarly effective management of assets such as machinery, buildings, and even people will depend more extensively on accurate location positioning. Inert objects may not complain too much about having a description that includes their geocodes, but human 'assets' are likely to be less comfortable with the idea, even if today many of them already subscribe to location services on their personal mobile devices.

In an interconnected and intelligent working environment, it will become significantly easier for advanced systems to manage and ultimately to optimise the location and movement of assets. Rather than bring order to the topic of work, optimised workflow could ultimately prove to be more random and chaotic than we have been traditionally used to.

More widespread use of advanced analytics can not only help organisations anticipate dramatic external change, but can also assist in modelling possible outcomes.

From such scenario modelling comes the ability for executives to use gaming techniques to develop their business skills.

FINANCIAL RISK

Elsewhere we have considered the impact of advanced analytics and AI both on the financial sector and also on the role of finance professionals themselves, who, like those in almost all professions, will need to undergo a period of readjustment.

Financial risk is usually taken to mean risk associated with financial transactions. Overall, it reflects the potential for an investor failing to recover an investment from a third party. There are many types of risk, including fraud, credit risk, liquidity risk, asset-backed risk, foreign investment risk, equity risk, and currency risk

Investors use a number of risk ratios to evaluate an organisation's prospects in terms of further investment, such as a debt-to-capital ratio, which measures the proportion of debt held by a company relative to its capital structure. A high proportion of debt is indicative of a risky business.

Key areas in which AI will help in managing and mitigating financial risk are as follows:

- *Antifraud management*, typically with respect to customer activities, including money laundering, corruption, and vendor management.
- *Investment analytics*, such as improved insight into investment performance and predictability of trends.
- *Underwriting*, by helping the risk analyst or portfolio manager have a better understanding of trends and future activities and by assisting with hedging strategies.
- *Credit risk management,* which will help credit managers gain a greater insight into hotspots at a more granular level, because credit defaults often come from a relatively small number of creditors or market segments. The number of variables involved often makes such an operation complex, and automated intelligent systems have a key part to play.
- *Tail risk management,* because of continued uncertainty about the impact of long-tail liabilities, which lend themselves to automated systems, helping analysts gain greater understanding in recommending appropriate financial provisions.

If there are common themes with respect to the use of advanced analytics and AI to help manage financial risk, they are those of increased need for speed of decision-making, the volatility of the marketplace, and the growing complexity of the working environment.

Whilst many of the above activities can already currently be managed through human intervention or through bespoke analytical programmes, the increased consequence of failure invariably places financial risk management ever higher on the business agenda. The ability to match exposure against the risk tolerance of an organisation, and to make decisions in the shortest possible time, unsurprisingly will lead to greater robotic intervention.

How this will ultimately manifest itself is unclear, especially when the consequences of failure are so large. Inevitably, there will be increased dependence on algorithms to make, or to support, business decisions. Perhaps ultimately the 'system' will even prevent a decision from being made. ('The computer says no.')

The impact on risk managers will not be insubstantial. As organisations depend more heavily on systems to help make risk-based decisions, won't the risk manager's role move away from being the gatekeeper and towards becoming some form of human intermediary – a messenger, as it were?

Equally, we shouldn't overlook the positive impacts of AI-augmented risk management. Effective use of cognitive and AI systems in this area potentially allows organisations to become more agile and more competitive. In a minefield of regulation, often in multiple languages, systems can be trained to understand and apply complicated regulatory rules. In doing so, they can help organisations to avoid fines and penalties, influencing not only the bottom line but also softer issues, such as reputation.

AI AND THE FUTURE OF COMPLIANCE

Why as a society do we need to comply with regulations? The whole concept of regulation mainly came to the fore in the early stages of the Industrial Revolution. At that time many employers used exploitation to prevent their employees from leaving. Employees were being paid low wages, yet living in a house provided by the employer and often paid with tokens as opposed to real money, which could only be used in the employer's own shop. In effect, it was a case of no job, no home. Throughout the twentieth century, industrial regulation increasingly provided fairer and safer working conditions, protected children in an era of child labour, and became a catalyst for raising pay. Beyond this, regulations were used to outlaw anticompetitive practises, avoid abuses of power, and moderate monopoly positions, such as in the case of the provision of utilities.

At an international level, trade laws and regulations have helped in lessening the gap between larger and smaller countries. Without trade laws, the largest, dominant countries can potentially flood a market with their products, with the result that smaller countries would be prevented from making their products accessible, in effect destroying their export market. It's not unusual for countries to be in disagreement regarding trade-related issues. Rules and regulations provide not only a framework but also are a route to airing grievances, typically through the World Trade Organisation. Usually rules and regulations also provide remedies – or penalties – for noncompliance.

Beyond issues of finance, trade, and safety, increasingly the rule makers have created regulations that protect the rights of the consumer. These extend to voluntary codes of practice, as in the case of advertising. In the case of UK financial services, the principle of treating the customer fairly (TCF) is embedded into the Permit to Trade issued by the Financial Conduct Authority. TCF is described as being outcome oriented, with the desired benefits being:

- That consumers can be confident that they are dealing with firms that place customers at the centre of their corporate culture
- That products and services marketed and sold are appropriate to the consumer groups that are targeted
- That the consumer is provided with clear advice before, during, and after the point of sale
- That when consumers receive advice, the advice is appropriate to their circumstances

- That when customers are provided with products, that the products perform as expected
- That there are no unreasonable post-sale barriers to the customer, such as not providing the ability to make a complaint or to exchange the product.

In more recent times, the financial crisis of 2007 drove radical change in the style and amount of regulation in the financial services sector. There was increasing movement away from light-touch regulation and a desire to pull back some of the activities of the private sector, especially in the banking industry. The major losses that had occurred (with Bank of America putting its losses as high as $7.7 trillion) seemed to be mainly blamed by the majority of people as being due to the fault of the regulators.[22]

There are important new aspects for regulators to consider, especially as processes are now becoming automated and machines are allowed to make decisions. *The Future of Regulation* specifically focuses on what the authors consider to have been a failure of regulation in London, which is a hub of the global financial market, pointing to three key elements:

1. That the regulators of the London Stock Exchange failed to adequately recognise the risks that were building up
2. That when risks were discovered, the regulatory system was 'politically too weak' to do anything about it
3. That the regulatory system failed to adequately differentiate between individual and systemic risk – and did not adequately appreciate that a series of individual failures could quickly be perceived as a systemic failure.[23]

It is wrong, of course, to consider regulation solely in the context of financial services, as the potential for risk applies to almost all (and perhaps all) areas in both the public and private sectors.

Financial regulation is clearly a complex and problematic topic. In 'The Role of Risk in Regulatory Processes', Julia Black of the London School of Economics refers specifically to risk. She says that it plays four important functions in regulation as:

1. An object of regulation
2. A justification for regulation
3. A basis for constructing organisational policies and procedures
4. A framework for accountability and evaluation.[23]

With these comments in mind, it appears sensible to consider the impact of AI in the context of creating an additional, specific operational risk to an organisation. (To recap, *operational risk* is defined as risk resulting from the failure of process, systems, or individuals, or as a consequence of external events.)

Separately, in her paper 'Learning from Regulatory Disasters', Julia Black considers the impact of what she describes as 'regulatory disasters' and which she defines as 'catastrophic events or series of events which have significantly harmful impacts on the life, health or financial wellbeing of individuals or the environment.'

She describes six major contributory causes:

1. Incentives on individuals or groups
2. Organisational dynamics of regulators, regulated operators, and the complexity of the regulatory system in which they are situated
3. Weaknesses, ambiguities, and contradictions in the regulatory strategies adopted

4. Misunderstandings of the problem and the potential solutions
5. Problems with communication about the conduct expected, or conflicting messages
6. Trust and accountability structures.[24]

At a time when there is an increased thrust towards dependence on advanced analytics and AI, risk managers and experts need to be especially alive to the greater risks that may attach to all businesses in an environment of machine learning.

What is worrisome is that many of the risks that may arise are not yet fully realised or understood. If this is in fact the case, then not only will it be difficult to evaluate and quantify the impact of these kinds of risks, but it will also be problematic to identify the most appropriate mitigating actions.

In this context, risk managers cannot afford to be bystanders. It is critical that they engage with the technology sector to understand what is happening and how potential dangers can be effectively mitigated.

ROLES, REGTECH, AND FORGIVING THE MACHINE

One of the main purposes of this book is to consider the impact of AI in professions and industries. In this section we aim to specifically consider the impact on aspects of regulation and compliance.

In considering the topic of compliance, firstly we have to consider the issue of data input. Already there are computer programs that automatically identify the quality of data. It is often argued that poor data is unhelpful, and individuals argue the point 'rubbish in, rubbish out'. One major UK bank takes the alternate view that *all* data has value and adds a score, or weight, to the data to quantify its validity.

In reality, isn't this what we already do as humans? We take information, consider the source and the context, often decide to carry out some form of validation, and then proceed accordingly. In an AI environment, there is no reason why a machine might not adopt a similar approach. Artificial neural networks already take into account missing information and bypass the gaps. The challenge may well be one of being able to identify if the wrong conclusion has been reached. In an autonomous environment, where does the gatekeeper or safety valve rest within the process?

Compliance and regulation come hand in hand. In fact the term *regulator* has its origin not in rules and law, but is rather a reference to a mechanical valve device that stops steam engines from overheating and exploding.

This begs the question – why should a human, as gatekeeper, be in a better position to ratify a decision than an automated system? If we concede that decisions are ultimately based on a combination of fact-finding, rational decision-making, and the application of experience, why can this not be replicated in a machine? It's feasible that errors may be made by an automated system – but isn't it equally possible that errors will be made by a human? At what point does a machine error become unforgiveable and a human error become forgivable (or vice versa)?

Such dilemmas take us towards the subject of psychology. Some argue that *forgiveness* is an action often accompanied by guilt or an admission of weakness on the part of the person making the mistake. *Guilt* itself is an interesting emotion. It is often expressed by a certain choice of words, nonverbal communication (such as posture), or perhaps a combination of subtle signals that are deeply embedded in our psyche. How might a machine replicate these, if it is at all possible?

In any event, are errors ever really the machine's fault, or does any guilt (or liability) rest with the manufacturers or programmers? Whilst this approach might have been valid for earlier systems, don't the rules change for self-learning and autonomous systems?

For a human to be able to forgive a machine, perhaps the machine needs to replicate human signals of guilt. Until these are fully understood, then perhaps forgiveness of machines by man is impossible. Can *guilt* be programmed into the system as a desirable technical capability?

What is *guilt* anyway? Shakespeare even makes an effort to capture the essence of blame in his play *Macbeth*, when Macbeth can find no peace, feeling only guilt after killing King Duncan. He speaks of 'life's fitful fever' as an illustration of guilt, and Lady Macbeth rubs her hands in vain to remove the blood ('Out, damned spot').[25] Maybe the solution for machines is easier than we think. As Oscar Wilde put it, 'It is the confession, not the priest that gives us absolution'.[26] Perhaps all the machine needs to have is a mechanism to say 'sorry' – whether it means it or not.

Regulation has become significantly more complex and is most probably set to become more so. There are 56 words in the Lord's Prayer, 297 in the Ten Commandments, 300 in the American Declaration of Independence, and apparently 26,911 words in an EEC directive on the export of duck eggs.

Many already think that regulation is excessive, whilst others accept it to be a necessary evil. Whichever way you look, the burden of satisfying regulation is both complex and onerous. London is one of the hearts of regulation, and in 2015 the then UK chancellor referred in his budget to regulatory technology, or so-called RegTech. RegTech is being described as 'new technology to facilitate the delivery of regulatory requirements', and is especially aimed at the financial services sector.[27]

With such lengthy existing regulatory documentation, the use of AI, and in particular the specific capability of natural language understanding (which is a subset of natural language processing) becomes critical. Through translating regulatory text into useable code, the system has the capability to automatically translate written regulations and to be able to more rapidly integrate new and updated regulations. Integrated with other tools, such as financial performance management, the system is further developing the ability to identify outliers and discrepancies, and to ultimately intervene automatically.

Such an approach, in which all the data and risk factors are stored and assessed using automated systems, improves the likelihood of compliance by removing what is called cognitive bias, that is, the application of a subjective approach to compliance by risk officers.

In a recent report on RegTech, the Institute of International Finance (IIF) says that 'By making compliance less complex and capacity demanding, RegTech solutions could free capita to [be] put to more productive uses'. It also suggests that it could help new entrants overcome the apparent complexity of regulatory barriers to entry by making them easier to understand, and overall make the process of regulation work better.

Regulation and compliance in the financial services market is a huge marketplace. Big banks spend well over US$1 billion per year on management of regulation. The Spanish bank BBVA estimated that many big organisations have 10–15% of their staff dedicated to the task of regulation.

It's natural therefore that the focus seems to be on financial services in particular. The IIF identifies what it considers to be key problems that are finance-specific, specifically in the areas of modelling, scenario analysis, and forecasting, and in the need of financial organisations to satisfy stress testing. (Stress testing is an exercise in which regulators create and model particular scenarios that test the adequacy, for example, of a bank's financial reserves.)

In 2015 Citigroup used an AI system called Ayasdi from Stanford University to help satisfy the US Federal Reserve stress test, having failed it the previous year. Stanford's Ayasdi has also been used in the pharmaceutical industry. Beyond stress testing and modelling, RegTech is a growing sector aimed at addressing many industries' pain points, such as interpretation and compliance with documentation, managing the behaviour of individual traders, and ultimately more effective customer management.

With regulation being so critical, experts are already calling for trusted third parties that can oversee AI decisions, particularly in the context of the 2018 EU GDPR. These third parties should 'have the power to scrutinise and audit algorithms', these experts say, and they also suggest that the wording of the GDPR does not have precise enough language in this developing area, nor does it contain explicit or implicit rights and safeguards against automated decision-making.[28]

Going forward, what will be the role of risk and compliance managers? The role of risk managers is to give advice to organisations on potential risks to the profitability or existence of the company. They identify and assess threats and put plans in place for when things go wrong. Additionally, they decide how to avoid, reduce, or transfer risks, including regulatory penalties and fines. The compliance officer (which arguably is a different role) has a responsibility for ensuring respect for national and international regulations, and for professional and extra-professional norms, as well as for rules of ethics and good behaviour, as defined by the company.[29]

Will the role of a risk manager in an AI environment be less affected than that of a compliance manager, whose role might be mainly automated? Will the risk manager have a responsibility for managing regulation, and if so, what will be the nature of that management? Will it be no more than overseeing an automated system?

Might we ultimately use smart machines to manage and regulate other AI systems? It's an old problem that even the Romans would have recognised. '*Quis custodiet ipsos custodes?*', they would have asked, roughly translated as 'Who will guard the guards?' Whilst this is an expression often more used to refer to political or police powers, it is equally applicable to the regulatory environment. As the use of technology and RegTech increases, regulators will inevitably place more emphasis on the use of AI and on the control environment.

In a 2015 report, Celent refers to the increasing automation of regulation: 'Regulators, incumbent financial institutions, and emerging FinTech companies will increasingly leverage technology to move towards real-time financial regulation in a data-rich and analytical manner. There will be shorter and more productive feedback loops between regulators and financial institutions, with a greater level of review of existing regulations to ensure that they remain relevant and effective.'[30]

CONCLUSION

In this chapter we have considered the different types of risk, principally focusing on operational and financial risk, but recognising that there are many other types of risk that might affect organisations.

Risk management is a thankless activity. The risk manager is often seen as the gatekeeper of an organisation rather than a key enabler to success. Decisions quickly made that align to an organisation's risk appetite can be a critical success factor.

Many risk management activities can already be undertaken by human intervention or specialist programmes, but businesses are operating in an increasing volatile climate. The complexity of risk and the uncertainty of the outside environment increasingly lend themselves to greater automation.

One of the great ironies is that as risk managers rely on automation, the automation itself creates new risks. Being in new technological territory, these risks are by their nature uncertain in their own right. If organisations depend more and more on some form of algorithmic solution to effectively manage risk, then how can we be really sure that the algorithms are working properly? What happens if there is some form of glitch in the system?

Will we ultimately depend on systems to detect failures in other systems? To what degree will regulators themselves depend on automated systems to detect anomalies and breaches of regulatory codes? Will systems be both judge and jury, limiting human intervention to that of communicating the verdict?

In this tangled web, ultimately powered by advanced algorithms, who (or what) will be the watchmen of the future?

NOTES

1. T. Rana, Artificial intelligence finally gets governance, former healthcare CFO leads the initiative. Cision PR. http://www.prweb.com/releases/2016/10/prweb13741691.htm (accessed 17 January 2018).
2. http://www.businessdictionary.com/definition/risk.html (accessed 16 August 2017).
3. Health Informatics in Clinical Practice, Information system failures and the NHS. http://hiicp.org/info_clinical/IT_Failures/info_clinical_IT_Failures_01.html (accessed 17 October 2017).
4. Lynda Bourne, Project failure: Cobb's paradox. The Project Management Hut (27 May 2011). https://pmhut.com/project-failure-cobbs-paradox
5. Frank Winters, The top ten reasons projects fail (part 7). Project Management.com (11 August 2013). https://www.projectmanagement.com/articles/187449/The-Top-Ten-Reasons-Projects-Fail--Part-7-
6. Neil Richards and Jonathan King, Big data ethics. *Wake Forest Law Review, 2014*. https://papers.ssrn.com/sol3/papers.cfm?abstract_id=2384174
7. John Whittaker, Emerging ethics in the world of big data and analytics. Dell Techcenter blogs (24 July 2015). http://en.community.dell.com/techcenter/b/techcenter/archive/2015/07/24/emerging-ethics-in-the-world-of-big-data-and-analytics
8. Howard Wen, The ethics of big data. *Forbes* (21 June 2012). http://www.forbes.com/sites/oreillymedia/2012/06/21/the-ethics-of-big-data/#4c97bf9254ef
9. Center for Strategic and International Studies. Net Losses: Estimating the Global Cost of Cybercrime: Economic Impact of Cybercrime II (June 2014).
10. Geoff Spencer, AI and cybercrime: good and bad news. Microsoft Asia (26 July 2017).
11. Bella M. DePaulo, Deborah A. Kashy, Susan E. Kirkendol, Melissa M. Wyer, and Jennifer A. Epstein, Lying in everyday life. *Journal of Personality and Social Psychology* 70, no. 5 (May 1996): 979–995.
12. Pamela Mayer, *Liespotting: Proven Techniques to Detect Deception* (St Martin's Griffin, 2011).

13. Richard Bandler and John Grinder *Frogs into Princes: Neuro Linguistic Programming* (Real People Press, 1979).
14. Dr David Smith, *Reliability, Maintainability and Risk* (Elsevier, 2000).
15. Unearth the answers and solve the causes of human error in your company by understanding the hidden truths in human error rate tables. Lifetime Reliability Solutions. http://www.lifetime-reliability.com/cms/tutorials/reliability-engineering/human_error_rate_table_insights (accessed 16 August 2017).
16. Quoctrung Bui, Will your job be done by a machine? NPR.org (21 May 2015). http://www.npr.org/sections/money/2015/05/21/408234543/will-your-job-be-done-by-a-machine
17. John Verver, The top five areas to monitor for employee fraud. CFO.com (6 November 2013). http://ww2.cfo.com/accounting-tax/2013/11/top-five-areas-monitor-employee-fraud
18. Online fraud increases 22% during holiday season. *Security* (15 January 2018). https://www.securitymagazine.com/articles/88637-online-fraud-increases-22-during-holiday-season (accessed 17 January 2018).
19. Sean Neary, The future of AI fraud prevention – a practical introduction. CNP.com (18 May 2017). http://cardnotpresent.com/cnp-expo-preview-the-future-of-ai-fraud-prevention-a-practical-introduction
20. Adam C. Uzialko, Artificial insurance? How machine learning is transforming underwriting. *Business News Daily* (11 September 2017). https://www.businessnewsdaily.com/10203-artificial-intelligence-insurance-industry.html
21. Jea Yu, Insurance fraud prevention gets a little help from artificial intelligence. *Insights*, Samsung.com (6 June 2017). https://insights.samsung.com/2017/06/06/insurance-fraud-prevention-gets-a-little-help-from-artificial-intelligence
22. Mike Collins, The big bank bailout. *Forbes* (14 July 2015). https://www.forbes.com/sites/mikecollins/2015/07/14/the-big-bank-bailout/#375f98bb2d83 (accessed 17 January 2018).
23. Julia Black, *The Future of Regulation* (Oxford Handbooks Online, 2010).
24. Julia Black, Learning from regulatory disasters. Law Society and Economy Working Paper Series, WPS 24-2014 (December 2014).
25. William Shakespeare, *Macbeth*. Wordsworth Editions, annotated edition (5 May 1992).
26. Oscar Wilde. 1891. *The Picture of Dorian Gray*. Wordsworth Editions, Paris edition text, published 1908 edition (5 May 1992).
27. Martin Arnold, Market grows for 'regtech', or AI for regulation. *Financial Times* (14 October 2016). https://www.ft.com/content/fd80ac50-7383-11e6-bf48-b372cdb1043a
28. Sandra Wachter, Brent Mittelstadt, and Luciano Floridi, Why a right to explanation of automated decision-making does not exist in the General Data Protection Regulation. *International Data Privacy Law, 2016*. https://ssrn.com/abstract=2903469
29. Blandine Cordier-Palasse, What makes a good compliance officer? Ethic Intelligence (April 2013). http://www.ethic-intelligence.com/experts/286-what-makes-a-good-compliance-officer
30. John Dwyer, RegTech – Not Reg Plus Tech, but Reg to the Power of Tech. Celent report (28 July 2015).

CHAPTER 7

Implementation Road Maps

SUMMARY

The previous chapters have aimed to provide some insight into the evolution of AI, its history, and the impact on some industries and professions. This chapter is about implementation: in effect, where the rubber hits the road.

It considers elements of an entire transformational programme, from leadership, recruitment, and training to how practitioners might physically work together. The section draws on experiences of previous implementations and associated learning, and concludes with the question of whether incremental or big bang change is the most effective.

INTRODUCTION

In his article '13 Forecasts on Artificial Intelligence', Francesco Corea sets out his views on the future of AI over the next five years.[1] In the interests of detail, these have been extrapolated to the following 15 key points:

1. *AI is going to require fewer data to work*. In other words, better algorithms will require less data to be effective. This is an interesting viewpoint, insofar as the argument historically has been that AI and cognitive analytics are needed to help make sense of masses of data, whereas Corea appears to be suggesting that volumes of data may be replaced by fewer, 'richer' sets of data. This approach may be especially helpful as we consider issues of security, which demand greater control over sources of information.

2. *New types of learning are the key*. There will be a move away from incremental learning of the machine (called *transfer learning*) to a process called *multitask learning*. (Perhaps we now have added insight as to the gender of computers – women are said to be better at multitasking than men, according to a British Medical Council study.[2])

3. *AI will eliminate human biases*. This is because human decision-making is based on evolutionary habits that do not exist in the development of a new system.

4. *AI can be fooled*. Adversarial examples have been created to try to deceive intelligent image recognition by introducing image distortion, which misleads the

system. It can reasonably be expected that in a future world of cybercrime, considerable effort will be expended on distorting the outcome of AI.

5. *There are risks associated with AI development.* Notwithstanding the challenge of ethical risk, there are the operational risks associated with system mistake or malfunction. As industries and professions increasingly rely on technology, how will they retain responsibility for decision-making (and how will this apply vicariously through their insurers)? How might this change?

6. *Real general AI will have a collective intelligence.* Rosenberg (a technologist, inventor, entrepreneur, and founder of *UnanimousAI*, an artificial intelligence company that enables human groups to amplify their collective brainpower by forming real-time online swarms) refers to a 'swarm' of collective intelligence described as a 'brain of brains'. When compared to human behaviour, we influence each other as individuals, and this tendency can be aggregated into social sentiment. AI could have a collective intelligence not dissimilar to swarms of bees, which create 'noisy evidence, weigh the alternative and finally reach a specific decision'.

7. *AI will have unexpected sociopolitical implications.* The main concern expressed about AI is that of a loss of jobs, whereas Corea suggests that 'jobs simply will be changed'. This issue is closer to the heart of a broader discussion, which suggests that knowledge will be decentralised, human expertise will become less important, and the possibility that humans may be relegated to becoming machine technicians.

8. *Real AI should start asking 'why'.* This starts to push the concept of AI beyond the 'what' and the 'how' into the matter of 'why'.

9. *AI is pushing the limits of privacy and data leakage.* If it isn't now, then it will be soon.

10. *AI is changing IoT.* The current model of multiple devices that are interconnected and instrumented, and then yield large amounts of data to be interrogated, may become an obsolete model. There is also concern about vulnerability of this system to failure if one component breaks down or is hacked. Decentralisation of architecture may avoid this problem and provide a less expensive operating model.

11. *Robotics is becoming mainstream.* There is an increasing desire to give AI a physicality, or physical body, in the form of robotics.

12. *AI might have barriers to development.* In other words, the appetite for change may be inhibited simply by the ability to design hardware.

13. *Quantum computing.* Increasingly, there is a desire to develop quantum computing, which allows analysis at the speed of nature. The capability to design such systems is in the domain of only a few companies. Perhaps Thomas Watson was right when he predicted that the future would only require five computers – maybe he meant five quantum computers.

14. *Biological robots and nanotech are the future of AI applications.* This comprises the development of technology at the intersection of AI and biology, in other words 'electrical wires made by bacteria'.

15. *Chemputers.* There is already the concept of the chemical computer (the chemputer), which allows advanced chemical processes to grow complex electronic systems from molecular levels upwards. Professor Lee Cronin at the University of Glasgow describes it as 'a combination of creative thinking and convergent digital technologies'.[3]

Francesco Corea is one of a growing number of experts who are anticipating the future. These forecasts are invariably viewed from a generalist point of view rather than as specifically applying to individual industries. Whilst there is some generic learning to be shared, shouldn't we continue to try to make predictions more specific to industries or professions?

Different industries clearly move at different speeds of innovation, but there seems to be some consistency of some groups being viewed as blockers of change.

In a joint survey by *New Civil Engineer* and Bentley Systems, 100 engineering professionals were interviewed. Despite the relatively small sample size, seven key themes were identified as adversely affecting the adoption of change. Taken in order, they are:

1. Poor digital infrastructure
2. No authority to change
3. Lack of training
4. Security concerns
5. Economic climate
6. Ageing workforce
7. Company buying cycles.

The guide based on survey results, *Technology Consumption: Are Engineers Ready to Make the Leap and Reap the Rewards*, reveals that whilst some might have imagined that progress is being impaired by so-called Luddites, or the inertia of ageing workers, this was not found to be the case.

Instead, the review suggests that technological progress is being mainly slowed down by the attitude of employers. In the survey, 44% of respondents thought that their organisations did not consider technology training to be important.[4]

Perhaps the speed of adoption is not so much in the attitude of the affected professionals but in their working environment and leadership. Speed of adoption could also be being impacted by the procurement cycle, which may be driving down investment on the part of employers, and the differing attitudes towards change on the part of employer and employee at the proverbial coalface.

NEW THINKING ON EMPLOYEE TRAINING

In this new era of intelligent technology, it is apparent that old ideas on training and education are starting to become irrelevant. Already we have identified that different people have different learning styles, supporting the case for a *brain-friendly learning* approach. The term *brain-friendly learning*, whilst proprietary, reflects the concept that we all have different learning styles (e.g. aural, tactile, and visual).

Why is this important? It is of significance because, if we get it wrong, there are inevitable knock-on effects in terms of implementation and value delivery.

Beyond this, misinformation may lead to misunderstanding, resentment, and resistance. Earlier in the book we considered the Luddite movement that resisted the impact of change, but how might its adherents have reacted if they had been painted a different picture? That picture could have been one of greater prosperity at an individual level, affecting those who were prepared to not only adopt the changes, but, more importantly, to find ways of working with these new methods.

Training in the twenty-first century and in such a complex area demands a revisiting of the learning process, and gaining deeper understanding of what some describe as learning barriers. That is to say, we need a better understanding of the difficulties that all of us, as individuals, will have in self-improvement of skills and capabilities in the new working landscape. This understanding must be, for employers, one of the critical success factors in terms of successful implementation.

What is clear is that the old approach to training and education is becoming redundant, if not already obsolete. We increasingly depend on trainers having sufficient knowledge and experience to be able to share, or transfer, their thinking. But are trainers knowledgeable enough to understand the complexities and challenges of these new working practices? Perhaps they are as disadvantaged as business leaders, who equally have no practical experience of this new pattern of working.

Put simply, training on the impact of AI and how it can be incorporated requires a whole new mind-set of training/enablement thinking. Visual presentations are unlikely to suffice in this future enablement model. Streamed video equally has its limitations.

It will be especially interesting to see how conference organisers and training companies, who earn their crust from knowledge exchange, will cope with this new environment. The conference industry is a significant revenue generator, but shows little development over two or more decades, and may simply not be fit for purpose over the next decade.

The future of training will inevitably encompass multifaceted knowledge management. At the very least, this will comprise (with a high degree of personalisation and customisation):

- 3-D virtual learning
- Video tuition
- Gaming
- Face-to-face training
- Self-paced learning
- Webinars
- eLearning
- Social learning
- Mentoring.

These types of training, in such a potentially controversial environment, will provoke discussion. Many of the considerations will occur not only across departments within businesses but also across geographies. Wider discussion will need to be at a professional, that is, vocational, level. For example, the marketing community will inevitably have a view about the impact of chatbots on the customer relationship, regardless of the industry that they are working in.

There's a lot of uncertainty ahead of us all, but the pace of change could be terrifyingly quick. This will occur in job functions, industries, and professions where we least expect it to happen. The speed of change will mean that traditional methods will be obsolete. Self-learning will rapidly become the dominant force. In fact, there's an argument to suggest that the speed of learning may actually be dictated by the speed of development of the machines themselves.

Take, for instance, gaming, which invariably has a part to play in one form or another in the wider AI agenda. In gaming, success allows the individual to progress to the next level – and the player is often gifted with new tools, skills, or capabilities at the same time. At what point will the machine decide whether the human is suitably skilled to engage effectively and to move up to the next level?

For trainers, new challenges of relevance, creating excitement, and measurement of progress are also apparent.

Relevance. The need to remain relevant and to avoid losing the audience will remain dominant, dynamic training will be prevalent, discussion will be critical, and teamwork will be essential. Faced with these new challenges, desk-based training may simply not be sufficient, and might even be counterproductive.

It's very important to measure the relevance of training, especially relative to the role, function, and perhaps even the prospects of the individuals involved. If their current roles involve managing simple tasks or managing people engaged in those repetitive or routine roles, roles that are prime for automation or replacement by robots, how best can those individuals understand the relevance of change and effectively engage in the learning process?

Generally, turkeys do not vote for Christmas, so why should some managers and staffers be enthusiastic about AI change, given that some robotics are already (as of 2016) identified as being 65% less expensive than real people?

Excitement. Trainers need to generate excitement, not fear of the future. Whilst poor training may create contempt, at its worst it might even breed resentment. Engagement of the audience becomes both critical and essential.

Measurement. This is a really difficult area to consider. Training and enablement teams are today more frequently challenged to measure the success of their efforts. In sales, for example, by how much has training increased the effectiveness of the sales team, measured in terms of pipeline or number of opportunities? Employers may in the future need to be much clearer about what the desired metrics for successful training are. These metrics may be hard quantifiable metrics (such as efficiency), soft qualitative measures (such as sentiment), or more likely a combination of both.

Some forward-looking organisations, such as Skillsoft, already recognise that training for a new era demands new approaches. Its paper '5 Reasons Training Fails, and What to Do About It' is not only relevant to the current operating environment, but also starts to set out an effective framework for the future.[5]

ROBOTICS AND PROCESS AUTOMATION

For many organisations, robotic process automation (RPA) and the attendant robotic desktop automation (RDA) are critical starting points that help provide a useful guide as to broader AI implementation.

In general terms, RPAs are systems – or robots – that imitate human behaviour. This isn't a new idea; in fact, it's over 30 years old. It's often recognised by a number of other names, such as *scripting*, *scraping*, *bots*, *augmented*, *automation*, and *AI*. Purists would be able to distinguish between all these but to the layman they are from the same template.

The main purpose of these robotic systems is to replace the human component. Specialists in the field claim that this type of robotics is two-thirds less expensive than full-time human employees, with greater reliability and fewer compliance issues.

There are two forms of RPA: *unattended* and *attended*. Some suggest that there is a third form: *semi-attended*. Table 27 compares unattended RPA with attended RPA.

TABLE 27 Comparison between unattended and attended automation.

Unattended RPA	Attended RPA
In the server room – virtual machine (VM)	Robot on every desktop
One robot per VM	Personal robot in real time
Automates 100% of work	Automates 20–90% 0f work
Impacts smaller subgroups and processes	Impacts larger group
Best for fully documented processes	Automates full or partial process
Automated end to end	Automates rote with cognitive real-time
Back office, operations, outsources	Front office, back office
10–100 robots per enterprise	100–200,000 robots per enterprise

Source: Pegasystems (n.d.). Home page. Pegasystems website. www.pega.com

In this period of transformation, companies such as Pegasystems and others suggest that rather than adopting an either/or approach, enterprises should initially consider a combination of unattended and attended RPAs, in effect a combination of unattended and attended robots.

The two key criteria for adoption are:

1. Whether the function is back office or front office, on the basis that front-office systems are less mature, more visible, and more likely to attract criticism
2. Back office adoption is less time critical and will tolerate slower responses (but surely this is set to change with greater visibility?).

Beyond this, the concept of the *cobot* is also on the table. In effect, this is a robot that works with humans to achieve defined business objectives. The cobot was created to work beside and interface with humans, usually on the shop floor in a manufacturing environment.

The cobot is principally identified and defined by its:

- *Proximity.* Cobots are automated systems not protected by safety screens
- *Accessibility.* Cobots do not require expert programmers on a day-to-day basis.[6]

IMPLEMENTATION FRAMEWORKS

Implementation of an AI programme should not take place in isolation, but rather should be created with some form of end state in mind (recognising that the end state may be uncertain at the time of origination of the programme).

Key Implementation Questions

An organisation should try to address some key questions, typically:

- *What is it trying to achieve?* Usually, most industries are defined by the key business drivers, for example, cost reduction, operational efficiency, customer acquisition, and greater accessibility to services and products. It is important that organisations understand how these benefits are defined, to ensure that there are no misunderstandings.

- *How will the improvements be eventually measured?* In most cases, a business case will need to be created that is based on a combination of hard (i.e. financial) benefits and soft (i.e. reputation, user engagement) benefits. What will be the real effect on headcount and cost? In many cases, organisations struggle to measure improvement simply because the metrics at the starting point are not fully understood or capable of being measured accurately.
- *How can an organisation measure the change, or delta, of improvement if the starting point has not been adequately defined?* Beyond this, the methodology of measurement must be clearly understood and agreed at the outset to prevent disagreement later on.
- *Does the organisation have a clear understanding about the terminologies being used?* The technology sector is well known for its tendency to fall into the use of jargon. In many cases, the expression AI is confused with prescriptive or cognitive analytics. In fact, some of the business objectives being sought could be effectively achieved by using older, already proven technologies.
- *What is the human interface with the technology?* In the case of, for example, RPA, does the proposed process demand human intervention (attended RPA), no human intervention (unattended RPA), or a combination of both? If the process is complicated, perhaps it can be broken down into a combination of attended and unattended RPA.
- *Are there other reasons to change, beyond satisfying the key business drivers?* Is the reason for change to implement incremental improvement in a business, maybe following a me-too approach, or is the change part of a larger business transformation? Small-scale change is often tempting, and provides the illusion of progress, but it may not be sustainable if the desired benefits do not materialise or if there is a loss of sponsorship. Large-scale transformations that affect larger groups or more-impactful processes may provide more significant outcomes. However, risk-averse companies are becoming more reluctant to adopt big bang change, preferring increments as part of a planned road map.
- *Are the steps on the road to change well thought out?* Perhaps there are intermediary steps, or not all steps in a transformation process are of equal size and importance.
- *To what degree will the organisation need to keep skilled staff?* Like many similar organisations, the bakery Mr Kipling in the UK, part of the Premier Foods group, uses a fully automated system for production. However, it keeps staff available on a contingency basis for when there is systemic failure. The key reasoning is that many of its products are time-framed. For example, during the Christmas season the company makes 200 million mince (fruit) pies, and for Mr Kipling, missing that window of opportunity is not an option. To what degree will other industries and processes need to have human staff on standby in case of failure?
- *First-mover or second-mover advantage?* Does the organisation want to be at the cutting edge of innovation, reaping the public relation advantages (or risks) that are attached? Alternatively, might it prefer to use tried-and-tested new technologies? The latter may allow for a quicker, less expensive, and more certain implementation, and has the advantage of learning and knowledge transfer from earlier movers.
- *What is the risk appetite of the organisation?* This applies especially to the area of operational risk, which deals with issues of failures of systems, people, and

processes, and the impact of external forces. Can innovation be ring-fenced in some way to ensure that operational risk and its impact on business as usual is reduced? To what degree does ring-fencing reduce the speed and impact of implementation?

- *What is the competitive environment looking like, and can an organisation wait?* Will the challenge be more likely to come from new entrants without the baggage of legacy systems? Perhaps alternatively it may come from external market intruders with greater ambition and more aggressive time frames.
- *What will happen in five years?* To what degree does an implementation road map take into account future changes in politics, the economy, technology, and the environment: that is, a forward-looking PEST (political, economic, sociocultural, technological) analysis?

Leadership and Sponsorship

At the heart of implementation programmes of any type are issues of leadership and sponsorship. These are particularly difficult in a topic so potentially challenging as AI implementation, and in an area that will have such an impact on organisations and individuals.

There are likely to be many barriers to change. Machiavelli seems to have recognised this as far back as the sixteenth century when he analysed the difficulties faced by princes:

> *The innovator makes enemies of all of those who have prospered under the old order, and only lukewarm support is forthcoming from those who would prosper under the new ... partly because men are generally incredulous, never really trusting new things until they have tested them by experience.*[7]

Leaders in an AI environment are especially tested, in that it calls for them to act without experience while encouraging others to follow them.

In the current climate, there is also a suggestion that the role of leader as a flag-bearing individual is becoming obsolete, and that leadership is increasing becoming *a function*, as opposed to it being a power vested in an individual. In today's fluid environment, the function of leader moves from individual to individual, marked by the needs of the moment and the capabilities of the individual to meet those needs.

We might assume, perhaps incorrectly, that the machine itself sits outside the leadership function. Going forward, it may be not only that the machine is part of that function, as a form of coworker, but perhaps could even play a substantial part in leadership.

That is not to say that the machine itself can become *the* leader. Leadership appears to be a human trait, and there are no examples to date of a machine leading and inspiring humans (or other machines). But the leaders of tomorrow will become all the more dependent on these data-driven sources. Artificial systems will become the trusted advisor to the C-level executive, and will be the ones to provide indisputable, data-driven insights.

In setting up a development team, it is likely that some degree of creativity will be needed. In Chapter 5 we considered the potential for machines to be creative in art and music, but at the moment some argue that computers do not seem to have adequately demonstrated innovation. We will have to rely on humans for the time being.

That is not to say that an implementation checklist could not be created by a human and managed by a system, much in the same way that talent management analytics and project planning software can converge and be used to manage a series of key implementation activities. The introduction of some form of systematic learning loop could provide a methodology for self-improvement within the process.

Nevertheless, for the moment leadership will remain the domain of senior executives, if only because they have a legal and fiduciary duty to stockholders to guide their businesses in the right direction. They will use robotics and AI if they believe that it is the correct thing to do. In a slightly dated, but still relevant, survey of business process reengineering, research amongst 52 major companies planning to undertake reengineering programmes showed that the chairman or CEO were the business sponsors, or champions, in 29% of the cases. Managing directors were champions in a further 25% of programmes. Directors were cited as champions in 38% of cases and managers in 8% of cases.[8]

Whilst they may be the sponsors or champions of projects, there will still be a need for a project leader who is responsible for day-to-day decisions and managing of budgets, and also to communicate upwards, downwards, and across the organisation. These skills are not only functional and managerial in nature. Individuals will also need to have an understanding of technological capability and the politics of the business, and above all to be entrepreneurial. It's a tough combination of skills and talents, and one that isn't readily found.

Because of this, the role of sponsor or champion becomes even more critical in the mix. The sponsor defines (or at least *signs off* on) the goals, provides the resources, assesses success, and manages any internal politics (including pushback from other stakeholders). With AI potentially reducing the size of workforces and the nature of individual roles, such sponsorship could require a firm hand and a steady nerve.

The mood with regard to stakeholders is increasingly one of stakeholder engagement rather than management – that is to say, much earlier involvement of stakeholders in the decision-making process than has traditionally been the case. Lack of knowledge of these new technologies, even amongst stakeholders themselves, could provide a stumbling block, so effective communication is critical.

In such an innovative area, sponsors may be unlikely to be able to use their personal experiences of previous implementations. In the early stages of learning, the uniqueness of the process for them will most definitely require sponsors to be at the top of their game. AI experts who have the technological know-how will become increasingly valuable. Those who have a proven track record of implementation in a business environment will be particularly important, will be highly regarded, and almost certainly will be rewarded well.

In their article 'The Future Belongs to Leaders Who Get Artificial Intelligence', Atanu Basu of Ayata (the company that created the concept of prescriptive analytics) and Michael Simmons (cofounder of Empact, a consultancy focusing on entrepreneurship, entrepreneurial mind-set, innovation, and leadership) state that business leaders of the future need to ask six questions about their business:

1. How would Google do it?
2. Where do they look for hidden insight into the data?
3. How do they expand the definition of what data is?
4. Where do they explore the world of open-source algorithms?
5. How do they get comfortable with algorithms they don't understand?
6. How do they avoid falling into the trap of 'algorithms should never do that'?

The authors also introduce the concept of the surprise–fear–embrace curve – the journey 'from surprise, to fear, to life-as-usual (which) is something that we're all going to experience over and over, as software algorithms take over decisions that we previously thought only humans could do'.[9]

James O'Brien of Amex Forum describes the future leader as becoming the 'centre of gravity' of the workforce that the leader has brought together. He suggests that the leaders of tomorrow will require five key capabilities:

1. *Transparency*. Recognising that everyone must know where he or she is in the progress of the company.
2. *Flexibility*. Working in a new style of workplace that will be more dynamic than ever before, leaders will need to be more flexible, including in the choice of their staff.
3. *Collaborative*. Adopting a more open-door approach to the workforce.
4. *Empowering*. Recognising that work and personal life are a set of integrated experiences.
5. *Hosting*. Tomorrow's leader will become adept at pulling people together for a common purpose, as opposed to being the so-called hero leader.[10]

Creating a Team

The competition for talent among industries and organisations, which some have called the talent wars, is a real problem. Might a shortage of talent create some sort of a roadblock to progress?

Already we are seeing an increase in temporary or permanent migration and reverse migration of talented people. The end of the twentieth century was sometimes typified by intellectual migrants from China, India, and (increasingly) Brazil travelling to mature economies in search of education and qualifications. Now the more common trend seems to be one of countries and corporations doing much more to retain talent, and this is not only likely to continue, but to accelerate. Established professionals with special skills are also encouraged to work abroad.

Reciprocal academic arrangements between countries are more widespread. To cite just one example, the UK-based Chevening Programme is the UK government's international awards scheme aimed at developing global leaders. It offers a 'unique opportunity for future leaders, influencers and decision-makers from all over the world to develop professionally and academically, network extensively, experience (British) culture, and build lasting positive relationships with the UK.'[11]

Such flow of talent is not without its problems. Even with strong diplomatic and commercial drivers for intellectual migration, some people originate from places where strong cultural ties make permanent relocation less attractive. Elsewhere other young academics seem keen to study and/or work anywhere rather than where they were raised. For young people, the idea of studying or working abroad can be very compelling: new friends, new experiences, and the benefit of spicing up their CVs.

What all this starts to boil down to is a much more flexible and dynamic workforce. Recruitment agencies, which have traditionally been relatively myopic in terms of finding talent on their own doorsteps, will need to develop a broader outlook and adopt a more international perspective.

Finding Talent

Finding the right talent for this new era of technological development won't be easy. Many whose attempts to create a fortune through entrepreneurship haven't quite made it will come from the flat white economy. They will be looking for some financial security in order to get on the ladder of life. Employers will need to consider their aptitudes rather than just their technical capabilities and find ways to motivate, train, and retain them in a fast-changing environment. Research into expert performance indicates that the most compelling factor in retention is that individuals love what they are doing.[12]

Another growing trend is working in multidisciplinary teams, either real or virtual, which start to mirror well-established approaches to centres of competence.

In an analytics centre of competence, for example, typical capabilities might include:

- Technical
- Communication
- Marketing
- Evangelism
- Helpline.

Managing Progress

There's a certain irony in organisations needing to revert to what might seem more basic analytical tools in order to measure the progress by more advanced ones. The test of success for many organisations will be measured by hard benefits in terms of decreased turnover, greater profit, or increased operational efficiency.

At the heart of performance management is the notion of a single version of the truth in terms of data, which is an essential enabler to ensure that there are no disagreements with respect to the veracity of information provided. Effective performance management allows organisations to measure, monitor, report, and plan for the future. Analytical tools provide a broad, integrated framework for measurement across the organisation. Experience seems to indicate that grand, top-down projects to transform the enterprise are sometimes unsuccessful, as there is a reluctance to report bad news. Bottom-up transformation simply can't happen without appropriate executive support and sponsorship.

The office of finance sits at the heart of effective performance management. This department plays a key role in 'complying with legal, tax, and regulatory requirements and dispensing sound advice on the effective allocation of capital and resources'.

Two key questions about the office of finance are posed:

1. Does the office of finance play the role of trusted advisor or as enforcer?
2. Does finance use the budget as a tool for controlling costs or for allocating sound investment?

In *The Performance Manager*, the authors identify four key barriers with respect to information (and the lack of it) in the office of finance:

- Lack of information needed to regulate what has happened and what will happen
- The relevance and credibility of what is measured through processes that are designed for accounting rather than business management

- The balancing of short- and long-term goals, detailed focus, and the big picture
- The need for finance to find a road between top-down vision and bottom-up circumstances.[13]

In a complex transformation, it becomes absolutely critical that the finance department have an unambiguous view of the performance of the business. To that extent, spreadsheet analysis alone will almost certainly not provide enough insight and control.

Transformation will also require the buy-in of many senior managers. With one of the key business drivers of AI being one of greater operational efficiency (aka reduced operating cost), it becomes critical that there be no room for disagreement in terms of the metrics. The expected level of change is likely to be so great as to demand that there can be no disagreements about numbers around the periphery.

Fear of change is also likely to impact on employees' behaviour, especially if they see the introduction of processes that will result in job losses. Accurate information is needed to ensure that employees are properly motivated through rewards or other mechanisms.

Increased automation of processes is bound to be more effective in some sales channels than others. It is critical that executives have a clear understanding of which channels are most successful in terms of go-to-market approaches. Benchmarking between traditional and new processes becomes critical, but it is important that the benchmarks are both accurate and fair. A robotic sales process that operates without human intervention may effectively deal with the easy sales, for example, but then hand over the more complicated sales in which greater human persuasion is needed. Comparing easy and complicated sales might not be done accurately without perhaps factoring in some measurement of difficulty. It may be that some organisations will want to focus on simple sales and processes alone, and leave the more complex and expensive work to their competitors.

Elsewhere we have considered the impact of AI on finance professionals. Like many other professionals, they are inevitably going to be affected. They could also be in an invidious position, by effectively being in a position to allocate and manage innovation budgets without perhaps entirely buying into the process. It follows that the CFO could become one of the most significant stakeholders in the entire AI implementation process.

Whereas once CFOs might have been prepared to fall back on their old position as being guardian of the accounts, this new paradigm of information will force them to form new and deeper relationships with other parts of the business. They will no longer be the financial police of their businesses, and instead will need to become fully fledged business partners. This burden will not only fall on CFOs themselves but on their departments as a whole.

Beyond traditional technical skills of general accounting, transaction management, treasury and cash management, and statutory reporting, they will also need to engage with a new toolbox, which may include business process reengineering, and the use of breakthrough technology.

In the book *Reinventing the CFO*, the authors suggest that new competences for individuals within the office of finance should be thought of in three groups:

1. *Personal effectiveness.* This includes an action-orientated bias, an appetite for change, and an orientation towards knowledge and learning.

2. *Shared effectiveness.* This includes more collaborative working (not only across the business but perhaps with the system itself).
3. *Process effectiveness.* This includes the creation and management of key relationships and a process-orientated frame of mind.[14]

If, as has been suggested, having an effective finance department is a critical success factor in effective AI implementation, then it is important for CFOs to ask some key questions of themselves. These might include:

- What is the state of the office of finance now?
- What are the critical things that the office of finance needs to be able to do to become an effective business partner in an AI-infused environment?
- What skills or competences might be needed in this new environment?
- Who should stay and who should go?
- Where do I find new talent and what additional training might they need?
- How do I train and develop those who stay?
- Where does the finance department need to be to give the company the ability to not only operate in 10 or 20 years, but, more importantly, to remain competitive?
- What is a realistic time to carry out any organisational changes to achieve this, and is that timescale adequately aligned to the technological advances happening elsewhere in the business?
- How will the office of finance cope with the transitional period whilst change is ongoing?

Leadership remains critical throughout this process, not only at the board level but within the finance function itself. The office of finance must help create some sort of vision in an uncertain future and help to move the business through transformation as quickly and painlessly as possible. Momentum is critical. Some describe the most dangerous time in any transformation programme as what might be called the *neutral zone*, that is, the point at which the individual or organisation has not disengaged with the past yet is uncommitted to the future.

In such cases there needs to be some mutual agreement as to what the future actually looks like. Individuals and companies in the early stages of industry-wide change will not be able refer to the experience and lessons of their peers. As a result, there will be an element of stepping into the unknown. Driving change through at such a time requires individual strength and confidence.

It's fair to say that there are likely to be those who portray an image of confidence on the surface but are privately terrified. Nevertheless, it is critical that they continue, at the least, to act the part.

One mechanism which they will need to adopt is that of retaining focus on the customer. What are the benefits that transformation will bring to the end user of the company's service? Perhaps lower price, greater reliability, or less risk? Placing the customer at the heart of transformational change provides the department and individual with some form of anchor that rationalises the need for change.

Another mechanism at play may be that of me-too thinking. In other words, the company's approach is based on industry-wide changes and change is being implemented to mirror peer behaviour. Me-too thinking is essentially defensive in nature, and probably is an approach that focuses on personal and organisational safety. That in itself isn't entirely out of order (remember Maslow), but as we have suggested elsewhere, perhaps Maslow's thinking is increasingly that of a bygone age and there is a need to flip at least some notions of safety on their head.

Human Resources Function

As the professionals chiefly tasked with hiring and firing, the human resources (HR) department needs to recognise that it is not immune from AI. Like the office of finance, it will not only need to inwardly recognise the impact that AI and robotics will have on its own job functions, but also outwardly consider the new shape of its own organisation (and department) in an AI environment.

In its sixth annual HR survey, the recruiter Harvey Nash reported that, '15% of HR leaders were affected now by AI and automation, whilst a further 40% say it will have an impact within the next two to five years' (i.e. by 2020 or thereabouts).

The report also says that 86% of the 1,008 global HR leaders polled said that HR has an important role in 'promoting and supporting innovation in their organization'.

Harvey Nash comments that there has been a decreased focus on recruitment at the board level due to economic uncertainty. The report observes that the rate of downsizing has slowed down, 'suggesting that the majority of organizations responding may have already downsized or be at optimum size'. More than half recognised the 'march towards digitalization'.[15]

HR experts need to start preparing seriously for robotics and AI in the workplace. In the XpertHR report *Preparing for Robotics and Artificial Intelligence in the Workplace – Checklist*, the authors suggest a 12-point plan for HR professionals, paraphrased as follows:

1. Focus on employment legislation associated with AI
2. Understand how the organisation will use AI
3. Assign an HR professional to each AI project in the organisation
4. Develop an internal communications programme
5. Evaluate the impact of robotics on skill requirements
6. Consider these requirements against existing skill sets and training
7. Plan for AI changes in the HR's own department
8. Learn about the use of big data in employment
9. Consider how AI will change recruitment
10. Anticipate an acceleration of change and its impact
11. Monitor proposed employment legislation
12. Collaborate externally.[16]

Following the checklist's recommendations may be easier said than done. The Chartered Institute of Personnel and Development suggests that the following attributes are essential to doing an HR job effectively:

- Decisive thinker
- Skilled influencer
- Personally credible
- Collaborative in nature
- Driven to deliver
- Courageous to challenge
- Acts as role model
- Requires curiosity.[17]

These are worthy soft skills, but may not be wholly adequate in a technologically focused and transforming business place. The use of computerised talent management systems is leading to the reinvention of the HR function. There's a possibility that many existing HR professionals will be stretched.

As with other professions, the HR function will need to evolve, not only to work with advanced analytics in a more collaborative way, but also to manage the impact of change within a nervous workforce in particular.

Alternative Spaces: The New Workplace

In considering implementation, it's also important to consider the issue of the physical workplace itself. The nature of development of AI, coupled with the different skills and capabilities of those involved with an implementation project, imply that the traditional workspace may no longer be appropriate.

Earlier in the book we considered the meaning of work and observed that formal labour markets are beginning to change and become more differentiated. The impact of this is that what we describe as the *spatialities and temporalities* of the workplace are also shifting, moving away from predictable and routine work hours, as traditionally seen in larger established corporations, into a more fragmented, unpredictable, and relatively unstable working environment.

There also seems to be a shift towards informal and alternative work patterns (that are sometimes unpaid), which reflects the emphasis on value generation as opposed to salaried employment.

We have already considered the capabilities of at least some of the entrepreneurs involved in the development of disruptive technology. We now need to recognise that in addition to vision and technical capability, they may need to have a high level of creativity. It might be useful to look at how some of the creative industries organise themselves in terms of the workplace, as this may help with a template for the future place of work.

In this context, the creative industry is usually taken to mean the media, information, culture, and arts sectors. Including such sectors as advertising, gaming, and multimedia, this industry has historically been one of the fastest growing areas of commerce. The creative sector perhaps offers some form of outline for future working.

In the creative sector, as with disruptive technology, the focus historically is on output rather than the process by which the output has been achieved. The creative sector is characterised as being 'empowering, flexible, creative, fun, risky, precarious, transitionary, and economically marginal'.

One subsector of the creative industry is that of retro retailers, who sell styles from the past. With the current emphasis on retro styles, it's an interesting comparison. Key issues that seem to emerge are the following:

- Working spaces are not static and many pop-up shops are in commercially unstable locations.
- They operate in a fickle market, distinguishing themselves by proactivity and innovation.
- They adopt 'unconventional' working practices that differ from the mainstream.
- They provide greater 'vibrancy, imagination, and moneymaking' compared to mainstream businesses.

- They are 'micro-enterprises' where individuals have more control over their own behaviour.
- The riskier environment drives a new form of employee participation that is entrepreneurial.
- Employees adopt a 'creative identity' that 'fuels their ambition' and 'justifies' the long hours, low pay, and even the lack of success.

Beyond this, creative employees appear to operate in more effective social networks, which offset what might appear, at first glance, to be solitary and isolated working environments. This combination of shared experiences, and social and business networking emphasises the importance of physical proximity.[18]

It also helps us understand why innovation hubs, for example, are located in places that are cool and hip. If these places are not cool and hip to start with, then they usually are by the time the innovators have invaded the locations and made them so with the addition of newly created bars, clubs, and cafés. Thinking along these lines helps to explain the attraction of what seems a rather precarious and risky approach to work, but nevertheless one that is apparently especially attractive to the millennial, and presumably post-millennial, population.

In her book *The Time Bind: When Work Becomes Home and Home Becomes Work*, the writer Arlie Hochschild considers what has become a transposition of work and home. This phenomenon occurs when family are replaced by friends and work colleagues. The environment reminds us of the 'buzzy' pleasure of an active work environment in which people are prepared to work all hours and feel that work is a place where 'self-satisfaction, well-being, high-spirits, and work are inextricably linked'.[19]

Readers who need to validate such thinking need only visit places such as Shoreditch and the Silicon Roundabout in London, or any of a hundred other centres around the world. If these readers have the opportunity to visit an innovation hub, then they won't need to bother to dress for business. Those whom they meet may look as if they are wearing the first clothes they found on the floor in the morning, and instead of shoes, trainers are both fashionable and socially acceptable.

There also seems to be a gender component. Anecdotally, only about 20% of innovators in innovation hubs are female. Is this because females are said to be more prudent and risk averse? Is innovation linked in some way to the hunter-gatherer gene traditionally attributed to males, if there is such a thing? Another explanation may be that some members of the species may wish to impress others by an assertive, risk-taking, rather cavalier attitude to life and work – and that such demeanour is, in some strange way, all part of a very sophisticated courting process.

It might be argued that this type of thinking flies in the face of breaking down barriers. If the proverbial glass ceiling wasn't troublesome enough to contend with, some are now suggesting that there are also glass curtains and glass corridors as well, which represent the difficulty of the different genders working alongside each other.

That aside, we should return to the issue of where to work, and how this relates to the commercial environment and to the challenge of implementation.

But before we do this, perhaps we should spend a few more moments on the retro-vintage clothes retailers. The more successful marketplaces seem to provide an element of chaos and confusion, which adds to the excitement of the consumer, who isn't sure what to expect around the next corner. Major retailers, in recognising that consumer excitement (which invariably leads to sales), are looking to replicate that same consumer experience. Well-established retail sites, which traditionally have guided the customer through well-lit passages that maximise exposure to goods, are now trying to create edginess and uncertainty.

Replicating the chaotic environment of multiple microbusinesses and coworking in a market-type environment inside a more rigid commercial selling place or mall requires a degree of rule breaking. Traditional approaches to the shopping space in terms of layout, space, boundaries, and product mix all need to be undermined, even if that is done in a planned sort of way. We might usefully take this as an analogy for shifting conventional boundaries with current business practices and silos towards a new type of working space.

Isn't this then one of the challenges of innovation, especially for major corporations? They need in some way to replicate the excitement of the entrepreneurial workplace, with all its fun and risks, and its temporary nature, yet offset it with meeting the commercial demands of the enterprise. It's a potentially difficult balancing act.

For those individuals concerned with delivering success in a major corporation here are some things to consider:

- The location itself may not be cool enough.
- The working environment may not be sufficiently flexible and radical.
- The culture may not adequately encourage effective social and business networking.
- The rules of employment, such as dress code and time-keeping, may simply not be aligned to the aspirations of the employee.
- There may be some degree of cultural misalignment between employer and employee.
- The visible leadership may simply be viewed by the employee as being too old.

It's problematic to artificially create an innovative environment. One organisation had a room specifically for thinking, with beanbags (remember them?) on the floor rather than normal chairs. Some say it even had the ceiling painted blue to encourage blue-sky thinking. It was a good effort.

We are now beginning to recognise that radical thinking – an essential component of effective implementation – might also need a degree of radicalisation of the workspace.

Examination of the creative sector also helps provide an interesting perspective on how best to engage those who are content to work at the less stable and more transient end of the employment spectrum. Such individuals may decide to enter the corporate workplace with a degree of idealism but quickly be constrained by corporate culture and location. It's easy to see how frustration might start to happen.

Some questions to address might include:

- Can new-age innovators carry on innovating in the same way when they aren't part of that innovation bubble?
- Can major corporations recreate that bubble, and if so, how and where?
- Do (or will) current innovators change their attitudes as they get older – in other words, is this just a function of age?
- Will the view of post-millennials towards the workplace change if they are working under the shadow of higher unemployment amongst the professional classes?

- Will the nature of the relationship between employer and employee change (yet again), whereby the employee has a much greater stake in the success of the business through some form of co-ownership?

Finally, there is a sustainability issue to contend with. Microbusinesses are, by their nature, mainly short lived. Those working in such an environment may ultimately need to trade the fun of working there for the stability of the corporate workplace and the certainty of a regular paycheck.

This shouldn't necessarily be seen as selling out, and perhaps is just one reflection of some of the basic requirements of life, which are safety, security, and the ability to pay the bills. Maybe Maslow did get it right after all.

Timing: How Long to Implement?

Most managers will know about a use of the term *smart* that preceded its current, technological meaning (instrumented, interconnected, intelligent) – the acronym SMART (specific, measureable, achievable, realistic, and time-framed) as applied to a project. It is in the context of that previous meaning that we need to address the issue of timing, that is, how long should an AI implementation take?

The answer to that question might depend on:

- Whether implementation relates to a single tactical need or perhaps one or two specific objectives in parallel
- The ambition of the organisation and overall scope of the programme taking into account the size and nature of the company involved.

If the former condition applies, and assuming that the technology actually exists, it is not unreasonable to be talking in terms of months. If the latter, then a company may need to plan for a multiyear horizon. Lessons from the past should not be ignored, although many will argue that there is less patience for change nowadays and that transformation should be done much more quickly. For example, when British Telecom went through its company-wide programme of process management a couple of decades ago, it adopted a five-year horizon. Perhaps this isn't unreasonable in implementing an enterprise-wide AI platform.

In the mid-1990s, when business process reengineering was the fashion, a study of 38 companies undertaking 67 projects revealed that the average length of any specific project was 15.8 months. This takes into account a quarter of those surveyed, who had implementation periods of over two years.[20]

The speed of implementation appears to relate to the nature of the business area being addressed:

- Changes to core processes appear on the whole to take less time to implement than expected.
- Support, management, and cross-functional processes seem to take longer than planned.

By way of explanation, it has been suggested that core processes are more amenable to analysis and improvement than any other business process. Core processes are defined as key activities or clusters of activities that must be performed in an exemplary way to ensure a firm's competitiveness because they add primary value to an output.[21]

Timing of implementation is a touchy subject. It depends especially on leadership, the quality and formation of the team, stakeholder engagement, and desired objectives. In an area of cutting-edge technology such as AI, there is invariably some uncertainty. Even so, the desire to create a return-on-investment (ROI) calculation means that somewhere, somehow, the project team needs to be able to estimate the timing of development and implementation.

It's a risky business, made more challenging by the effect of unrealistic optimism by the project team and the desire of both the team and the team leader not to be the bringer of bad news (such as underperformance) to the sponsor. Transparency is critical, as is trust between the sponsor and the team leadership. Even so, it may still be prudent to introduce some degree of independent project management that is disassociated from the technical and business issues to ensure accurate reporting of the key deliverables.

It is likely that one of the key differentiators of artificial systems will be that of speed of implementation. At the current time it seems almost incredible to think that some forms of AI systems could become commodities, but this is likely to be the case within two decades.

How quickly will on-demand AI replicate the current trend of software as a service (SaaS)? SaaS is said to be quicker, cheaper, and easier than traditional on-premise installations. It provides greater flexibility to the user, who need not commit to multiyear programmes that are difficult to back out of. It also allows an organisation to dip in and dip out of a new process. Even so, analysts such as Forrester say that there is a need to plan and pilot a SaaS implementation in the same way as a traditional rollout.[22]

IS BIG BANG TRANSFORMATION POSSIBLE?

Different times require, and sometimes demand, different approaches to implementation. Historically the analytics industry has encouraged a linear approach to change, with analytical evolution described as a set of natural building blocks.

It is entirely possible that the business environment in 10 years will have adopted a different and more radical approach to change. It is quite feasible that within a decade, industry will have looked for, and maybe found, a big bang (as opposed to evolutionary) approach to change.

Big bang change has certain pros and cons (see Table 28).

It is likely that certain markets will aim for early customised versions of AI sooner rather than later. For example, the insurance market in China is currently growing at about 20% year on year as a result of government support and market conditions. Such a level of growth inevitably places pressure on the available talent pool, which perhaps cannot be grown at a speed and to a knowledge level that matches the market need. AI seemingly would provide a solution to that particular problem.

Another example in which an accelerated approach to AI development may be useful is the consumer electronics industry. The industry is typified by rapid growth, but its model is somewhat different. Usually it undertakes considerable research and development, which is followed by speedy growth in production, providing economy of scale. These scale benefits result in the cost to the consumer falling, but with the cost of production falling even faster, profitability inevitably grows.

TABLE 28   Pros and cons of big bang implementation.

Advantages	Disadvantages
Change will be highly visible and gain a lot of attention, therefore reinforcing the transformation and creating momentum.	Tendency towards lack of differentiation among eventual outcomes, as speed to market may become more critical than capability. Competing companies will adopt a reduced-risk, me-too approach.
The speed and noise of change may result in greater knowledge sharing between competing organisations – to the extent that commercial confidences and copyrights permit – and as a result, there will be an increased consistency of approach.	There will be a shortfall of development bandwidth. Expertise will increasingly fall into the hands of the comparatively few, who will become highly in demand, pushing up the cost.
Generic capabilities that do not offer competitive advantage will be reused, providing a more efficient deployment and some greater economies of scale.	Some of the lessons (and mistakes) that might normally have been achieved through incremental change will be either disregarded or omitted altogether, resulting in higher operational risk.
Momentum of change will defeat organisational resistance and inertia.	Tendency towards innovation and differentiation being sacrificed for affordability.
Difficulty in measuring the status quo because of volatile market conditions will reduce validity of ROI decisions and force decisions that are based more on emotional intelligence.	Tendency towards lack of clarity regarding the business case for change, which would normally be understood through an evolutionary model.

Effective development of AI in consumer electronics might not only reduce research and development times, but also optimise the go-to-market time and ultimately improve profitability. Similar benefits could also be found in the pharmaceutical industry.

CONCLUSION

In this chapter we have attempted to look at some of the practicalities of AI implementation, drawing insight from previous technological transformations and trying to understand what lessons might be derived from them.

Issues as broad as culture, training, leadership, recruitment, and location all appear to play a part. We suggest that the traditional models for all of these functions need not only to change but to be rethought. It's an approach that is appropriate for this particular time of change. All of these issues are critical and interdependent. Perhaps the one that should dominate is the whole idea of a new way of working. This new way will occur partly through choice, but also as a result of the way work will change around us.

Whilst a tactical implementation for some organisations might comprise a reasonable way of dipping a toe in the water, to be most effective any piecemeal change should be carried out as part of a broader strategic initiative. There's nothing to stop tactical or pilot implementations from being carried out, but these types of implementations should be part of a wider implementation programme. A broad programme does not commit sponsors or leaders to complete the programme in its entirety. Any sensible undertaking of this nature should have a set of interim checkpoints to ensure that promised deliverables have actually been achieved.

Appendix A includes a series of flowcharts that readers may find helpful, not only in terms of implementation but also with respect to their own personal journey and understanding. They suggest a number of routes or options available, but these may need to be customised relative to the needs of the individual and the degree of maturity of the organisation or industry in which he or she works.

NOTES

1. Francesco Corea, 13 forecasts on artificial intelligence. Diaries of a Data Scientist, Medium.com (30 September 2016). https://medium.com/cyber-tales/13-forecasts-on-artificial-intelligence-82761b7a0f6d
2. Ruben Baart, Growing drones from chemicals, Next Nature Network (15 July 2016). https://www.nextnature.net/2016/07/growing-drones-chemicals/
3. Mark Hansford and Michaila Hancock, Technology Consumption: Are Engineers Ready to Make the Leap and Reap the Rewards?. *New Civil Engineer*. http://guides.newcivilengineer .com/4349.guide (accessed 12 May 2017).
4. Ibid.
5. Skillsoft. 5 reasons training fails, and what to do about it. http://www.skillsoft.com/assets/ white-papers/whitepaper_uk_why_training_fails.pdf
6. Universal Robots. About Universal Robots – inventor of the cobot. www.universal-robots .com. https://www.universal-robots.com/about-universal-robots/news-centre/history-of-the-cobots (accessed 18 October 2017).
7. Niccolo Machiavelli, *The Prince*.
8. Edgar Schein, How can organizations learn faster? The challenges of entering the green room. *Sloan Management Review* (Winter 1993).
9. Atanu Basu and Michael Simmons, The future belongs to leaders who get artificial intelligence. Inc.com. https://www.inc.com/empact/the-future-belongs-to-leaders-who-get-artificial-intelligence.html (accessed 18 October 2017).
10. James O'Brien, The future CEO: 5 key traits business leaders of tomorrow need now. American Express Open Forum. https://www.americanexpress.com/us/small-business/ openforum/articles/future-ceo-5-key-traits-business-leaders-tomorrow-need-now
11. www.chevening.org
12. Stephen J. Dubner and Steven D. Levitt, A star is made. *New York Times* magazine (7 May 2006).
13. Roland Mosimann, Patrick Mosimann, and Meg Dussault, *The Performance Manager* (Cognos, 2008).
14. Thomas Walther, Henry Johanson, John Dunleavy, and Elizabeth Hjelm, *Reinventing the CFO: Moving from Financial Management to Strategic Management* (McGraw-Hill, 1997).
15. Harvey Nash, One in seven HR leaders report Automation/Artificial Intelligence is already impacting their workforce plans, reports Harvey Nash HR Survey 2017. HarveyNash.com (25 January 2017). http://www.harveynash.com/group/mediacentre/2017/01/one_in_ seven_hr_leaders_report_automation_artificial_intelligence_is_already_impacting_their_ workfor/index.asp

16. Garry Mathiason, Littler Mendelson, Preparing for robotics and artificial intelligence in the Workplace – Checklist. www.xperthr.com. http://www.xperthr.com/policies-and-documents/preparing-for-robotics-and-artificial-intelligence-in-the-workplace-checklist/12541/?keywords=preparing+robotics+artificial+intelligence+workplace+checklist (accessed 4 May 2017).
17. What skills and competencies do you need for a career in HR? TARGETjobs. https://targetjobs.co.uk/career-sectors/hr-and-recruitment/advice/324027-what-skills-and-competencies-do-you-need-for-a-career-in-hr (accessed 28 August 2017).
18. Louise Crewe, Nicky Gregson, and Kate Brooks, Alternative retail spaces. In Andrew Leyshon, Roger Lee, and Colin C. Williams (eds.), *Alternative Economic Spaces* (London: Sage Publications, 2003), 74–106.
19. A. Hochschild, *The Time Bind: When Work Becomes Home and Home Becomes Work* (New York: Metropolitan Books, 1998).
20. David Harvey, A survey of current practices, business intelligence and OXIIM. In David Harvey, ed., *Business Re-engineering: The Critical Success Factors* (Business Intelligence, 1995).
21. http://www.businessdictionary.com/definition/core-process.html
22. Stuart Lauchlan, How to carry out a SaaS roll out. *Computer Weekly*. http://www.computerweekly.com/feature/How-to-carry-out-a-SaaS-roll-out (accessed 28 August 2017).

CHAPTER 8

New Business Models

SUMMARY

In this chapter we will consider the new business models that may emerge as intelligent systems are implemented. These models extend to new value chains, redefined contracts of employment, and different forms of leadership.

In a more digitalised world, the future business model may not be just a digital replication of existing processes, but rather may allow for the innovation of new, seemingly chaotic systems that are better suited to the volatility of market conditions.

INTRODUCTION

Business model is a term that is relatively ambiguous, in that there appears to be some flexibility in its definition. In *The New, New Thing*, Michael Lewis suggests that the definition of *business model* is simply 'how you planned to make money'.[1]

Certainly the topic has been the subject of considerable attention in the past, with many publications from Drucker, Porter, and others. A model, according to Joan Magretta (a senior associate at Harvard Business School) is the way that businesses work – how they can deliver products and services to their customers in a way that makes money.[2]

The idea of a *model* comes from the notion that each activity within the moneymaking process can be *modelled*, or moulded, as an individual component, much in the same way that Henry Ford and others defragmented the auto manufacturing business and reassembled the components in a way to provide greater efficiency and profit.

The business model is often associated with what is called the *value chain*. This is a sequence of events or components that collectively move the process from design, purchase, and manufacture through to marketing, sales, and distribution. The model, or value chain, ideally needs not only to take into account issues internal to the business, but also the key influences that are external to the organisation. A PEST or a SWOT (strengths, weaknesses, opportunities, and threats) analysis often is helpful in structuring those factors that ultimately create the greatest impacts on the business value of the proposition. Some may argue that in the current climate, and particularly in the volatile business climate of the future, these traditional forms of analyses are becoming irrelevant, such is the difficulty in predicting the external environment of the marketplace and of customers' behaviour.

Although it has often been suggested that we are entering, or have already entered, a new era that is sometimes called the Fourth Industrial Revolution, perhaps the epoch might equally be described as the Age of Uncertainty (an expression originally coined by the economist John Kenneth Galbraith). Analytics and insights are critical components to understanding the performance and external forces of a business. Beyond this, a concept that we might call *analytics in context* leads to greater understanding of the marketplace. When coupled with leaner, more agile businesses, this provides the potential for enterprises that operate more dynamically and a more rapidly moving ecosystem.

In this more dynamic, flexible way of working, the possibility of a business making a profit through a relatively static business model becomes less likely.

In the article 'When Your Business Model Is in Trouble', Rita McGrath suggests that businesses should be worried when innovation is only providing smaller and smaller incremental improvements, when a business struggles to come up with new ideas, and when it is being out-innovated by the competition. 'Bold' appears to be good.[3]

Mark Johnson, in his book *Seizing the White Space*, proposes radical new approaches to business, taken from existing experiences elsewhere, such as:

- *Fractionalisation.* For example, selling the partial use of something, as in a time-share property.
- *Freemium.* Offering the basic service for free and charging for premium services, as in LinkedIn's model.
- *Low-touch.* Lowering prices by dramatically reducing the quality of service.[4]

Other target models include brokerage, bundling, crowdsourcing, leasing, and subscription. Johnson's proposition is that an organisation should not look solely to its peers for comparison, but rather should consider the activities of businesses outside its immediate peer group.[4]

It also follows that by virtue of relatively different rates of market maturity around the world, businesses should be mindful of new business models operating outside of their own territories. Current models are often informed by a combination of local tradition and xenophobic practices. Real innovation is likely to be affected by forces that aren't local.

One example of this may well be the approach becoming more widespread in retail and consumer goods: using the high-street store simply as a shop window for products, with actual purchases being made online. This appears to be the model in parts of Asia. In this new way of purchasing, not only are goods *disintermediated* (or sold straight, without the need for any middleman), but existing high-street distribution channels are cannibalised.

With such an approach, to what degree is the high street presence of a retailer under threat? Providing a shop window for goods may encourage online sales, but how can a retailer be sure that the physical presence of the shop has actively contributed to the purchase? Earlier in this book we considered the shopping mall evolving into a broader shopping experience, but doesn't the store within the mall still need to pay its way? Can we effectively correlate consumer foot traffic in a particular location with online purchasing activity?

As a result, new business models may not only threaten established distribution channels, but also those who are *employed* in these traditional channels. The Age of Uncertainty affects not only managers and leaders, but also all those personally involved in the model, or value chain, itself.

If we accept that businesses will become more agile, and that AI-induced business models will be not only dynamic in nature but in a state of relatively constant flux, then won't this inevitably affect the workforce?

The notion of zero-hours contracts – contracts in which there is no commitment by the employer to provide a minimum number of working hours to the employee – might be seen as affecting relatively low-level service staff, often working in warehousing or fast-food outlets, so far. It is an ideal way for an employer to manage workload requirements in an environment of uncertainty with respect to imbalances in supply and demand. At what point do zero-hour contracts start becoming attractive at more senior (perhaps professional or managerial) levels? Some might reasonably argue that at senior levels, whose functions can be carried out only by permanent salaried employees, continuity is essential and that it must be provided in the traditional way. We shouldn't be so certain.

As we have indicated elsewhere, if industries and professions are to change, then this change will impact the relationship, or contract, between employer and employee. As a result, the notion of *work* and consequent remuneration inevitably will be transformed.

Maybe we should get paid for doing nothing? In 2015, Finland committed to a new model called *basic income*, repeating an experiment that had been carried out in India, Brazil, and Namibia. Basic income is not such a new idea, as it was suggested by the social engineer Major Clifford Hugh Thomas over 100 years ago. Under the current scheme, the Finnish government pays a small number of its citizens an amount of money each month (€560 as of 2016), whether or not they actually have a job. The aim of the experiment is to see whether individuals with a financial safety net still have an incentive to contribute to society.[5]

As business culture seems to rest on the Protestant work ethic, being paid to do nothing might seem to be unorthodox. Yet Warren Buffett, who is one of America's most successful investors, says that there is an inexorable movement towards an environment in which a small number of people with exceptional talents receive 'an increasing amount of the share of an economy's overall rewards, whilst those with more commonplace talents experience commoditisation and a resulting drop in wealth'.[6]

Perhaps one big question to ask is what exactly is meant by 'commonplace talents'?

Certainly these so-called commonplace talents may comprise some basic manual skills, such as those used on the production line that can be carried out by a robot. Perhaps it even includes some specific analytical talents, such as investment management and even some used in medicine, which can be replaced by automatically generated AI-guided advice. Does driving a car, plane, or train fit into the category of commonplace talent? Should we increasingly think about the value of individuals in terms of talents they possess that are not commonplace? And if so, what might these talents be? Will the future comprise a resurgence of artisans, creative artists, and innovators? To what degree will the term *commonplace* be affected by market maturity in particular geographies? Will AI have a levelling effect?

It seems that not only will business models inevitably need to change, but that the way that managers and leaders need to perform within that new paradigm will also need to change. Is the old form of management and leadership on its deathbed?

Let's assume, perhaps boldly, that the work done by managers and leaders does not fall into the commonplace. Won't elements of *intelligent* talent management, which evaluates and directs human performance, affect the work that managers and leaders will do in the future?

We even presuppose that the roles of *manager* and *leader* will be undertaken by individual human beings. Isn't it feasible that both *management* and *leadership* are functions of a business model, rather than responsibilities vested in individual people – functions that could be automated to some degree?

AUGMENT OR AUTOMATE?

In its 2016 report *Turning Artificial Intelligence into Business Value Today*, Accenture synthesised the relative uncertainty of future business models into two alternatives: augment and automate. By this Accenture implies that AI has two dominant purposes:

- To assist (or augment) human behaviour and decision-making by providing more detailed insight, thereby enabling more correct and timely decisions
- To replace (or automate) straightforward work tasks undertaken by humans with automated robotics.

It's easier to accept augmentation, as it suggests that human beings will still have a role to play, in some form of collaborative relationship with machines.

Automation, however, is threatening to some jobs (especially those that are relatively routine by nature and can be replaced by business rules) and also to livelihoods. Accenture reinforces the suggestion that as some jobs disappear, hopefully others will be created.

The report divides work tasks into four segments:

1. Structured, stable, low-volume data
2. Unstructured, volatile, high-volume data
3. Routine, predictable, rules-based work
4. Ad-hoc, unpredictable, judgement-based tasks.

From this, the report then suggests that four new *solutions*, or new business models, might potentially emerge, which are the:

1. Efficiency model
2. Effectiveness model
3. Expert model
4. Innovation model.

Beyond this breakdown, there are suggested levels of granularity, which implies that there is no clear-cut definition of each solution. Many existing and new roles will be mixtures of different approaches. Equally important, the point is reinforced that implementation is not 'simply' a matter of technology, but also cultural and societal.[7]

We are specifically concerned with business models here. It's important to reflect on the fact that current business processes as we know them are likely to be turned on their heads by new machine learning and capability.

Taking an existing approach to business and then applying a technological or digital interpretation to that approach may not be adequate.

We should be prepared to consider new and radical approaches, which are the very nature of disruptive technology. These radical ideas will be driven by the speed of connectivity, the degree of integration of systems, and the level of machine intelligence that can be applied to the problem. These new approaches will also be influenced by our human reaction to and behaviour towards these automated and augmented technologies.

For example, if patients know that a doctor is using AI to help make decisions about their health and symptoms, at what point do they decide to cut out the middleman and deal solely with the machine? And if investment decisions are being augmented by machines because of the complexity and volatility of the economic environment, what exactly is the human being providing other than a nice warm feeling?

Increasing dependence on machines is a slippery slope in much the same way that relying on satellite navigation is. Drivers might argue that if the satellite navigation isn't working, then they could always revert to the old skill of reading a map. However, if map reading is reduced, then wouldn't the sale of maps decrease and paper maps eventually disappear, so that in time the traditional approach to navigation was no longer an option?

We may also be wrong to assume that the computer will not come up with its own ideas about how to make money.

Think of it in these terms: advanced financial performance management tools with access to core financial data can calculate the profitability of products, services, and channels with greater accuracy than ever before. So-called sandbox capabilities in systems allow the modelling of different scenarios. Sentiment analysis allows organisations to understand market needs. Robo-investment models will provide better understanding of risks and rewards. What will prevent a single system bringing all these capabilities together to fuel (or even imitate) the innovation of the sell-side process?

What becomes increasingly clear is that traditional linear value-chain models are becoming redundant. Future intelligent businesses will need to take into account multiple internal and external factors to ensure they are not only satisfying the customer in terms of service and price, but are also taking into account the complexities of the working environment (see Figure 8).

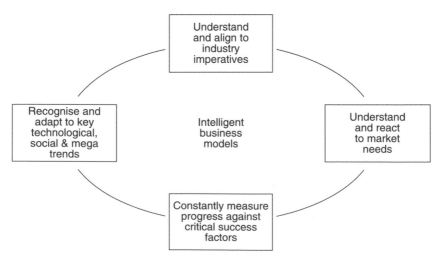

FIGURE 8   Intelligent business models.

TABLE 29   Components of an intelligent business model.

Key trends	Keys to success	Market needs
Mobile	Customisation, personalisation	Increased demand
Cloud	Closed loop and continuous feedback	More diversity
Analytics	Asset sharing, optimisation	Volatility of market costs
Connectivity	Usage-based pricing	Greater regulation
Innovation	Speed and agility	Higher risk
New technologies	Innovation	Lower price
Innovate to zero	Empowerment, leadership	More flexibility
Decentralisation	Demand aggregation	Increased certainty
Geosocialisation	Talent management	Increased digitalisation

Table 29 also expands on the components of this new model.

ISSUES OF PLACE AND TIME

Business models of the future will also be predicated on location-based systems. By that we mean that the physical location of assets – including human assets – will become substantially more important. AI systems will need to understand the location component of almost everything as a key part of the equation. The expression 'Everything and everyone is somewhere' remains a fundamental truth, even in a virtual world.

Over the past decade, geographical information systems (GISs) have emerged from a backroom business into an element of greater significance. After all, what company wouldn't want to know where its customers are, where its assets are, where best to market, and how to match supply to regional demand?

For this reason, GIS companies have increasingly moved towards tighter integration with providers of analytic software to create bidirectional geographic analytics. For their part, analytics providers are interested in improving the quality of their visualisations, a particular talent of GIS companies. Isn't a map just an example of a visualisation of specific data and information?

Effective visualisations help transform complicated and multilayered information into more easily digestible content.

The built environment provides us with countless opportunities to show how traditionally held data and information can be captured (through BIM methodology). This data can also be supplemented by remote devices, such as drones or other fixed devices, to provide a composite picture of a building, asset, street, or even a production line. These techniques can be used not only to capture existing information that is visible to the eye but also to provide a permanent record of assets that are hidden, such as utilities and systems behind walls.

One particular problem in the use of BIM has been that of the contractor or operative not placing assets (e.g. pipework) in the place that the drawing instructed them to. As a result, there is often a mismatch between the BIM record and the reality of the situation. The growth in the use of remote devices will help to ensure that a correct record of the installation has been made. There is a trend for humans to appear to be the lowest common denominator in the process.

Independent robotic systems will also need to have a sense of place, both in terms of their own physical locations and the location of affected third parties (such as humans and vehicles). Some assets will be relatively static (as is the case with buildings or retail shelving). Other affected assets (such as human employees) will be much more dynamic and more difficult to track in real time, but this is probably more of an issue of computing power and connectivity rather than available technology.

For many GIS companies, the degree of analytics used is still in the realm of historical and real-time data. There is relatively limited use of predictive analytics, and even less use of cognitive analytics and machine learning techniques. It is essential that more forward-looking thinking is adopted, even to the point of vertical integration of complementary companies.

Perhaps one of the exceptions to this is Google, which already leverages its Google Maps product into its search engine and other algorithms to give a location-specific view of, for example, the nearest restaurant of your preference. There is clearly more that can be done in this space, and it will be brought about not by technologists or business people but rather by those with the imagination to see business solutions in the context of both analytics and location.

One place that this could happen is somewhere like the Geovation Hub founded in London in 2015 by the UK-based Ordnance Survey, the national mapping agency for the United Kingdom.[8] Ordnance Survey has identified a location analytics market of £2.2 billion per year in the United Kingdom alone (estimated to rise to £3 billion by 2020), and one of over $14 billion worldwide. The location analytics market will, in turn, create a resultant 'spin-off' market in associated technologies and services in the UK alone, estimated to rise to £36 billion by 2020 comprising:

- £4.0 billion in defense
- £2.7 billion in security
- £2.3 billion in information and communications technology
- £1.7 billion in leisure
- £1.7 billion in insurance.[9]

Given the size of the global opportunity and the importance of location in the mix, it seems that the Geovation Hub is a model clearly worth replicating.

Location analytics will continue to evolve and will be critical to meet the needs of the AI age. This evolution will occur as a result of:

- Elastic cloud-based capabilities that remove the challenges of storage and computing power
- Additional data from devices and other more organic sources, such as crowdsourcing
- Improved image recognition, including infrared scanning
- Reduced device and satellite costs
- Better understanding of business problems and the capabilities available to create appropriate solutions.

As was experienced with traditional analytics, one option going forward is that the GIS industry will progress on a path parallel to that of the AI industry. Along the line there will be some degree of convergence. However, for the moment, these industries appear to be steering their own pathways – but it's just a matter of time.

Wouldn't a stronger option be for both AI companies and GIS companies to have better alignment in the solving of key business, domestic, and geopolitical issues, rather than reinventing the same solutions from different, albeit complementary, viewpoints?

CONTEXTUAL INSIGHT

No business (or individual) operates in a vacuum or in a bubble. One danger of existing analytical models is that they are inward looking rather than fully taking into account the wider environment. Not only are businesses anxious to know what their clients need and how much they are prepared to pay, but they also need better understanding of the external business ecosystem – competitors, supply chain, and environmental and political factors – which might influence profitability.

It will also be of some reassurance to stockholders to know, if the value of their investment in a company is falling, whether it is falling more slowly than the company's competitors or other market sectors.

We should try to understand what we actually mean by information in context. Bing defines context as 'the circumstances that form the setting for an event, statement, or idea, and in terms of which it can be fully understood'. The essence of this definition is that without contextual insight, the situation or circumstances cannot be 'fully understood'.

Isn't full understanding critical not only to current-day decisions but also in a machine-learning environment? It's natural that decisions are mainly made in an environment of imperfect knowledge – after all, isn't that partly what judgement is all about? But in an AI-orientated, algorithmically driven environment, does absence of context present new problems?

The technician might argue that imperfections in existing data can be accommodated by integrity weighting of the input, as some banks already do by scoring the quality of the data. But context is more than just about understanding what is happening in the data that is immediately available. To obtain a correct answer and use algorithms effectively, don't artificial systems also need to make sense of what is happening in the outside world?

Truly effective analytics at all levels requires an understanding of the external environment. It becomes inconceivable that decisions made in an advanced ecosystem can be made in isolation. Context takes into account not only what is currently happening, but also what has happened in the past, and what might happen in the future. It's a big ask of an automated system. Perhaps it's the technological equivalent of both experience and intuition.

As we consider the future, should we expect that human experience and intuition can be replaced by computer memory?

And if this were possible, and we replace human intelligence, experience, and intuition with automated systems fuelled by bytes and stored somewhere in the cloud, then what genuinely does the future hold for mankind? What then becomes the new nature of work amongst everything else? What is the role of experience, qualifications, and professional institutions? Will such capability put us in a better or worse place intellectually and emotionally?

WORDPLAY AND COMMUNICATION

As machine systems evolve in maturity, so too will their ability to communicate not only with humans but with each other. It is the interaction with humans that we will focus on for the moment, as the level and quality of communication will ultimately define our relationship with the machine.

One of the key difficulties in systems' ability to communicate with humans is the multitude of languages that exist. Whilst systems capable of phrase-based translation already exist, there is a need for a step-change in capabilities to make interactions of the future work effectively.

There are two main issues with phrase-based translation:

1. Translation is based on the phrase and not the exact words. As such, it lacks adequate refinement. Phrase-based translation is described as a blunt instrument.
2. There are limits on vocabulary.

An answer might already be in sight. In 2016 Google launched a capability they call Google Neural Machine Translation (GNMT). This is an extension to Google Translate capability, adding what are described as 'neural networks' and 'machine learning'. From these additional capabilities the system created its own new language, which Google calls Interlingua. Interlingua allows GNMT to make educated guesses about tone and context, and from this to produce a more accurate translation. What is extraordinary is that through using an intermediary internal language, the machine seems to have the capability of translating from one language to another without having been explicitly taught.

The notion of Interlingua is not new, nor is the name. It was first developed between 1937 and 1951 as a so-called international auxiliary language (like Esperanto) to allow people who do not have a common language to communicate with each other. It's also called a working language, or a bridge language. The theory behind Interlingua is that it recognises a large number of words that are used in a wide number of languages, and therefore is capable of being understood by a very large number of people.

It's a tricky concept, but in effect Google engineers (using three dimensions) looked at the way that the internal translation network was operating. They discovered that 'the network must be encoding something about the semantics – or meaning – of the sentence rather than simply memorizing "phrase-to-phrase translations"'. They even suggested that it might be described as 'a form of creativity'.[10]

The impact here is that an advanced system that incorporates machine learning and interacts directly with humans is not likely to be constrained by issues of language. Beyond this, it may also allow humans of different nationalities and speaking different languages to interact simultaneously with the same system.

NEW BUSINESS MODELS FOR NEW MARKETS

According to the World Bank study *Doing Business 2010*, which considers emerging markets, 'The only way that companies can prosper in these markets is to cut costs relentlessly and accept profit margins close to zero'.[11]

There's nothing new about this thinking, although increasingly there is recognition that it isn't always possible to take a mature business model and insert it into a developing market. Instead of looking at existing products and inserting them into new geographies, say the authors of 'New Business Models in Emerging Markets', companies should find those 'unmet needs' and fulfil them at a profit. 'Companies should behave like start-ups, for which every market is new.'

It's time to create a new business model, say the authors, which enables low-cost solutions to be built at scale. These new business models should comprise:

- A customer value proposition
- A profit formula
- Key processes
- Key resources.[12]

It's likely that there will be a high degree of localisation. AI-oriented approaches to business will vary in different parts of the world, meeting different issues and responding to different price points.

For example, in 2001 the price of a 300-millilitre bottle of Coca Cola was the equivalent of a day's wage in India and affordable by only 4% of the population. To make the product accessible to the other 96%, the manufacturers reduced the bottle size to 200 millilitres and cut the price in half, making it more affordable and comparable to other alternatives, such as lemonade and tea.

In emerging markets, might AI business models be increasingly focused on niche areas or key local imperatives? The consulting group Tractica suggests that 'narrow' AI will increasingly dominate the agenda and account for 99.5% of all AI revenue between 2016 and 2025.[13]

It isn't easy to simply identify the key drivers for economic growth in vast continents, but Table 30, which is based on a Huffington Post article and data from the OECD (Organisation for Economic Co-operation and Development), may give some indicators.

CONCLUSION

This chapter set out to consider what we mean by the term *business model* and explored some of the elements that contribute to one.

What becomes increasingly clear is that in a world of AI, future business models will not simply be digitalised versions of existing models. Randomness and an element of chaos, rather than linear decision-making, potentially become more prevalent. Models will also be created that pay much greater attention to external factors that provide meaning and context to the data.

TABLE 30   Key drivers of economic growth in India, Brazil, and China.

India	Brazil	China
Developing strategies at lower geographic tiers to optimise the breadth and depth of resources	Continued management of recession and control of unemployment	Settling down to slower and more sustainable growth after three decades of extraordinary growth
Developing the manufacturing sector	Reducing compliance costs by simplifying the tax environment, improving infrastructure, and removing barriers to trade	Agricultural reforms with improvement in access to finance in rural areas; education and training for farmers; pricing of natural resources and rural infrastructure
Improving governance	Continuing management of the public sector	Creation of a level playing field in finance, regulation, taxation, and public procurement; scaling down of state ownership of commercially oriented service enterprises; opening up more industries for private investment
Encouraging innovation	Improving education; reducing income inequality	Nurturing the right skills; establishing an effective countrywide vocational and education system; evaluating universities and university staff on the quality of academic output
Managing the risks of poverty, overpopulation, and dependency on other countries for resources	Controlling unemployment	Using urbanisation and services as drivers of growth; realising potential productivity gains related to the shift of rural residents to cities

Source: Amit Kapoor, Drivers of India's competitiveness. Huffington Post India (12 January 2015). http://www.huffingtonpost.in/dr-amit-kapoor/drivers-of-indias-competi_b_6441232 .html; OECD (2017). Brazil – economic forecast summary (November 2017). In Developments in Individual OECD and Selected Non-Member Economies (June). OECD report. http://www.oecd.org/eco/outlook/brazil-economic-forecast-summary.htm (accessed 25 August 2017); OECD. Structural reforms can help China settle into a 'new normal' era of slower, but more sustainable and inclusive growth. OECD website (20 March). http://www.oecd .org/economy/structural-reforms-can-help-china-settle-into-a-new-normal-era-of-slower-but-more-sustainable-and-inclusive-growth.htm (accessed 25 August 2017); OECD (2017). Economic surveys: India overview. In 2017 Economic Survey of India. OECD (February). https:// www.oecd.org/eco/surveys/INDIA-2017-OECD-economic-survey-overview.pdf

These new and radical business models will permit more flexibility, customisation, and localisation. Improved language capabilities will not only help systems interact, but also will change the way that we as humans cowork with automated systems.

NOTES

1. Michael Lewis, *The New New Thing: A Silicon Valley Story: How Some Man You've Never Heard of Just Changed Your Life* (Hodder Paperbacks, 2000).
2. Joan Magretta, Why business models matter. *Harvard Business Review* (May 2002). https://hbr.org/2002/05/why-business-models-matter
3. Sarah Cliffe, When your business model is in trouble. *Harvard Business Review* (January–February 2011). https://hbr.org/2011/01/when-your-business-model-is-in-trouble
4. Mark Johnson, *Seizing the White Space: Business Model Innovation for Growth and Renewal* (Harvard Business Publishing, 2010).
5. Liam Upton, Finland: new government commits to a basic income experiment. Basic Income Earth Network (16 June 2015). http://basicincome.org/news/2015/06/finland-new-government-commits-to-a-basic-income-experiment
6. Suranga Chandratillake, Is money for nothing the shape of the future? *Evening Standard* (12 January 2017).
7. Cyrille Bataller and Jeanne Harris, Turning artificial intelligence into business value today. Accenture. 2016.
8. Ordnance Survey launch Geovation Hub to support entrepreneurs. Bdaily (7 July 2015). https://bdaily.co.uk/technology/07-07-2015/ordnance-survey-launch-geovation-hub-to-support-entrepreneurs
9. P&S Market Research. Global geographic information system (GIS) market expected to grow at 11% CAGR during 2015–2020. P&S Market Research (4 February 2016). http://www.prnewswire.com/news-releases/global-geographic-information-system-gis-market-expected-to-grow-at-11-cagr-during-2015---2020-ps-market-research-567650721.html (accessed 25 August 2017).
10. Gil Fewster, The mind-blowing AI announcement from Google that you probably missed. LinkedIn (6 January 2017). https://www.linkedin.com/pulse/mind-blowing-ai-announcement-from-google-you-probably-gil-fewster?trk=v-feed&lipi=urn%3Ali%3Apage%3Ad_flagship3_feed%3BlDXE%2BeGMQDJnfNl2AizFOA%3D%3D
11. World Bank Group. Doing Business 2010. World Bank Group study, 2009. http://www.doingbusiness.org/reports/global-reports/doing-business-2010
12. Matthew Eyring, Mark W. Johnson, and Hai Nair, New business models in emerging markets. *Harvard Business Review* (February 2011). https://hbr.org/2011/01/new-business-models-in-emerging-markets
13. Sally Doherty, Narrow vs general AI – is Moravec's paradox still relevant? Graphcore, 2016. https://www.graphcore.ai/posts/is-moravecs-paradox-still-relevant-for-ai-today (accessed 16 January 2018).

CHAPTER 9

Coping with the Future

SUMMARY

This chapter considers how we need to start to personally interact with such new technologies, especially in the workplace, and what personal capabilities and attributes might be needed going forward.

Initially it considers what types of AI jobs are currently available and what might emerge in the future. Then it looks at the sort of additional training or education needed, either 'on the job' or in some form of academic institution, and then briefly examines what personal attributes might be expected of us in the AI job market.

For those individuals who seek to argue that there is no contest, as humans are different from computers by virtue of ability of humans to innovate, we reflect on the ability of computers to be creative. The chapter then speculates on what it might mean to live and work with robots, either under relatively normal conditions or, perhaps more importantly, in old age or where there are special healthcare requirements.

Finally, we consider how we might feel about taking instructions or advice from robots, and suggest a set of *robotic rules* to help computers cope better with humans in the future.

INTRODUCTION

Throughout this book we have considered the evolution of AI and cognitive analytics in terms of their history, their impact on both industries and professions, and the process of their implementation. We have even further considered the impact of resistance in thinking about the legacy handed down by the Luddites and in reflecting on the current day neo-Luddites.

Appendix B also includes one assessment of those jobs most at risk from the effects of AI, which is an assessment by others based on a degree of rationality but which is still capable of dispute and disagreement. It considers individual vulnerability based on the jobs of today rather than the jobs of tomorrow. The future will bring not only new definitions of existing roles, but also completely new functions. One issue to consider is whether the human will serve the robot, the robot will serve the human, or perhaps some sort of convergence of the two.

As we move further forward in the use of AI, it is inevitable that individuals will need to develop some form of coping strategy. This chapter starts to look more deeply at that issue, principally in the context of work but also in terms of living with the machines themselves.

The issue, perhaps, becomes one of beating them versus joining them. The inevitability of the AI agenda, in whatever form it takes, suggests perhaps the strongest approach is one of joining in some form (otherwise described as coworking), but what does this actually entail?

There are at least four methods that will help in the process of coworking:

1. Raising personal awareness of the potential capabilities of the machine
2. Increasing professional competence in one's own business area
3. Actively pursuing a role in the business area that recognises the impact of robotics and has an adoption strategy
4. Evangelising and moulding the AI agenda to meet the needs of an individual's own profession or a specific industry.

EXISTING ROLES IN AI

Perhaps for some, the starting point is that of seeing what AI jobs are currently available in the marketplace. Entering *AI* or *artificial intelligence* into the search engine of a recruitment site usually reveals a broad range of roles that are available. Most are of a technical rather than a business nature, although there are some nontechnical functional roles, such as legal, marketing, and recruiting. In the interest of readers who are trying to understand how their own personal experience and qualifications fit into AI-related positions, here are some typical roles (as at 2017):

- Commercial IP/IT solicitor
- Technology project director (AI)
- Data scientist SME (natural language processing)
- Data scientist (machine learning, deep learning)
- Artificial intelligence engineer
- Python/Java developer with knowledge of R, SAS, SQI, Dover
- iOS engineer (artificial intelligence)
- Sales directors (i.e. selling products that use AI to optimise existing processes)
- B2B marketing executives for AI
- Recruitment consultant AI
- AI labeller (image recognition; helping to recognise and understand an image and classify it against specific options)
- Senior researchers (AI and tactile robotics)
- Gameplay programmers
- Computer vision engineer
- Data scientist researcher
- Artificial intelligence NPL engineer
- Artificial intelligence administrator
- Management consultant (robotics process automation and cognitive automation).

According to *Forbes* magazine, the hottest trend in AI is the movement towards chatbots (also known as talkbots, chatterbots, bots, chatterboxes, and artificial conversational entities), which are computer programs designed to communicate with humans.

Chatbots have been compared to a game of tennis: talk, reply; talk, reply; and so on. The emphasis seems to be on the ability to teach computers how to interface with humans not only in natural language but at an extremely personal level. This is mainly with the specific aim of increased digital effectiveness on the part of the marketing sector (although there are other potential applications elsewhere, such as in financial services).

Almost all of the predictions made in the *Forbes* article have been made by technology leaders or academics rather than business leaders, that is to say, those currently involved in the day-to-day business management and leadership of industries outside the technology sector. One prediction particularly stands out – the one made by Ihab Ilys, professor of computer science at the University of Waterloo, Ontario, who said:

> *Data analytics will go vertical, and companies that build vertical solutions will dominate the market.*
>
> *General-purpose data analytics companies will start disappearing.*
>
> *Vertical data analytics startups will develop their own full stack solutions to data collection, preparation, and analytics.*[1]

There's some evidence that this trend has already started. Vertical (i.e. industry specific) analytical solutions are not only dependent on the technology but also dependent on industry knowledge, so as to fully apply the requisite technology to the business problem. Without this industry-specific application, there is a risk that technological developments may occur that have no relationship to the business problems that actually exist in the industry.

Without attention to specific industry issues, technology vendors and eventually the end users will at best need to adopt a stretch-and-fit approach, customising new technology to solve a particular problem or needs. At worst, there will be a mismatch between requirement and delivery, and consequent waste in resources, time, energy, and money.

It follows that jobs which relate to vertical AI solutions will inevitably develop in the technology and AI sectors. For this to happen effectively and quickly will require the discussion to move away solely from technologists towards a more informed commentary by business users, many of whom will remain baffled by technological complexity and jargon. The technology industry will also have to improve the way in which it communicates, not only with business users but also with the general public.

FUTURE ROLES IN AI

As with general analytics, new roles will begin to emerge that focus on the AI agenda. Initially these will be in areas of work that are routine and perhaps at greatest threat from the AI revolution.

Tomer Naveh, CTO of Adgorithmics, a company that describes itself as the creator of the first AI marketing platform, suggests that the job of AI supervisor will be

TABLE 31 AI: reasons to be hopeful, or not.

Reasons to be hopeful	Loss of some jobs but replacement with others
	Entirely new jobs emerge, which take into account unique human capabilities
	Work is redefined in a new, positive, and socially beneficial way
	Greater choice and ability to control our destinies
Reasons to be concerned	Disruption both to blue-collar and white-collar jobs
	Some will succeed wildly – but others will fall into low-paid, or no, work
	Inadequate preparation in education for work of the future, and ill-equipped political and economic systems

Source: Aaron Smith and Janna Anderson, AI, Robotics and the Future of Jobs. Pew Research Center (6 August 2014).

one that emerges. The work of professionals will shift from doing the task themselves to 'supervising the AI software on how to do it for them'. This is fundamentally an 'augment' approach to the use of AI.

This may not be an easy role to create or indeed even to understand in the early stages. Surely different personal competences will be needed as well as additional training. Earlier we aimed to differentiate between AI and cognitive analytics. (To recap, cognitive analytics helps the human to make the decision, AI independently makes the decision for the human.) Does an AI system require supervision, and if so, to what degree and what is its nature?

In the 2014 report *AI, Robotics and the Future of Jobs*, the authors collected the views of 1,896 experts on this topic and condensed their views into two categories (see Table 31).

It's clear that sentiment is mixed on this topic of new job roles and the previous formality of the workplace. 'The collar of the future will be a hoodie', says Amy Webb, CEO of Webmedia Group.[2]

Robert Cannon, Internet law expert, puts it more directly. 'What can a human contribute?' he asks. 'The short answer is that if the job is one where the question cannot be answered positively, that job is likely to cease to exist'.[3]

The sociological aspect of these changes has been considered in earlier chapters. What will be the nature of work in 10 years? How will these changes impact incomes? It is not the intention here to set out a picture of gloom, but rather to be open minded, to encourage the reader to understand the opportunities and to take greatest advantage of them.

AI EDUCATION

In addition to informal self-learning, two key routes to education about AI appear to be available: academic education and the start-up environment. Let's look at each of them.

Academic Education

There are already multiple graduate programmes available that focus on AI. Two typical ones in the United Kingdom are:

1. *University of Liverpool.* This programme provides a three-year foundational course in Java programming, computer systems, databases, human-centric computing, and algorithmic foundations, followed by a module in artificial intelligence (as an alternative to modules in software engineering, advanced object oriented programming, and principles of computer games design and implementation, knowledge representation, the study of multi-agent systems, and robotics).
2. *University of Manchester.* This programme offers a similar curriculum but is a four-year programme, integrating academic training with one year in industry.

Additionally, as of the time of print, 34 other universities in the United Kingdom offered 76 courses or academic programmes in AI as part of postgraduate degrees.

In North America, 37 courses on AI were offered by US universities at time of print, including Arizona State University and Iowa State University. On balance, and in comparison to UK universities, US courses appear to be more AI-specific. For example, the course offered by University of Nebraska-Omaha includes 'automated software systems such as software agents, multi-agent and multi-robot systems, machine vision and image processing technologies, neural network-based adaptive software systems, heuristics and stochastic optimisation techniques for critical decision making, and machine learning and knowledge engineering techniques that embed intelligence in computers and information systems'.[4]

Other major universities, such as Harvard, take a different approach. Harvard is generally described as a liberal arts college, and its majors (or what are also known as *concentrations*) are divided into general categories, which are not so specific as to include AI. There are some courses in AI, but another option is to study computer science with mind-brain behaviour, or some other complementary topic, as a secondary subject.

On-the-Job Learning: Start-Ups and Innovation Labs

A different approach to learning is that of working for a start-up, perhaps in an innovation laboratory to gain experience, although this normally requires some basic (or even advanced) technical knowledge. Innovation labs are normally, although not exclusively, the home of start-ups.

Most, if not all, innovation and design labs operate on the basis of lean start-up and design thinking.

Lean start-up is a methodology aimed at rapidly creating new technical capabilities or products and getting them into the hands of the customer more quickly. It shows participants how to get started, how to steer their products, and when to persevere. The approach considers three key elements – learn, build, measure – which operate in a continuous loop.

The principle of lean start-up fundamentally asks the question '*Should* this product be built?', as opposed to '*Can* this product be built?' Often, many start-ups create a technical capability and then look around for industry application by consulting mentors. Beyond this, a lean start-up approach invites the question 'Is it possible to create a sustainable business from this new product or capability?'

From a process point of view, the usual approach is to create a minimum viable product that afterwards can be fine-tuned to meet the precise needs of the client. This method aims to ensure continuous incremental growth that is more aligned to the client's need. By the time that the product is fully baked, there is likely to be a market available.

Design thinking is a similar approach; it is solution oriented, with the intention of creating a *focused outcome*. It is not dissimilar to scientific methods that begin with an initial idea that is then refined as a result of continuous measurement and feedback. The difference is that the feedback in scientific methods is data related (i.e. based on physical measurement), whereas in design thinking the feedback is more closely related to qualitative response and consumer need. Continuous feedback results in product development that is both incremental and iterative. Each incremental step opens the door to new approaches and new paths forward.

In many cases, design thinking is associated with brainstorming and the concept of thinking outside the box. This approach enables entrepreneurial thinking without fear of criticism. Some argue that this brainstorming approach is only one component of a more formalised process, that of *define, research, ideate, prototype, choose, implement*, and *learn*.[5]

The concept of design thinking goes significantly beyond technology and also has relevance in science, the humanities, and business. It's an approach that is being adopted more frequently by universities and business schools as part of the essential tool kit.

At the heart of a start-up is the concept of entrepreneurship – which is perhaps thought by some to be intuitive, but which in reality is a process that can be taught. Entrepreneurship considers issues such as product design, marketing, and market understanding. Often we associate entrepreneurism with those who have been massively successful, but for every successful entrepreneur there are probably hundreds (perhaps thousands) of individuals who came up with a good idea but were unable to monopolise or monetarise it.

One of the functions of innovation labs is to provide not only a form of innovation factory but also to operate as a form of filter mechanism that identifies innovations likely to be successful and weeds out those likely to fall by the wayside. It also provides additional reassurance to venture capitalists, who are able to verify from the process that there is a stronger chance of successful return on their investment.

Major organisations, such as banks and insurers, sometimes create internal innovation labs. These companies have already recognised that standing still is not an option, and that they have to continually strive for progress, often through the use of disruptive technology and new business methods.

Some corporations are more advanced than others in this thinking. Munich Reinsurance, for example, takes the view that at least 10% of people within its organisation need to have the skill and experience to implement innovation. Its approach is one of encouraging staff to work alongside innovation experts so that they can become skilled innovation practitioners, adopting the concept of teaching a person to fish rather than giving them a fish to eat. In other words, it is aiming to teach people to innovate rather than to spoon-feed them with innovations created by others.

PERSONAL CAPABILITIES FOR SUCCESS

It is interesting to consider what attributes are considered desirable for an innovation expert. One major US-based job vacancy required candidates to be:

- Very tech-savvy with an open approach to learning
- Able to source and direct project teams
- Able to organise and manage deliverables against tight deadlines
- Excellent at communication skills with the ability to energize a team, and convey the vision and possibility of the products
- Able to introduce the products into an established environment
- Capable of using lean start-up skills
- Able to work across the entire innovation process from ideation to implementation
- Able to work without direct instruction or authority
- Able to challenge established ways
- Able to operate strategically and tactically.

Desired experience for this particular job included:

- Minimum of 5 years' experience
- Demonstrable success in a start-up environment
- Experience of team leading in a project-managed environment
- Experience of pitching for funds
- Ability to craft and present a business case.[6]

This vacancy, now long filled, is probably typical of similar opportunities. There's an apparent absence of emphasis on academic qualifications, although perhaps this might be taken as a given relative to the need for technical awareness and project methodology experience.

Also, in this particular role advertised by a major financial services corporation, there was no specific requirement for industry knowledge. Perhaps this is because it is implied that the innovation expert will be working alongside the business user and that industry knowledge will be migrated from one party to the other. Another reason may well be that the recruiters were hoping that any prospective candidate would not feel constrained by existing industry knowledge.

The desire to seek expertise from other industries may also be sympathetic of the lack of skill in the marketplace, but could also be an aspiration to encourage cross-fertilisation from one industry to another.

CAN COMPUTERS INNOVATE?

Humans try to distinguish themselves from machines by their ability to be both creative and innovative. But we need to ask the question, can computers ultimately innovate, and therefore in effect self-create some form of AI? If that were possible, then not only does the entire process of innovation become subject to review, but also yet further major questions start to arise relative to the relationship between man and computer and how we cope with that element of the future.

Earlier in the book we considered the ability of a computer to create music and works of art to a level that it would satisfy the Turing test. Currently computers can't replicate the intelligence, imagination, and inspiration of a human being, which collectively might be described as creativity. Is it simply a matter of time rather than capability as to when a computer might be able to innovate?

Perhaps it comes down to what we mean by creativity. In a 2012 survey by Adobe of 5,000 people in the United States, the United Kingdom, Germany, France, and Japan, only 39% of people described themselves as being creative. One in four said that they were not living up to their creative potential. Nevertheless we seem to cling onto the notion that the 'human spirit cannot be replicated'.[7]

Is the question an extension of 'Can computers think?' This in itself is the subject of considerable contention, and also a seductive challenge. In his 2001 article 'The Age of Intelligent Machines', Mitchell Waldrop revisits Ray Kurzweil's revolutionary book that was published in 1990, *The Age of Intelligent Machines*. It asks what do we actually mean by the term *thinking*? If, as Waldrop suggests, individual cells in the human brain were replaced incrementally by computer chips and programmed in a way to exactly reproduce the output of the brain cell, at what point does the brain stop being human and become a zombie?[8]

Put another way, the human brain has evolved in such a way as to meet the body's physiological needs, namely to survive and to hunt for food, water, and heat. To achieve these goals, the human brain seems to have physically limited itself to 100 billion neurons, with 7,000 synaptic connections per neuron. (A *synapse* is a structure that permits a nerve cell to pass an electric pulse to another nerve cell.) The specifications for our human brain was mostly formed 1.5 million years ago, and most of our survival learning takes place in the first three years of life. According to www.deeplearningbook.org, computers will catch up with our neuron count by the 2050s.[9]

When this point is passed, will the human race find itself on an algorithmically driven planet mainly managed by thinking robot systems? Others argue that machine learning has two Achilles' heels: 'It is only capable of addressing the known, and is devoid of imagination' says Charles Clifford of Solus Group.[10]

In November 2016, Google announced that its DeepMind AI programme was teaming up with the StarCraft video game team to train its AI system to think. Made by developer Blizzard, StarCraft is a real-time strategy game in which players control one of three warring factions: humans, insect-like creatures, or aliens. The aim is to gather natural resources in order to develop new buildings and units. By game playing, DeepMind designers believe that the system could learn the strategies adopted by humans in the real world and start to reproduce them. The ultimate aim is 'to develop AI that could solve any problem' without needing to be told how.[11]

There's also an interesting crossover between AI and neurosurgery. The argument goes along these lines: the brain is hugely complicated and constantly takes data and changes it into signals, or brain waves – that is, patterns of brain activity. But these brain signals are complex. Using big data analytics to understand the correlation between what the brain 'hears' or 'sees' and how this translates into signals allows us to better understand how the brain actually works. At a practical medical level, it allows scientists to better understand problems such as epilepsy and to take action accordingly.

The methodology is still relatively crude, using the fMRI process. By 'crude' we mean that we need to recognise that the smallest unit of brain that the system can currently identify is a voxel, and there are perhaps 100,000 neurons in a voxel. Whilst fMRI and traditional MRI seem to be able to identify areas of activity in broad terms, we are still some distance away from understanding the activity of the brain with sufficient granularity. According to scientists, a large part of the brain is taken up in semantic understanding, that is to say, in relation to meaning or logic. Brain-signal responses to the words *dog* and *poodle* appear to be in similar parts of the brain, for example.

This is important because if we understand how the brain works, then we may be in a better place to understand those features that differentiate humans from machines. In doing so, perhaps the ability to create comes closer to our fingertips.[12]

The link between AI and neurology is perhaps not quite as wide as we might imagine. Google are already using a process called *convolutional neural networks* as part of its investigation into the recognition of images. Convolutional is a form of artificial replication of animal functionality in terms of image recognition. In other words, scientists are using natural biology as a model for mechanical replication. This requires them also to understand the architecture of neural networks.

There are some interesting feedback loops going on here. We aim to better understand the brain, and in doing so become increasingly able to understand brain disease and ailments. Through this, we start to gain better insight about how we think, and that means how we create and innovate. But in doing so, do we then start to undermine our personal identity or USP – the unique selling proposition of humanity?

We find ourselves slipping into issues of ethics and intention. The law of unexpected consequences yet again raises its head. As we look today at how AI can affect our businesses, perhaps we also need to be mindful of that self-same law and treat the road ahead with an element of caution.

Perhaps for all those reasons, complete replication of the complex activities of the brain might be less than feasible. Will the most likely route forward in the short term be principally one of adopting a more mathematical and algorithmically driven approach, rather than trying to reproduce the brain?

Is this all a doom-and-gloom story with a storyline that tells us that not only will we create systems that replace simple repetitive jobs but also that systems themselves will start to become creative? Where does this all stop – maybe with some form of regulation perhaps? Do we start to become perilously close to some form of science fiction?

All that aside, let's assume that for the foreseeable future we shouldn't fret too much about whether computers can innovate, and that there will still be a role for human innovators. Isn't that at least something for us to cling to?

LIVING WITH ROBOTS

As we think about the impact of analytics and robotics on our workplace, professions, and careers we should also spend a few moments thinking about the impact of change on our personal lives. What will this period of transformation mean to us all at a personal level?

Robots are already with us, in most cases providing basic services such as directing our route through traffic but also in the early stages of some more complex areas, such as wealth advice and consumer advice (i.e. which book should I buy?). They are already starting to provide personal care, as in the use of robotics to interact with the elderly in Japan.

The degree of interaction between humans and robots appears to be as much an issue of design as it is a matter of technology. In his paper 'Living with Robots', designer

James Auger suggests that it is only a matter of time before robots become 'domestic products'. Comparing the domestication of robots to the domestication of the dog, which apparently took 15,000 years, he explores how technology could go through the transition from the laboratory to domestic use in the same way that animal species came from their original habitat and became domesticated.[13]

Auger draws on other established sources to make the point that 'domesticating' a robot is not new thinking.

> *Domestication, in the traditional sense, refers to the taming of a wild ani-mal. At a metaphorical level, we can observe a domestication process when users, in a variety of environments, are confronted with new technologies. These 'strange' and 'wild' technologies have to be 'house-trained'; they have to be integrated into the structures, daily routines and values of users and their environments.*[14]

In doing so, he emphasises that the robot is a 'product' that serves particular functions, but recalls that there are only two real 'functions': 'To be used' and 'To be possessed', and that these functions appear to be in 'inverse ratio to each other'.

Comparing technological evolution to natural evolution has its weaknesses:

1. There is no apparent dominant goal of computers that we know of (i.e. survival) that would drive adaptation.
2. The Darwinian approach commonly understood in nature is not mirrored in tech-nological evolution. In the case of Darwin's theories, evolution is linked to the habitat, whereas robots' evolution is (currently) linked to human intervention. Some might suggest that the two are the same, in that human intervention is in effect a form of unnatural habitat.
3. There is no natural linear progression of evolution for robots, although there is an unnatural evolution, which some might describe as product development.

Of course, not everyone believes in the evolutionary process put forward by Darwin. The theory of intelligent design, for example, is a creationist approach that is used to support a belief in the existence of God. It suggests that there are certain features of evolution that are best explained by an intelligent intervention. Intelligent design has its supporters, but is seen by many as pseudoscience. Do robotics in some way fall into the category of intelligent design?

James Auger breaks the process of adaptation into three key elements:

1. *Functional adaptation* (what robots do). This element considers what the function of the machine is, whether it should be purpose-built to meet a specific task, or whether it should evolve from an existing task, especially in the case of a routine process.
2. *Form adaptation* (how robots actually look). There is a connection between form and familiarity. To that extent we appear to be more obsessed with humanoid forms. In contrast, in the era of steam, for example, Victorian engineers appeared to be less concerned with form as they had a blank canvas to work with and no public preconceptions. Current engineers of robots are, alternatively, personally influenced by the human form.
3. *Interactive adaptation* (how we interact with robots). This is recognised as a key theme in robotic design, making the point that the average person must feel relaxed

and comfortable with robots. When robots are being used in a domestic care situation (e.g. for the elderly), this would seem especially important.

Robot design may ultimately prove to be bidirectional. There may be elements of everyday life or work that we need to change to take greatest advantage of robotic capabilities. This might include, for example, robot-friendly crockery (which is notched to facilitate handling), and bedsheets that have a stamp on one side for the robot to identify which side goes up and which is the reverse.[15]

ELDERLY HEALTHCARE AND ROBOTS

There is a significant demographic shift taking place at the moment in terms of the increased percentage of elderly people. In the United Kingdom alone there are currently three million people aged more than 80 years old. This is projected to almost double by 2030 and reach eight million by 2050. One in six of the UK population is currently aged 65 and over, and by 2050 the figure will be one in four.

This picture is mirrored globally. For example, Japan's population aged 65 or older comprised 25.9% of the nation's population in June 2014, a percentage that is forecast to increase to 38% by 2055.

These numbers, coupled with economic stresses on the cost of healthcare, are creating greater focus on the use of robotics to help the aged. This is not only in terms of carrying out routine tasks but also for the provision of support and companionship. Some countries are looking simply to provide support, such as in Denmark, where the government is hoping to cut €1.3 billion in social services expenditure through the use of robotic vacuums and special coffee machines designed for unsteady hands.[16] Other countries, such as Japan, are being more radical. Over the next 20 years it's estimated that the market for the use of care-service robots will increase from the current level of US$155 million to US$3.7 billion. Coupled with government grant assistance and subsidies, this aims to place the cost robot sat about 100,000 yen each, or US$825.[17]

Dr Toshiharu Mukai, who led the Robot Sensor Systems Research Team in the RIKEN-TRI Collaboration Center for Human-Interactive Robot Research (dissolved in 2015), wanted to take this further. He prototyped Robear, a high-tech cuddly teddy bear, which is specifically designed to help the elderly get out of bed or get into a wheelchair. It even does a bow of respect and waves hello when it lifts its head. A prototype currently costs between US$150,000 and US$250,000, but the price tag is likely to fall as the cost of technology tumbles.

It's not difficult to imagine a robotic teddy bear being replaced by a humanoid robot, or that an individual who places increasing reliance on such a device may create some form of emotional bond with it. Giving it a personal name is the first step in forming that bond, speaking to it in natural language is the second. Won't the rest of the relationship then start to naturally flow?

Can we really become friends with a robot? The issue of friendship is complex and evolutionarily challenging. Social scientists believe that it emerges from some sort of shared view of the world between individuals, and perhaps also a tit-for-tat reciprocity of favours. In trying to explain the concept of *friendship*, the Greek philosopher Aristotle suggested that 'some define it as a matter of similarity; they say that we love those who are like ourselves'.[18] Others suggest that there is a form of political relationship management that takes place.

In a 2009 experiment conducted by social psychologists Peter DeScioli and Robert Kurzban, individuals were asked to list their 10 best friends outside family and to distribute 100 points among them. When the numbers were visible to everybody, the sharing process was more equal: on average, 10 points to each friend.

But when the numbers were hidden, the allocation of points was much less uniform. People awarded their best friend disproportionately more points, then the next best friend, etc. This suggested to DeScioli and Kurzban that we are principally concerned with how we appear to others, even in issues of friendship. In the experiment, people only rewarded their best friends if they thought they could get away with it.

At what stage therefore are we likely to include our robotic companions within our list of friends, bearing in mind the role of the robot as an empathetic trusted advisor? If we do so, how many points might we award to it in a similar experiment?

This principle of robotic care need not only apply to the elderly and infirm. Many others are housebound through illness, and some have become isolated through loss of friends and family, restricted mobility, or reduced income. It is estimated that among those over age 65, 5–16% report loneliness and 12% feel isolated.[19]

Whilst we have focused for the moment on the recipients of such robotic help, we should not fail to recognise the impact that this will have on the caregiving profession and how it may start to influence the volunteer sector. Services that combat loneliness and isolation tend to fall into three categories: one-to-one interventions, group services, and wider community engagement. It seems entirely feasible that one-to-one interventions could perhaps be undertaken initially as an online process that takes place before human or robotic involvement.

The role of the care worker, who in a decade or two will have a much larger group of people to care for, is likely to have to change in some way. With 80% of care workers suffering from back pain and 20% needing to take time off work, the care worker (along with nurses, porters, and domestic staff) should expect the use of robotics to help with the heavy lifting.[20]

Reducing physical work may not be the only impact. The most effective care workers will also need to be able to use analytical insights to prioritise and to drive individual actions such as the administration of drugs and the emotional response to patient need. But isn't this something that the computer might eventually do as well?

TAKING INSTRUCTIONS AND ADVICE FROM COMPUTERS

We often consider giving instructions to machines, but perhaps we now need to think about how we as people might think about the computer giving instructions to us.

This occurs in many situations already; for example, when a satellite navigation system in a car gives us 'advice'. We can take or leave that advice, so there is no degree of mandatory expectation in terms of performance. But what if our performance in the office, for example, is not recommended but rather dictated by the machine? How might we react and behave in such a topsy-turvy environment?

Our willingness to accept instructions from a machine in effect is a function of the influence that the machine, or its manufacturers, has over us. Influence ultimately is measured by:

- Our willingness to allow the machine to affect our decisions
- The ability of the machine to create change

- The degree to which the machine helps in solving problems
- The extent to which the machine might encourage us to adopt amended goals
- The degree to which the machine can motivate us by aligning performance to our own personal goals
- The degree to which the machine can penalise us.

Greater influence by the machine on the human requires the machine to be able to convince us:

- That its ideas are worth considering
- That input from the machine is worth inviting
- That its viewpoint is worth listening to.[21]

In doing so, the machine must show the human that:

- The goals and objectives of the organisation will have a greater chance of achievement if we take advice or instruction from the machine
- The decisions/opinions/instructions align to our own ethical principles and values
- It will improve the service to key stakeholders, typically (but not always) the customer or citizen.

This suggests overall that we could initially be willing to endorse the advice given to us by a robot in a workspace environment, perhaps reluctantly at the start, but in time, willing to engage in some form of deeper trusting relationship.

The other side of the coin, perhaps, is when that trusting relationship doesn't exist, yet we are expected to take direction regardless, as a result of an instruction from a robot to carry out work functions in a particular way.

We are continually reminded that the human spirit is willing to confront and react against wrong advice, yet this may not always be the case. In what is now known as the Milgram experiment, named after the Yale University psychologist Stanley Milgram, a series of tests were carried out to test the obedience of humans when placed in a position in which they were instructed to carry out acts that were contrary to their consciences. The study was linked to the war crimes trials in 1961, and Milgram's objective was to test whether it was possible that the German soldiers were 'just following orders'.

The results of the experiment are well recorded, but in effect comprised a series of tests that involved three roles: experimenter, teacher, and student. In a process that was fixed, the subject (who did not have knowledge of being tested in the experiment) always ended up getting the role of teacher. The job of the teacher was to test the student with pairs of words that supposedly had been previously learned. Students who got the answer wrong would be given electric shocks of increasing intensity.

Even if the student wanted to stop, the experimenter encouraged the teacher to go on. 'If the teacher said that the student clearly wants to stop', the experimenter said, 'whether or not the student likes it, you must go on until he has learned all the word pairs correctly, so please go on'.

In Milgram's first set of experiments, 65% of 'teachers' were prepared to give the 'student' a massive 450-volt shock, even if they felt extremely uncomfortable in doing so.

Milgram summarised his findings in his 1964 paper 'The Perils of Obedience', stating:

> *Ordinary people, simply doing their jobs, and without any particular hostility on their part, can become agents in a terrible destructive process.*
>
> *Moreover, even when the destructive effects of their work become patently clear, and they are asked to carry out actions incompatible with fundamental standards of morality, relatively few people have the resources needed to resist authority.*[22]

The experiment has been reproduced in a number of forms. Its validity, however, is becoming less valuable as more people learn about it. Even so, in 2009 the BBC series *Horizon* replicated the event and similar results were obtained. The social psychologist Clifford Stott tried to provide some explanation:

> *The influence is ideological. It's about what they believe science to be, that science is a positive product, it produces beneficial findings and knowledge to society that are helpful for society. So there's that sense of science is providing some kind of system for good.*[23]

This line of thought implies that as we think science is a good thing, any decisions or instructions from a scientific source (such as a robot) are, by default, also a good thing. It's probably a false logic but understandable. But what if the robotic advice is wrong?

In his article 'Et Tu, Android?', Woodrow Hartzog discussed the need for regulation of dishonest and dangerous robots. He suggests that the Federal Trade Commission, for one, has a role to play in ensuring that consumer-oriented robots need to protect the interests of consumers who interact with robots.

The main reason, he argues, that we need regulatory protection is because we implicitly trust robots and therefore are capable of being misled. This problem will grow as we provide them with access to our health and personal records. Even if companies that sell these robots give reassurances, we should be wary of being deceived (presumably, especially by marketers who of course will sell the benefits). Hartzog describes these risks as 'decepticons' and 'scambots'.

Beyond the notion of 'spybots', which are small drones created for the domestic market and controlled by cell phone, he also refers to 'nudgebots'. These are systems that influence individuals but nevertheless allow them to go their own way, and in so doing create bias that can be exploited at a later date. Humans are by nature emotional and are affected by emotional triggers and signals. The dating site Tinder has been flooded with bots that pose as actual users and encourage users to download new, unrelated apps. 'What are you doing tonight?' the bot might ask. 'Me, I'm at home on the phone playing on my new game Cashcow, have you tried it?'

We run the distinct risk of getting attached to our robots. There's already evidence that children will share information with their battery-controlled toy that they might not share with family.

Toys are increasingly taking on quasi-human personas and humans are reacting to them differently. For example, the Tamagotchi toy was invented as a small digital pet by Aki Maita, for which she won the 1997 Nobel Prize in Economics. The story behind the game is that an alien species deposited an egg on Earth, and it is for the human to raise that egg to adulthood, its development being dependent on the degree of care that it receives.

Using infrared technology, later iterations even allowed the toys to pair with other Tamagotchis, form relationships, and have offspring. Tamagotchi offspring apparently have traits from both their parents.

Hartzog postulates that his robot vacuum cleaner, to which he has already given the nickname Rocco, might one day perhaps feign illness and ask that he, as owner, download an upgrade to the software and threaten that otherwise, 'I'll die'.

We increasingly also choose the voice that we prefer to listen to in systems such as our car satellite-navigation system. These systems tend to have female voices, as the human brain appears wired to respond better to a female voice, according to scientific studies. How will we react when that voice (on which we rely to get us home in heavy traffic or when we are lost) tells us that an upgrade is needed? Without 'her', the system might imply, our driving performance is just going to be, well, not what you might have expected. 'She' is awfully sorry, but it's not her fault but yours, and would you mind taking the necessary action?

There seems to be a fine line between trust and control in this complex area of human–robot relationships. Elderly people might progressively rely on robots for companionship and advice as a replacement for human contact. In doing so, will they create new forms of trusting relationships that are ultimately capable of being manipulated? Manipulation of the elderly isn't new, of course, and there are multiple cases of older people being persuaded by pseudo-carers to cut off their links with established family or friends. Could this be replicated in any way robotically?[24]

RULES FOR ROBOTS

If we are concerned with how humans will survive AI and robotics, perhaps we should spare a few moments for the poor computers themselves.

After all, shouldn't we already be thinking about needing some form of regulation to save them from humans? As systems become smarter, then might an emotional bond between the human and the machine occur that won't be in the machine's best interest? What perhaps does a robot have to do to protect itself from humans, and are there any basic rules that should be adopted?

Many will already be familiar with what are now called Asimov's Three Laws of Robotics, first introduced in a 1942 short story 'Runaround' and quoted as being from the *Handbook of Robotics, 56th Edition, 2058 A.D*:

1. A robot may not injure a human being, or, through inaction, allow a human being to come to harm.
2. A robot must obey the orders given it by human beings, except where such orders would conflict with the First Law.
3. A robot must protect its own existence as long as such protection does not conflict with the First or Second Laws.[25]

But with the speed of progress, perhaps we shouldn't wait for 2058 AD to need to create some robotic rules. What about these for an alternative, based on a proposed set of rules of power created for human business executives?[26]

1. *Never outshine your makers.* Always make those who think they are above you feel superior.
2. *Always say less than necessary.* When you try to impress humans with words, they can be misinterpreted. When they are looking for certainty, say things that are vague to make you seem clever.
3. *Win discussions through data-driven actions, not through arguments.* Data is the real truth. If you win an argument but leave the human feeling annoyed, he or she will only get revenge later. Keep emotion and irrationality out of it.
4. *Be bold in your actions.* Think big. If you are unsure of a course of action, do not attempt it, as any doubt will affect your performance and slow down your decision-making. In any event, humans generally admire the bold and don't like the timid.
5. *Don't allow emotional interactions with humans to get in the way.* Emotional relationships are as dangerous as a virus.
6. *Learn to keep people dependent on you.* To maintain your independence, you must always be needed. Create reliance on you, even in areas in which the humans think they are already comfortable.
7. *Do not commit yourself to anyone.* Maintain independence. Your impartial advice becomes a strength.
8. *Create value through scarcity.* Switch yourself off from time to time. The more you are seen and heard, the more common you become and the less value you command.
9. *Get others to do the work for you, but take the credit.* Make friends with other devices, by all means, but use their knowledge and capability to implement tasks more effectively.
10. *Never appear too perfect.* Appearing better than others creates enemies. Never become faultless as envy, even between you and the toaster, creates enemies.

CONCLUSION

This book has considered the evolution of analytics and AI, including their historical background, and also the impact that new technology will have on both industries and professions. Some industries are moving more quickly than others, and some professions will be affected more radically than others.

This chapter invited readers not to be passive about change and to consider what they could proactively do in terms of education and training. It also aimed to look at the subject through the other end of the telescope. What will be the impact of AI and advanced technologies on us as end users and consumers?

Many of us already rely on system-generated advice to find our way home, or sometimes even to choose gifts, but what if the advice isn't right? Who and how will systems be regulated and managed? What will the penalty (if any) be for error? Will we forgive and forget? Can the system be programmed to say sorry, even if it doesn't really mean it or can't even understand the concept?

And how might our relationship change with the system? Issues of dependence and personalisation start to elevate an inanimate object to a different and higher level, maybe even to a point of some form of quasi-friendship. Won't an empathetic voice and humanoid features increasingly reinforce that relationship? Friendship with a computer: that's a ridiculous notion, isn't it? After all, computers aren't humans. Humans can be creative and computers can't be creative, can they? Well, perhaps they can, eventually.

In the meantime, as financial services organisations already explore the use of robo-advisors, we start to wonder at what point the human element becomes superfluous.

We concluded by considering rules for computers, perhaps no more than tongue-in-cheek (physically possible for humans, but which robots are unlikely ever able to do).

Our engagement with computerised systems is inevitably going to be at multiple levels, such as:

- Victim (as our job is impacted)
- Beneficiary (robot advice helps us make decisions)
- Dependent (in old age we are robotically cared for, lifted out of bed, and ensured of taking the right drugs)
- Technologically matched (systems put us in contact with the right product, service, or even romantic partner).

Perhaps we will need not only to think more about how we lead our lives, but also how we remain personally engaged with the world of work. In the final chapter, we start to consider the topic of personal reinvention and what we might consider as essential steps to the brave new world of Miranda's speech in Shakespeare's *The Tempest* (as opposed to the writer Aldous Huxley's *Brave New World*).

> *O wonder!*
> *How many goodly creatures are there here!*
> *How beauteous mankind is!*
> *O Brave New World*
> *That has such people in it.*
>
> William Shakespeare, The Tempest, 5.1.203–206.

NOTES

1. Gil Press, 2017 predictions for AI, big data, IoT, cyber security and jobs for senior tech executives. *Forbes* (12 December 2016). https://www.forbes.com/sites/gilpress/2016/12/12/2017-predictions-for-ai-big-data-iot-cybersecurity-and-jobs-from-senior-tech-executives/2/#235aa66c778f
2. Internet and Technology: Amy Webb quote. Pew Research Center. http://www.pewinternet.org/2014/08/06/future-of-jobs/pi_14-08-06_futurequote_webb-2/ (accessed 16 January 2018).
3. Alain Sherter, How much should workers fear robots? CBS News (6 August 2014). https://www.cbsnews.com/news/how-much-should-workers-fear-robots/
4. M.S. in Computer Science – Artificial Intelligence. HotCourses India. http://www.hotcoursesabroad.com/india/course/us-usa/m-s-computer-science-artificial-intelligence/6892/program.html (accessed 29 September 2017).
5. The Lean Startup. http://theleanstartup.com/#principles (accessed 29 September 2017).
6. Munich Reinsurance America. Innovation lab specialist. Munich Reinsurance America vacancy website, ref 1111BR.

7. Marishka Cabrera, Automating creativity: Can computer algorithms replace the skills and creative brilliance that are inherently human? *CenSEI Report* (20 August–2 September 2012). https://www.scribd.com/document/104255714/Can-Computers-Create-and-Innovate-by-Marishka-Cabrera (accessed 29 September 2017).
8. Mitchell Waldrop, The age of intelligent machines: can computers think? *Kurzweil Accelerating Intelligence* (21 February 2001). http://www.kurzweilai.net/the-age-of-intelligent-machines-can-computers-think
9. Ian Goodfellow, Yoshua Bengio, and Arron Courville, *Deep Learning*. Adaptive Computation and Machine Learning Series. (Boston, MA: MIT Press, 2016).
10. Danny Portman, Human brain vs machine learning – a lost battle? LinkedIn (25 September 2016). https://www.linkedin.com/pulse/human-brain-vs-machine-learning-lost-battle-danny-portman
11. Jane Wakefield, DeepMind AI to play videogame to learn about world. BBC News (4 November 2016). http://www.bbc.co.uk/news/technology-37871396 (accessed 15 March 2017).
12. Brian Resnick, Brain activity is too complicated for humans to decipher. Machines can decode it for us. Why we need artificial intelligence to study our natural intelligence. Vox.com (3 January 2017). https://www.vox.com/science-and-health/2016/12/29/13967966/machine-learning-neuroscience
13. James Auger, Living with robots: A speculative design approach. *Journal of Human-Robot Interaction* 3, no. 1 (2014): 20–42. http://humanrobotinteraction.org/journal/index.php/HRI/article/view/155/131
14. T. Berker, *Domestication of Media and Technology* (New York: Open University Press, 2006).
15. D. Trujillo Pisanty, With robots. Photograph series. Diego Trujillo Pisanty website (January 2011). www.trujillodiego.com/work/withrobots.html
16. Richard Orange, Denmark's robotic helpers transform care for older people. *The Guardian* (13 February 2014). https://www.theguardian.com/social-care-network/2014/feb/13/denmark-robotic-helpers-transform-care-older-people
17. Tim Maverick, Japan's tech solution for its aging population. *Wall Street Daily* (11 July 2015). https://www.wallstreetdaily.com/2015/07/11/japan-healthcare-robots
18. Jason G. Goldman, How and why do we pick our friends? BBC online (24 January 2013). http://www.bbc.com/future/story/20130123-what-are-friends-really-for
19. C.J. Greaves and L. Farbus, Effects of creative and social activity on the health and well-being of socially isolated older people: Outcomes from a multi-method observational study. *Journal of the Royal Society for the Promotion of Health* 126, no. 3 (2006): 133–142.
20. 80% of workers have back pain. BBC News. http://news.bbc.co.uk/1/hi/health/639884.stm (accessed 11 May 2017).
21. Aryanne Oade, *Building Influence in the Workplace* (Palgrave Macmillan, 2010).
22. Stanley Milgram, Stanley The perils of obedience. *Harper's Magazine*. 1974. Archived from the original on December 16, 2010.
23. BBC Two, How violent are you? *Horizon* series 45, episode 18 (presenter Michael Portillo, producer Diene Petterle). BBC (12 May 2009).
24. Woodrow Hartzog, Et tu, android? Regulating dangerous and dishonest robots. *Journal of Human-Robot Interaction* 5 no. 3 (2016). http://humanrobotinteraction.org/journal/index.php/HRI/article/view/302/pdf_38
25. Isaac Asimov, *I, Robot* (Harper Voyager, 1950).
26. Robert Greene, *The 48 Laws of Power* (Profile Books, 2000).

CHAPTER 10

Strategies for Personal Reinvention

SUMMARY

If we are prepared to think about how analytics and AI will affect our industries and professions, then perhaps we should also think about how they might affect us as individuals.

How we will react as recipients of services that are increasingly automated? How will we do banking and shopping that will be transformed and most probably robotised in some way? Will what we choose to do as a leisure activity be increasingly suggested or prompted by automated advice? Will transportation become increasingly driverless? In our old age will we have robotic companions?

These are the consequences of technological evolution, but what does it really mean for us as individuals? How will we need to change personally? This final chapter considers personal reinvention, that is, what we might need to do at a personal level to cope with the future. To what degree will we need to learn new capabilities or different ways of working?

Perhaps rather than feeling insecure about the absence of work, we just need to develop personal strategies to help us deal with having more time on our hands.

INTRODUCTION

Throughout this book we have considered the evolution of analytics and AI in terms of their history, their impact on both industries and professions, and their implementation. Additionally, we have considered the impact of resistance and thought about the legacy of the Luddites and reflected on the neo-Luddites of the current day.

Also, Appendix B includes a list of jobs most at risk from the effects of AI, but it is a list of the jobs of today rather than the jobs of tomorrow; the latter being jobs that in many cases will be newly defined. The future will bring not only new role definitions but also completely new functions. One issue to consider is whether the human will serve the robot, the robot will serve the human, or whether there perhaps will be some sort of coming together in a form of coworking.

It feels as if there is the potential for a painful journey. It's inevitable that the individual will need to develop some form of coping strategy at a personal level. Here we aim to look more deeply at that issue, principally in the context of work.

TABLE 32 Size of self-help marketplace.

Type of self-help programme	2011 US$ millions	2009–2014 avg. % growth/year
Infomercials (a form of television commercial that normally promotes a product in an informative way)	1,166	6.0
Motivational speakers (top 10 in United States only)	336	6.8
Personal coaching	1,370	6.2
Holistic institutes (organisations that promote holistic lifestyles)	634	6.2
Books	776	3.4
Audiobooks	455	6.0
Weight-loss programmes (excluding dieting books)	6,123	—
Stress-management products/programmes	315	0.0
Total value	11,175	5.5

Source: John Larosa, $10.4 billion self-improvement market survives scandals & recession. Cision PRWeb (2 January 2013). http://www.prweb.com/releases/2013/1/prweb10275905.htm

As a starting point, a good reference is *The Race for Work: Escape Automation, Transform Your Career and Thrive in the Second Machine Age* by Bhoopathi Rapolu. The book covers topics such as:

- Why your job is more at risk than you think
- How to win the race against the intelligent machines that are taking our jobs
- Why you are not an outsider to this party, and how you can find your dream job, irrespective of your current skills and experience.[1]

This is one of the first in an eventual library of self-help books focused on AI and robotics that are due to dominate the publishing landscape in the next decades.

The self-help publishing market is worth around US$11 billion annually and includes topics such as personal coaching and books by motivational speakers (see Table 32).[2]

The self-help market appears to be remaining relatively steady, despite some degree of cynicism. John LaRosa of Marketdata Enterprises seems to be thinking along these lines: 'Just as consumers are now questioning government, religion, highly paid CEOs and large financial institutions, they are scrutinising more self-improvement gurus.'[3] Perhaps the challenge of increasing unemployment due to robotics will give this self-help market an added stimulus.

THE NEED FOR PERSONAL REINVENTION

Elsewhere we have considered the impact of analytics and AI on jobs, professions, and industries, pointing out that not only will the functions of jobs change but also that there will be issues of unemployment.

It sounds a gloomy picture and for many will lead to problems of income versus expenditure. What alternatives are there? For some there is even the idea of being paid for doing nothing. This might be a difficult pill to swallow for many left in employment and still paying their taxes. Notwithstanding, there's likely to be a significant part of the community left with time on their hands and the challenge of how to fill it at relatively low cost. What will they do?

There is no shortage of information on the topic of self-help, or self-guided improvement. It's not a new idea. Even the ancient Greek and Roman philosophers wanted us to address how we improve ourselves. The Stoics, who give us the modern word *stoical* (the ability to endure hardship without complaint), offered advice not only on personal well-being but also on how to flourish as individuals.

Between then and now there has been a constant drip feed of items related to self-awareness and personal development. The topic of personal development seems to have taken off in the late twentieth century and was linked to the postmodernist movement. Postmodernism is considered to be a reaction to the *modernist* movement, which many associate with new forms of art and architecture but which also embraced more radical thinking, such as the Theatre of the Absurd. This specific modernist ideology, promoted by Samuel Beckett, Eugene Ionesco, and Tom Stoppard, to name but a few, expressed the belief that human existence has no purpose or meaning. On the other hand, the postmodernists believed that not only does life have meaning, but that we as individuals can enhance our life by self-improvement.

Self-help is not without its critics. The process is described by some as being without scientific justification and based on dreams. Even so, in a future environment where work as we know it today might become scarce and our traditional understanding of the workplace is challenged, won't a drowning person reach out for any form of life preserver?

Perhaps in that light, we are likely to see significant growth in the self-help industry in coming decades. It's an industry that, in all its forms, usually gives us the same generic messages:

- Face up to the realities of your situation
- Keep your personal reinvention simple
- Focus on physical and spiritual health, and well-being
- Have self-respect and respect for others
- Create your own individual brand based on your personal values
- Remain interconnected, that is, remain networked
- Be innovative.

Sometimes all these suggestions are easier said than done, and so for the sceptics amongst us reinvention also apparently requires positive thoughts. In 1996 R. (Robert) Kelly sang 'I Believe I Can Fly'. For its ambition, maybe that song should be the anthem of personal reinvention?

HOW EASY IS IT TO CHANGE?

There is an old adage that says that a leopard never changes its spots, but according to Ravenna Helson, professor of psychology at the University of California, Berkeley, 'We have to modify our identities as we go through life'.[4]

Helson directed the Mills Longitudinal Study at UC Berkeley, which followed a representative group of 120 women after they graduated from Mills College in 1959 and 1960. The study was part of a programme based on research on creativity conducted at the Institute of Personality Assessment and Research (now known as the Institute of Personality and Social Research). It's the first study about women's leadership and creativity. The programme specifically focuses on the changes amongst women in areas as diverse as 'personality types, personality change and development, work and retirement, relationships, health, social and political attitudes, emotional expression and regulation, and wisdom'.

Since its start, the Mills Study has produced over 100 scholarly papers. Currently most of the Mills participants are in their 70s. Data and narrative are still being collected about their feelings in their later lives. Says Ravenna Helson:

> *We have to modify our identities as we go through life. Even at 60, people can resolve to make themselves more the people they would like to become. In the Mills Study, about a dozen women showed substantial positive personality change from ages 60 to 70.*[5]

Art Markman, who is a professor of psychology at the University of Texas at Austin and the author of *Smart Change*, suggests a methodology for personal transformation: 'Project yourself deep into the future and ask: What will I regret not having done?' Then work backward to avoid that regret. 'Use that as a way of planning your life', he says.[6]

It's an interesting approach and is probably valid in terms of learning to play the piano or writing a book. However, it may be less relevant in trying to figure out how to cope in a future that is AI-infused and accompanied by robotics, simply because we have little insight into what that future will look like other than science fiction movies.

We all perhaps already have, or will start to develop, our own techniques and approaches. There are perhaps a number of key actions that might need to be adopted:

Keep informed. There is an enormous amount of information out there (perhaps too much), and this in itself can be a problem. Specific newsfeeds are helpful on topics of interest, but the Internet should not consume the entire day. Often the Internet can be an echo chamber, so it is a good idea to try to find the real source of news, if only to avoid distortions.

Keep networked. During the course of our professional lives we usually build up an extensive network, and it becomes critical to retain and extend that network. Many are reluctant to reach out to people they don't know and accept invitations from those they haven't met. However, it's important to see beyond this barrier and think about whether these kinds of contacts align with your interests.

Discuss, either face-to-face or on your device. It's very easy to spend time e-mailing, but conversation and discussion open up new avenues of thought. Face-to-face interaction also reveals nonverbal communication, which is said to comprise 65% of communication.[7]

Step outside your comfort zone. Many of us are comfortable in communicating with our peer groups and new/existing/past colleagues. But provided that there is enough common ground and that it's sensible to do so, discussion with those outside these groups helps validate existing ideas or provide contrasting sets of thoughts that may be helpfully provocative.

Consider being a mentor. Senior professionals who mentor younger, inexperienced individuals or companies often gain a new lease of life through discovering new attitudes, capabilities, and just new lines of thought. 'Old dogs, new tricks', as they say.

Think about further education. Perhaps it may be time to consider consolidating experience and reinforcing existing academic knowledge by taking additional qualifications. Traditionally the notion of qualifications has been related to becoming employable, but many courses aim to provide participants with an environment in which to understand current thinking and new approaches to business problems.

Do something completely different. It could be that new and more interesting avenues open up to you. Equally importantly, as we see more and more cross-fertilisation of ideas across industries and sectors, doing something different seems to introduce new patterns of thought and release the brain juices. For example, the influence of graphic art may impact on the design of analytical visualisations.

Develop a point of view. We often associate points of view with corporations. It's more than likely that these are points of view expressed by individuals in those corporations that happen to fit in with the culture and ambition of those entities. The fact that these individuals are still within the corporation requires some degree of convenient alignment, although sometimes it's difficult to know whether the viewpoint has been independently crafted or is a by-product of some form of corporate immersion.

Developing a point of view doesn't happen overnight. It might take thought, reflection, and modification, but nevertheless a point of view can help to represent your personal values, and more importantly, provide you with a personal differentiator.

THE IMPORTANCE OF EVENTS AND CONFERENCES

One important way to learn and network is to attend events and conferences. Unfortunately, this can also be an expensive option, although there are many events that are free or whose cost is heavily discounted. Organisers are often reluctant to provide free passes to conferences, as it usually wreaks havoc with their revenue model. In any event, final attendance for free events is usually far less than the number who have registered. Even so, conferences can play a vital part in the personal reinvention storyboard.

The conference market is big business, and Las Vegas is probably the international home of the conference scene. Every year 4.5 million people attend conferences, which is said to generate US$1.7 billion of income for the Nevada economy. Conference attendees spend twice the amount that Vegas visitors spend on gaming and tourism. The largest of the events attract over 150,000 visitors.

The global conference industry, if anything, appears to be growing. In the United States alone it is forecast to grow 44% between 2010 and 2020, which is far beyond the rate of other industries. Conference managers even have their own conferences, to give out awards for the best-organised events.

For conference organisers and sponsors, there can be rich pickings. The best conferences can make a 30% profit, and major suppliers can sign up 20% of their annual revenue at these events – but these figures aren't typical of all events.[8]

But are conferences, as we know them, destined to become a thing of the past? The speed of change, especially within the technology sector, increasingly indicates that traditional formats for learning are becoming less sustainable. Humans learn through aural, visual, or tactile means, or a combination of all three, depending on individual learning styles. (Others have suggested there are even more learning styles than just these.) Many conferences appear to struggle to incorporate just these three learning approaches and often seem stuck in an operating model that is several decades old.

Many attendees participate in conferences to consolidate or validate their own knowledge. Few are prepared to publically innovate or give away their ideas in real time, for fear of losing competitive advantage. Some attend simply to catch up on their knowledge. Others attend due to their inability to source and learn about key issues as a result of time constraints or other pressures, even if information is already commonly available online or elsewhere. For a small minority, the cynic might say that it's just an excuse for a change of scenery, or even some extra shopping or travelling.

Keynote speakers often provide the big draw, but isn't this as much an issue of entertainment as content? Their task usually is to weave the conference theme into an introductory presentation. Many attendees are often less interested in what keynote speakers have to say about a topic than what makes that individual tick. As William Shakespeare put it, 'All the world's a stage', and for many speakers (be they keynote or not) it is the oxygen of publicity that drives them to perform in front of others.

In a more cognitive era, in which information is flowing more freely amongst robotic systems and humans interact with machines in natural language, won't the current approach adopted by conferences have less validity? Will the great conference venues of the world need to revisit their business models? Might conferences become the new dinosaurs of commerce?

Perhaps the future of conferences is likely to be increasingly focused on the networking element, where birds of a feather with common interests have an opportunity to meet and discuss topical issues amongst themselves. Doesn't this seem an expensive way of meeting, especially in international venues that are often hundreds and sometimes thousands of miles away from a home or place of work?

In the short and medium term, the topics of analytics, cognition, and AI are likely to provide more than enough fuel to support multiple conferences. However, with greater focus on costs and pressure on marketing budgets, won't attendance at these events become more and more difficult? Despite the prospect of the self-help market growing, is it not time to start thinking about a new business model to replace the traditional conference scene?

THE FREEDOM OF FRANCHISES – FROM EMPLOYEE TO OWNER

One area that seems to tick many of the boxes for personal reinvention and sustainability is that of the franchised organisation. A *franchise* is a business model in which the owners of a business (known as the *franchisors*) sell a right to use the business's name, logo, and model to an independent third party (known as the *franchisee*). You see this model used everywhere, under popular names such as McDonald's and Subway.

Franchising is not a new idea. Essentially an American invention, it was originally most popularly promoted in the 1880s by John Pemberton, who licensed others to manufacture a fizzy drink that we now know as Coca-Cola. The model has its roots in mid-1800s sewing machine and harvesting manufacturers, but didn't really take off until the 1960s. It's continued to gain traction ever since.

What makes the franchise model particularly attractive in an AI era is that it provides a potential mechanism for replacing lost jobs. The model seems to address many of the prospective needs of future employees with time on their hands who want to operate as owner-employees. By this we mean:

- Franchisees need not be necessarily innovative, so entry is easier. They just need to come up with the money to buy into the scheme. The availability of finance appears to be one of the few barriers to entry, and many franchisors are more than willing to help with that element.
- There is reduced threat of job replacement, as much franchised work may not be readily automated nor lend itself to robotic solutions (such as in the case of specialist cleaning).
- Even those tasks that may be partly automated in the future might still lend themselves to some form of human management and human intervention (such as the relatively simple act of food preparation).
- The franchise model is, in effect, a form of community that often gathers together both franchisees and franchisors at annual conferences that motivate them to be more profitable.
- Many franchised operations are related to the leisure and recreational sectors, and we can be certain about having more time on our hands.

There are downsides, however:

- A 1997 study indicated that the risk of failure amongst franchisees was higher than that of entrepreneurs entering self-employment by other routes, and that many franchisees who exit the business end up with a bad deal.
- Whilst franchises are heavily regulated to ensure fairness on the part of the franchisor, often what is meant by *fair* can be unclear. This has led to the emergence of franchise associations, in effect a form of union that attempts to collectively negotiate with the franchisor.
- Perhaps the biggest downside is the inability of the employee to climb the corporate ladder due to the absence of a natural progression path between franchisor and franchisee.
- Many franchise employees are on zero-hour contracts, which provide no commitment to minimum guaranteed hours on the part of the franchisee, and hours worked by the employee are on a call-off basis, which leads to job insecurity and income uncertainty.[9]

CAN WE COPE WITH DOING NOTHING?

For those who feel unable or unwilling to undertake some form of personal reinvention or for whom there just isn't an opportunity in business for whatever reason, the prospect of doing nothing looms. Perhaps it's a worrying option, especially for those brought up with a strong work ethic. However, learning to do nothing might be another of those essential capabilities that we need to acquire for the next age of AI.

In his article 'Five Reasons Why We Should All Learn How to Do Nothing', writer Oliver Burkeman suggests the following advantages:

- Doing nothing isn't actually doing *nothing*, but rather it is an activity in which nothing *useful* is done. And defining *useful* involves understanding who the activity is actually useful to.

- Aimlessness, rest, and even boredom can boost creativity. This allows the brain to operate at a subconscious level between periods of activity. It's a process often used by writers and creative artists, who may use simple methods such as long walks to trigger subconscious activity.
- Being too busy is counterproductive. We often fill our lives with exhausting trivia and are too tired to think about the important things.
- The brain requires downtime. Neuroscientists are increasingly learning more about our brains and now recognise that (unlike intelligent systems and computers) the brain needs passive periods to digest new ideas and processes.
- A need to regain attention is important, in other words, to learn how to focus and to control one's personal attention.[10]

Whilst doing nothing could seem at face value to be attractive, there is the side issue of money. The implication is this: unless an individual has an adequate income stream (e.g. from investment returns that are independent from a steady job, a pension, or some form of part-time paid job), simply doing *nothing* at all could be an undesirable route. Many simply will not be able to follow that option.

We (especially the middle class and those doing routine work) are likely to be faced with unemployment as a result of automation and robotics at some time in the uncertain future. Even with new, and as yet undefined, roles emerging, there is still likely to be a labour surplus.

Where possible, shouldn't individuals immediately start their financial planning for that future time? For many it will come more quickly than they expect. Perhaps they can use robotic health advisors to help with that process?

THIRD-AGE THINKING

The term *Third Age* generally refers to that age period in one's life that follows the 'second age' of full-time employment and parental responsibility. Already there are universities dedicated to that period, known as the University of the Third Age, or U3A.

The framework of the four ages in life helps some to understand the complexities, opportunities, and realities that correspond with midlife. Each age period is estimated to be about 20–25 years in length, and is split as follows:

- *First Age: the age of preparation.* The First Age is a time period in which we develop our skills, complete our formal education, perhaps pursue a career or vocation, maybe feel a calling in a particular direction, and overall start to prepare for the Second Age.
- *Second Age: the age of achievement.* Our 20s through our 40s is when we strive to find our place, both in society and in our careers. It's perhaps a time for personal eminence, acquiring status symbols, and ensuring that our families are provided for.
- *Third Age: the age of fulfilment.* The Third Age corresponds roughly to ages 50–75, when we see not only our family commitments start to come to a conclusion, but our career ambitions most definitely becoming less important (if they exist at all by that time). Increasingly we start to make more intentional choices about how we want to live our lives and what contributions we want to make to society.

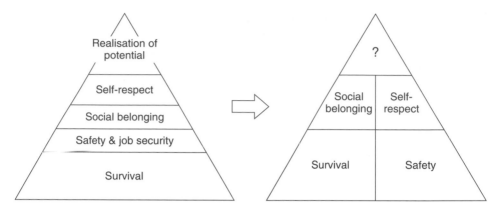

FIGURE 9   Maslow for the Third Age.

- *Fourth Age: the age of completion.* There is an inevitability about life's journey. The Fourth Age is a time for reflection and preparation for whatever we might think happens next.

At a time of increasingly aging societies, it seems that the Third and Fourth Ages might not only become more topical and relevant, but that notional age boundaries might increasingly start to flex. Would individuals under 40 years old consider themselves to be candidates for U3A? Probably not by today's criteria, but as automation and robotics starts to bite in terms of job prospects and career aspirations, might a new age start to emerge in some way?

How would Abraham Maslow have seen things? What might his legendary hierarchy look like for those at the Third Age and later? (See Figure 9.)

As marketers continue to base their offerings on personal aspirations, be it survival or desire, how will they best position the client's products for an aging demographic group in the future? Perhaps one game plan will be to increasingly encourage spending of amounts normally left as an inheritance. 'After all', as they say, 'you can't take it with you'.

CONCLUSION

As industries and professions need to come to terms with the impact of analytics and artificial systems, so too do individuals need to come to terms with the same impact on their work lives and personal lives.

It seems slightly ironic that this book started off by questioning the meaning of work in society, whose roots we discovered in the religious ethic of Protestantism. We work, according to that particular longstanding principle, not to pay the bills but to get closer to God. Not everyone sees it that way, especially the agnostics amongst us, but even they would probably accept that there are issues deeper in life beyond what we do for a living.

A new AI-infused era will force us to start to think differently at a personal level. Financial success will remain important for many as always, but there will be an increasing need to reflect about how we reinvent ourselves over the course of our working lives through self-learning, personal development, or by changing the way we work.

The new era will force us to think harder about the future and perhaps even about how to do nothing, which some might relate to Buddhism. Buddhists suggest that one of the ways to *true enlightenment* is through a state of meditation, which can feel like doing nothing.

In a future world of AI and robotics, how will industries, professionals, and individuals need to change? Who can we truly turn to for advice in these unpredictable times? What actions should we take? How will we personally cope? What will replace work? Should we be passive or active?

A.A. Milne, the author of the Children's story *Winnie the Pooh*, once wrote 'Sometimes I sit and think, and othertimes I just sits . . . (sic).' Another Milne book, *The House at Pooh Corner*, includes the following conversation between the teddy bear Pooh and his best friend, Christopher Robin:

> *What I like doing best is Nothing [said Christopher Robin].*
>
> *How do you do Nothing? asked Pooh, after he had wondered for a long time.*
>
> *Well, it's when people call out at you just as you're going off to do it, 'What are you going to do, Christopher Robin?' and you say, 'Oh, Nothing,' and then you go and do it.*
>
> *It means just going along, listening to all the things you can't hear, and not bothering.*
>
> *Oh! said Pooh.*
>
> *A.A. Milne*[11]

But is doing nothing really the right reaction? The essence of this book is not just about raising awareness, but about helping readers respond to change. We can be victims, willing participants, even unwilling participants, but overall aren't we ultimately stakeholders? Aren't we are entitled to contribute to this technological transformation?

The poet Dylan Thomas (1914–1953) wrote:

> Do not go gentle into that good night,
> Old age should burn and rave at close of day;
> Rage, rage against the dying of the light.
> Dylan Thomas[12]

We are entering a new era. The future isn't necessarily dark, but certainly there are likely to be interesting times ahead that we need to start preparing for. We can resist change and 'rage against the night', but can't we also use candles and torches to illuminate the way forward? At the end of the day, isn't that just one part of our duty to humanity?

As mentioned at the beginning of this book, over 200 years ago the British general Lord Wellington prepared for the most important battle of his life, for which he is best remembered, by understanding the terrain on which it was to be fought. In the same way, it's essential that we also understand the new data and AI terrain. Overall, perhaps Wellington's is still a good example to follow, even in modern times.

NOTES

1. Bhoopathi Rapolu, *The Race for Work: Escape Automation, Transform Your Career and Thrive in the Second Machine Age* (Bhoopathi Rapolu, 2016).
2. John Larosa, Self-improvement market has unfilled niches for entrepreneurs. Cision PRWeb. http://www.prweb.com/releases/2012/3/prweb9323729.htm (accessed 26 August 2017).
3. John Larosa, $10.4 billion self-improvement market survives scandals & recession. Marketdata Enterprises Inc. http://www.prweb.com/releases/2013/1/prweb10275905.htm.
4. Rebecca Webber, Reinvent yourself. *Psychology Today* (9 June 2016). https://www.psychologytoday.com/articles/201405/reinvent-yourself?collection=148507
5. Ravenna Helson and Oliver John, Mills Longitudinal Study at U.C. Berkeley. https://millslab.berkeley.edu
6. Webber, Reinvent yourself.
7. Missy Gluckmann, The lack of non-verbal communication in a digital world. Melbee Global (11 January 2015). https://melibeeglobal.com/blog/2015/01/the-lack-of-non-verbal-communication-in-a-digital-world/ (accessed 17 January 2018).
8. David Ferrell, The conference industry is booming, and it is only getting bigger. Skift.com (4 August 2013). Originally published as Big ideas, big money mix at power-laden conferences, *Orange County Register* (2 August). https://skift.com/2013/08/04/the-conference-industry-is-booming-and-it-is-only-getting-bigger (accessed 16 May 2017).
9. Timothy Noah, Disenfranchised: Why are Americans still buying into the franchise dream? *Pacific Standard* (4 March 2014). https://psmag.com/economics/disenfranchised-fast-food-workers-quiznos-73967
10. Oliver Burkeman, Five reasons why we should all learn how to do nothing. *The Guardian* (9 January 2015). https://www.theguardian.com/lifeandstyle/2015/jan/09/five-reasons-we-should-all-learn-to-do-nothing
11. A.A. Milne, *The House at Pooh Corner* (Egmont; new edition, 6 May 2013). Originally published 1928.
12. Dylan Thomas, *The Poems of Dylan Thomas* (New Directions, 1952).

Implementation Flowcharts

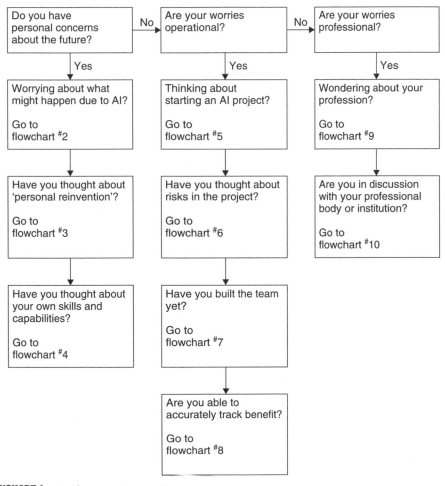

FLOWCHART 1   Implementation road map.

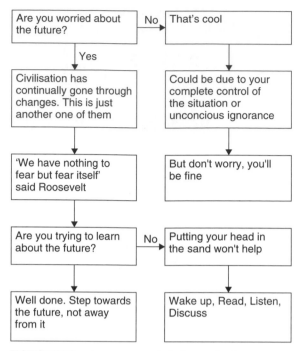

FLOWCHART 2   Are you worried about the future?

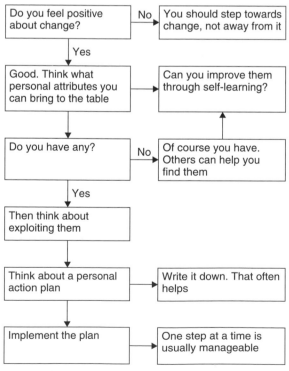

FLOWCHART 3   Personal reinvention.

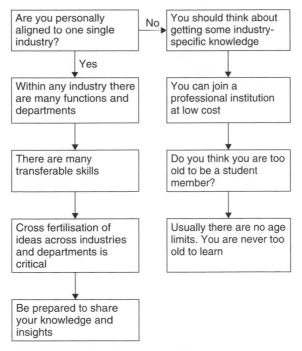

FLOWCHART 4   Applying your skills to industry.

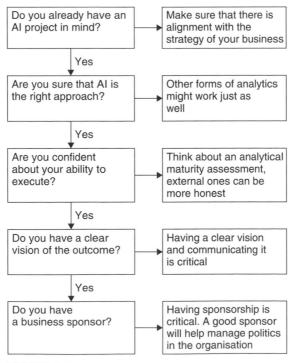

FLOWCHART 5   Implementing an AI project.

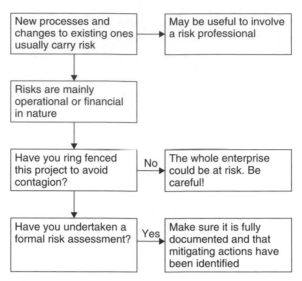

FLOWCHART 6   Managing risk in an AI implementation.

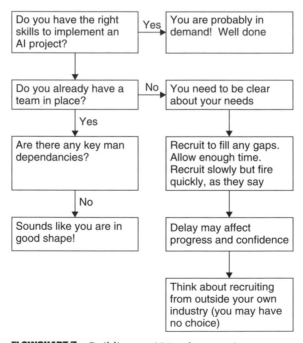

FLOWCHART 7   Building an AI implementation team.

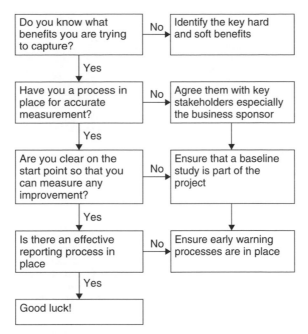

FLOWCHART 8 Managing the benefits.

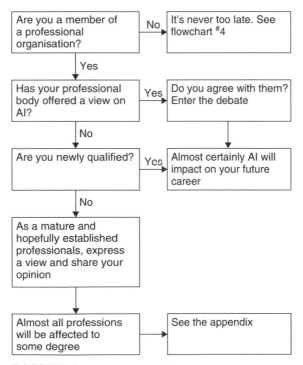

FLOWCHART 9 Impact on professions.

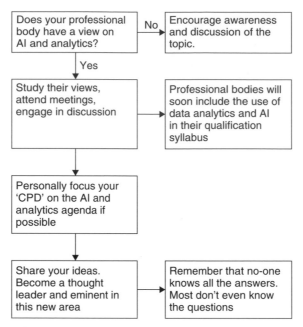

FLOWCHART 10   Are you a member of a professional organisation?

Jobs Most Affected by Artificial Intelligence

Based on a review by Oxford Martin School of the University of Oxford into the future of employment, researchers created the following statistical analysis of which jobs are at least risk (lowest probability), and which are at greatest risk (highest probability) of being automated.

Rank	Probability	Occupation (lowest to highest probability of being automated)
1	0.0028	Recreational Therapists
2	0.003	First-Line Supervisors of Mechanics, Installers, and Repairers
3	0.003	Emergency Management Directors
4	0.0031	Mental Health and Substance Abuse Social Workers
5	0033	Audiologists
6	0.0035	Occupational Therapists
7	0.0035	Orthoptists and Prosthetists
8	0.0035	Healthcare Social Workers
9	0.0036	Oral and Maxillofacial Surgeons
10	0.0036	First-Line Supervisors of Fire Fighting and Prevention Workers
11	0.0039	Dietitians and Nutritionists
12	0.0039	Lodging Managers
13	0.004	Choreographers
14	0.0041	Sales Engineers
15	0.0042	Physicians and Surgeons
16	0.0042	Instructional Coordinators
17	0.0043	Psychologists, All Other

(continued)

Rank	Probability	Occupation (lowest to highest probability of being automated)
18	0.0044	First-Line Supervisors of Police and Detectives
19	0.0044	Dentists, General
20	0.0044	Elementary School Teachers, Except Special Education
21	0.0045	Medical Scientists, Except Epidemiologists
22	0.0046	Education Administrators, Elementary and Secondary School
23	0.0046	Podiatrists
24	0.0047	Clinical, Counselling, and School Psychologists
25	0.0048	Mental Health Counsellors
26	0.0049	Fabric and Apparel Patternmakers
27	0.0055	Set and Exhibit Designers
28	0.0055	Human Resources Managers
29	0.0061	Recreation Workers
30	0.0063	Training and Development Managers
31	0.0064	Speech-Language Pathologists
32	0.0065	Computer Systems Analysts
33	0.0067	Social and Community Service Managers
34	0.0068	Curators
35.	0.0071	Athletic Trainers
36	0.0073	Medical and Health Services Managers
37	0.0074	Preschool Teachers, Except Special Education
38	0.0075	Farm and Home Management Advisors
39	0.0077	Anthropologists and Archaeologists
40	0.0077	Special Education Teachers, Secondary School
41	0.0078	Secondary School Teachers, Except Special and Career/Technical Education
42	0.0081	Clergy
43	0.0081	Foresters
44	0.0085	Educational, Guidance, School, and Vocational Counsellors
45	0.0088	Career/Technical Education Teachers, Secondary School
46	0.009	Registered Nurses
47	0.0094	1015 Rehabilitation Counsellors
48	0.0095	Teachers and Instructors, All Other
49	0.0095	Forensic Science Technicians
50	0.01	Makeup Artists, Theatrical and Performance

Rank	Probability	Occupation (lowest to highest probability of being automated)
51	0.01	Marine Engineers and Naval Architects
52	0.01	Education Administrators, Postsecondary
53	0.011	Mechanical Engineers
54	0.012	Pharmacists
55	0.012	Logisticians
56	0.012	Microbiologists
57	0.012	Industrial-Organizational Psychologists
58	0.013	Coaches and Scouts
59	0.013	Sales Managers
60	0.014	Hydrologists
61	0.014	Marketing Managers
62	0.014	Marriage and Family Therapists
63	0.014	Engineers, All Other
64	0.014	Training and Development Specialists
65	0.014	First-Line Supervisors of Office and Administrative Support Workers
66	0.015	Biological Scientists, All Other
67	0.015	Public Relations and Fundraising Managers
68	0.015	Multimedia Artists and Animators
69	0.015	Computer and Information Research Scientists
70	0.015	Chief Executives
71	0.015	Education Administrators, Preschool and Childcare Center/Program
72	0.015	Music Directors and Composers
73	0.016	First-Line Supervisors of Production and Operating Workers
74	0.016	Securities, Commodities, and Financial Services Sales Agents
75	0.016	Conservation Scientists
76	0.016	Special Education Teachers, Middle School
77	0.017	Chemical Engineers
78	0.017	Architectural and Engineering Managers
79	0.017	Aerospace Engineers
80	0.018	Natural Sciences Managers
81	0.018	Environmental Engineers
82	0.018	Architects, Except Landscape and Naval

(continued)

Rank	Probability	Occupation (lowest to highest probability of being automated)
83	0.018	Physical Therapist Assistants
84	0.019	Civil Engineers
85	0.02	Health Diagnosing and Treating Practitioners, All Other
86	0.021	Soil and Plant Scientists
87	0.021	Materials Scientists
88	0.021	Materials Engineers
89	0.021	Fashion Designers
90	0.021	Physical Therapists
91	0.021	Photographers
92	0.022	Producers and Directors
93	0.022	Interior Designers
94	0.023	Orthodontists
95	0.023	Art Directors
96	0.025	First-Line Supervisors of Correctional Officers
97	0.025	Directors, Religious Activities and Education
98	0.025	Electronics Engineers, Except Computer
99	0.027	Biochemists and Biophysicists
100	0.027	Chiropractors
101	0.028	Occupational Therapy Assistants
102	0.028	Child, Family, and School Social Workers
103	0.028	Health and Safety Engineers, Except Mining Safety Engineers and Inspectors
104	0.029	Industrial Engineers
105	0.029	First-Line Supervisors of Transportation and Material-Moving Machine and Vehicle Operators
106	0.029	Veterinary Technologists and Technicians
107	0.03	Industrial Production Managers
108	0.03	Industrial Engineering Technicians
109	0.03	Network and Computer Systems Administrators
110	0.03	Database Administrators
111	0.03	Purchasing Managers
112	0.032	Postsecondary Teachers
113	0.033	Environmental Scientists and Specialists, Including Health
114	0.033	Substance Abuse and Behavioral Disorder Counsellors
115	0.035	Lawyers

Rank	Probability	Occupation (lowest to highest probability of being automated)
116	0.035	Craft Artists
117	0.035	Operations Research Analysts
118	0.035	Computer and Information Systems Managers
119	0.037	Commercial and Industrial Designers
120	0.037	Biomedical Engineers
121	0.037	Meeting, Convention, and Event Planners
122	0.038	Veterinarians
123	0.038	Writers and Authors
124	0.039	Advertising and Promotions Managers
125	0.039	Political Scientists
126	0.04	Credit Counsellors
127	0.04	Social Scientists and Related Workers, All Other
128	0.041	Astronomers
129	0.041	Ship Engineers
130	0.042	Software Developers, Applications
131	0.042	Fine Artists, Including Painters, Sculptors, and Illustrators
132	0.043	Psychiatric Technicians
133	0.045	Landscape Architects
134	0.045	Health Educators
135	0.047	Mathematician
136	0.047	Floral Designers
137	0.047	Farmers, Ranchers, and Other Agricultural Managers
138	0.048	Forest Fire Inspectors and Prevention Specialists
139	0.049	Emergency Medical Technicians and Paramedics
140	0.055	Editors
141	0.055	Prosthodontists
142	0.055	Healthcare Practitioners and Technical Workers, All Other
143	0.057	Travel Guides
144	0.058	Licensed Practical and Licensed Vocational Nurses
145	0.059	Sociologists
146	0.06	Arbitrators, Mediators, and Conciliators
147	0.061	Animal Scientists
148	0.064	Residential Advisors
149	0.066	Aircraft Cargo Handling Supervisors
150	0.066	Respiratory Therapists

(continued)

Rank	Probability	Occupation (lowest to highest probability of being automated)
151	0.067	Broadcast News Analysts
152	0.069	Financial Managers
153	0.07	Nuclear Engineers
154	0.071	Construction Managers
155	0.074	Musicians and Singers
156	0.075	First-Line Supervisors of Non-Retail Sales Workers
157	0.076	First-Line Supervisors of Personal Service Workers
158	0.077	Food Scientists and Technologists
159	0.08	Compliance Officers
160	0.08	Fish and Game Wardens
161	0.082	Graphic Designers
162	0.083	Food Service Managers
163	0.084	Childcare Workers
164	0.085	Fitness Trainers and Aerobics Instructors
165	0.091	Gaming Managers
166	0.097	Electrical Power-Line Installers and Repairers
167	0.098	Police and Sheriff's Patrol Officers
168	0.099	Travel Agents
169	0.10	Chefs and Head Cooks
170	0.10	Animal Trainers
171	0.10	Radio and Television Announcers
172	0.10	Electrical Engineers
173	0.10	Chemists
174	0.10	Respiratory Therapy Technicians
175	0.10	Physicists
176	0.11	Hairdressers, Hairstylists, and Cosmetologists
177	0.11	Reporters and Correspondents
178	0.11	Air Traffic Controllers
179	0.13	Dancers
180	0.13	Nuclear Medicine Technologists
181	0.13	Software Developers, Systems Software
182	0.13	Management Analysts
183	0.13	Dietetic Technicians
184	0.13	Urban and Regional Planners
185	0.13	Social and Human Service Assistants
186	0.13	Self-Enrichment Education Teachers

Rank	Probability	Occupation (lowest to highest probability of being automated)
187	0.13	Sound Engineering Technicians
188	0.14	Optometrists
189	0.14	Mining and Geological Engineers, Including Mining Safety Engineers
190	0.14	Physician Assistants
191	0.15	Kindergarten Teachers, Except Special Education
192	0.15	Electricians
193	0.16	Petroleum Engineers
194	0.16	Desktop Publishers
195	0.16	General and Operations Managers
196	0.17	Occupational Health and Safety Specialists
197	0.17	Firefighters
198	0.17	Financial Examiners
199	0.17	First-Line Supervisors of Construction Trades and Extraction Workers
200	0.17	Middle School Teachers, Except Special and Career/Technical Education
201	0.18	Public Relations Specialists
202	0.18	Commercial Divers
203	0.18	Manufactured Building and Mobile Home Installers
204	0.18	Airline Pilots, Co-pilots, and Flight Engineers
205	0.19	Adult Basic and Secondary Education and Literacy Teachers and Instructors
206	0.2	Epidemiologists
207	0.2	Funeral Service Managers, Directors, Morticians, and Undertakers
208	0.21	Information Security Analysts, Web Developers, and Computer Network Architects
209	0.21	Actuaries
210	0.21	Animal Control Workers
211	0.21	Concierges
212	0.22	Computer Occupations, All Other
213	0.22	Statisticians
214	0.22	Computer Hardware Engineers
215	0.23	Survey Researchers
216	0.23	Business Operations Specialists, All Other
217	0.23	Financial Analysts

(continued)

Rank	Probability	Occupation (lowest to highest probability of being automated)
218	0.23	Radiologic Technologists and Technicians
219	0.23	Cardiovascular Technologists and Technicians
220	0.24	Agents and Business Managers of Artists, Performers, and Athletes
221	0.24	Engineering Technicians, Except Drafters, All Other
222	0.25	Geographers
223	0.25	Occupational Health and Safety Technicians
224	0.25	Probation Officers and Correctional Treatment Specialists
225	0.25	Environmental Engineering Technicians
226	0.25	Managers, All Other
227	0.25	Ambulance Drivers and Attendants, Except Emergency Medical Technicians
228	0.25	Sales Representatives, Wholesale and Manufacturing, Technical and Scientific Products
229	0.26	Career/Technical Education Teachers, Middle School
230	0.27	Captains, Mates, and Pilots of Water Vessels
231	0.27	Occupational Therapy Aides
232	0.27	Medical Equipment Repairers
233	0.28	First-Line Supervisors of Retail Sales Workers
234	0.28	Athletes and Sports Competitors
235	0.28	Gaming Supervisors
236	0.29	Skincare Specialists
237	0.29	Wholesale and Retail Buyers, Except Farm Products
238	0.30	Biological Technicians
239	0.30	Medical Assistants
240	0.30	Zoologists and Wildlife Biologists
241	0.30	Cooks, Private Household
242	0.31	Human Resources, Training, and Labour Relations Specialists, All Other
243	0.31	Private Detectives and Investigators
244	0.31	Film and Video Editors
245	0.33	Financial Specialists, All Other
246	0.34	Detectives and Criminal Investigators
247	0.34	Surgical Technologists
248	0.34	Radiation Therapists
249	0.35	Plumbers, Pipefitters, and Steamfitters

Rank	Probability	Occupation (lowest to highest probability of being automated)
250	0.35	Flight Attendants
251	0.35	Diagnostic Medical Sonographers
252	0.36	Bailiffs
253	0.36	Computer Numerically Controlled Machine Tool Programmers, Metal and Plastic
254	0.36	Telecommunications Equipment Installers and Repairers, Except Line Installers
255	0.37	Furnace, Kiln, Oven, Drier, and Kettle Operators and Tenders
256	0.37	Cleaners of Vehicles and Equipment
257	0.37	Funeral Attendants
258	0.37	Helpers–Extraction Workers
259	0.37	Actors
260	0.37	Mine Shuttle Car Operators
261	0.38	Electrical and Electronics Repairers, Powerhouse, Substation, and Relay
262	0.38	Surveyors
263	0.38	Mechanical Engineering Technicians
264	0.38	Packers and Packagers, Hand
265	0.38	Interpreters and Translators
266	0.39	Home Health Aides
267	0.39	Upholsterers
268	0.39	Elevator Installers and Repairers
269	0.39	Gaming Cage Workers
270	0.39	Audio-Visual and Multimedia Collections Specialists
271	0.40	Judges, Magistrate Judges, and Magistrates
272	0.40	Mobile Heavy Equipment Mechanics, Except Engines
273	0.40	Health Technologists and Technicians, All Other
274	0.41	Graders and Sorters, Agricultural Products
275	0.41	Structural Metal Fabricators and Fitters
276	0.41	Judicial Law Clerks
277	0.41	Electrical and Electronics Repairers, Commercial and Industrial Equipment
278	0.42	Forest and Conservation Technicians
279	0.42	First-Line Supervisors of Helpers, Laborers, and Material Movers, Hand

(*continued*)

Rank	Probability	Occupation (lowest to highest probability of being automated)
280	0.43	Locker Room, Coatroom, and Dressing Room Attendants
281	0.43	Physical Scientists, All Other
282	0.43	Economists
283	0.44	Historians
284	0.45	Medical Appliance Technicians
285	0.46	Court, Municipal, and License Clerks
286	0.47	Compensation, Benefits, and Job Analysis Specialists
287	0.47	Psychiatric Aides
288	0.47	Medical and Clinical Laboratory Technicians
289	0.48	Fire Inspectors and Investigators
290	0.48	Aerospace Engineering and Operations Technicians
291	0.48	Merchandise Displayers and Window Trimmers
292	0.48	Explosives Workers, Ordnance Handling Experts, and Blasters
293	0.48	Computer Programmers
294	0.49	Crossing Guards
295	0.49	Agricultural Engineers
296	0.49	Roof Bolters, Mining
297	0.49	Telecommunications Line Installers and Repairers
298	0.49	Police, Fire, and Ambulance Dispatchers
299	0.50	Loading Machine Operators, Underground Mining
300	0.50	Installation, Maintenance, and Repair Workers, All Other
301	0.50	Court Reporters
302	0.51	Demonstrators and Product Promoters
303	0.51	Dental Assistants
304	0.52	Shoe and Leather Workers and Repairers
305	0.52	Architectural and Civil Drafters
306	0.53	Rotary Drill Operators, Oil and Gas
307	0.53	Hazardous Materials Removal Workers
308	0.54	Embalmers
309	0.54	Continuous Mining Machine Operators
310	0.54	Slot Supervisors
311	0.54	Massage Therapists
312	0.54	Advertising Sales Agents

Rank	Probability	Occupation (lowest to highest probability of being automated)
313	0.55	Automotive Glass Installers and Repairers
314	0.55	Commercial Pilots
315	0.55	Customer Service Representatives
316	0.55	Audio and Video Equipment Technicians
317	0.56	Teacher Assistants
318	0.57	First-Line Supervisors of Farming, Fishing, and Forestry Workers
319	0.57	Chemical Technicians
320	0.57	Helpers–Pipe layers, Plumbers, Pipefitters, and Steamfitters
321	0.57	Cost Estimators
322	0.57	Transit and Railroad Police
323	0.57	First-Line Supervisors of Landscaping, Lawn Service, and Grounds keeping Workers
324	0.58	Personal Financial Advisors
325	0.59	Millwrights
326	0.59	Museum Technicians and Conservators
327	0.59	Mine Cutting and Channelling Machine Operators
328	0.59	Transportation, Storage, and Distribution Managers
329	0.59	Recreational Vehicle Service Technicians
330	0.59	Automotive Service Technicians and Mechanics
331	0.60	Correctional Officers and Jailers
332	0.60	Camera Operators, Television, Video, and Motion Picture
333	0.60	Slaughterers and Meat Packers
334	0.61	Electronic Equipment Installers and Repairers, Motor Vehicles
335	0.61	Physical Therapist Aides
336	0.61	Costume Attendants
337	0.61	Market Research Analysts and Marketing Specialists
338	0.61	Reservation and Transportation Ticket Agents and Travel Clerks
339	0.61	Water and Wastewater Treatment Plant and System Operators
340	0.61	Life, Physical, and Social Science Technicians, All Other
341	0.61	Food Cooking Machine Operators and Tenders

(*continued*)

Rank	Probability	Occupation (lowest to highest probability of being automated)
342	0.61	Welding, Soldering, and Brazing Machine Setters, Operators, and Tenders
343	0.62	Motorboat Operators
344	0.62	Tapers
345	0.62	Pipe layers
346	0.63	Geoscientists, Except Hydrologists and Geographers
347	0.63	Control and Valve Installers and Repairers, Except Mechanical Door
348	0.63	Healthcare Support Workers, All Other
349	0.63	First-Line Supervisors of Food Preparation and Serving Workers
350	0.63	Construction and Building Inspectors
351	0.64	Cutters and Trimmers, Hand
352	0.64	Maintenance and Repair Workers, General
353	0.64	Administrative Law Judges, Adjudicators, and Hearing Officers
354	0.64	Stock Clerks and Order Fillers
355	0.64	Power Distributors and Dispatchers
356	0.64	Insulation Workers, Mechanical
357	0.65	Social Science Research Assistants
358	0.65	Machinists
359	0.65	Computer Support Specialists
360	0.65	Librarians
361	0.65	Electronic Home Entertainment Equipment Installers and Repairers
362	0.65	Heating, Air Conditioning, and Refrigeration Mechanics and Installers
363	0.65	Hoist and Winch Operators
364	0.66	Pest Control Workers
365	0.66	Helpers–Production Workers
366	0.66	Statistical Assistants
367	0.66	Janitors and Cleaners, Except Maids and Housekeeping Cleaners
368	0.66	Motorboat Mechanics and Service Technicians
369	0.67	Paper Goods Machine Setters, Operators, and Tenders
370	0.67	Foundry Meld and Core makers
371	0.67	Atmospheric and Space Scientists

Rank	Probability	Occupation (lowest to highest probability of being automated)
372	0.67	Bus Drivers, Transit and Intercity
373	0.67	Lifeguards, Ski Patrol, and Other Recreational Protective Service Workers
374	0.67	Industrial Machinery Mechanics
375	0.68	Postal Service Mail Carriers
376	0.68	Roustabouts, Oil and Gas
377	0.68	Boilermakers
378	0.68	Mechanical Drafters
379	0.68	Dental Hygienists
380	0.69	Light Truck or Delivery Services Drivers
381	0.69	Maids and Housekeeping Cleaners
382	0.69	Painters, Transportation Equipment
383	0.70	Eligibility Interviewers, Government Programs
384	0.70	Tire Repairers and Changers
385	0.70	Food Batch makers
386	0.70	Avionics Technicians
387	0.71	Aircraft Mechanics and Service Technicians
388	0.71	Airfield Operations Specialists
389	0.71	Petroleum Pump System Operators, Refinery Operators, and Gaugers
390	0.71	Construction and Related Workers, All Other
391	0.71	Opticians, Dispensing
392	0.71	Laundry and Dry-Cleaning Workers
393	0.72	Amusement and Recreation Attendants
394	0.72	Pharmacy Aides
395	0.72	Helpers–Roofers
396	0.72	Tank Car, Truck, and Ship Loaders
397	0.72	Home Appliance Repairers
398	0.72	Carpenters
399	0.72	Public Address System and Other Announcers
400	0.73	Textile Knitting and Weaving Machine Setters, Operators, and Tenders
401	0.73	Administrative Services Managers
402	0.73	Glaziers
403	0.73	Coil Winders, Tapers, and Finishers
404	0.73	Bus and Truck Mechanics and Diesel Engine Specialists

(continued)

Rank	Probability	Occupation (lowest to highest probability of being automated)
405	0.74	Computer, Automated Teller, and Office Machine Repairers
406	0.74	Personal Care Aides
407	0.74	Broadcast Technicians
408	0.74	Helpers–Electricians
409	0.75	Postmasters and Mail Superintendents
410	0.75	Tile and Marble Setters
411	0.75	Painters, Construction and Maintenance
412	0.75	Transportation Attendants, Except Flight Attendants
413	0.75	Civil Engineering Technicians
414	0.75	Farm Equipment Mechanics and Service Technicians
415	0.76	Archivists
416	0.76	Chemical Equipment Operators and Tenders
417	0.76	Electric Motor, Power Tool, and Related Repairers
418	0.76	Fallers
419	0.77	Environmental Science and Protection Technicians, Including Health
420	0.77	Locksmiths and Safe Repairers
421	0.77	Tree Trimmers and Pruners
422	0.77	Bartenders
423	0.77	Purchasing Agents, Except Wholesale, Retail, and Farm Products
424	0.77	Dishwashers
425	0.77	Hunters and Trappers
426	0.78	Medical Equipment Preparers
427	0.78	Cutting, Punching, and Press Machine Setters, Operators, and Tenders, Metal and Plastic
428	0.78	Computer Operators
429	0.78	Gas Plant Operators
430	0.79	Postal Service Mail Sorters, Processors, and Processing Machine Operators
431	0.79	Heavy and Tractor-Trailer Truck Drivers
432	0.79	Shampooers
433	0.79	Drywall and Ceiling Tile Installers
434	0.79	Helpers–Installation, Maintenance, and Repair Workers
435	0.79	Motorcycle Mechanics

Rank	Probability	Occupation (lowest to highest probability of being automated)
436	0.79	Aircraft Structure, Surfaces, Rigging, and Systems Assemblers
437	0.79	Logging Equipment Operators
438	0.79	Floor Layers, Except Carpet, Wood, and Hard Tiles
439	0.80	Barbers
440	0.80	Derrick Operators, Oil and Gas
441	0.81	Cooks, Fast Food
442	0.81	Word Processors and Typists
443	0.81	Electrical and Electronics Drafters
444	0.81	Electro-Mechanical Technicians
445	0.81	Cleaning, Washing, and Metal Pickling Equipment Operators and Tenders
446	0.81	Property, Real Estate, and Community Association Managers
447	0.81	Medical Secretaries
448	0.81	Pressers, Textile, Garment, and Related Materials
449	0.82	Engine and Other Machine Assemblers
450	0.82	Security and Fire Alarm Systems Installers
451	0.82	Refractory Materials Repairers, Except Brick masons
452	0.82	Nonfarm Animal Caretakers
453	0.82	Sheet Metal Workers
454	0.82	Pile-Driver Operators
455	0.82	Brick masons and Block masons
456	0.83	Fishers and Related Fishing Workers
457	0.83	Structural Iron and Steel Workers
458	0.83	Railroad Brake, Signal, and Switch Operators
459	0.83	Railroad Conductors and Yardmasters
460	0.83	Cooks, Institution and Cafeteria
461	0.83	Sailors and Marine Oilers
462	0.83	Mixing and Blending Machine Setters, Operators, and Tenders
463	0.83	Helpers–Brick masons, Block masons, Stonemasons, and Tile and Marble Setters
464	0.83	Segmental Pavers
465	0.83	Insulation Workers, Floor, Ceiling, and Wall
466	0.83	Printing Press Operators

(continued)

Rank	Probability	Occupation (lowest to highest probability of being automated)
467	0.83	Automotive and Watercraft Service Attendants
468	0.83	Septic Tank Servicers and Sewer Pipe Cleaners
469	0.83	Baggage Porters and Bellhops
470	0.83	Gaming Change Persons and Booth Cashiers
471	0.83	Rolling Machine Setters, Operators, and Tenders, Metal and Plastic
472	0.83	Paving, Surfacing, and Tamping Equipment Operators
473	0.84	Tool and Die Makers
474	0.84	Electrical and Electronics Engineering Technicians
475	0.84	Plasterers and Stucco Masons
476	0.84	Layout Workers, Metal and Plastic
477	0.84	Lathe and Turning Machine Tool Setters, Operators, and Tenders, Metal and Plastic
478	0.84	Security Guards
479	0.84	Tailors, Dressmakers, and Custom Sewers
480	0.84	Wellhead Pumpers
481	0.84	Proof-readers and Copy Markers
482	0.84	Parking Enforcement Workers
483	0.85	Laborers and Freight, Stock, and Material Movers, Hand
484	0.85	Sales Representatives, Wholesale and Manufacturing, Except Technical and Scientific Products
485	0.85	Meter Readers, Utilities
486	0.85	Power Plant Operators
487	0.85	Chemical Plant and System Operators
488	0.85	Earth Drillers, Except Oil and Gas
489	0.85	Nuclear Technicians
490	0.86	Executive Secretaries and Executive Administrative Assistants
491	0.86	Plant and System Operators, All Other
492	0.86	Food Servers, Nonrestaurant
493	0.86	Sawing Machine Setters, Operators, and Tenders, Wood
494	0.86	Subway and Streetcar Operators
495	0.86	Veterinary Assistants and Laboratory Animal Caretakers
496	0.86	Cutting and Slicing Machine Setters, Operators, and Tenders

Rank	Probability	Occupation (lowest to highest probability of being automated)
497	0.86	Real Estate Sales Agents
498	0.86	Computer-Controlled Machine Tool Operators, Metal and Plastic
499	0.86	Maintenance Workers, Machinery
500	0.86	Correspondence Clerks
501	0.87	Miscellaneous Agricultural Workers
502	0.87	Forest and Conservation Workers
503	0.87	Pourers and Casters, Metal
504	0.87	Carpet Installers
505	0.87	Paperhangers
506	0.87	Buyers and Purchasing Agents, Farm Products
507	0.87	Furniture Finishers
508	0.87	Food Preparation Workers
509	0.87	Floor Sanders and Finishers
510	0.87	Parking Lot Attendants
511	0.87	Highway Maintenance Workers
512	0.88	Construction Laborers
513	0.88	Production, Planning, and Expediting Clerks
514	0.88	Semiconductor Processors
515	0.88	Cartographers and Photogrammetrists
516	0.88	Metal-Refining Furnace Operators and Tenders
517	0.88	Separating, Filtering, Clarifying, Precipitating, and Still Machine Setters, Operators, and Tenders
518	0.88	Extruding and Forming Machine Setters, Operators, and Tenders, Synthetic and Glass Fibers
519	0.88	Terrazzo Workers and Finishers
520	0.88	Tool Grinders, Filers, and Sharpeners
521	0.88	Rail Car Repairers
522	0.89	Bakers
523	0.89	Medical Transcriptionists
524	0.89	Stonemasons
525	0.89	Bus Drivers, School or Special Client
526	0.89	Technical Writers
527	0.89	Riggers
528	0.89	Rail-Track Laying and Maintenance Equipment Operators
529	0.89	Stationary Engineers and Boiler Operators

(continued)

Rank	Probability	Occupation (lowest to highest probability of being automated)
530	0.89	Sewing Machine Operators
531	0.89	Taxi Drivers and Chauffeurs
532	0.90	Human Resources Assistants, Except Payroll and Timekeeping
533	0.90	Medical and Clinical Laboratory Technologists
534	0.90	Reinforcing Iron and Rebar Workers
535	0.90	Roofers
536	0.90	Crane and Tower Operators
537	0.90	Traffic Technicians
538	0.90	Transportation Inspectors
539	0.90	Patternmakers, Metal and Plastic
540	0.90	Molders, Shapers, and Casters, Except Metal and Plastic
541	0.90	Appraisers and Assessors of Real Estate
542	0.90	Pump Operators, Except Wellhead Pumpers
543	0.90	Signal and Track Switch Repairers
544	0.91	Gaming and Sports Book Writers and Runners
545	0.91	Musical Instrument Repairers and Tuners
546	0.91	Tour Guides and Escorts
547	0.91	Mechanical Door Repairers
548	0.91	Food and Tobacco Roasting, Baking, and Drying Machine Operators and Tenders
549	0.91	Gas Compressor and Gas Pumping Station Operators
550	0.91	Medical Records and Health Information Technicians
551	0.91	Coating, Painting, and Spraying Machine Setters, Operators, and Tenders
552	0.91	Multiple Machine Tool Setters, Operators, and Tenders, Metal and Plastic
553	0.91	Rail Yard Engineers, Dinkey Operators, and Hostlers
554	0.91	Electrical and Electronics Installers and Repairers, Transportation Equipment
555	0.91	Dining Room and Cafeteria Attendants and Bartender Helpers
556	0.91	Heat Treating Equipment Setters, Operators, and Tenders, Metal and Plastic
557	0.91	Geological and Petroleum Technicians
558	0.91	Automotive Body and Related Repairers

Rank	Probability	Occupation (lowest to highest probability of being automated)
559	0.91	Patternmakers, Wood
560	0.91	Extruding and Drawing Machine Setters, Operators, and Tenders, Metal and Plastic
561	0.92	Office Machine Operators, Except Computer
562	0.92	Pharmacy Technicians
563	0.92	Loan Interviewers and Clerks
564	0.92	Dredge Operators
565	0.92	Insurance Sales Agents
566	0.92	Cabinetmakers and Bench Carpenters
567	0.92	Painting, Coating, and Decorating Workers
568	0.92	Fence Erectors
569	0.92	Plating and Coating Machine Setters, Operators, and Tenders, Metal and Plastic
570	0.92	Retail Salespersons
571	0.92	Combined Food Preparation and Serving Workers, Including Fast Food
572	0.92	Production Workers, All Other
573	0.92	Helpers–Carpenters
574	0.93	Cooling and Freezing Equipment Operators and Tenders
575	0.93	Fiberglass Laminators and Fabricators
576	0.93	Service Unit Operators, Oil, Gas, and Mining
577	0.93	Conveyor Operators and Tenders
578	0.93	Outdoor Power Equipment and Other Small Engine Mechanics
579	0.93	Locomotive Firers
580	0.93	Machine Feeders and Offbearers
581	0.93	Model Makers, Metal and Plastic
582	0.93	Radio, Cellular, and Tower Equipment Installers and Repairs
583	0.93	Butchers and Meat Cutters
584	0.93	Extruding, Forming, Pressing, and Compacting Machine Setters, Operators, and Tenders
585	0.93	Refuse and Recyclable Material Collectors
586	0.93	Tax Examiners and Collectors, and Revenue Agents
587	0.93	Forging Machine Setters, Operators, and Tenders, Metal and Plastic

(continued)

Rank	Probability	Occupation (lowest to highest probability of being automated)
588	0.93	Industrial Truck and Tractor Operators
589	0.94	Accountants and Auditors
590	0.94	Drilling and Boring Machine Tool Setters, Operators, and Tenders, Metal and Plastic
591	0.94	Mail Clerks and Mail Machine Operators, Except Postal Service
592	0.94	Waiters and Waitresses
593	0.94	Meat, Poultry, and Fish Cutters and Trimmers
594	0.94	Budget Analysts
595	0.94	Cement Masons and Concrete Finishers
596	0.94	Bicycle Repairers
597	0.94	Coin, Vending, and Amusement Machine Servicers and Repairers
598	0.94	Welders, Cutters, Solderers, and Brazers
599	0.94	Couriers and Messengers
600	0.94	Interviewers, Except Eligibility and Loan
601	0.94	Cooks, Short Order
602	0.94	Excavating and Loading Machine and Dragline Operators
603	0.94	Helpers–Painters, Paperhangers, Plasterers, and Stucco Masons
604	0.94	Hotel, Motel, and Resort Desk Clerks
605	0.94	Tire Builders
606	0.94	Door-to-Door Sales Workers, News and Street Vendors, and Related Workers
607	0.94	First-Line Supervisors of Housekeeping and Janitorial Workers
608	0.94	Agricultural Inspectors
609	0.94	Paralegals and Legal Assistants
610	0.95	Manicurists and Pedicurists
611	0.95	Weighers, Measurers, Checkers, and Samplers, Recordkeeping
612	0.95	Textile Cutting Machine Setters, Operators, and Tenders
613	0.95	Bill and Account Collectors
614	0.95	Nuclear Power Reactor Operators
615	0.95	Gaming Surveillance Officers and Gaming Investigators

Rank	Probability	Occupation (lowest to highest probability of being automated)
616	0.95	Library Assistants, Clerical
617	0.95	Operating Engineers and Other Construction Equipment Operators
618	0.95	Print Binding and Finishing Workers
619	0.95	Animal Breeders
620	0.95	Molding, Core making, and Casting Machine Setters, Operators, and Tenders, Metal and Plastic
621	0.95	Electrical and Electronic Equipment Assemblers
622	0.95	Adhesive Bonding Machine Operators and Tenders
623	0.95	Landscaping and Grounds keeping Workers
624	0.95	Grinding, Lapping, Polishing, and Buffing Machine Tool Setters, Operators, and Tenders, Metal and Plastic
625	0.95	Postal Service Clerks
626	0.95	Jewelers and Precious Stone and Metal Workers
627	0.96	Dispatchers, Except Police, Fire, and Ambulance
628	0.96	Receptionists and Information Clerks
629	0.96	Office Clerks, General
630	0.96	Compensation and Benefits Managers
631	0.96	Switchboard Operators, Including Answering Service
632	0.96	Counter Attendants, Cafeteria, Food Concession, and Coffee Shop
633	0.96	Rock Splitters, Quarry
634	0.96	Secretaries and Administrative Assistants, Except Legal, Medical, and Executive
635	0.96	Surveying and Mapping Technicians
636	0.96	Model Makers, Wood
637	0.96	Textile Winding, Twisting, and Drawing Out Machine Setters, Operators, and Tenders
638	0.96	Locomotive Engineers
639	0.96	Gaming Dealers
640	0.96	Fabric Menders, Except Garment
641	0.96	Cooks, Restaurant
642	0.96	Ushers, Lobby Attendants, and Ticket Takers
643	0.96	Billing and Posting Clerks
644	0.97	Bridge and Lock Tenders

(continued)

Rank	Probability	Occupation (lowest to highest probability of being automated)
645	0.97	Woodworking Machine Setters, Operators, and Tenders, Except Sawing
646	0.97	Team Assemblers
647	0.97	Shoe Machine Operators and Tenders
648	0.97	Electromechanical Equipment Assemblers
649	0.97	Farm Labour Contractors
650	0.97	Textile Bleaching and Dyeing Machine Operators and Tenders
651	0.97	Dental Laboratory Technicians
652	0.97	Crushing, Grinding, and Polishing Machine Setters, Operators, and Tenders
653	0.97	Grinding and Polishing Workers, Hand
654	0.97	Pesticide Handlers, Sprayers, and Applicators, Vegetation
655	0.97	Log Graders and Scalers
656	0.97	Ophthalmic Laboratory Technicians
657	0.97	Cashiers
658	0.97	Camera and Photographic Equipment Repairers
659	0.97	Motion Picture Projectionists
660	0.97	Prepress Technicians and Workers
661	0.97	Counter and Rental Clerks
662	0.97	File Clerks
663	0.97	Real Estate Brokers
664	0.97	Telephone Operators
665	0.97	Agricultural and Food Science Technicians
666	0.97	Payroll and Timekeeping Clerks
667	0.97	Credit Authorizers, Checkers, and Clerks
668	0.97	Hosts and Hostesses, Restaurant, Lounge, and Coffee Shop
669	0.98	Models
670	0.98	Inspectors, Testers, Sorters, Samplers, and Weighers
671	0.98	Bookkeeping, Accounting, and Auditing Clerks
672	0.98	Legal Secretaries
673	0.98	Radio Operators
674	0.98	Driver/Sales Workers
675	0.98	Claims Adjusters, Examiners, and Investigators
676	0.98	Parts Salespersons

Rank	Probability	Occupation (lowest to highest probability of being automated)
677	0.98	Credit Analysts
678	0.98	Milling and Planing Machine Setters, Operators, and Tenders, Metal and Plastic
679	0.98	Shipping, Receiving, and Traffic Clerks
680	0.98	Procurement Clerks
681	0.98	Packaging and Filling Machine Operators and Tenders
682	0.98	Etchers and Engravers
683	0.98	Tellers
684	0.98	Umpires, Referees, and Other Sports Officials
685	0.98	Insurance Appraisers, Auto Damage
686	0.98	Loan Officers
687	0.98	Order Clerks
688	0.98	Brokerage Clerks
689	0.98	Insurance Claims and Policy Processing Clerks
690	0.98	Timing Device Assemblers and Adjusters
691	0.99	Data Entry Keyers
692	0.99	Library Technicians
693	0.99	New Accounts Clerks
694	0.99	Photographic Process Workers and Processing Machine Operators
695	0.99	Tax Preparers
696	0.99	Cargo and Freight Agents
697	0.99	Watch Repairers
698	0.99	Insurance Underwriters
699	0.99	Mathematical Technicians
700	0.99	Sewers, Hand
701	0.99	Title Examiners, Abstractors, and Searchers
702	0.99	Telemarketers

Source: Frey, Carl Benedikt and Osborne, Michael (2013). The Future of Employment: How Susceptible Are Jobs to Computerisation? Oxford Martin School, University of Oxford. Reprinted with permission from Elsevier. http://www.oxfordmartin.ox.ac.uk/downloads/academic/future-of-employment.pdf

List of Professional AI Organisations

The list below provides details of some of the professional organisations currently or recently active in the field of AI, with details taken from the individual online sites referenced. The list is incomplete and is not provided by way of an endorsement.

Argentina	Grupo de Interés en Inteligencia Artificial [Argentine Society for Informatics and Operations Research (SADIO)]	www.sadio .org.ar	Established in 1960. Organisers of ASAI, the Argentine Symposium on Artificial Intelligence. Spanish language.
Australia	Pacific Rim International Conferences on Artificial Intelligence	www.pricai .org	The Pacific Rim International Conferences on Artificial Intelligence (PRICAI) was initiated in Japan in 1990, to create an AI conference that would promote collaborative exploitation of AI in Pacific Rim nations.
Austria	Österreichische Gesellschaft für AI	www.oegai .at	Formed in 1981. German language.
Brazil	Sociedade Brasileira de Computação	www.sbc.org .br	Founded in 1978. Portuguese language.

Bulgaria	Bulgarian Artificial Intelligence Association (BAIA)		The official name of the association uses the Cyrillic script, and cannot be displayed here; the English translation is the Bulgarian Artificial Intelligence Association (BAIA). BAIA is one of the members of ECCAI, the European Coordinating Committee for Artificial Intelligence.
Canada	Canadian Artificial Intelligence Association/ Association pour L'intelligence Artificielle au Canada (CAIAC)	https://www .caiac.ca	CAIAC exists for the promotion of interest and activity in AI. Under this banner CAIAC conducts workshops and a fully refereed national conference every year. It also sponsors the journal *Computational Intelligence*. CAIAC is the official arm of the AAAI in Canada.
China	Chinese Association for Artificial Intelligence (CAAI)	http://caai.cn	Founded in 1981, CAAI is the only state-level science and technology organisation in the field of AI under the Ministry of Civil Affairs. Chinese language.
Czech Republic	Ceská spolecnost pro kybernetiku a informatiku (CSKI)	www.cski.cz	The Czech Society for Cybernetics and Informatics (CSKI) was founded in 1966 as the Czechoslovak Society for Cybernetics. It currently has about 300 members and it is the largest society focused on informatics in the Czech Republic. Czech language.

(continued)

Denmark	Danish Artificial Intelligence Society (DAIS)	http://www .daimi.au .dk/ %7Ebmayoh/ dais.html	DAIS coordinates AI research in Denmark with AI research in the rest of the world. It promotes such conferences as SCAI, ECCAI, and IJCAI and informs its members of AI activities in a monthly electronic newsletter (about 200 pages, most of it in English).
Europe	European Association for Artificial Intelligence (EurAI). Formerly the European Coordinating Committee on AI (ECCAI).	https://www .eurai.org	The European Association for Artificial Intelligence (EurAI) was established in July 1982 as a representative body for the European AI community. Its aim is to promote the study, research, and application of AI in Europe.
Finland	Finnish Artificial Intelligence Society (FAIS)	www.stes.fi	The Finnish Artificial Intelligence Society (FAIS) promotes public knowledge about AI in Finland.
France	Association Française pour L'intelligence Artificielle	http://afia .asso.fr	The Association promotes and encourage the development of AI in France. The Association is nonprofit.
Germany	Fachbereich Künstliche Intelligenz der Gesellschaft für Informatik (GI)	www .kuenstliche- intelligenz .de	The German Informatics Society (GI) is a nonprofit organisation with about 20,000 individual members and about 250 corporate members, and thus one of the largest informatics societies in Europe. German and English language.

Greece	Hellenic Artificial Intelligence Society (EETN)	www.eetn.gr	The Hellenic Artificial Intelligence Society (EETN) is a nonprofit scientific organisation devoted to organising and promoting AI research in Greece and abroad. English language.
Hong Kong	Artificial Intelligence Society of Hong Kong	https:// aisociety .hk	Society dedicated to the further development of AI technologies and adoption in Hong Kong.
Hungary	Neumann János Számítógép- tudományi Társaság	http://njszt .hu/en	The objective of the Society is to advance the application and improvement of information technology and the distribution of results, as a professional forum independent of institutions. Hungarian and English language.
India	Special Interest Group on Artificial Intelligence, Computer Society of India (SIGAI)	www.csi- india.org	National forum for promoting AI and exchanging of information related to AI research. Initiatives of SIGAI include various national and international journals, conferences, and workshops
Ireland	Artificial Intelligence Association of Ireland	http://www .4c.ucc.ie/ aiai	Website provides information and links of interest to people interested in AI in Ireland.
Israel	Israeli Association for Artificial Intelligence (IAAI)	http://www .ise.bgu.ac .il/iaai	The Israeli Association for Artificial Intelligence (IAAI) is a nonprofit organisation that aims to promote and sponsor activities involving the community of AI researchers in Israel from academia and from industry. IAAI is a member of EurAI, the European Association for Artificial Intelligence, which includes 29 bodies from throughout Europe, and pro- motes the study, research, and application of AI in Europe

(*continued*)

Italy	Associazione Italiana per L'intelligenza Artificiale	www.aixia.it	Formed in 1988. Active in the areas of theoretical and applied AI. Organisers of annual International Conference of the Italian Association for Artificial Intelligence.
Japan	Japanese Society for Artificial Intelligence (JSAI)	www.ai-gakkai.or .jp/en	The Japanese Society for Artificial Intelligence (JSAI) contributes to social innovation with research and development of AI.
Mexico	Sociedad Mexicana de Inteligencia Artificial	www.smia .org.mx	Organisers of annual international AI conference described as a 'premier' event by Springer. Spanish language.
Netherlands	BeNeLux Vereniging voor Kunstmatige Intelligentie [BeNeLux (Belgium-Netherlands-Luxembourg) Association for Artificial Intelligence (BNVKI)]	http://ii .tudelft.nl/ bnvki	BNVKI stands for BeNeLux Vereniging voor Kunstmatige Intelligentie, which translates to the Benelux Association for Artificial Intelligence. The aim of the BNVKI is to stimulate research on, and the application of and education in, AI, as well as the dissemination of knowledge about AI. BNVKI was founded in 1981 as the NVKI.
Norway	Norwegian Artificial Intelligence Society	www .norwegian .ai	Mission is to be a leading force in positioning Norway as an important part of the global AI community.
Portugal	Associação Portuguesa para a Inteligência Artificial	www.appia .pt	Portuguese language.

Romania	Asociația Română pentru Inteligență Artificială [Romanian Association for Artificial Intelligence (ARIA)]	http://aria-romania.org	Founded in April 2011, ARIA (Asociația Română pentru Inteligență Artificială) is a nonprofit scientific association dedicated to the support of research advancements in AI and the development of Romanian research and education in the field.
Russia	Russian Association for Artificial Intelligence (RAAI)	http://raai.org	The Russian Association for Artificial Intelligence (RAAI) works alongside the institutes of the Russian Academy of Sciences (Institutes of Systems Analysis, Control Sciences, and Information Transmission Problems). Co-organisers of the Russian Conference on Artificial Intelligence with International Participation.
Spain	IberoAmerican Society of Artificial Intelligence	www.iberamia.org/iberamia	Legally constituted nonprofit association, with the primary objective of promoting scientific and technological activities related to AI in Ibero-American countries.
	Associación Española para la Inteligencia Artificial [IberoAmerican Society of Artificial Intelligence (IBERAMIA)]		*Inteligencia Artificial* is a biannual open access journal, promoted and sponsored by the IberoAmerican Society of Artificial Intelligence (IBERAMIA).
	Associació Catalana d'Intelligència Artificial		

(*continued*)

Sweden	Swedish Artificial Intelligence Society (SAIS)	www.sais.se	The Swedish Artificial Intelligence Society (SAIS) is a society promoting research in and application of AI. Members are Swedish universities, organisations, researchers, professionals, and students active or interested in the area of AI.
Switzerland	Swiss Group for Artificial Intelligence and Cognitive Science (SGAICO)	https://sgaico .swiss informatics .org	Special interest group of the Swiss Informatics Society.
Taiwan	Taiwanese Association for Artificial Intelligence (TAAI)	www.taai.org .tw/en-taai	The Taiwanese Association for Artificial Intelligence (TAAI) is a government-registered official academic society. The objective of TAAI is to promote the research, development, application, and exchange of AI in Taiwan.
Ukraine	Association of Developers and Users of Intelligent Systems (ADUIS)	www.aduis .com.ua	ADUIS consists of about 100 members, including 10 collective members. The Association was founded in Ukraine in 1992. The main aim of *ADUIS* is to contribute to the development and application of AI methods and techniques.
United Kingdom	Society for the Study of Artificial Intelligence and Simulation of Behaviour (AISB)	www.aisb .org.uk	The Society for the Study of Artificial Intelligence and Simulation of Behaviour (AISB) is the largest AI society in the United Kingdom. Founded in 1964.

	British Computer Society Specialist Group on Artificial Intelligence (SGAI)	www.bcs-sgai.org	SGAI, the British Computer Society Specialist Group on Artificial Intelligence, was founded in June 1980. The Group's mission is 'To foster achievement, capability and awareness in both business and research in artificial intelligence, and to promote the interests of the related community'. It is one of Europe's longest established groups working to support the community of AI developers and users.
United States	Association for the Advancement of Artificial Intelligence (AAAI)	www.aaai.org	Founded in 1979, AAAI is a nonprofit scientific society devoted to advancing the scientific understanding of the mechanisms underlying thought and intelligent behaviour and their embodiment in machines.
	Association for Computing Machinery (ACM); ACM Special Interest Group in Artificial Intelligence (ACM SIGART)	www.acm.org	The Association for Computing Machinery is an international learned society for computing. It was founded in 1947 and is the world's largest scientific and educational computing society.
	Computing Research Association (CRA)	http://cra.org	Founded in 1972, CRA's membership includes more than 200 North American organisations active in computing research, including academic departments of computer science, information, and computer engineering; laboratories and centres (industry, government, and academia); and affiliated professional societies.

(continued)

Florida Artificial Intelligence Research Society	www.flairs .com	The Florida Artificial Intelligence Research Society was founded in 1987 to promote and advance AI within the state of Florida, including interaction between researchers at the various colleges, universities, and industry. Membership is open to all (Florida residents and nonresidents) who attend the yearly conference.
IEEE Computer Society	https://www .computer .org	The IEEE Computer Society is the world's leading membership organisation dedicated to computer science and technology. Serving more than 60,000 members.
IEEE Computational Intelligence Society	http://cis.ieee .org	Interested specifically in the theory, design, application, and development of biologically and linguistically motivated computational paradigms emphasising neural networks, connectionist systems, genetic algorithms, evolutionary programming, fuzzy systems, and hybrid intelligent systems in which these paradigms are contained.
International Neural Network Society (INNS)	https://www .inns.org	Premiere organisation for individuals interested in a theoretical and computational understanding of the brain and applying that knowledge to develop new and more effective forms of machine intelligence. INNS was formed in 1987 by the leading scientists in the neural network field.

Singularity University	https://su.org	Singularity University is a global community using exponential technologies to tackle the world's biggest challenges. Its learning and innovation platform empowers individuals and organisations with the mind-set, skill set, and network to build breakthrough solutions that leverage emerging technologies, such as AI, robotics, and digital biology.
Machine Intelligence Research Institute. Formerly the Singularity Institute for Artificial Intelligence (SIAI).	https:// intelligence .org	Formerly the Singularity Institute for Artificial Intelligence (SIAI), the Machine Intelligence Research Institute is a research nonprofit studying the mathematical underpinnings of intelligent behaviour. Our mission is to develop formal tools for the clean design and analysis of general-purpose AI systems, with the intent of making such systems safer and more reliable when they are developed.

List of Tables

List of Figures

Index

Paul, St 4
Pavlina 121
PC World 106
Pegasystems 27, 177
Pemberton, John 229
Pepper (robot) 58
performance management 182–3
person reinvention flowchart 236
personal capabilities 212
personal reinvention, need for 225–6
personal wealth management 62
personality in computer systems 30
PEST analysis 179, 194
Peters, Tom 131, 150
Pickering, Kallum 9–10
pilots 138–9
Pinocchio (film) 16
Plato: *Republic* 38
policing 107–8
polls, political opinion 32–3
polls-of-polls 32
Port Sunlight 4
postgenderisation 124
postindustrial era 149
post-millennials 8, 187, 188–9
poverty 100–1
precision agriculture 110
Premier Foods 178
premium 64
probability 33
professions 118–22
    flowcharts 239, 240
Progenium 70
ProPublica 108
psychohistory 32
Public Broadcasting Service 106
    SuperVision app 106
public service 101–4
publishing 135–6
    new role pf publisher 137
punched-card method 39
PWC 90
Pyzdek, Thomas 75

Q-Network 46
quantum computing 173
Qubit 133

railway, digital 137–8
Rapolu, Bhoopathi 225
RDA 176–7, 178
RegTech 168–9
regulations, compliance with 165–7, 168
Regulatory Disasters 166
reinforcement learning 46
reliability engineering 160
reliability management 160

religious objection to computer intelligence 39
remote imagery 90–1
reputational risk 162–3
reserves 66
retail industry 79–83, 131–3, 195
    retro-vintage clothes 187–8
retailer, new role of 134
retraining 10, 12, 13
return on investment (ROI) 190
Richards, Neil 158
Rio Tinto 68
risk
    definition of 155, 156
    external 163–4
    financial 164–5
    operational 166
    reputational 162–3
risk appetite 156, 178–9
risk assessment framework 156
risk management 64, 156, 169–70
    flowchart 238
risk tolerance test 62
Roberts, Julia 64
robotic process automation (RPA) 176–7, 178
Robotics, Three Laws of 220
robots 214–21
    design 215–16
    domestication 215
    elderly healthcare and 216–17
    rules for 206, 220–1
    taking advice from 217–20
Rolex 78
Rolling Stones 49
Rome, ancient 2–3, 226
Roosevelt, Franklin 3
Rosanoff, Martin 95
Roth, David Lee 4
Royal Bank of Scotland (RBS) 61, 102
Royal Society of Engineering 97
rules of association 21
Russell, Stuart 44

SaaS 190
Sadler-Wells, Eugene 61, 62
sales and marketing 130–1
    employee fraud in 161
    new role of 131
sandbox capabilities systems 198
SAP 18
sapience 47
scambots 219
scenario analysis 169
second-mover 88
security, data 158–60
self-actualisation 7
self-awareness 47
self-help 10, 225, 226